METHODOLOGIES OF
COMPARATIVE PHILOSOPHY

SUNY series in Chinese Philosophy and Culture

Roger T. Ames, editor

METHODOLOGIES OF COMPARATIVE PHILOSOPHY

The Pragmatist and Process Traditions

ROBERT W. SMID

STATE UNIVERSITY OF NEW YORK PRESS

Published by
STATE UNIVERSITY OF NEW YORK PRESS, ALBANY

© 2009 State University of New York

For information, contact
State University of New York Press, Albany, NY
www.sunypress.edu

Production, Laurie Searl
Marketing, Anne M. Valentine

Library of Congress Cataloging-in-Publication Data

Smid, Robert W., 1974–
    Methodologies of comparative philosophy : the pragmatist and process traditions / Robert
W. Smid.
        p. cm. — (SUNY series in Chinese philosophy and culture)
    Includes bibliographical references and index.
    ISBN 978-1-4384-2829-1 (hardcover : alk. paper)
    1. Philosophy, Comparative.   I. Title.

B799.S65 2009
101—dc22   2009003430

10 9 8 7 6 5 4 3 2 1

~ To Robert Cummings Neville ~

CONTENTS

PREFACE

When the idea of writing a book of my own was a faint, distant notion at best, I remember reading the following comment in the preface to my advisor's first book. "My philosophical debts are the heavy ones of a young man," he wrote. "It is especially true that what is good in this book is what my teachers have taught me and that what is bad comes from my own incorrigibility" (Neville 1992a [1968]). At the time, this impressed me as an admirable expression of modesty with which to launch a book—and an especially easy one when followed by such a strong philosophical argument as the one presented in that text. Having now written my own text, however, I feel the modesty in that statement all the more palpably and am quite sure that it was intended with all sincerity when he penned it now forty years ago.

In the text at hand, I have not only all of the inexperience of youth but also all of the inexperience of one writing at the outset of a subfield's development. As it stands, while there is a growing literature pertaining to the actual practice of comparative philosophy, there has been very little written on the subject of methodology for such comparisons. Ideally, this text would have been written by someone much older than me and someone with much more experience in comparative philosophy. Yet such a text has not been forthcoming, and it has seemed to me too important a task to let waste away waiting for someone with more experience to pick it up. Thus, while any contributions this text might make can ultimately be attributed to the sound guidance I have received from my teachers, its shortcomings will be due less to any incorrigibility on my part (as if I were writing in a field where counterarguments were clear and compelling) than to my own lack of adequate creativity and foresight with respect to an emerging subfield that is anything but well defined.

It is thus with tremendous appreciation for his exceptional guidance in the development of this project, combined with a genuine humility concerning the final product, that I dedicate this work to my primary doctoral advisor, Robert Neville. Throughout this project, he has been consistent in his insistence that this work pay him no deference, always reminding me that the success of the project will require a relatively evenhanded assessment of all methodological alternatives. As he has told me on numerous occasions, he is not interested in attracting disciples but in cultivating a new generation of thinkers who can make their own constructive contributions to pressing philosophical (and other) concerns. I hope that this project honors that request and thus honors his guidance, by assessing his work on par with all of the other approaches considered in this study.

Plato was surely right in the *Theaetetus*, however, when he compared the development of an idea to the birth of a child. My wife and I have often joked about this, as my dissertation was completed at about the time our first child, Dalia Jean, was born, and this book will be published at about the time that our second child is born. Anyone who has had a child knows how much support is needed and appreciated around the birth of a child, and so thanks must go out not only to my primary philosophical midwife (so to speak) but also to the many others who have aided in the delivery of this project.

First, I bear great debts to my former teachers at Boston University, John Berthrong and Wesley Wildman, both of whom have provided guidance at important points in the development of this book; they should likewise be credited with the successes of this project and exempted from its shortcomings. Sincere thanks is also due to Roger Ames, who has been more than generous with his time and the opportunities he has provided in the development of this volume; I hope that he will also be honored by the evenhandedness with which I have tried to address his work, as well as the extent to which his work has influenced my own. I would also like to express my gratitude to my colleagues at Curry College, including Les Muray, Bette Manter, Alan Revering, and Russ Pregeant, who have been a constant source of inspiration, encouragement, and understanding as I have tried to jump the many high hurdles of completing this work. Special thanks in this respect is due to Alan, who has been a great help in the final stages of editing for publication, as well as to Nancy Ellegate and Laurie Searl at SUNY Press, who have been more than patient with the few hurdles I have tripped along the way.

Finally, of course, I would like to thank my loving wife, Lora, who is perhaps as happy to be on the other side of childbirth (for once!) as she is to see this book's completion. Being married to someone writing a book seems to be almost as hard—and perhaps sometimes harder—than being the person who writes it, so I would like to thank her for her remarkable patience and understanding throughout this process. Without it, this project would likely have never come to fruition.

INTRODUCTION

THE BALLAD OF EAST AND WEST

Oh, East is East, and West is West, and never the twain shall meet, Till
Earth and Sky stand presently at God's great Judgment Seat.

—Kipling, "The Ballad of East and West"

Such are the often-quoted words of Rudyard Kipling just prior to the twentieth
century. At first glance, Kipling appears to have been sorely mistaken, as the
"twain" of East and West have now clearly met and even interpenetrated on
almost every conceivable level. Yet what most fleeting citations of Kipling's
"Ballad of East and West" fail to include are the concluding two lines of the
quatrain: "But there is neither East nor West, Border, nor Breed, nor Birth,
when two strong men stand face to face, tho' they come from the ends of
the earth!" (1994, 245). These additional lines furnish the poem with an
important sense of ambivalence, suggesting that cultures may come together
productively, but they also may not, with the difference being determined by
the "strength" of those who represent them. In this sense, Kipling appears to
have been largely correct, as East and West would meet in countless venues
over the next century with decidedly mixed results.

Kipling had his own ideas of what constituted "strong men," but if
one can look past his nineteenth-century romanticism he raises a crucial
question for contemporary consideration: if there are better and worse ways
for diverse cultures to engage one another, what differentiates the former
from the latter, and how can we more successfully bring about the former?
This is, at its most basic, a methodological question, and one that would
plague comparativists throughout the twentieth century. Indeed, this question
is hardly settled even now in the twenty-first century. At the same time,
however, scholars over the last century have made a number of important

1

contributions that must be understood and critically appraised if the question is to be addressed with any more success in the current century.

This text examines one small but important source of such contributions: namely, comparative philosophers. While cross-cultural influence is hardly unprecedented in the study of philosophy, twentieth-century philosophers experienced this influence on a scale far beyond that of any previous century: more cultures converged in a greater variety of venues and to a greater extent than had ever done so before. The rise of comparative philosophy in the twentieth century represents the attempt of many of these philosophers to understand these cross-cultural influences and consider their philosophical implications. Perhaps as a validation of their efforts, comparative philosophy has grown in both interest and influence and now represents a vibrant subfield in the discipline of philosophy.

WHAT IS COMPARATIVE PHILOSOPHY?

Comparative philosophy can be defined by its attempt to move across the boundaries of otherwise distinct philosophical traditions—especially insofar as these traditions are divided by significant historical and cultural distance—thus enabling a comparison of what lies on either side of the boundary. By this definition, a comparison of Descartes and Locke would constitute no less an instance of comparative philosophy than one of Mencius and Aquinas (e.g., Yearley 1990), although the latter would likely be of greater interest to comparative philosophers because of the greater historical and cultural distance among the traditions represented.

This fluidity in the content of comparative philosophy stems from the fluidity of the very notion of a "tradition" (philosophical or otherwise). The word *tradition* is derived from the Latin verb *tradere*, which literally means "to hand over" or "to transfer."[1] This suggests that, within a tradition, something—usually an idea or a practice—is being passed on from one person or group to another. Yet there are few things that are passed on with all of their original integrity still intact and just as few things that are not passed on to at least some extent. In other words, strictly speaking, each person is a tradition unto him/herself, while each is also part of a panoply of broader, common traditions. What the use of 'tradition' seems intended to designate is that something *distinctive* and *of particular importance* has been passed on from one person or group to another. That is, it is a practical designation rather than a metaphysical one.

This distinction is an important one because it suggests that, in attempting to cross the boundaries of these otherwise distinct philosophical traditions, comparative philosophers are not attempting to do something that is either unprecedented or *prima facie* impossible. The boundaries between traditions are not impenetrable ones; they simply become more difficult to traverse as the historical and cultural distance between them increases (i.e., where what is being passed on is held less and less in common). As aware of these difficulties as anyone, comparative philosophers take as their subject matter traditions whose historical and cultural distance from one another is especially significant, paying particular attention to the implications of trying to traverse that distance while still remaining faithful to the traditions compared.

Within this general aim of comparative philosophy, there are two distinct but interrelated dimensions of the subfield that must be distinguished if one is to have a clear conception of the whole. On the one hand, comparative philosophy can mean the comparison of ideas, texts, or aims of different philosophical traditions, where the primary focus is the comparisons themselves. Understood in this sense, comparative philosophy entails the "comparison of philosophies," where the term *philosophies* is taken to represent the philosophical ideas, texts, or aims compared. The comparison of philosophies is often taken to represent the whole of comparative philosophy and easily accounts for the overwhelming majority of works published in the field.

On the other hand, however, comparative philosophy can also mean philosophical reflection on the nature of comparison itself, where the primary focus is the development of a philosophic account of what comparison is and how it is best carried out. In this conception of comparative philosophy, *what* is compared is not as important as *how* it is compared. Thus, the subject matter of the comparisons considered might be philosophical ideas, but they might also be religious practices or standards of ritual decorum; what the comparativist is most concerned with in this case is improving the comparative process itself by subjecting it to philosophical scrutiny. Conceived in this sense, comparative philosophy is best understood as the "philosophy of comparison," where "comparison" refers to the question of how one set of things is understood with respect to another.

These two dimensions—the "comparison of philosophies" and the "philosophy of comparison"—are both crucial components of comparative philosophy, and comparative philosophers at their best incorporate both dimensions in their work. It is as difficult to compare philosophical traditions well without reference to a critically refined comparative method as it is to develop such a method without an adequate awareness of the similarities and differences among philosophical traditions. Each dimension needs the other in order to flourish and by flourishing aids the other in its further development. The two exist in dialectical relationship with one another, each informing the other for mutual benefit and improvement over time.

It is thus for good reason that almost all those who have made significant contributions to the philosophy of comparison have also made contributions to the comparison of philosophies. Unfortunately, however, this mutual commitment has not hitherto been very reciprocal: only a small number of those who have made contributions in the comparison of philosophies have given substantive consideration to the development of a philosophy of comparison. As a result, while there has been a proliferation of texts comparing philosophical ideas from different cultures, there has been a relative dearth of texts concerned with the notion of comparison itself.

This disparity would be acceptable if the few texts that take up the task of methodology were exhaustive of the available possibilities or were so well known within the academy as to require little further elaboration. Yet neither of these alternatives seems to be an accurate portrayal of the state of comparative philosophy. Those who have made contributions to a philosophy of comparison know well that their contributions are still very much works in progress, as is clear from the fact that they continue to publish new and enterprising texts on the topic. At the same time, many of the texts that take up the comparison of philosophies seem to proceed without an adequate awareness of the full variety of methodological options available to them. Indeed, the assumption seems far too often to be that "what comparison is" is sufficiently obvious that it requires little further attention; yet the diversity of approaches actually taken demonstrates that the methodology of comparison is far from a settled question.

The purpose of this book is to make a small contribution toward restoring the balance between these two aspects of comparative philosophy by aiding in the further development of the philosophy of comparison. It seeks to do this in four ways: by shedding light on an ongoing methodological conversation among philosophers of comparison; by providing a concise account of the comparative methods of some of that conversation's most prominent participants; by offering a critical assessment of each of these methods with respect to its strengths and weaknesses; and, finally, by considering the implications of the results of this inquiry for the nature of the philosophy of comparison.

The reason for the first move is that, while there has been an ongoing conversation among philosophers of comparison, only parts of it have been documented in the available literature, and there exists no organized record of its development. Unless one is already familiar with it, this conversation can be difficult to trace through the literature. As a result, it has remained largely obscured from the broader population of comparative philosophers. This is an unfortunate loss for all comparativists because their conversation sheds additional light not only on how comparative methods develop but also on the strengths and weaknesses of each method as illuminated by the critiques of other conversation partners. In order to help bring this conversation to light, each of the first four chapters will begin by placing its respective method in the historical context of its development, paying particular attention to any points of connection that exist with other methods considered in the book. In addition to the methods, the text will also pay attention to the relationships among their authors, who relate to each other variously as teachers, students, classmates, colleagues, and friends.

There is a very human dimension to this conversation, and this text will seek to illuminate these relationships as appropriate.

The second move follows from the first: because there is a lack of awareness of the ongoing conversation, there is consequent unfamiliarity with many of the available methods of comparison. Typically, each of these methods has been laid out over the course of multiple publications and entails multiple stages of development, making it difficult for those who do not take the philosophy of comparison as their primary area of expertise to establish and maintain a mastery of them. Additionally, the few sources that examine multiple comparative methods—thus constituting methodologies in their own right—tend to do so only as a secondary feature of a larger project (e.g., Hall and Ames 1987; Neville 2000).[2] Without a source that takes as its primary task the explication of some of the leading methods of comparison, scholars have often been left to simply perpetuate the method most prominent in their respective academic communities. In the interest of raising awareness of a broader array of comparative methods, each of the first four chapters will follow its historical introduction with a detailed explication of its respective method. My hope is that, by providing these detailed accounts in a single study, this text can serve as a more central-ized resource for understanding some of the methodological options that are available.

The third move is the most important and most difficult one for this project: namely, providing a critical evaluation of the methods previously described by drawing attention to the relative strengths and weaknesses of each approach. Hitherto, there has been almost no sustained critical evaluation of the available comparative methods. Of course, philosophers of comparison have often responded to both their critics and their competitors (who are usually one and the same), but these responses often take their own method for granted and do little more than elaborate and further develop their own positions. This study seeks to press the assessment further by *applying the comparative process to the comparative methods themselves*. Accordingly, each of the first four chapters will conclude with an assessment of the strengths and weaknesses of the method under consideration.[3]

Following the historical contextualization, explication, and assessment of each of these methods, all that remains is to try to understand each of them in relation to one another. That is, what remains is the comparison of the comparative methods themselves. Careful consideration will be given to what they suggest collectively about the development of the philosophy of comparison, what advantages each method has relative to the others, and what all of this suggests about the nature of comparative philosophy itself. The fifth and final chapter of this text will have as its sole focus the investigation of these issues. While the conclusions reached in this last chapter will be the most tentative and least completely formulated, it is also the chapter that should prove most fertile for the further development of comparative philosophy as a whole. Its accomplishments and its limitations are those of the current state of comparative methodology.

SCOPE OF THE LITERATURE

As noted earlier, the primary concern of this study is with the dimension of comparative philosophy that is concerned with the philosophy of comparison rather than that concerned with the comparison of philosophies. Accordingly, the subject matter for this study is not the literature *of* comparison (i.e., literature that takes as its primary task the practice of comparing religious and philosophical ideas) but rather the literature *about* comparison (i.e., literature that takes as its primary task philosophical reflection on the nature of comparison itself). This distinction will inevitably be blurred, as virtually every text that discusses comparison in its own right also engages in comparison for sake of exemplification; some of these comparisons may even be highlighted in this study for illustrative purposes. Ultimately, however, texts are included or excluded primarily on the basis of their concern with the methodology of comparison, and their claims about such methodology constitute their chief interest here.

While the amount of literature in comparative philosophy that is self-consciously concerned with the philosophy of comparison is noticeably limited relative to the literature concerned with the comparison of philosophies, it nonetheless constitutes a significant body of work that extends beyond the possible purview of a study of this size. Accordingly, not all methodological approaches in the philosophy of comparison will be considered here. Rather, this study will consider only a very small subset of the larger group: namely, those that arise out of the American pragmatist and process philosophical traditions.[4] Specifically, it will examine the methods of four leading philosophical comparativists in those traditions: William Ernest Hocking, F. S. C. Northrop, David Hall and Roger Ames (in collaboration), and Robert Cummings Neville (along with the Comparative Religious Ideas Project). There is a line of continuity running through these figures—largely due to their historical and biographical connection with one another—that grants this selection an integrity of its own and ensures a coherent focus throughout the project.

The study begins with the work of William Ernest Hocking (1873–1966), a second-generation pragmatist and student of William James. The reasons for beginning with Hocking are twofold. First, while some first-generation pragmatists and other early representatives of American philosophy expressed an interest in non-Western culture and incorporated this interest into their own work, the comparative philosophical implications of this interest were not carefully addressed let alone developed in their own work.[5] Second, while Hocking was not the most orthodox of pragmatists, he was the representative of that tradition that was first and most directly involved in the second-order reflection on comparison considered in this study. All things considered, while it has strong philosophical and cross-cultural roots in previous thinkers, comparative philosophy proper began in the American traditions with Hocking.

The second figure addressed in this study, F. S. C. Northrop (1893–1992), provides a natural progression from Hocking's work. Northrop was Hocking's prize pupil, who launched his initial foray into comparative philosophy with the assistance of his teacher. While he was still less of an orthodox pragmatist than Hocking, he was even more of a figurehead for comparative philosophy among his generation of American philosophers. Moreover, while there is a line of continuity between him and Hocking, he also moved the study of comparative philosophy in a new direction and ultimately developed his own comparative methodology. While Northrop's approach was somewhat controversial among the growing body of comparative philosophers, it was nonetheless well respected and one of the most prominent approaches; indeed, it would be difficult to discuss midtwentieth-century comparative philosophy without sustained reference to Northrop.

The third set of figures addressed is David Hall (1937–2001) and Roger Ames (1947–), as exemplified most significantly in their collaborative work. There is a noticeable gap between their work and that of Northrop, both in time and in the character of their methods. Hall and Ames began their comparative work about a quarter of a century after Northrop had written his most influential books and have been much more concerned with highlighting the profound differences among philosophical traditions than with exploring their potential complementarity. This change can be traced to two changes that occurred in the intellectual landscape in the middle of the twentieth century.

The first change was the rise of analytic philosophy and the simultaneous decline of traditional American philosophy. The early analytic tradition had been cultivated primarily in the European context, but many of its leading representatives emigrated to the United States in the wake of World War II (e.g., the logical positivists Rudolf Carnap, Carl Hempel, and Hans Reichenbach) and fostered the growth of a vibrant analytic tradition on American soil. Additionally, there was a surging interest in mathematics and the natural sciences, initially spurred by the drive for technological superiority over Nazi Germany in that same war and intensified by the continuation of that drive against the Soviet Union in the Cold War that followed. This interest was only further amplified when the Soviet Union launched *Sputnik* in 1957, thus initiating a "space race" that threatened to leave the United States vulnerable if it fell behind. The net result of this change was a shift of interest and resources toward traditions that cultivated the level of precision and demonstrability prized in mathematics and the natural sciences—in short, toward analytic philosophy and away from American philosophy.

The second change was an increase in the availability of critical translations of non-Western philosophical texts, along with more careful and informed historical studies of the traditions from which they emerged. As a result, earlier comparative conclusions were called into question for their inability to account for this new information, and it became clear that these comparisons tended to assert facile similarities where more profound differences prevailed. The result of this development was a growing distrust of comparative philosophy and a tendency to focus on areas studies, allowing for only the most minute and text-based comparisons.

The result was that, at least within American traditions of philosophy, comparative philosophy languished, and when it reemerged it took on a noticeably different character. This change is represented well in Hall and Ames' work, which represents both the late-twentieth-century reemergence of American philosophy and the redoubled concern with maintaining the highest standards in the interpretation of non-western texts and traditions. With Hall and Ames, process philosophy (and, to a lesser extent, pragmatism) has been brought to the fore of the comparative philosophical discussion in America, and while they may not have even been orthodox Whiteheadians (or Rortyans, for that matter) any more than Hocking or Northrop were orthodox pragmatists, they have nonetheless been less among the most prominent comparativists in the American tradition for their generation.[6] Moreover, because they have been explicit about their partial debts to Northrop, the chapter after Northrop's appropriately moves to consider their work.

Finally, the work of Robert Neville (1939–) reflects many of the same changes in comparative philosophy as those encountered by Hall and Ames, though he responds to them in very different ways. Like Hall and Ames, Neville begins writing on comparative philosophy in the last quarter of the twentieth century and represents the vanguard of the reemerging American traditions of philosophy; yet while he also draws on the pragmatist and process traditions, he draws on very different aspects of those traditions. Likewise, while Neville also remains sensitive to the shortcomings of previous approaches to comparative philosophy (especially with respect to assertions of similarity), he sees the recognition of these shortcomings as evidence of improvement within comparative philosophy—and as a spur toward further improvement—rather than as grounds for restriction of any further synoptic reflection. Indeed, Neville represents in many respects the opposite end of the methodological spectrum from Hall and Ames and thus can be used in conjunction with them to frame the broader contemporary debate about comparison within American philosophy.

While this choice of figures represents only four points in the history of comparative philosophy, they are four of the most influential developments in comparative methodology within the American tradition and thus provide a telling snapshot of its development over time. For example, if one takes the East-West Philosophers' Conferences as a measure, almost every one of its nine conferences has been attended by at least one of the figures examined in this study.[7] The only gap, as noted above, is the later midtwentieth century, during which American philosophy itself was on the decline; yet, again, if the aforementioned conferences were any indication, comparative philosophy itself encountered difficulties during this period as well: the conference did not meet from 1969 to 1989.[8]

Furthermore, while these figures have been among the most prominent comparativists in American philosophy to consider comparison on a second-order basis (as well as prominent comparativists in their own right), they have also shared another important characteristic: namely, the awareness of a continuity and ongoing conversation among them. Northrop was explicit about his debts to Hocking, Hall, and Ames about their debts to Northrop, Neville about his debts to Hocking, and Neville and Hall/Ames about their ongoing debate with one another.[9] The ongoing conversation that has persisted among these figures—heightened by their *awareness* of its ongoing nature—ensures a line of continuity throughout this project. Our awareness of that conversation will help us to understand the contemporary state of comparative philosophy in America and may help us to enter into that conversation in our own right as well.

LIMITATIONS OF THE PROJECT

Limiting the scope to the pragmatist and process philosophical traditions admittedly ignores the important contributions of a number of traditions of comparison. The most notable exclusions arise out of the disciplines of religious and theological studies. Religionists and theologians have been interested in comparison far longer than philosophers have, in large part facilitated by religions with an impetus for cross-cultural missions (including, though not exclusively, Buddhism, Christianity, and Islam). The comparative study of religions has followed on this history of interaction and has gone a long way toward bringing greater sophistication and even-handedness to the comparisons that arise out of it.[10]

Although not highlighted here, the connection with comparative religions is important for the current project because it informs much of the current interest in the philosophy of comparison. The comparative study of religion arguably now dominates the philosophy of religion by defining the context of all of its traditional questions: one cannot address the question "what is/are religion(s)?"—let alone any of the more subtle philosophical questions about religions that follow—without understanding religions in comparative context. Yet one of the things that philosophers of religion have found in the context of comparison is that the religious is not as distinguishable from the philosophical as was previously believed (as seen, for example, in the case of Confucianism). Understood in this light, it is only natural to take the developments in comparative religions and apply them to comparative philosophy—and, in fact, each of the comparative philosophers discussed in this study also maintains an interest in the religious dimensions of their comparisons.

What comparative philosophy can bring back to the comparative study of religions is a more self-conscious and critical philosophical concept of comparison to employ in its own comparisons. While the focus of this text is on comparative philosophy—understood as both the comparison of philosophical ideas and the development of a philosophical conception of comparison—the hope is nonetheless that the results of this project will prove helpful in spurring such self-conscious and critical reflection about methodology in the comparative study of religion as well.

The other noticeable exclusions that follow from the scope of this project are the many other traditions of comparative philosophy. For example, the analytic and Continental philosophical traditions both have their own traditions of comparison, as do a number of non-Western traditions; any one of these could have served as the subject matter for this text; they have been excluded simply because they do not conform as quickly to my own background and expertise. This limitation notwithstanding, I hope that this study will serve as a model for similar projects with alternative foci that will be undertaken in the near future.

IN DEFENSE OF METACOMPARATIVE PHILOSOPHY

As should now be evident, this text is not merely *about* comparison but is moreover an exercise *in* comparison. The thesis of this book is that, if it is possible to compare philosophical traditions in ways that lead to a better and more critical understanding of those traditions, it should also be possible to compare comparative methods with a similar result. Comparative philosophy seeks to give common voice to various philosophical traditions while remaining as faithful to each of those traditions as possible throughout the process of comparison. If it is critical and self-reflective throughout that process, then it should be no less critical and self-reflective when it considers questions of methodology. By shifting the focus of comparison from philosophical traditions to the comparative methods themselves—thus moving from comparative philosophy to metacomparative philosophy—this study simply presses the comparative process one step further.

This move, however, brings with it a number of unique challenges that might seem to call into question the very viability of this project. Of these, three are particularly pertinent and merit careful consideration.[11] The first pertains to the decision to take a further step back from the comparative process to subject such processes to comparative scrutiny. In an academic climate in which things "meta-" are as routinely maligned as they are proliferated in publications, the reader might be concerned that this move to a metacomparative philosophy is merely a gratuitous attempt to supersede the already difficult task of comparative study. What is there, one might ask, to stop further steps back—a comparison of comparisons of comparative methods, perhaps, or some regression *ad nauseum* to ever more "meta" stages of comparison?

The answer to this question is entirely practical: there is very little need for any comparisons further removed from the one at hand simply because there are hardly any comparisons like the one at hand to be compared. If there was already such sustained critical reflection on comparative methods, then a comparison one further step removed might be warranted. At the same time, because there is already a wide variety of well-developed methods of comparison, there is clearly something to be gained from a comparison of those methods. Far from being a fanciful feat of intellectual gymnastics that is simply one step more abstract than the others, this project has very concrete goals: namely, the cultivation of a better understanding of the available comparative methods, the development of a better sense of each method's relative strengths and weaknesses, and perhaps even the generation of new insights about the nature of comparison itself.[12]

A second concern pertains to the fact that this project attempts to make comparisons when its very subject matter is comparison. The reader would be right to ask at this point whether the project is not therefore fatally self-referential. What method does one use in making these comparisons, if not a method that is at least potentially—if not actually—one of the ones being compared? This would seem akin to counting ways of counting: how does one begin to enumerate these without conforming to one or another tradition of counting? Yet comparison is still more dangerous, because it not only enumerates but also represents and even evaluates. Thus, the entire project would seem to be in danger of ceasing to be comparative in any legitimate sense, devolving instead into a mere reflection of its own methodological biases.

This concern is not entirely unfounded: the comparison of comparisons *is* self-referential and is so by necessity. As Thomas Nagel rightly pointed out, there is no "view from nowhere" (1986), no neutral position from which to make comparisons; instead, one must start the process of making comparisons with some particular conception of comparison, and one's results will inevitably reflect that conception to some degree. Yet the plight of meta-comparative inquiry is no different than the plight of comparative inquiry more generally: every comparative philosopher has a particular philosophical background, and it would be naïve to think that this background does not influence the results of his or her comparative work. The problem of self-reference is thus hardly peculiar to metacomparative inquiry; it plagues all who undertake the task of comparison.

Drawing on this similarity, then, this second concern can be resolved by taking a page from comparative inquiry more generally. Biases—methodological or otherwise—cannot be avoided, but they can be dealt with responsibly and even productively. In comparative inquiry, this entails being open and honest about those biases, minimizing them where they seem to interfere with the inquiry, and drawing on them insofar as they enable one to engage the subject matter in question.

As noted earlier, my own philosophical background is heavily informed by the American pragmatist and process philosophical traditions, and I have drawn on this background in the selection of the particular set of comparative methods considered in this text. Appropriate to this subject matter, the method I employ here is also drawn broadly from these two interrelated traditions. I say *broadly* because, while each of the methods considered in this text has strong roots in American pragmatism and process philosophy, each interprets those traditions very differently and with notably different results. The aim of this text is to employ a method that is broad enough to register the insights of each of these methods without excessively biasing them in favor of one particular reading of the philosophical traditions underlying them.

From this broad reading of American pragmatism and process philosophy, the argument for comparative philosophy is that comparisons among traditions take place whether in accordance with carefully and critically constructed methods or not. Furthermore, at least some of those comparisons (though not necessarily all of them) enable a better understanding of the traditions compared, as evidenced from the fact that at least some understanding exists among the world's philosophical traditions, and that this generally seems to increase as interactions among traditions—which are all at some level comparative—also increase. From this perspective, a comparison can be considered good (and perhaps even true) to the extent that it enables a better understanding of the traditions compared. Comparative philosophy, then, has as its task the cultivation of "good comparisons," both encouraging and developing comparisons that enable greater understanding among traditions and critiquing comparisons that stand in the way of achieving that end.

The argument for metacomparative philosophy, in turn, is that if it is possible to identify good comparisons, then it should be at least possible to identify what is good about the method that produced the comparison. Identifying what it is about a method that enables the production of good comparisons—what I will call the "strengths" of a method—can thus facilitate the production of more good comparisons and perhaps better ones as well. Moreover, carrying out this analysis across a variety of comparative methods can allow for a comparative understanding of the strengths of each method, thus providing a more informed sense of each method's relative strengths, another venue for the improvement of those methods, and a critically informed basis for the development of new and improved comparative methods.

This understanding of the possibilities for metacomparative philosophy is built into the method of the current project as follows: rather than forcing each comparative method to measure up to a static and external measure, each one is presented on its own terms, in accordance with its own intentions, developments, and achievements. It is then assessed with as unbiased a rendering of its strengths and weaknesses as possible, seeking to remain as faithful as possible to the goals and values of that method. It is only in the final chapter that these assessments of each method will be considered in conjunction with one another. There, the intent will not be a matter of trying to identify the strongest method, since this would inevitably distort the methods under consideration by forcing them to adhere to a common, external standard.[13] Rather, the purpose will be to clarify the points of comparison among each of the methods considered and to indicate something of their strengths relative to one another.

In sum, a comparative method arising out of the pragmatist or process traditions would never simply *assert* the possibility of comparison; rather, it must *demonstrate* it by the results of its comparisons. Metacomparative inquiry takes the additional step of trying to identify what it is that allows for demonstrably good results in each method and to provide a context for consideration of whether and how these can contribute to the further development of comparative methodology as a whole. Like each individual comparative method, however, metacomparative inquiry in this tradition must also be based on its ability to provide insightful results. Accordingly, this study—and the method it employs—should be judged on the basis of its stated goals and values, namely, the cultivation of a better understanding of the available comparative methods, the development of a better sense of each method's relative strengths and weaknesses, and perhaps even the generation of new insights about the nature of comparison itself.

A third concern about metacomparative inquiry arises in contradistinction to the second: without drawing on a single, well-developed, and thoroughly tested method, does this project not run the risk of falling victim to all the vulnerabilities of any new method? Indeed, does the intentional broadness and openness of its method not make it susceptible to aimlessness and vacuity? It would seem that, in the absence of a clearly defined and well-tested method, the best that can be hoped for is a muddling through of the data in a simple, unrefined way.

However, it is by no means clear that the comparison of philosophical positions and the comparison of comparative methods are the same sort of activity, and it is therefore questionable that a method developed for the one would be appropriate for the other. There is an important difference between interpreting alternative comparative methods from the perspective of one method and attempting to mediate in an even-handed manner among competing methods. In the former, alternative methods are judged on the basis of the values of the method used to compare them, and because the values used to judge them are not necessarily intrinsic to them, there is a much higher propensity for distortion in the comparative process. In such instances of comparison, it would be difficult to distinguish the comparison of comparative methods from the mere self-expression of the particular method employed. Metacomparative inquiry tries to move beyond this in the same way that comparative inquiry tries to move beyond the mere expression of philosophical positions. Although one cannot be certain from the outset that such a metacomparative philosophy is possible—and much less exactly what it should look like if it is—this project proceeds into the unknown with the same pragmatic optimism that has characterized the development of the methods it compares.

With respect to the development of this new method, it will inevitably face challenges throughout its development. However, although this may run the *risk* of naïveté and make the method *susceptible* to aimlessness and vacuity, it does not necessarily *condemn* the method to these ends. The pragmatism in which the method of this project is rooted is nothing if not optimistic about the productive power of vulnerability when it is coupled with the possibility for correction and improvement, and this is a virtue that is largely carried over into the process tradition as well. Taking for granted that it is at least possible that metacomparative inquiry is different in important ways from standard comparative inquiry, the thrust of the pragmatist and process traditions is to encourage the development of new approaches capable of determining whether such a difference exists and—if so—what sorts of methods are best able to address it.

The current project is admittedly novel and may thus have to "muddle through" its data to some extent at least initially. Yet comparative philosophy itself is also a relatively new endeavor—at least in the large-scale, self-conscious way it has been undertaken over the course of the last century. If it has taken American philosophy three generations to cultivate the comparative methods that are extant today, why should one expect that it would be any different for the comparison of these comparative methods? Indeed, what one finds when one looks to the history of the comparative philosophy is that the development of methods is hardly a seamless endeavor, perfect from its beginnings. Rather, it is an inherently messy affair that starts from modest beginnings but emerges over time as an increasingly sophisticated affair through perpetual correction and improvement.

Ultimately, any conclusions that are reached by a project of this sort can only be incomplete and inadequate when considered in an absolute sense, since they are but the perspectives of a single individual inaugurating the larger task of the comparison of comparisons. Yet the value of the following chapters should arguably be judged only on a basis relative to the extent to which they are able to advance the burgeoning study of comparative philosophy. The task at hand is to initiate the comparison of comparative methods on reasonably solid footing so that it can continue on the long process of correction and improvement that has hitherto sustained the comparison of philosophies itself. To the extent this project inaugurates that task and launches it on a productive trajectory, it will have been worth the effort.

CHAPTER ONE

WILLIAM ERNEST HOCKING

Comparative Philosophy for the "Emerging World Culture"

In the course of a lifetime of imprudent undertakings, one maxim I have been led to adopt is that no task is to be evaded merely because it is impossible. The relevant questions: whether it requires to be done, and whether the circumstances point a finger in one's direction.

—Hocking, *Strength of Men and Nations*

William Ernest Hocking (1873–1966) personifies the maturing of American philosophical interest in comparison. Although he had many important predecessors in American philosophy who nurtured a growing interest in non-Western religious and philosophical traditions (e.g., Ralph Waldo Emerson, William James, Josiah Royce, George Santayana), Hocking was the first to provide any substantive critical reflection on the nature of comparison and the first to develop and apply a deliberate comparative philosophical method.[1] While the lack of any established tradition of comparative philosophy in America might have made the development of a comparative method seem impossible, Hocking understood both that the increasing interpenetration of world cultures required its development and also that the vagaries of historical context had pointed a clear finger in his direction. It is because of his inaugural and influential role in the development of comparative philosophy in America that this study begins with a careful consideration of his life and works.

Hocking's interest and involvement in comparative philosophy was what it could only have been at the outset of that subfield's development: serendipitous. In the absence of any established tradition of philosophical comparison, few if any of his contemporaries could have been considered experts in comparative philosophy, and none of them—including Hock-ing—could have received formal training in it. Rather, to the extent that any of them could have been interested and involved in comparative phi-losophy, it could only have been by virtue of the exceptional opportunities afforded to them over the course of their careers.

For Hocking, the starting point for his own interest can be traced back to his attendance at the World's Columbian Exposition in 1893. There, at the World's Parliament of Religions, he had the opportunity to hear Swami Vivekananda speak on Advaita Vedānta, and the event had—as it would for many Americans at the time—a significant influence on the young philo-sophical idealist. To be sure, Advaita Vedānta is not the same as Western philosophical idealism, but the apparent similarities between the two sug-gest that these two early interests may not have been entirely unrelated for Hocking. He would go on to examine Vedānta and other non-Western traditions with much greater sophistication later in his career, although his subsequent readiness to take seriously these other traditions can arguably be traced back to the seriousness with which they were considered at the World's Parliament of Religions.

While his encounter with Vivekananda whetted his appetite for Indian philosophy, Hocking's primary interest remained in Western philosophical idealism and—upon the publication of William James' *Principles of Psychology* (2007 [1890])—in its connection with the budding new discipline of psy-chology.[2] To pursue these interests to their fullest extent, Hocking resolved to study under Royce and James and so enrolled at Harvard University in 1899. He was pleased to find that both mentors shared his interest in Indian philosophy and religion and surely benefited in his understanding of those traditions as a result.

Following his graduate education, it is noteworthy that Hocking's first professional position was as an instructor of comparative religion at Ando-ver Theological Seminary (1904–1906). Although this would be followed by general appointments in philosophy at the University of California at Berkeley (1906–1908) and Yale (1908–1914), it indicates that the early Hocking's philosophical interests were at least accompanied by a burgeoning interest and aptitude in cross-cultural comparison. This is consistent with the character of his seminal text, *The Meaning of God in Human Experience* (1912), which was published at this time: although its primary purpose was not with comparison per se, it does exemplify a broad interest in and familiarity with non-Western traditions.

Two events occurring in 1914, however, marked a definitive turning point in Hocking's readiness and ability to address issues beyond the purview of his own Western philosophical idealism. The first, of course, is the onset of the First World War. As Bruce Kuklick notes in his *Rise of American Philosophy* (1977), although the United States would not become involved in the war until 1917, "the spectacle of civilized Europeans slaughtering one another preoccupied all thoughtful Americans [in the intervening period], and the role of the United States in the conflict dominated public discussions" (435). That this was true for Hocking can be seen in his many war-related publications from 1914 to 1917 (about one-third of which dealt directly with issues concerning the war),[3] as well as his enlistment in the Civilian Training Camp at Plattsburgh, New York, in 1916.[4] Upon American entry into the war, Hocking volunteered for service and, according to Leroy Rouner, traveled with "the first detachment of American military engineers to reach the front" (1966, xii–xiv).[5] Following this, he served as the district director of War Issues Courses for colleges in the American northeast.[6]

In many respects, this "war to end all wars" can be understood to have had an effect on Hocking not unlike that which it had on America more generally: just as it forced the nation to attend to political and military challenges in the international arena, so it compelled Hocking—as it did many of his peers—to attend to the challenges of political philosophy on a global scale. What differentiates Hocking from most of his peers in this respect is that, even after the war was over, these issues remained among his foremost concerns (see, e.g., Hocking 1926a, 1926b, 1932, 1947, 1956, 1959).[7]

The year 1914 is also important for Hocking's development as it marks his return to his alma mater, Harvard, as a professor of philosophy. In doing so, he filled the position vacated by Santayana in 1912 upon the latter's retirement. Although he was not the first choice for that position, he quickly demonstrated his merit and subsequently accepted the prestigious Alford Chair of Natural Religion, Moral Philosophy and Civil Polity (1920), a position previously held by his advisor, Royce. He would hold this position for the remainder of his prolific career (1920–1943). Although he had already published the book that would be his magnum opus (Hocking 1912), it was during his time at Harvard that he would establish his reputation as one of the preeminent philosophers of his generation.

Moreover, it was at Harvard that he was able to carry on and develop further the comparative interests of his predecessors James, Santayana, and Royce. There, he was able to maintain an ongoing conversation about such things not only with Royce (during the latter's remaining years) but also with Charles Rockwell Lanman of the Sanskrit department (Riepe 1967, 127).[8] More broadly, his prominent position also enabled him to take as conversation partners such formative figures in the American tradition as John Dewey and A. N. Whitehead as well as prominent international scholars such as Sarvepalli Radhakrishnan, P. T. Raju, and Hu Shi.[9] This cross-section of interests and professional connections positioned Hocking to be at the forefront of a growing American philosophical interest in comparative philosophy.[10]

DESCRIPTION OF METHOD

Re-Thinking Missions, Pre-Thinking Comparisons

For all of Hocking's longstanding interest and involvement in global politics and cultural pluralism, his first substantive publication on issues pertaining directly to cross-cultural comparison found their place in a work on missiology. In 1930, he was asked to serve as the chairman of the Commission of Appraisal for the Laymen's Foreign Missions Inquiry, an organization of laypersons from seven different American Protestant denominations brought together in the context of a precipitous decline in interest in and support for foreign missions. Their purpose was to determine whether such missions should continue at all and, if so, in what manner.[11]

Hocking was asked to fill this role on the basis of his already-established fame as a prominent Harvard philosopher, and his accession provided him with the opportunity to travel through India, Myanmar (then Burma), China, and Japan over the course of more than nine months to observe and evaluate the ongoing effects of the missionary enterprise in each country. In the course of its investigations, the commission had the opportunity to meet not only with missionaries but also with indigenous Christians and non-Christians alike. This provided Hocking with a rare opportunity to cultivate his interest in other cultures and religions in the context of direct, physical engagement.

The results of the commission were published under the title *Re-Thinking Missions: A Laymen's Inquiry after One Hundred Years* (1932). While the book was technically a collaborative work by all fifteen members of the commission, Hocking was clearly the most influential of its members—both on the project and on the subsequent publication. Most important, scholars generally agree that he bore primary if not sole responsibility for the first four chapters: those that detail the relation of Christianity to other religions. These chapters are necessarily comparative and as such provide the first glimpses of Hocking's comparative method (albeit a method that was at this point very much still in formation).[12]

The publication of *Re-Thinking Missions* marked a significant change in the debate about Christianity's relationship with other religions. It rejected the traditional model for that relationship—which it termed the "conquest" model, but which might also be termed the "conversionary" model—whereby the purpose of Christian missions is the conversion of non-Christians. The commission's report described this model as follows: "The original objective of the mission might be stated as the conquest of the world by Christianity: it was a world benevolence conceived in terms of a world campaign. There was one way of salvation and one only, one name, one atonement" (1932, 35). It is important to note that the conquest model does not assume that other religions have nothing of religious value to offer; rather, it proceeds on the belief that *only the clearest and most complete revelation should prevail*, as less complete revelations only blind others to the full potential of religion (36). The result, in any event, is more or less the same.

The problem with this model, according to the commission, was that it had become increasingly problematic as a means for engaging other cultures. Whereas earlier missionaries had enjoyed a cultural advantage (insofar as political, social, economic, and medical advances tended to accompany Western missionaries), many non-Western nations were becoming capable of providing these advantages for themselves.[13] Likewise, the resurgence of local religions amid national pride meant that Christian missionaries had to contend with revalorized religious alternatives. Indeed, the fact that Christianity was associated with Western influences now tended to count against it. Add to this the apparent waning of Christian fervor in the West, and the "conquest" model left many wondering why it was worthwhile to continue sending missionaries overseas.

In place of the conquest model, the commission proposed an "ambassadorial" model of missions, whereby Christians are still called to share their faith with other cultures but, after introducing it, must leave it to those cultures to develop that faith as they will. The commission employed a fitting analogy: "The 'foreign' mission must regard as its task the planting of a seed, not the final growth of a tree" (1932, 24). By leaving church planting at the planting, "foreign" churches are allowed to develop their own indigenous character (82), thus reducing their dependency on Western institutions while also allowing for a greater richness and diversity in the Christian engagement of "the emerging world-culture" (19). Following the initial church "planting," then, the Christian missionary should serve as an ambassador to the host country—as a guide, advisor, and resource on behalf of Christianity, helping the indigenous church to cultivate the meaning of Christianity in its environment without losing its own cultural heritage.

In allowing "foreign" churches to develop their own indigenous character, the commission did little in the way of restricting the ways in which such churches could develop. As *Re-Thinking Missions* made clear, it is entirely acceptable and appropriate for indigenous churches to draw on surrounding religious truths and religiously meaningful practices, as these are not only a part of their cultural heritage but also a part of the broader heritage of human religiosity. This openness to other religious traditions stemmed from a conviction on the part of the commission that religions are—at their most basic—expressions of a common human quest and that the religious intuitions of all of humankind are best served when all religions are allowed to develop to their fullest extent.

In asserting an underlying commonality among religious traditions, the commission also recognized that there are significant differences among existing religious traditions. However important these differences may be, the commission saw its task as drawing attention to the truth of the similarities among traditions. "It is a matter of truth," the commission wrote, "not because the assertion of likeness, where likeness exists, is any truer than the assertion of the difference that also exists" (1932, 31–32); rather, attention had been focused so heavily on the differences among religions that the underlying similarities had become obscured. Focusing on the similarities in this case was thus simply a matter of balancing the scales of religious understanding.

This notion of the similarities among religions, as it pertains to missions and other forms of religious interaction, was developed in terms of a "principle of growth." The commission argued, "The more of religious insight there is in any group of mankind, the more favorable the conditions are for one who has further insight to contribute. It is not what is weak or corrupt but what is strong and sound in the non-Christian religions that offers the best hearing for whatever Christianity may have to say."[14] Historically, the argument continued, religions—including Christianity—have been able to spread only because they have encountered and built upon the common "germ" of human religiosity—"the inalienable religious intuition of the human soul" (1932, 37). From a mission perspective, then, Christianity not only gains nothing by disparaging other religions but also undercuts its own potential for growth in areas where those religions are prominent.

The implications of this position become clear when the focus shifts to the borrowing of beliefs and practices from one tradition by another. The commission noted that such borrowing is not only to be expected (as any historical inquiry will reveal) but also encouraged, since it is in large part through such borrowing that religious traditions experience growth and development. Accordingly, if some feature of Christianity were adopted and adapted by another religion, this should not be seen as an impoverishment of the Christian message but rather a validation of the basic religious intuition underlying it. Indeed, this should be seen as a "striking success" for the Christian message:

> It is time for the Christian to have overcome these unworthy fears springing from a sense of proprietorship. The unique thing in Christianity is not borrowable nor transferable without the transfer of Christianity itself. Whatever can be borrowed and successfully grown on another stock does in fact belong to the borrower. For a part of the life of any living religion is its groping for a better grasp of truth. The truth which rectifies the faults of any religious system is already foreshadowed in its own search. (1932, 44)

Any concern with religious propriety, then, merely stands in the way of the growth of the religious intuition in humankind—or, to put it in Christian terms, the salvation of human souls. "With what are we concerned," the commission asked, "except for the spread through the world of what Christianity *means?"* (43, italics original). If we are really concerned with spreading the meaning—the truth—of Christianity, then concern with the name under which it spreads can only impede the growth of its meaning.[15]

The concern among more conservative Christians regarding *Re-Thinking Missions* centered on the apparent loss of primacy for Christianity among the world's religious traditions, which appeared to undercut one of the most compelling justifications for foreign missions. Such fears seem to be realized in the conclusions of the commission:

> We desire the triumph of that final truth: we need not prescribe the route. . . . The Christian who would be anxious in view of such a result displays too little confidence in the merits of his own faith. Whatever is unique in it, and necessary to the highest religious life of men can be trusted to show its value in due time and in its own way. Meantime, if through growing appreciation and borrowing, the vitality of genuine religion is anywhere increased he may well rejoice in that fact. He will look forward, not to the destruction of these religions, but to their continued co-existence with Christianity, each stimulating the other in growth toward the ultimate goal, unity in the completest religious truth. (1932, 44)

This suggests that "the completest religious truth" is neither Christianity nor any other presently existing religion but rather some new formulation that represents the complete growth of all religions in their interactions with one another. In the meantime, then, the goal of Christian missions should be the cultivation of its own meaning (which includes borrowing from other religions), as well as the encouragement of such cultivation within other religions.

Re-Thinking Missions is most often remembered for its place in the development of twentieth-century Protestant missiology. However, it is at least as important for the inauguration of cross-cultural comparison. When the commission stripped Western Christianity of its privileged position, it decentered not just Christianity but also Western culture more generally. If no tradition can claim a privileged position among other traditions, then *any interaction among traditions must begin with comparison.* Although this was not its primary goal, *Re-Thinking Missions* outlined a bold new vision for cross-cultural comparison, one that saw in all traditions the same basic quest for truth and meaning while also recognizing the distinctive differences among those traditions that constitute their contribution to the broader quest. Although it was written in the language of comparative religion, it suggested a basic framework for comparison that Hocking would develop in his subsequent philosophical works.

Before moving to those works, it is worth pointing out four of the distinctive features of this approach to comparison. Perhaps the most immediately evident of these features is the religious essentialism that pervades *Re-Thinking Missions*: the conviction that all religions are, at least at their most basic, effectively about the same thing, however broadly conceived. The commission wrote that "within the piety of the common people of every land . . . there is this germ, the inalienable religious intuition of the human soul. The God of this intuition is the true God: to this extent universal religion has not to be established, it exists" (1932, 37).[16] Quoting C. B. Olds, the report affirmed that "we *are* brothers in a common quest, and the first step is to recognize it, and disarm ourselves of our prejudices" (31, italics original).[17] Religions may be unique insofar as they embody a particular set of religious truths, but these truths need not be limited to the religions that first express them; to the contrary, it is both possible and desirable to learn from those truths and thus improve one's own religion.

The second notable feature of *Re-Thinking Mission* that would carry over into Hocking's later work is his account of *how* one religion can learn from another. The commission employed the metaphor of "borrowing" to explain how religions both take things from other religions and yet make them their own. "Whenever two vigorous religions are in contact," it notes, "each will tend to borrow from the other—terms, usages, ideas, even gods and articles of faith" (1932, 42). As noted above, such borrowing often entails creative alterations on the part of the borrower due to its integration into a different context, with the result that borrowed terms (etc.) tend to mean something somewhat different to the borrowing tradition than they did in the host tradition. What is revolutionary in this approach is that what is actually borrowed is less important than the change that comes about in a tradition as a result of the borrowing.

A third significant feature of *Re-Thinking Missions* for Hocking's future work is its focus on "the emergence of a world-culture" (1932, 19)—the development of a single, common culture that could draw on the contributions of all local cultures and develop them into a stronger, more unified culture befitting the challenges facing a world whose cultures were coming increasingly into contact with one another.[18] This concern is best understood in light of the broader "internationalist" movement: a political movement in America that arose at the close of the First World War and took as its goal the eradication of any further international wars through the establishment of a unified world order.[19] Hocking was a vigorous supporter of the internationalist movement—especially as it pertained to U.S. entry into the League of Nations—and this commitment found ready expression in his approach to cross-cultural comparison in this and his later works.[20]

One final feature of *Re-Thinking Missions* that should be considered is the uproar within American Protestantism that followed its publication. This fury had little to do with the practical proposals of the report (on which there was eventual consensus). Instead, it centered on the theological assertions pertaining to the relation of Christianity with other religions.[21]

Many conservative Protestants felt that the inclusivist position laid out in the report compromised the integrity of their faith: sin, grace, redemption, the virgin birth, the person and work of Christ, the Trinity, all of which seemed to many to be rendered arbitrary expressions of a much more basic and amorphous (if not vacuous) religious idea. Indeed, many people failed to see how any other tradition could have the truth and meaning they knew their own tradition to have.[22]

Holding aside, for the moment, whether or not American evangelicals were correct in this reading of Hocking's report, it is worth noting that Hocking and his comparative heirs would face much the same resistance in philosophical circles. Many contemporaries are hesitant to give Confucius and Laozi a place next to Plato and Aristotle, let alone Wang Yangming and Dai Zhen a place next to Kant and Hegel. One must ask, with Hocking, whether anything of the validity of one's own tradition is really lost in recognizing the validity of other traditions as sources of insight as well, and whether it is so impossible to recognize these insights in the context of a broader—and perhaps improved—philosophical frame of reference.

In closing, it should not be surprising that cross-cultural comparison in American philosophy has its roots in missions. Missionaries have often been among the first points of contact among different cultural traditions, as well as the earliest conduits through which texts and ideas flow between cultures. Moreover, by virtue of their advance engagement, they have often been harbingers for broader impending concerns in cross-cultural engagement.[23] This being the case, understanding the history and experience of these missions should play a major role in the self-understanding of academic comparativists, who have shown up relatively late in the discussion. Despite this, attitudes toward mission are typically uninformed, incomplete, and overwhelmingly negative. Comparative philosophers shun missions only at the peril of misunderstanding their own disciplinary roots and remaining ignorant of some of the best early examples of cross-cultural engagement.

For his part, Hocking would remain involved in the ongoing debate about missions for the rest of his life and would write a number of additional works on religion (see esp. 1940). However, soon after *Re-Thinking Missions*, Hocking came to maintain a stronger distinction between philosophy and religion that would inform all of his later works. Philosophy, he argued, pertains to universal truths, such that any differences in philosophical positions can ultimately be resolved by means of further inquiry. Religion is similar insofar as it has a universal goal—"living well," as he described it (1940, 26)—but it does not share the appeal to a universal standard of judgment. Religion is thus less capable of moving beyond its cultural context and rendered at least partially irrational.[24]

The cash value of this distinction for Hocking was that, while philosophical traditions can be expected to work together toward the development of a single, fullest expression of metaphysical truth, religions can only become universal if they make their particular cultural experiences the norm for all people. Thus, he came to see the prospects for comparative thought to be much more promising in philosophy than in religion. Accordingly, he proceeded to publish a number of texts in comparative philosophy, including the development of a more robust and specifically philosophical comparative methodology. It is to these texts that we now turn.

Hocking as Comparative Philosopher

Hocking's first specifically philosophical work in comparison was an essay entitled "Chu Hsi's Theory of Knowledge" (1936).[25] It demonstrates a surprising familiarity with the Chinese Confucian tradition, given that Hocking was not a sinologist, read Chinese texts only in translation, and was largely self-taught in Chinese philosophy. "Hocking is rare indeed among major Western philosophers," wrote Charles Moore. "He not only has comprehensive and detailed knowledge of the great Oriental philosophies—he spent some time in concentrated study in this area—but also understands them—and knowledge does not always produce understanding, as much work in this field reveals" (Rouner 1966, 342).[26] Hocking may not have been a sinologist, but he was of the conviction that a philosopher should be concerned with reality in all of its richness—including the many perspectives from which it has been engaged and expressed.[27] Accordingly, he wrote a remarkable amount for his time on Asian culture, politics, and religion and took advantage of every opportunity to learn more about other traditions. Indeed, it was his fortuitous involvement with a growing consortium of Chinese students at Harvard that led him to write his monumental article on Zhu Xi for publication in the inaugural issue of *The Harvard Journal of Asiatic Studies* (1936).

In this article, Hocking argued that Zhu Xi has an important contribution to make to the contemporary discussion about the nature of scientific knowledge. Although Zhu Xi was writing several centuries before the Western "scientific revolution," Hocking maintained that he "was closer than any other before [the twentieth] century to an anticipation of what we now call 'scientific method' " (1936, 111). Moreover, while he possessed all of the rational and empirical sensitivities of the modern sciences,[28] he also incorporated additional sensitivities that enabled him to expound a more robust philosophy of nature.[29] Specifically, he incorporated into his theory of knowledge categories such as *li* (principle) and *xin* (heart/mind) that have an integrated ethical dimension, which enables them to address not only what a thing is but also the implications of knowing that thing. Thus, the "investigation of things" (*gewu zhizhi*)—originally emphasized in *The Great Learning* (*Daxue*) and championed by Zhu Xi—should result not only in a greater factual knowledge of things but also in the moral cultivation of the knower.

The significance of this broader epistemological purview is that it expands the possibilities for further knowledge. As Hocking pointed out at the beginning of his essay, "If not an axiom, it is at least a reasonable presumption in the theory of knowledge that ways of knowing must vary with the nature of the objects to be known. . . . It is a direct application of this principle that if anything like mentality or purpose is a factor in the wider world, what we call 'scientific procedure' would not be likely to discern it." Rather, if such things are real, "it would not be unreasonable to suppose that some disciplinary preparation of the organ of perception would be necessary in order to apprehend it" (1936, 109). Zhu Xi's significance, according to Hocking, lies in having provided such disciplinary preparation by means of the development of a more comprehensive set of categories for understanding nature.[30] These categories enabled him to cultivate "a finer degree of receptivity to the realities operating in the given world" (123) by rendering the knower open to both facts *and* values as potential sources of knowledge. What Zhu Xi's theory of knowledge has to offer the modern sciences, then, is a way of interpreting reality that is no less rational and empirical but that can also incorporate ethical considerations. In short, Zhu offered a way beyond the reductively mechanistic understanding of nature that has dominated the modern sciences.

This chance to learn from Zhu Xi is not a merely gratuitous one, Hocking insisted; it addresses identifiable needs in the struggle to achieve a flourishing democracy. The sciences are crucial to a healthy democracy because they encourage and reinforce the universality of knowledge: scientific knowledge can—at least in principle—be known and verified by anyone. Not only does such universality level the playing field in a world where knowledge is power, but it also allows democratic participants to hold each other accountable for that knowledge and thus to build more responsible and trusting communities. By enlarging the purview of the scientific method, Zhu Xi provides the means for the ethical dimensions of reality to be incorporated into this democratic discourse as well, with all of the legitimacy and universality hitherto afforded to modern science.

This essay constitutes an important foray for Hocking into the venue of comparative philosophy, and several of its features deserve further comment insofar as they are characteristic of his approach to comparison. The most remarkable feature of this essay is the ease with which it brings Zhu Xi into the conversation about contemporary Western concerns. Zhu Xi was writing in a different context, to a different audience, for different purposes; he was certainly neither a scientist nor a democrat in the modern sense. Yet these differences, according to Hocking, pose no greater challenges than the differences that accompany the ancient Greek philosophers, or modern Continental philosophers for that matter. As Neville notes, Hocking "read Zhu Xi as a philosopher alongside Kant, Fichte, and Bergson, improving upon them in crucial respects" (Lachs and Hester 2004, 368).[31] Moore concurred when he wrote that Hocking "distinctly appreciates those 'alien' concepts and perspectives in the philosophies of the East. . . . He also apparently feels quite deeply that some of the insights of the East can enlighten and provide correctives of the narrow points of view of philosophers in the Western traditions—and that philosophy itself, in its broadest sense, can be significantly enriched by some of the deep convictions of Eastern philosophies and philosophical traditions" (Rouner 1966, 342). Hocking's task was ultimately the task of the comparative philosopher: to understand the insights of multiple traditions and bring them to bear on one another, with the ultimate goal of developing better ways of thinking in general.

It is also worth noting that Hocking's appraisal of Zhu Xi is not an uncritically enthusiastic one, as would characterize many of the early encounters with non-Western traditions. His appraisal was informed and balanced, identifying both where Zhu Xi has contemporary contributions to make and where his ideas run into difficulty. For example, he noted that Zhu Xi's categories are pre-Cartesian ones, insofar as they do not make a strong distinction between the mental and physical worlds. While he maintains that Cartesian dualism needs to be overcome, he notes that it can only be overcome by being passed through. This, he pointed out, is something that Zhu Xi did not have the opportunity to do, and—while no fault of its own—it does pose an important challenge for the application of his thought to contemporary philosophy. Hocking's readiness to draw on Zhu Xi's work, however, demonstrates that he believed the potential contributions are sufficiently great and the challenges sufficiently surmountable to merit careful consideration.

Finally, although this is not immediately evident, Hocking's purpose in drawing attention to Zhu Xi is entirely consistent with his earlier work in *Re-Thinking Missions*: to strengthen and advance the "emerging world-culture" (1932, 19). Hocking knew that the sciences would play an integral role in that world culture, and he was keenly interested in rendering a vision of these sciences that was capable of acknowledging the full breadth and depth of reality. This, as Neville points out, was an overarching concern in most of Hocking's works, and his essay on Zhu Xi offered him a distinctly cross-cultural means for expressing it (Lachs and Hester 2004, 377).

It may seem strange that Hocking would publish such a concrete cross-cultural comparative work before producing a more theoretical account of the approach he would take. This, however, is merely a testament to the significance of his comparative work in religion and missions for his philosophical work: the theory was already completed in its most basic form in *Re-Thinking Missions*. That this is the case can be seen in the prominence of some of the themes introduced there in his piece on Zhu Xi. I have already highlighted his continued focus on the cultivation of a world culture in the essay. No less evident, however, is his exemplification of what "borrowing" among cultures entails in his "use" of Zhu Xi to inform modern scientific theory. Note, for instance, how there is no concern with whether Zhu Xi's insights are applied only as originally intended; the sole concern is whether modern science has something to learn by engaging Zhu Xi. As is the case with religions, any concern with intellectual propriety only impedes the growth of traditions—philosophical, scientific, or otherwise—and it is with the growth of these traditions that Hocking was primarily concerned.

The Value of the Comparative Study of Philosophy

Hocking's most complete account of comparative methodology would come almost a decade later, in an essay written for the first East-West Philosophers' Conference, held at the University of Hawaii in 1939. This conference was of immense importance in the history of comparative philosophy: it was the first to take this emerging new subfield of philosophy as its primary focus, and it sought to do so by bringing together some of the most influential philosophers of its time. Gregg Sinclair, president of the University of Hawaii and initial organizer of the conference, described its intent in the following excerpt of his letter to Sarvepalli Radhakrishnan (1936):

> I have in mind a conference of Eastern and Western philosophers of the very first rank—who in sessions here would consider Eastern and Western philosophy, would endeavor to find common ground, or would make clear points of difference, the understanding of which would make for keener intelligent appreciation of Eastern and Western thought. . . . We should do something as important as the Conference of World Faiths was in Chicago in 1893. Our aim would be to make Eastern points in Eastern philosophy clear to the leaders in Western philosophy, so that they would show a more planetary perspective in future books.

While Sinclair had originally hoped to have a conference of about twenty philosophers—including John Dewey, A. N. Whitehead, and Henri Bergson—in the end only six were able to attend: Wing-tsit Chan (Hocking's former student and one of the founders of the conference), Charles A. Moore (another founder and director of the conference), Junjirō Takakusu (a prominent Buddhologist from Japan), Shunzō Sakamaki (a Japanese and American historian), George P. Conger (scholar of Indian philosophy), and F. S. C. Northrop (another of Hocking's former students, the topic of chapter 2).

Hocking had originally been invited by conference organizers in the "hopes that he [would] organize it from the Western point of view" (Sinclair 1936) and thus attract other prominent scholars to the conference.[32] Unfortunately, he was prevented from attending due to an unknown, last-minute conflict. He did, however, write an essay for the conference, which was published as the opening piece in the collection of essays put together for publication at the close of the conference. This essay, "Value of the Comparative Study of Philosophy" (1944b), served as both a concise defense of Hocking's comparative methodology and an apology for the conference as a whole.[33]

He began the essay by noting the sea change in East-West relations taking place at the beginning of the twentieth century. "The Western world," he quipped, "is beginning to take the Orient seriously."[34] Certainly, over the course of the previous two centuries, there had been a growing interest in things non-Western, but to the extent that this interest was scholarly—as opposed to merely exploitative—it pertained primarily to historical and linguistic studies. The East was seen as a curiosity: something that merited further examination sheerly for interest's sake, and which might at best fill out one's understanding of the diversity of human civilization. Yet, he notes: "In all of this scholarly work, there has been very little assumption that the philosophies of the Orient have something important for us. With the outstanding exception of Schopenhauer, no Western philosopher of the first rank has incorporated major Oriental ideas into his system of thought" (1944b, 1).[35] All polite demurrals to the "wisdom of the East" aside, it had been generally taken for granted that any prospects for "real knowledge" were best pursued by means of Western philosophy. Indeed, philosophy proper was seen in the West to be precisely, if not solely, what Western philosophers had accomplished to date.

Yet all of this, Hocking argued, is beginning to change. He pointed to a "new spirit of respect" emerging among scholars in the East and the West. Eastern thinkers continued to learn from Western traditions, especially in the natural sciences; Western thinkers, however, had also begun to learn from Eastern traditions, especially in aesthetics.[36] By virtue of this cross-fertilization of ideas, all traditions were being enriched, and to the extent that these interactions brought traditions closer together, they pointed to "a truth which is above race and nation" (1944b, 1).

This "truth above race and nation" is the philosophical side of the "emerging world-culture" anticipated in Re-Thinking Missions and aimed at in "Chu Hsi's Theory of Knowledge." It was also the long-range goal of the first East-West Philosophers' Conference as a whole. Charles Moore wrote of the conference that "[t]he underlying purpose was to determine the possibility of a world philosophy through a synthesis of the ideas and ideals of East and West, and to reach conclusions in the form of specific suggestions concerning the most fruitful ways in which such a synthesis could be effected" (1944, vii). Hocking could not have said it better himself: in Living Religions and a World Faith, he wrote that "[t]here is universal science; there should be universal law; why may we not also expect a world faith?" (1940, 21). Indeed, one should expect him to add, "Why may we not also expect a world philosophy?"

This is not to say that everyone at the conference agreed with every aspect of Hocking's approach. Moore noted that the essays written in conjunction with the conference include a number of provocative proposals "upon which the several writers do not always agree." However, there does seem to have been at least a broad consensus on the general points of Hocking's approach. For example, Moore wrote: "Among these [essays] is the constant theme that neither Orient nor Occident is philosophically self-sufficient, each lacking that total perspective which is characteristic of philosophy. Specifically, it is held that the West needs new and wider perspectives, and that the East . . . may provide inspiration as well as specific doctrines for this new Renaissance" (1944, vii). This is just about as concise a statement of Hocking's position in "Chu Hsi's Theory of Knowledge" as is possible: he was trying to bring about just such a Renaissance in scientific thinking by supplementing it with insights from the Chinese Confucian tradition. Hocking's intended participation in the East-West Philosophers' Conference, then, was more than just another event in a prolific career; it demonstrated that his vision for comparative philosophy was one that was becoming increasingly shared within the academy and one that he had no small part in spreading.

This essay, however, is more than a mere rehashing of Hocking's previous work in comparative philosophy; it is an apology for comparative philosophy itself, based on a critical appraisal of similarity and difference among philosophical traditions. Comparative studies "show how much akin the minds of men are under all circumstances," he wrote. "But they show also, and sometimes with startling contrast, differences in the very bases of our world views" (1944b, 2–3). The question for comparative philosophy, then, is whether these similarities and differences are sufficiently balanced as to make comparative inquiry both possible and worthwhile.

Hocking began by considering the belief that the differences among philosophical traditions are so pervasive that there is no common basis by which to compare them. The most prominent version of this argument is that the categories of thought themselves differ among traditions (something typically attributed to nonphilosophical peculiarities in one's starting point), thus eliminating any possibility of thinking about common philosophical problems in the same way across traditions. He noted, for instance, the argument that Western philosophy, thanks to the subject-predicate structure of the Greek language, has been saddled by recurrent difficulties with the concept of "being." Chinese philosophy, as the argument goes, has been able to avoid this difficulty since the Chinese language has no linguistic equivalent to the vague infinitive "to be" (1944b, 3). If differences were really this fundamental, there could be no place for comparative philosophy; there could only be an enumeration of different philosophical traditions whose relative merits would be impossible to determine.

Hocking would readily admit that there are often substantial differences among philosophical traditions; in fact, he said as much in the opening lines of his essay. Yet these differences can never be absolute ones, but rather only matters of *emphasis*. With respect to the Chinese tradition's evasion of the question of being, he wrote: "It may be true that Chinese thought is more naturally relational. But it is a question of emphasis. The basic categories both of being and of value are the same everywhere. If it were not so, there would be no hope of an international understanding nor of international order. Nor could scholars write about these differences articles which would be understood in both hemispheres" (1944b, 3). In other words, if there were no similarities underlying the differences among traditions, then comparison would not be possible. The fact that comparison is in fact taking place productively among the most diverse of philosophical traditions is thus testament not only to the possibility of comparative philosophy but also to the existence of more fundamental similarities underlying the differences among traditions.[37]

Having established his argument for a basic level of commonality among traditions, Hocking then turned to address their differences. The difficulty here for comparative philosophy lies with those who hold that philosophy is a process of linear development. "If philosophy were a simple deductive science," he wrote, "both Western and Eastern philosophy could regard themselves self-sufficient and in no absolute need of light from any other quarter of the globe. The original premises ought to agree, and the inferences from them would constitute a body of truth indifferent to time and place" (1944b, 6). In short, comparative philosophy would be pointless, as any differences would merely indicate errors on the part of one (or both) of the different traditions.

Yet philosophy is not a simple deductive science, he argued; it is "primarily a matter of *what a person sees*, and then of his capacity to make a rational connection between what he sees and what he otherwise knows; his premises are his original observations about the world" (1944b, 7). This, of course, is Hocking's argument for differences among traditions as matters of emphasis taken from a different tack: all perspectives—even philosophical ones—are necessarily selective, so philosophical traditions should be expected to differ even in their original observations. Yet these original observations need not be fundamentally opposed to one another; they can come together on the basis of the common categories of thought. Accordingly, differences among philosophical traditions are best seen as differences of perspective, which are not so much right or wrong as they are comparable and potentially supplementary.

This is not to say that differences among traditions do not sometimes indicate errors, or that one tradition cannot be, as a whole, stronger and more fully developed than another. Indeed, this is very likely to be the case, as there is no apparent force or principle regulating the development of philosophical perspectives. Hocking's point, however, is that this should not be decided in advance but rather made the subject of comparative inquiry. "The real question," he wrote, "is whether each is *capable of recognizing* that his moral judgments are defective; for if so, he is judging his judgments by a standard more nearly universal, and common ground can be reached" (1944b, 4). It is only after such cross-traditional modesty has been achieved that one can engage productively in comparative inquiry, although the focus will inevitably shift from pointing out defects to working constructively to improve traditions—especially one's own.

The value of comparative philosophy thus lies in strengthening each philosophical tradition by bringing it into constructive dialogue with other philosophical traditions. In this sense, it is *fortunate* that these traditions have developed in relative isolation from each other for so long: the result is a number of different answers to many of life's most difficult questions—and, indeed, answers to questions that some traditions may not have even thought to ask (1944b, 7).[38] As Hocking wrote, "We need not two eyes but many eyes; and those very differences which constitute the felt strangeness of the Orient are precisely the differences which make its thought indispensable for us" (11).

As laid out in "Value of the Comparative Study of Philosophy," then, comparison is possible only because traditions have both similarities and differences: they have similarities at least with respect to their basic categories of thought (although there may be greater similarities than this) and are different at least with respect to their philosophical purview (although they may also differ due to their respective errors). Overemphasizing the differences or the similarities renders comparative philosophy impossible and consequently strips philosophy of its full potential. Taken together, however, these similarities and differences provide the grounds for the supplementation of all philosophical traditions and the gradual emergence of a stronger philosophical vision on the part of all traditions.[39]

Hocking closed his essay with a brief review of comparative philosophy to date and proposed a constructive vision looking forward. He wrote:

> There are three historic attitudes in dealing with what is beyond our own circle of ideas. First, "This is strange and alien—avoid it." Second, "This is strange and alien—investigate it." Third, "This appears strange and alien—but it is human; it is therefore kindred to me and potentially my own—learn from it." Until two centuries ago, we were for the most part acting upon the first maxim. For another two centuries, the eighteenth to the twentieth, we have acted on the second: we have been concerned with an objective study of the East. The two centuries ahead of us must be devoted to the third, an attempt to pass beyond the scholarly objectivity to . . . the common pursuit of universal truth. (1944b, 11)

Looking over the decades since the publication of his essay, Hocking would perhaps have been pleased with the significant advances that continue to be made in the detailed study of each of the world's great philosophical traditions. He would arguably have been far less impressed, however, with the development of the comparative study of those traditions. While some progress has been made, it has been slow at best: cross-cultural comparative work is still eyed with suspicion in many philosophical circles and tends to persist only at the margins of the academic world; perhaps this is why he allowed two centuries for its proper development. Fortunately, there is some indication that, over the course of the last decade or two, this trend has started to change, with comparative philosophy moving more and more into the mainstream—especially among younger generations of scholars. With more than a century remaining, Hocking's mandate may yet see its fulfillment.

Whether or not his mandate is realized, Hocking's significance for comparative philosophy lies in his bold new vision and compelling rationale for its development. Taking into consideration that, prior to his time, comparative work among American philosophers was at best an occasional and tangential affair, his contributions to the field are particularly stunning. His work not only marks the advent of sustained comparative work in American traditions of philosophy but also inaugurates it with remarkably subtle and sophisticated reflection on the nature and content of comparison. It is thus in his work that one sees the maturing of American philosophical interest in comparison.

ANALYSIS AND APPRAISAL

Hocking's approach to comparative philosophy is rooted in his philosophical commitments to what might be called a "pragmatic idealism" (Hocking, 1912). As noted earlier, Hocking studied with both James and Royce while at Harvard. Of the two, Royce clearly had the more significant influence, passing on to him a strong idealist commitment to the importance of the Absolute for philosophy—something that would dominate all of Hocking's later work (even when only implicitly).[40] However, he also received from James a pragmatist's commitment to the importance of immediate experience for forming and testing any philosophical formulation. Although he would never become a full-fledged pragmatist himself, Hocking did believe that pragmatism revealed a significant shortcoming in traditional idealism, namely, its inability to impart any final significance to immediate experience.[41]

Yet Hocking saw the pragmatist critique not as doing away with idealism entirely but rather serving as an important corrective for it. Pragmatism, he maintained, has its own shortcoming, namely, its inability to provide any significant purpose or meaning for experience; that is, it was incapable of forming any ideals. For that, he maintained, one must engage the *ideas* underlying and driving experience, and this only idealism could do. Accordingly, he sought to create a fusion of pragmatism and idealism that would preserve the strengths of each while avoiding their respective weaknesses.[42] In the final analysis, his work remained an expression of philosophical idealism, but one profoundly modified by its pragmatist influences.

The influence of Hocking's particular brand of pragmatic idealism is readily apparent in his approach to comparison. On the one hand, his pragmatist side had him withhold judgment on any philosophical tradition in advance, allowing the truth of these traditions to prove themselves in the experience of their adherents. Hocking's self-described "negative pragmatism" maintained that any idea that, when acted on, fails to work itself out as predicted must be false.[43] Thus, the fact that the many world traditions in philosophy are so longstanding can be taken as a testament to their general truth (1944b, 7).[44] Accordingly, Hocking was less interested in discrediting traditions than he was in improving the ability of traditions to engage human experience in its fullness.

On the other hand, his idealist side retains the conviction that all philosophical traditions are engaging the same reality—the same Absolute—and that they all therefore possess a fundamental commonality as philosophical traditions. Because of this commonality, it is possible for all such traditions to engage one another productively. Even differences among traditions exist only as differences following upon more basic commonalities (Hocking 1944b, 3). Therefore, it is at least theoretically possible for various traditions—no matter how different—to engage one another productively, not only addressing common issues but also broadening the range of issues each tradition engages.

Brought together, this combination of pragmatism and idealism forged a tempered idealism of a distinctly twentieth-century variety. Gone is the confident optimism in the inevitable progress of ideas, replaced with a humbling recognition of the diversity of human experiences and ways of knowing. The result is a philosophical method that sees as much to be lost as gained in the development of ideas, so it places a premium on cultivating positive developments. It is a method that enables one to look broadly for new insights and to think creatively about how to develop those insights among traditions. It is a method that can find as much insight for Western science in Zhu Xi as it can in Newton or Galileo. In short, it is a philosophical method that is ideally situated to be developed into a robust comparative method.

Hocking's comparative method embodies all of this, but because he is seldom explicit about how that method operates it will take some interpretive generalization to unpack. He starts by taking for granted an underlying commonality to all traditions, which makes available the data from any philosophical tradition. He then proceeds from a position of epistemological modesty, recognizing the inevitability of shortcomings within his own tradition and anticipating the possibility that other traditions have fared better where his own tradition has struggled. Actual comparison begins, then, with a searching glance across traditions to find instances in which the advances of other traditions shed light on the shortcomings of one's own. This seems akin to Peirce's notion of "musement" (1998, 2:436), the results of which are easy to recognize in retrospect but nearly impossible to proscribe in advance. Upon identification of this productive difference, the difficult work of comparison lies in identifying what it is about the other tradition that has enabled its success in the respect in question and then demonstrating how the source of the success of that tradition might be incorporated into one's own.

This is the methodological structure best exemplified in Hocking's essay on Zhu Xi and most ably defended "Value of the Comparative Study of Philosophy." There are two points that merit particular attention. First, while the method may seem to focus primarily on the differences among traditions, the focus of the method is ultimately on the more basic similarities between the two. One must remember that, for Hocking, the beginning and end of all knowledge consists in a single "truth above race and nation" (1944b, 1); differences among traditions can thus only be indications of limited perspectives or errors. Thus, one may look to points of disparity among traditions to find productive loci of comparison, but the hard work of comparison lies in trying to overcome these differences to achieve a higher unity.

Second, Hocking's method is primarily one for improving one's own tradition. He did not set out to fix other traditions or point out where they fall short: this, he realized, is not how traditions are developed; rather, they must be developed from within. To use the terms of *Re-Thinking Missions*, traditions should serve as ambassadors to one another, making their resources available to one another for the sake of mutual improvement; but the primary responsibility of each tradition is to learn from other traditions and improve itself accordingly. For Hocking, the comparativist's role in bringing about the "coming world civilization" lies in strengthening his or her own tradition as much as possible by virtue of its cross-cultural interactions, with the knowledge that it is precisely such strength—among all traditions—that will sustain that coming civilization.

Strengths of Hocking's Approach

There are a number of strengths to this approach, but they can be summarized under four main points. The first is its open engagement with other traditions and its complementary readiness to decenter Western philosophical traditions. It was true in Hocking's day no less than in our own that Western culture dominated the global intellectual agenda, and Hocking could easily have argued—as many others have—for the superiority of Western philosophy on the basis of Western philosophical criteria.[45] Yet Hocking realized that every philosophical tradition is by necessity selective in its focus and that every tradition was therefore able to be supplemented by other traditions just as it was able to supplement those traditions in turn. What philosophy needed was not more claims to superiority but rather a commitment to growth within and among all traditions. Rouner summed up his contribution as an American philosopher as follows:

> He is a distinctively American philosopher, but perhaps his greatest contribution to American philosophy is his detailing of *The Coming World Civilization* in which American thought and action must now take place. Heretofore we have taken characteristic pride in being among the leading nations in the world, but in a world community, competitiveness must increasingly find its way to co-operation. . . . America's world-involvement is therefore requiring . . . an adaptation—some would say a maturing—of the American character. (1966, 18)

Hocking's contribution to American philosophy was encouraging its maturation by virtue of a productive engagement with non-Western traditions. His contribution to world philosophy, by extension, was the cultivation of a richer discourse among all traditions that should ultimately be able to help shape the "coming world civilization."

A second strength of this approach is the freedom it affords the comparativist in bringing one tradition into constructive conversation with another. Assuming proper care and insight on the part of the comparativist and his or her audience,[46] there are no two traditions that cannot be brought into conversation with one another to some extent. Moreover, since the diversity among traditions is precisely the locus for productive comparison (1944b, 7), the differences among traditions actually increase the possibilities for comparison rather than decreasing them. Certainly, strong differences among traditions may pose a particular challenge for comparativists who—like Hocking—would place a premium on interpreting traditions accurately, but with those greater difficulties come greater rewards. Indeed, the more diverse the array of longstanding philosophical alternatives, the richer the possibilities for comparative philosophy.

A third and related strength of this method is its readiness to differentiate between philosophical ideas and their particular, cultural expression. In Hocking's view, although any philosophical tradition will inevitably be couched in the particularities of its local context, its unique features—whether ideas or practices—can nonetheless be "borrowed" by other traditions without a necessary loss in their meaning. Naturally, the adopted features of another tradition may be altered somewhat as they take on a new set of cultural accoutrements, but the underlying idea remains for the most part intact. When applied across cultures, this process allows for a clear, traceable, and exploitable means of improving traditions one upon the other. Scholars are becoming increasingly aware of the extent to which such borrowing occurs; Hocking's approach has the singular distinction of having first made a general principle of it.

The fourth and final strength of this approach is its ability to envision the relevance of comparative philosophy beyond the bounds of the academy. Hocking carried on the commitments of his teachers, James and Royce, that philosophy reaches full expression only when it is related directly to real life situations. Accordingly, he was able to tie his comparative work to broader questions of diplomacy, global justice, and world peace.[47] This was of particular importance for Hocking, who lived to see the rapid spread of global economics and politics and the comparably lackluster spread of global philosophy. The difference, he maintained, had to do not with differences among the disciplines, but rather with the amount of effort exerted.[48] That difference was all the more tragic because of the important role that philosophy and religion can—and should—play in creating a just and peaceful world order. For Hocking, then, all philosophical traditions have an obligation to engage one another constructively and develop their common ideas in pursuit of a philosophy that has relevance to the "coming world civilization." One of his great contributions in comparative philosophy was not only to follow through on this obligation but also to set that task before all subsequent comparativists.[49]

Weaknesses of Hocking's Approach

While Hocking's work marks an important point in the development of comparative philosophy in America, his interests were not primarily those of a cross-cultural comparativist. As a result, following the two philosophical essays discussed above, Hocking turned his sights back to his more longstanding philosophical interests in idealism, international politics, and religion and wrote occasional pieces that were only peripherally concerned with comparative method. As a result, whatever strengths his approach has—and, indeed, whatever other weaknesses—it is marked by a certain incompleteness that ultimately calls into question the viability of the entire approach.

This incompleteness is manifested most prominently in the lack of development of the basic categories of his approach, something pointed out by almost every significant interpreter of Hocking's works.[50] As noted earlier, the precise structure of his method is vague at best. For example, while he was able to suggest in his essay on Zhu Xi that Western science has something to learn from Chinese philosophy with respect to the relevance of ethical sensitivities, he never indicated how he came to that realization in the first place. Moreover, he never said anything about how to actually incorporate these sensitivities into contemporary scientific practice. Similarly, in his essay "Value of the Comparative Study of Philosophy," he did well to point to social identification and otherworldliness as fruitful ideas for any civilization but failed to determine precisely how to incorporate these ideas into Western civilization.

It is unfortunate that Hocking was unable to develop his thought more completely, because what he accomplishes in his few comparative works is remarkable for its time. There is little doubt that Hocking himself would have liked to have had more time to refine his thought along systematic lines. However, his career was characterized by a relentless application of his philosophical ideas to the problems of ordinary life (as he would put it), such that the opportunity for the more austere—though nonetheless important—task of systematizing his thought never presented itself (Rouner 1969, 312). Rouner characterizes Hocking's situation as follows: "[M]any contemporary philosophers have spent too much time sharpening their tools and too little time working with them. Hocking's problem has been the reverse. It was only toward the end of his life that he began carving out his basic categories of fact, field, and destiny in detail" (313). In view of Hocking's prolific career of philosophic engagement, it is clear that he never stopped working constructively with his philosophical interests. Thus, if his tools are not as sharp as they might otherwise be, this can be safely attributed not to their inherent inadequacy or neglect but rather to their assiduous application.

This defense notwithstanding, the undeveloped status of his approach still creates significant problems for those who follow after him. A prime example of this can be seen with respect to the balance necessary in comparative philosophy between mastery of each of the traditions that would be compared and the speculative oversight that guides the way the traditions are brought together. Hocking, for his part, had surprisingly little difficulty mastering both sides of the process; as exemplified in "Chu Hsi's Theory of Knowledge," he was able to bring together disparate traditions with remarkable skill and apparent ease. For most comparativists, however, such skill and ease are more difficult to come by, and Hocking provides little direct guidance concerning where proper comparison starts, what skills it requires, what constitutes a "good" comparison, and so on.

The weakness in his approach, therefore, manifests itself primarily in the work of those who came after him, who often lacked his ability to master other traditions but who nonetheless sought to provide speculative insights across those traditions. Devoid of any established framework for comparison to hold their conclusions accountable, they tended with disturbing frequency to distort the traditions they compared and thus reach mistaken and misleading conclusions. At least in part as a reaction against these abuses, there has been a backlash in comparative philosophy against speculative oversight and a move instead toward area studies and specialization in single traditions.

The move toward area studies has allowed for a significant increase in knowledge about the world's many and diverse traditions and as such has constituted a positive contribution to comparative philosophy. No less important for comparison, however, are the insights of those who provide the speculative oversight pertaining to how these traditions can be brought together. The weakness of Hocking's approach, then, manifests itself both in the poorly grounded comparative conclusions of Hocking's less capable heirs and more recently in the suppression of the role of speculative oversight in comparison. Both of these developments have had a negative effect on comparative philosophy as a whole, and—perhaps appropriately—have together been responsible for much of the decline in Hocking's status in comparative philosophy.[51]

CONCLUSION

Hocking was undoubtedly one of the most prominent philosophers of his time, holding one of the most prestigious philosophical chairs in what was arguably the strongest philosophy department in the first half of the twentieth century. He was president of the Eastern Division of the American Philosophical Association for two terms (1926–27, 1927–28), and delivered the prestigious Hibbert Lectures (1936) and Gifford Lectures (1938–39). He was also a prolific writer, producing almost twenty monographs—many of them widely read and significant in their own right—as well as nearly three hundred essays and articles whose subject matter spanned every conceivable field in relation to philosophy. As John Howie notes, Hocking has certainly "earned himself a place among the best American philosophers" (Lachs and Hester 2004, 217).[52]

This being the case, it is remarkable that he has fallen as far out of favor in the current philosophical discussion as he has. At this point, there are few left who are still interested in Hocking's work, and among them most are interested in his significance as a historical figure. There is a sad irony to this status, since one of the most remarkable things about Hocking was his willingness to treat philosophers from all times, places, and commitments as peers for philosophical conversation.[53] It is not going too far to suggest that Hocking would ask his heirs to give him the same respect he gave to Zhu Xi: to recognize not only his historical significance but also what he has to offer contemporary philosophy. In deference to Hocking, I offer both of these in closing.

With respect to his historical significance, it is difficult to say enough about the role he has had in shaping comparative philosophy. His work in *Re-Thinking Missions* leveled the playing field for comparative inquiry with other cultures and traditions in a way that opened the door to comparative philosophical inquiry. His article on Zhu Xi was one of the first genuinely comparative works on a Chinese philosopher by a prominent American philosopher. His leading essay for the first East-West Philosophers' Conference was symbolic of the inauguration of a comparative philosophical discussion within the American philosophical tradition that has continued to the present day. By virtue of these three accomplishments alone, it is no overstatement to argue—as suggested at the start of this chapter—that he personifies the coming to maturity of comparative philosophy in America.

With respect to his potential contributions to the contemporary conversation about comparative philosophy, Hocking's method serves as a vitally important example of what comparative methods can—and perhaps should—look like early in their development. Writing at early stages of comparative philosophy, he did not have the privilege of knowing in advance the "proper bounds" for comparison, so he could press the creative boundaries of what was possible in comparative philosophy. In this sense, the loose-fitting style of his work actually serves to encourage precisely the bold vision that is required at the outset of any new philosophical venture.

In one of his later texts, Hocking likened himself to a philosophical explorer, whose thoughts "chart the forward passage" (1956, xiii). This is largely what the current text seeks to do, and if it seems vague in its definition this will only be because it has learned from Hocking's own experience. Placing a priority of rigorous precision and exhaustive development is not only a good way to stifle creativity in a novel project, but a good way to ensure that it never gets off the ground as well. Not unlike Hocking's works, this text submits its best insights to the broader community of inquirers as a way of initiating the conversation, with the hope and expectation that that community will follow up on that offering by further cultivating and improving it—much as Hocking tried to do with philosophical traditions in their own right.

As noted above, Hocking's philosophical heirs were questionable in their success at following up on his work and perhaps did his contributions—and, by extension, comparative philosophy—more harm than good by their contributions. Not all of his heirs, however, were so unsuccessful: his prize pupil, F. S. C. Northrop, would influence the development of comparative philosophy in equally significant—if fundamentally different—ways. Appropriately, then, it is to Northrop's work that we now turn.

CHAPTER TWO

FILMER S. C. NORTHROP

Comparative Philosophy as Comparative Ideology

> East and West can meet, not because they are saying the same thing, but because they are expressing different yet complementary things, both of which are required for an adequate and true conception of man's self and his universe. Each can move into the new comprehensive world of the future, proud of its past and preserving its self-respect. Each also needs the other.
>
> —Northrop, *The Meeting of East and West*

Filmer Stuart Cuckow Northrop (1893–1992) begins the first chapter of his most famous work, *The Meeting of East and West* (1946), by arguing that World War II was really the first "world war." Whereas World War I was "primarily a Western conflict, in which a few Oriental peoples found it expedient to participate" (1946, 1), it was only in the Second World War that both Western and Eastern forces were integrally involved. Such diverse involvement reflected not only the strong influence of Western ideologies in the Orient but also Eastern forces bringing their own ideologies to bear upon the Occident.[1]

> This means that for the first time in history, not merely in war but also in the issues of peace, the East and the West are in a single world movement, as much Oriental as Occidental in character. The East and the West are meeting and merging. The epoch which Kipling so aptly described but about which he so falsely prophesied is over. The time is here when we must understand the Orient if we would understand ourselves, and when we must learn how to

41

combine Oriental and Occidental values if further tragedy, bitterness, and bloodshed are not to ensue (1946, 4).

This is the task to which Northrop set himself in all of his comparative works: first, to identify the distinctive features of Western cultures; second, to identify those of Eastern cultures; and finally, to understand how those features can be understood and appreciated within the context of a world that has become pluralistic on a global scale.

It would be difficult to overestimate the influence of the Second World War on the development of Northrop's approach to comparative philosophy. His first significant reflections on cross-cultural comparative philosophy took place in the context of the first East-West Philosophers' Conference in Honolulu, Hawaii, in 1939, during which time the primary antecedents for the war were already in place. By the outset of that conference, the Japanese had already instigated the Second Sino-Japanese War by invading China (July 7, 1937); Germany had already annexed Austria (March 12, 1938) and occupied Czechoslovakia (March 1939). Although the war had not broken out in its full scale at the time of the conference, it would have been clear to most of those in attendance that whatever peace still existed was tenuous at best. In fact, it would be only a few weeks after that conference that Germany would invade Poland (September 1, 1939), which set off the Second World War in Europe.[2] Although it would be more than two years before the United States would become involved in the war, these international—and, indeed, cultural—conflicts would have been prominent concerns in 1939 for an American intellectual such as Northrop.[3]

Whatever the extent of its influence on his thought, the impending war could not have been the driving reason for Northrop's involvement in the conference concerning cross-cultural comparison. The conference had been in planning stages since at least 1936—prior to all of the aforementioned antecedents—and Northrop's involvement would have had to have been secured some time in advance. Given this, and the lack of any published interest in comparison prior to this point, Northrop's involvement in the conference seems due instead to the direct influence of his dissertation advisor and mentor, W. E. Hocking.[4] Northrop was the closest thing that Hocking had to a direct philosophic heir (at least in comparative philosophy), and there is good reason to believe that the latter's interest in cross-cultural comparison influenced the former's interests and attunement.[5] Moreover, given Hocking's prominent place in the initial planning of the conference, it is likely that Northrop's inclusion was at least in part the result of his teacher's influence.[6]

However, Northrop quickly established his own place as one of the foremost comparative philosophers of his time. He not only produced one of the most innovative essays of the conference, but soon thereafter he published an extended version of that essay in what would become his most famous book, *The Meeting of East and West* (1946). Indeed, this text burst onto the intellectual landscape at precisely the time when there was a felt need among many for new ways of relating to the global diversity of world cultures.[7] Northrop provided such a way in the *Meeting*, and in doing so he provided the framework for all of his subsequent work in comparative philosophy.

It is the purpose of this chapter to examine the comparative method of Northrop in careful detail. As with the chapter on Hocking, it will begin with a brief review of Northrop's works—including both early and later works but focusing on the *Meeting*—and culminate in an analysis and appraisal of the key features of his method. By the end of this chapter, it should be clear that Northrop developed one of the most innovative comparative methods from the middle of the last century, but one that is for the most part misunderstood and hence neglected by contemporary comparativists.

DESCRIPTION OF METHOD

Early Works

Prior to the *Meeting*, Northrop published only one explicitly comparative work, namely, the essay published in conjunction with the first East-West Philosophers' Conference in 1939. However, his early work figures so prominently in the *Meeting* that the latter is better understood as a natural extension of his earlier work than as a separate project altogether. Indeed, it would be difficult to fully appreciate the distinctive features of his comparative method without an adequate understanding of the broader method he developed in that earlier work. Accordingly, this description of his method begins with a brief review of what is perhaps the most significant collection of his early work, *The Logic of the Sciences and the Humanities* (1947).[8] This review will focus on two influential features of Northrop's early thought: the centrality of the scientific method and the emphasis on technical terminology.

The primary purpose of the *Logic* was to examine the question of method as it pertains to a diverse spectrum of disciplines. Accordingly, when Northrop wrote about "logic," he did not mean only the specialized subfield in philosophy by that name; rather, he conceived of it "in the broadest possible manner" (1947, vii), referring to the scientific method as it applies to any given discipline. Strictly speaking, there is no one "scientific method," according to Northrop; rather, there is a variety of scientific methods, each of which is designed to address a particular type of problem. Because different disciplines address different kinds of problems, they each use different methods or sequences of methods.

While there is no single scientific method that applies to every discipline, Northrop argues, each method is best understood as one part of a broader, cross-disciplinary theory of inquiry.[9] This broader theory of inquiry, if successful, should be able to draw on the insights of each discipline to address all factual and normative problems in a unified manner. The intended result is "a procedure which may bring scientific verification and attendant human agreement into the present demoralized world of ideological humanistic controversy" (Northrop 1947, x–xi).

This unified theory of inquiry consists of three stages. The first stage is the "problem stage," wherein one recognizes that there is a problem for which traditional theories appear to be inadequate and analyzes that problem to determine what sort of facts are relevant for its resolution. Northrop argued that problems of fact are different from problems of value and therefore require different methods for their resolution but that both types of problem must come down to some set of determining facts if they are to be "cognitive and true, rather than merely persuasive and hortatory" (1947, 32).[10]

The second stage is the "natural history stage," which consists of a consideration of the facts identified by the first stage. This stage draws on three methods: observation, description, and classification. The observational method entails immediate apprehension of the facts independent of any conceptual overlay; appealing to preestablished concepts only blinds the observer to potentially relevant facts, and thus is best held off at least momentarily.[11] It is only in the next method, description, that these facts (and their interrelations) are expressed in terms of concepts; yet even here, the overlay is not speculative but limited to what is given by means of immediate apprehension; Northrop referred to these concepts as "concepts by intuition" (1947, 36). Finally, classification seeks to systematize the described facts according to a common framework for further consideration.

The third and final stage is that of deductively formulated theory, during which new hypotheses are formed to explain the facts collected in the second stage. This may require the postulation of new (i.e., not observed) entities or relations to provide a satisfactory explanation of the observed phenomena; Northrop referred to these as "concepts by postulation" (1947, 60). These hypotheses, along with the new concepts, are tested by deducing their necessary consequences and then performing the appropriate experiments to verify or disprove them, a process that continues until a verifiable hypothesis is identified that is sufficient to resolve the problem identified at the initiation of inquiry.

Again, not every instance of inquiry requires the use of every stage and/or method described above, and many disciplines characteristically employ only a select few. Yet this unified theory is intended to include every relevant facet of inquiry understood in the broadest possible respect, something that becomes particularly important when one conducts inquiry over a wide variety of subject matter. Accordingly, Northrop noted that this theory of inquiry should have particular relevance to comparative philosophy, which takes as its subject matter a discipline (i.e., philosophy) that not only has the broadest variety of subject matter but also engages in the greatest variety of ways.

In addition to a unified theory of inquiry, the *Logic* also includes a reprint of the essay that Northrop originally presented to the first East-West Philosophers' Conference.[12] That essay, retitled in this collection as "The Possible Concepts by Intuition and Concepts by Postulation as a Basic Terminology for Comparative Philosophy," argued that one of the necessary preconditions for comparative philosophy is the development of "an unambiguous, commensurable terminology" (1947, 77) by means of which to give expression to the distinctive characteristics of the world's diverse philosophical traditions. Because comparative philosophy is as broad-ranging a form of inquiry as is possible, the terminology of his universal theory of inquiry effectively becomes the terminology for comparative philosophy.

Of course, comparative philosophy was not without terminology prior to Northrop's essay, so one of his primary concerns was to lay out a critique of the two most prominent sources of this terminology in order to clear the ground for his own position. First, in a marked rejection of the most common source for comparative terms, he argued that such terms should not be taken directly from merely linguistic translations of philosophical texts. Such translations typically only provide dictionary correlations of a term and tend to overlook the philosophical ramifications of its use. Accordingly, two terms might be granted equivalency in translation, even though they express very different, and even contradictory, philosophical ideas. Thus, he concluded, "the trustworthy student of comparative philosophy must be more than a mere linguist or possess more than trustworthy translations by linguists; in addition he must have a professional mastery of the problems, methods and theories of philosophy" (1947, 168). Although critical philological translations are also important for comparative study, they are not sufficient to provide a philosophically reliable basis for comparison; comparative terminology must account for philosophic similarities no less than linguistic ones.[13]

Second, focusing on the second most prominent source, he argued that comparative terminology should also not be derived from the commonsense terminology of any given culture. Typically, philosophy takes its terms from ordinary usage and then assigns the term a precise meaning within that system. It has done this in the hope of making itself more applicable to the common concerns of everyday life; yet the result is the same as with the linguistic translators: "[T]he same word in different philosophical systems often designates quite different and even opposite technical philosophical meanings, and different common-sense terms in different systems often denote the same meaning" (1947, 81). Thus, while it is not sufficient to be a linguist to compare philosophical terms, neither is it sufficient to be a philosopher, according to Northrop, since this only secures an understanding of the terms as employed in that philosopher's tradition. For the comparative philosopher, the terms of comparison must be able to account for the meaning of its terms in every philosophical tradition.

From whence, then, should comparativists derive their terminology? Northrop provided a distinctive solution: it must be derived from an understanding of the world's philosophical traditions that is able to account for each of the insights of each of those traditions. In his words, "A theory of any kind, whether scientific or philosophic, is a body of propositions, and a body of propositions is a set of concepts. Concepts fall into different types according to the different sources of their meaning. Consequently, the designation of the different possible major types of concepts should provide a technical terminology with the generality sufficient to include within itself as a special case any possible scientific or philosophical theory" (1947, 82). For Northrop, one of the primary tasks of comparative philosophy is to provide the terminology for use in any comparative inquiry. Accordingly, for the remainder of the essay, he laid out just such a technical terminology, based on the distinction between concepts by intuition and concepts by postulation. It is not necessary to understand the details of each type of concept to understand this aspect of Northrop's method. He specified each concept into four meticulously defined subtypes. It is important to note, however, that he claimed to give systematic expression to all of the "major *possible* types of concepts" (82, emphasis mine), thus giving expression to precisely the "unambiguous, commensurate terminology" that he claimed is necessary for comparative philosophy (77). This is a bold claim, to be sure, but it is one that is developed and defended most ably in *The Meeting of East and West*. We therefore turn our attention to that work now.

The Meeting of East and West

Written after the first East-West Philosophers' Conference (1939) but prior to the end of the Second World War (1945), the *Meeting* (1946) gives full expression to the war's influence on Northrop's thought, especially with respect to his understanding of its ramifications for philosophy.[14] As he wrote: "The state of mind following the recent war differs from that subsequent to the previous one. Then everyone supposed there were no ideological conflicts. The war had been fought to "save the world for democracy" and with the defeat of the Kaiser democracy supposedly had won. Only later did disillusionment appear. . . . Now ideological conflicts are present everywhere" (1946, ix). The Second World War made it clear that ideological differences are a real feature of the global community and that cultures are both willing and increasingly able to resort to tremendous violence against one another in the pursuit of their own ideals.[15] These ideological conflicts were neither peculiar to the war nor eliminated by it; to the contrary, the postwar era witnessed a proliferation of such conflicts throughout the world.[16]

It was clear to Northrop that ideological conflicts were a tremendous threat to the emerging global community and that they were likely to only intensify as the world's cultures increasingly overlap. "The time has come," he wrote, "when these ideological conflicts must be faced and if possible resolved. Otherwise, the social policies, moral ideals and religious aspirations of men, because of their incompatibility one with another, will continue to generate misunderstanding and war instead of mutual understanding and peace" (1946, ix). If further world wars are to be avoided, he suggested, it will be necessary to develop a better model for cross-cultural engagement.

The problem in ideological conflict, he maintained, is not primarily that different cultures have different understandings of what is good, true, or otherwise worth pursuing; difference itself is not a sufficient reason for engaging in war or otherwise pursuing the eradication of another culture. Rather, the problem lies chiefly in the way that cultures engage one another in light of these differences. Referring to the long list of contemporary ideological conflicts, Northrop wrote that "it is literally true in all these instances that, at least in part, what the one people or culture regards as sound economic and political principles the other views as erroneous, and what the one envisages as good and divine the other condemns as evil or illusory" (1946, ix). In Northrop's view, then, these conflicts are not due to the specific beliefs of any particular tradition but rather the general beliefs among traditions about how to relate to other traditions.

If the problem is not primarily with a culture's ideals but rather with the way they pursue them vis-à-vis other cultures, then the solution cannot be to simply replace the ideals of one culture with those of another. Historically, this has been the road most traveled, as cultures seek—by force, if necessary—to supplant the "inferior" ideals of surrounding cultures with their own. Not surprisingly, it is also one of the most popular proposals in the contemporary world; the world's most powerful nations continue to assert that peace, justice, and prosperity depend on the world's adoption of their own cultural norms, whether political, economic, or religious. Yet this does not solve the problem, Northrop explained, but only exacerbates it. "[W]e are confronted, not with a simple issue between the good and the bad, but with a complex conflict between different conceptions of what is good. It is in the provincialism and inadequacy of the traditional ideals that the trouble in considerable part centers" (1946, 458). The problem is precisely the inability to appreciate the ideals of other cultures, and this is at the very heart of a culture's desire to impose its own ideals on others.

It is surely a paradox that the ideals we hold most dear are precisely those that must be left aside in addressing this problem, and this is not lost on Northrop. He wrote: "Ours is a paradoxical world. The achievements which are its glory threaten to destroy it. The nations with the highest standard of living, the greatest capacity to take care of their people economically, the broadest education, and the most enlightened morality and religion exhibit the least capacity to avoid mutual destruction in war. It would seem that the more civilized we become the more incapable of maintaining civilization we are" (1946, 1). One must remember that the Second World War, like the First, was not fought among the most "primitive" nations; rather, it was fought among precisely those nations that considered themselves the most advanced and "civilized" in the world, each of whom was confident in the superiority of its respective ideals and committed to their promulgation. Ironically, the war brought most of those nations to embody ideals that ran directly counter to their professed ideals. "This," he wrote, "is the basic paradox of our time: our religion, our morality and our 'sound' economic and political theory tend to destroy the state of affairs they aim to achieve" (6). If the contemporary slew of ideological conflicts is to be resolved peacefully, Northrop maintained, then nations must find ways to engage one another without imposing even their most cherished ideals.

A proper solution to these problems must change the way that cultures understand their differences from other cultures. The key to such a solution, according to Northrop, lies in the realization that the problem is, at its most basic, a *philosophical* problem. Cultures each have their own understanding of what is good, and each is surely at least partially right in its characterization; what they do not have, however, is a framework whereby they can relate themselves productively to other cultures in this respect. Any solution to the problem at hand must therefore be able to conceive of such a framework, wherein "what is good" is not specific to any particular culture but is specified to some extent in every culture. In short, what is needed is a conception of what it is to be a culture among other cultures; what is needed is a *philosophy of culture* (1946, x).

What Northrop offered the global community in *The Meeting* was just such a philosophy of culture. This project was undertaken on a truly Herculean scale, consisting of an attempt to analyze all of the world's major cultures and to bring them all under a more comprehensive cultural framework. Northrop argued that, while ideological conflicts abound in the contemporary world, the most important such conflict is to be found, as the title indicates, in the "meeting of East and West." These two civilizations, broadly conceived, demonstrated their mutual relevance in the Second World War, and their interpenetration is only increasing in the postwar context. "This means that for the first time in history, not merely in war but also in the issues of peace, the East and the West are in a single world movement, as much Oriental as Occidental in character. *The East and West are meeting and merging*" (1946, 4, emphasis mine).[17] All other ideological conflicts, he argued, are subsets of this broader global encounter of Oriental and Occidental civilizations: "It happens by good fortune," he wrote, "that the problem in the one case is identical with that in the other" (x). Thus, if a solution can be found for the broader and more complicated ideological conflict between East and West, then that solution can be applied to all other such conflicts as well.

The method he undertook for the development of this philosophy of culture is complex and multifaceted, but it follows the unified theory of inquiry laid out in the *Logic*. The first stage of the method—the "problem" stage—is meant to highlight specific ideological conflicts and to indicate "how an analysis of this normative problem guides one to the specific factual information which must be determined before further effective discussion of the problem can occur" (1947, 31). Inquiry is not a gratuitous problem, for Northrop; there are always specific problems that initiate inquiry. This first step seeks to identify the ideological conflicts spurring the inquiry, as well as the range of data relevant to understanding and resolving those conflicts. For ideological conflicts, this will always pertain to an identification of the specific ideals underlying the conflict as well as the facts and values that may support them.

The second stage—the "natural history" stage—consists of the presentation of that data, and it constitutes most of the content of the *Meeting*. It consists of a detailed description of every culture that had a significant influence on the major ideological conflicts of Northrop's time, including the culture of Mexico, the culture of the United States, British democracy, German idealism, Russian communism, the tension between Roman Catholic culture and Greek science, and Oriental culture.[18] Each study recounts developments not only in the history of philosophy (Northrop's primary area of expertise) but also in science, religion, politics, economics, and aesthetics. Moreover, each of these studies is remarkable for the breadth of its purview, as well as its cultural sensitivity and attention to detail; there are few thinkers, in Northrop's day or in our own, that can provide such depth of insight over so broad a range of materials. Over the course of these detailed studies of different cultures, he makes five notable points about the nature of cultures in general:

1. Cultures each have their own particular characteristics that can be characterized in more general terms (e.g., Mexican culture is predominantly "aesthetic," while that of the United States is predominantly "pragmatic").

2. Cultures are not monolithic but are ever-changing, ever-adapting frameworks that reflect their many influences. Cultures are not only capable of interacting productively (and thus overcoming mere ideology), but have been doing so—with varied success, of course—for as long as they have encountered one another.

3. Each culture is typically both more and less advanced than the cultures around it, depending on which aspect of the culture is highlighted. It is the responsibility of each culture to recognize its

own weak points and learn from other cultures how to improve them.

4. The ideals of one culture can have devastating effects when imposed on other cultures, especially when imposed with an ignorance about the truth and value of the ideals of other cultures.

5. Intercultural conflicts can be overcome only in a manner that takes seriously the ideals of each of the cultures involved.

These five points find exemplification in the rich detail Northrop provided for each culture, and even though they are not his main concern in each study, they nonetheless set the stage for the framework of cultural relations that is to follow.

These individual studies on Eastern and Western cultures are brought together in summary chapters designed to further classify cultures by highlighting their most fundamental ideals. In Northrop's terminology, this consists of identifying the "meaning" of Western and Eastern civilization.[19] The meaning of Western civilization, according to Northrop, is that the good is associated with the logical, theoretically formulated factor in knowledge. As far back as the pre-Socratics, the early Greeks found that it was possible to extend knowledge beyond immediate sensory perception by proposing and testing speculative hypotheses; furthermore, it was possible derive further knowledge from these hypotheses through proper logical deductions. This insight was cultivated throughout the history of Western thought and has resulted in a flourishing of theoretical knowledge, especially in mathematics and the natural sciences, but also in politics, economics, and religion. All of these developments, Northrop maintained, are rooted in a commitment to the possibility of a knowledge that is rooted not in sensory perception but rather in the imageless, intellectual perception of the mind.

These developments, however, have not come without a cost: they have been attended by an overconfidence in the West with respect to the power of theoretical knowledge. Western thinkers have traditionally been very impressed with the predictive and explanatory power of theories; Greek thinkers as early as Parmenides, Democritus, Plato, and Aristotle began to distinguish between "real" theoretical knowledge and "illusory" sensory experience, and their bias has persisted into modern Western civilization. Yet theoretical knowledge, taken by itself, has a largely unacknowledged vulnerability: its validity can only be determined with respect to its ability to account for empirical data. Theories are only ever *indirectly verified*, such that one never knows if a theory is true (or, better, the extent to which it is true) but only that it has not yet been proven untrue (i.e., that it continues to be able to account for all of the available data). Theoretical knowledge, then, is properly understood only as provisional knowledge pending further data. Yet the overconfidence that has accompanied theoretical knowledge in the West, Northrop argued, has led to a tendency to overlook the tentative nature of theoretical knowledge and to treat such knowledge instead as absolute.

Applied on a cultural level, this overconfidence manifests itself in the West in the persistent pursuit of utopias, each of which is pursued zealously until it proves faulty and is replaced with a new, revised vision. This recurrent pattern, Northrop maintained, is both the strength and weakness of Western culture. On the one hand, these recurrent reconceptualizations continue to improve theoretical knowledge, as each failed ideal is replaced with an improved ideal. On the other hand, it leads Western cultures to hold often contradictory ideals and to defend them as if they were absolute rather than tentative. The challenge for Western civilization in the context of ideological conflicts is to realize the tentative nature of its ideals and put aside ideological conflicts, seeking instead to improve its theoretical formulations by broadening its cultural perspective.

The meaning of Eastern civilization, by contrast, is that it "has concentrated its attention upon the nature of all things in their emotional and aesthetic, purely empirical and positivistic immediacy" (1946, 375). Eastern cultures, he explained, have tended to take what he calls the "differentiated aesthetic continuum" as the sum total of all existent things expressed in their most knowable form. According to this view, each thing is what it is in immediate experience, such that to know a thing in its fullness is to know it in its immediacy. There is only one thing that is indeterminate (i.e., eternal and unchanging), and that is what Northrop terms the "undifferentiated aesthetic continuum" (which he associates alternately with the Dao, Brahman, Qi, and Nirvana). This focus on the concrete lends to Eastern thought a stark realism, by which pain and suffering are taken at face value rather than explained away in some larger theory. At the same time, however, it brings them to meet all such differentiations with a complementary disregard due to their impermanent and transitory nature as determinate things. Taken together, this has allowed for the cultivation of a highly developed aesthetic sense among Eastern cultures.

Since cultural ideals are typically understood as fleeting and impermanent, Northrop argues, there has been little temptation for absolute commitment to any such ideals in Eastern culture; hence, the East has been far less plagued by utopian visions and their attendant exclusivism than has the West. This reticence, however, has brought with it its own challenges for Eastern cultures, namely, a lack of interest in cultivating those skills associated with identifying and controlling the determinate features of reality. Thus, it has been traditionally unable to compete with Western cultures in the areas of economic prosperity, political conviction, and scientific progress. The challenge for Eastern cultures within the context of ideological conflicts is to learn to compete with Western cultures in these areas *without* sacrificing their aesthetic sensitivity and tempered appraisal of cultural ideals.[20]

Northrop was consistent in affirming the distinctiveness and importance of the contributions of both East and West: the West has a theoretical emphasis that has been largely overlooked in the East, while the East has cultivated an aesthetic sensitivity that has been underdeveloped in the West.[21] There are exceptions to each characterization, of course, and Northrop made note of these at various points throughout his work. In fact, without a certain level of overlap, no synthesis of world ideologies would be possible. Yet it is not the commonalities but the differences that are the problem for cross-cultural relations, so his descriptions and categorizations focus primarily on those.

Northrop's foremost interest, however, lies in conceiving of a broader framework through which the distinctive insights and contributions of both East and West can be mutually recognized, cultivated, and brought together for a more peaceful and productive interaction of world cultures. The third and final stage of his comparative method—the "deductively formulated theory" stage—considers whether the ideals just described are complementary or contradictory and how they can be understood within the context of a broader theory of cultural ideals. He wrote:

> In the case of diverse but compatible cultures the task will then be that of correctly relating the compatible elements of the two cultures by enlarging the ideals of each to include those of the other so that they reinforce, enrich and sustain rather than convert, combat or destroy each other. Between diverse and contradictory doctrines . . . the problem will be to provide foundations for a new and more comprehensive theory, which without contradiction will take care, in a more satisfactory way, of the diverse facts which generated the traditional incompatible doctrines. (1946, 6)

Whether these ideals are complementary or contradictory, the ultimate goal is to develop "a more inclusive truly international cultural ideal" (1946, x). This broader ideal should include the distinctive insights of each culture, but should also bring them together in ways that transform those insights and allow for additional insights. This gives each culture not only no reason *not* to accept the broader ideal (since it reflects their best insights) but every reason to actually *do* so (since it also reflects additional insights).

With this end in mind, Northrop proposed a framework based on a new, broader theory of knowledge that he termed "epistemic correlation." This theory is meant to stand as an alternative to the predominant three-termed relation of appearance, which consists of an object as it "really exists" (in the mathematical, space-time world of theoretical knowledge), the person who observes the object (whose observation distorts the object), and the object as it is observed (which is rendered "mere appearance"). Epistemic correlation, by contrast, is a two-termed relation, consisting of concepts by intuition and concepts by postulation. Concepts by intuition refer to the aesthetic, purely empirical, given component of knowledge for their complete meaning. Concepts by postulation do likewise for the theoretically designated and indirectly verified component (1946, 447). What is significant about epistemic correlation is that neither the aesthetic (intuitive) nor the theoretic (postulative) is given priority, nor are the two reduced to the same thing; rather, the two are taken as complementary components of knowledge, each of which must be correlated to the other to be more fully understood.[22]

By way of explanation, Northrop addressed the longstanding philosophical distinction between universals and particulars. Concepts by postulation, he noted, can provide a wealth of knowledge about the universal qualities of things but nothing about what it would be to actually experience such a thing in its aesthetic immediacy. Alternately, concepts by intuition can provide a wealth of knowledge about a thing as experienced in aesthetic immediacy but nothing about what that experience has in common with an experience of similar things. Both aspects—a knowledge of the universal and of the particular—are necessary for a more complete knowledge of a thing.[23] "It is one of the errors of traditional science and of traditional philosophy," he wrote, "that most of their adherents felt constrained for some inexplicable reason to regard all concepts as either universal or particular" (1946, 449). A more comprehensive truth, he concluded, is possible when the available knowledge of both aesthetic and theoretic factors is taken into account.[24]

By identifying these two components of knowledge and providing a precise account of how they relate to one another, Northrop provided a basic framework for relating Eastern and Western cultures: "[I]t indicates each of the diverse modern, medieval, Eastern and Western cultures to be giving expression to something which is in part true, and it shows precisely how to relate and reconcile them all without conflict or contradiction so that a peaceful comprehensive world civilization approximating more closely to the expression of the whole truth is possible" (1946, 449). This more complete truth, he maintained, is both consistent with and available to all cultures and identifies what each culture must learn to take full account of all of the available knowledge. What the West has to learn from the East is how to better recognize and appreciate things in their aesthetic immediacy: how to make writing more than just a means of communication, make art more than mere representation, make rituals more than a means of efficacy, and so on. Moreover, it must eliminate its bias against the wisdom of the ancients, since the strongest impetus for aesthetic knowledge is typically the initial insight. What the East has to learn from the West is how to better utilize its knowledge: how to harness the power of the natural sciences, envision and commit to broader social and political ideals, increase economic productivity, and so on. Moreover, the East must eliminate its bias against innovation and progress, since the validity of theoretical knowledge relies on its ability to address the most up-to-date information. To take full account of all available knowledge is not only to become a stronger, more informed culture; it is also to become more consistent with all other cultures that do likewise. If East and West could accept the fact that neither has possession of truth in its most complete form and consent to learn from each other, Northrop was confident that both civilizations can not only improve but also move toward the formation of a stronger, unified world civilization.[25]

At the end of inquiry, then, what initially seemed to be problems of conflicting values—which are thus unable to be mediated by any culture-neutral perspective—are thus found only to be problems that have at their root an inability to account for the full range of available evidence.[26] Northrop reached this conclusion in what is perhaps the most cohesive—and perhaps also the longest—sentence of his text:

> It appears, therefore, when the paradoxically confusing and tragic conflicts of the world are analyzed one by one and then traced to the basic philosophical problem underlying them, and when this problem of the relation between immediately apprehended and theoretically inferred factors in things is then solved by replacing the traditional three-termed relation of appearance by the two-termed relation of epistemic correlation, that a realistically grounded, scientifically verifiable idea of the good for man and his world is provided in which the unique achievements of both the East and the West are united and the traditional incompatible and conflicting partial values of the different parts of the West are first reconstructed and then reconciled, so that *each* is seen to have something unique to contribute and *all* are reformed so as to supplement and reinforce instead of combat and destroy each other. (1946, 478)

It was Northrop's implicit hope that, when different cultures realize that their most deeply held truths are preserved in his broader framework, they will be not only able but moreover inclined to forego their own limited ideals in favor of "a more comprehensive and adequate idea of the good for our world" (1946, 458).

Later Works

The Meeting of East and West would remain Northrop's most influential text, although he would publish a number of subsequent works in a variety of different disciplines. Most of these works sought to provide additional development and defense to ideas originally laid out in the *Meeting*, but some of those ideas change in the process, thus providing additional insight into

Northrop's method, as well as its strengths and weaknesses. In the interest of highlighting these changes, brief consideration will be given to the most prominent of his subsequent comparative works, *Philosophical Anthropology and Practical Politics* (1960).

The basic argument of this book, as its title implies, is that philosophical anthropology plays an important but largely misunderstood role in practical politics. More precisely, Northrop was interested in pointing out how political initiatives—especially those involved in the formation of a world government—inevitably fail when they are imposed on cultures that hold political, legal, or other norms that conflict with those initiatives. Following Eugene Ehrlich (1936), Northrop distinguished between two types of law: positive law (the official law of a people) and living law (the law people hold to irrespective of official laws). Living law is basic in the local customs of a culture and informs positive law; positive law, by contrast, reflects and yet also shapes living law in turn. Applied to political initiatives, this indicates that a new positive law can be effective only if it conforms in the short run to the living law of a people, while simultaneously educating them to affirm a new positive law. In short, politics can be successful only when it takes local customs seriously: "[S]ince customs are anthropological and sociological," he wrote, "contemporary politics must be also" (1960, 15).

Perhaps the most distinctive feature of *Philosophical Anthropology* is the extensive support it seeks in the social, political, and biological sciences. For example, he continued to maintain the argument, originally laid out in the *Meeting*, that philosophical commitments are a real and relevant part of ordinary human life. In the text at hand, however, he defended this argument primarily with respect to recent developments in anthropology, neurophysiology, and epistemology. For example:

1. He referred the reader to the work of anthropologists such as Clyde Kluckhohn (Northrop 1949, 356–84), who argued that all cultures, even those of nonliterate peoples, have an underlying "philosophy": a specific set of shared meanings derived from a set of "primitive postulates."[27]

2. He drew heavily on McCulloch and Pitts (1943), which found that cortical neurons not only fire as a result of immediate stimuli but also contain "trapped universals." These universals constitute "remembered" associations that can be recalled under similar circumstances and thus allow for a concept of human neurophysiology that extends beyond immediate, private experience.

3. He directed the reader's attention to Rosenblueth, Wiener, and Bigelow (1943), which showed that, because goal-oriented actions

require recurrent attention vis-à-vis the same goal, ideas must have direct relevance to human behavior.

Northrop drew these three discoveries together to argue for a conception of the human nervous system as "the hierarchically ordered, cortically trapped persisting impulses that are the epistemic correlates of that person's set of elemental concepts and postulates, i.e., his cognitively true or false philosophy" (1960, 71). In short, *Philosophical Anthropology* seeks to advance much the same hypothesis as the *Meeting* but in such a way as to provide it with additional scientific support and credibility.

This additional reference to developments in the natural and social sciences, however, also caused Northrop to alter some of his initial assertions. For example, in his original rendering of the unified theory of inquiry in the *Logic* (and as played out in the *Meeting*), he had argued that the "natural history" stage of inquiry consisted initially of a brief moment of immediate observation (without the influence of theory), which was then followed by theory-laden description and classification. In *Philosophical Anthropology*, however, he deferred to the work of Pitirim Sorokin (1937; 1949)—which argued that *all* observations are theory-laden and that any attempt to simply "observe the facts" only further distorts the observation by smuggling in unacknowledged theoretical commitments—and effectively eliminated observation from the second stage. Instead, he argued that proper description of a culture must seek to describe the facts *as that culture observes the facts*, taking into consideration not only how people *actually* relate to their world but moreover how they *believe they ought* to relate. This change demonstrates an additional sensitivity to the cultural location of all beliefs and also provides an added emphasis on presenting other cultures and their beliefs at their best.

Ultimately, however, Northrop mustered this information together to reach largely the same conclusion as the *Meeting*: that ideological conflicts are ultimately philosophical conflicts and that if those conflicts are to be resolved most effectively then they must be understood, at least in large part, philosophically. *Philosophical Anthropology* might just as well have kept the subtitle of the *Meeting*, *An Inquiry concerning World Understanding*, as it sought no less than its predecessor to defend such an understanding. As it stands, it takes the subtitle *A Prelude to War or to Just Law*. This is reflective of the fact that, whereas the *Meeting* was written during the Second World War in the hope of avoiding further such conflicts, *Philosophical Anthropology* was written during the Cold War with the Soviet Union in the hope of stemming the policy of "power politics" undertaken by both sides. It remained Northrop's great though ever unrealized hope that State Department officials and foreign diplomats alike would be trained in philosophical anthropology so that they could learn to recognize not only the validity of the insights of other cultures but also the limitations of their own culture and could thus contribute to the development of a more wholesome—in the most profound sense of that word—means of global cultural interaction.

ANALYSIS AND APPRAISAL

Northrop inherited a number of traits from his teacher, W. E. Hocking, that are characteristic of early attempts at comparison within American philosophy. What can be considered virtues for an early innovator like Hocking, however, should be able to be taken for granted by Northrop and his generation of comparativists. For Northrop, comparative philosophy is no longer an interesting aside that provides new intellectual and spiritual resources for an otherwise traditional American philosopher; rather, it is a vibrant philosophic subfield that finds expression within an ongoing, critical discussion among committed comparativists from a wide array of cultures. To make his own contributions, Northrop needed to move beyond the avant-garde virtues of his teacher, and this is a challenge he took on with notable, if controversial, results.

The initiatives that Northrop undertook constitute both the strengths and weaknesses of his method: it is precisely in his moves beyond Hocking that Northrop both made distinctive contributions and also ran into practical and methodological difficulties. Because the strengths of his approach are so difficult to separate from its weaknesses, they will be considered in tandem in this chapter with respect to the following three themes: his broad-ranging expertise, his cross-cultural sensitivity, and his comprehensive, systematic framework.

Broad-Ranging Expertise

Although Northrop was first and foremost a Western philosopher, he exhibited mastery in a remarkable breadth of areas, spanning multiple disciplines and diverse cultures. Naturally, he brought this broad mastery to bear on his comparative work, and it had a distinctive effect on his method. While this allowed him to develop what is arguably the most intricately developed and empirically tested comparative method of his time, it also opened him up to critique from an equally wide array of disciplines and cultures. Despite his proficiency, Northrop would ultimately prove unable to keep pace with this onslaught of critique, with the result that his comparative method—along with his broader philosophical program—would be considered highly questionable by many within the academy. His expertise will be considered here with respect to both his cross-disciplinary proficiency and his cross-cultural competency.

CROSS-DISCIPLINARY PROFICIENCY

Northrop's cross-disciplinary prowess is first exemplified in his early work in the natural sciences. While he earned his doctoral degree in philosophy, his dissertation was "The Problem of Organization in Biology" (Harvard, 1924), a combination that evinced his commitment to an interdisciplinary approach to philosophy from the very beginning.[28] Indeed, he would take as his conversation partners—quite literally—some of the most prominent physical scientists and mathematicians of his time, including but not limited to A. N. Whitehead[29] and Albert Einstein.[30] His close relationship with these two intellectual giants is evident in his first major publication, *Science and First Principles* (1931), which seeks to provide a logical analysis of the first principles of science with a particular focus on atomicity, motion, and change. Specifically, he argued that the covariant chronogeometrical tensor in Einstein's 1916 general relativity equations did not allow for a common referent for such first principles, and that without this common referent these features of ordinary experience were left without theoretical explanation. As an alternative to Einstein's tensor, Northrop proposed his own "macroscopic atomic theory," which effectively interpreted all of the atomic elements of reality as ultimately unified in a single, unifying atom.

Although Northrop's theory was eventually superseded by Einstein's move to field theory in 1929, this need not take away from the significance or originality of Northrop's contribution; to the contrary, both Einstein[31] and Whitehead[32] affirmed its validity as a theoretical alternative. Thus, as Andrew Reck observed, "Whether the macroscopic atomic theory is a tenable hypothesis or not, it may be viewed as an ingenious attempt to overcome difficulties in Einstein's physics prior to the development of field theory concepts" (1968, 200). Northrop would continue to publish on issues in the philosophy of science (e.g., 1947, 1960, 1962, 1985), keeping a close eye to developments in the sciences and updating his philosophical methods as appropriate.[33]

While his connections in the philosophy of science are difficult to outclass, Northrop was actually more influential in legal studies, especially in the area of international law. As Reck noted, "[f]rom his chair in the Yale Law School Northrop has wielded immense influence in directing the minds of his students, foreign as well as American, to a theory of law adequate to the needs of the international situation" (1968, 208). Most of Northrop's later publications took as their primary concern contemporary challenges in global politics, focusing on the need for a defensible legal foundation and a diplomatically effective means for applying it (see, e.g., 1947, 1952, 1954, 1959, 1960).[34] His significant influence in the area of legal studies can be seen from the fact that, in contemporary literature, he is as likely to be cited for his contributions there as to any other field (including comparative philosophy).

Northrop's other areas of expertise spanned the disciplinary spectrum, including religion, mysticism, history, poetry, linguistics, economics, and education.[35] These interests were often integrated into his larger works (esp. the *Meeting*). They were also expressed in essays published as parts of explicitly interdisciplinary works (see esp. 1962 and 1985). As a result, it is often difficult to associate any of his works with a single discipline. Yet Northrop was explicit from the very beginning that, although disciplinary boundaries identify important differences among modes of inquiry, disciplines are best understood as facets of a broader process of inquiry and that it is the philosopher's responsibility to critically assess these facets and facilitate their interaction as appropriate. This cross-disciplinary commitment not only places him in direct lineage with his predecessors James, Royce, and especially Hocking but also marks him as their superior with respect to his level of mastery in these many disciplines.[36]

CROSS-CULTURAL COMPETENCY

As noted earlier, Northrop was neither initially nor primarily a student of other cultures; he was trained in the Western philosophical tradition, and he used his expertise in that field to address concerns across cultures. At the same time, however, he did this with an extraordinary degree of insight into other cultures for a nonspecialist. For example, the *Meeting* provided a brief yet insightful analysis of a remarkable number of the world's most influential traditions and demonstrated a level of competency that goes beyond that of the interested philosophical bystander. "Competency" is the right word here, too, because Northrop never claimed to be an expert on non-Western traditions: what his works were intended to communicate was that he had an unquestionably solid grasp of the defining features of the world's major traditions that was sufficient to provide a reliable basis for his cross-cultural comparative conclusions, and they demonstrate this surprisingly well.

To contemporary scholars, Northrop's analyses leave much to be desired. In the wake of the vociferous pursuit of area studies over the last half-century, much more has been learned about non-Western cultures than is reflected in his midcentury work. Taken in context, however, it represents in many respects the state of the art for comparative studies at his time. For example, his distinguished research on the history and character of Mexican culture—much of which is represented in its respective chapter of the *Meeting*—led the Mexican government to award him in 1949 the Order of the Aztec Eagle (Orden Mexicana del Aquila Azteca), the highest decoration it can award a foreign national. The chapters pertaining to other Western traditions in the *Meeting* demonstrate a similar level of insight and appreciation and attest to Northrop's mastery of his broad tradition. While the chapters that address Eastern traditions are noticeably scant, already in his first comparative work they demonstrate a remarkable familiarity with these traditions for a nonspecialist.

That his understanding of non-Western traditions cannot have been entirely misplaced can be seen from his prominence at the first, second, and third East-West Philosophers' Conferences: Northrop offered more than his share of conference papers and provided an exceptional number of additional public lectures surrounding the conferences. These conferences consisted of many of the leading interpreters of non-Western traditions, and the fact that he was able to maintain a prominent place in each of these conferences speaks to the level of respect he earned from his colleagues by means of his contributions. Indeed, over the many weeks spanning each conference, Northrop was not only able to demonstrate his competence in non-Western traditions, but he was also able to enhance it by means of his interactions there.

Although Northrop's expertise was certainly not limitless across either disciplines or cultures, he exemplified a surprising amount of expertise in the many areas he engaged. This capacity is relevant to his method because he brought all of this to bear on his comparative conclusions. When Northrop examined cross-cultural problems, he examined them in the broadest possible respect, taking account of the problem in all of its many facets. In this respect, Northrop was a comparativist's comparativist: he may not have had enough expertise in any one of the areas he engaged to provide a precise specification of how a general trait applies to a particular culture, but he had enough of an understanding to recognize when a trait seemed to have bearing in a given culture. Thus, he was capable of providing a broad overview and general orientation for comparative philosophy that a specialist in just one tradition would not be able to provide.

The downside of this broad expertise is that, while it brought a new richness and depth to his comparative work, it ultimately prevented Northrop from keeping pace with both the critiques and the new developments in the disciplines and cultures he incorporated. As a result, he was not able to adequately defend all of his initiatives in those areas, and the credibility of his broader method suffered as a result.

In his cross-disciplinary expertise, this can be seen by the shifting prominence of nonphilosophical disciplines in his comparative work. Although this can be seen in other fields, it is nowhere more evident than in his persistent struggle with the natural sciences.[37] Although Northrop's initial grounding in the natural sciences was unquestionable, these disciplines changed so quickly over the course of his career that there was no guarantee of continuing proficiency. Indeed, while he was always well-informed in the natural sciences, he always struggled to maintain his credibility in the scientific community, especially as it pertained to some of his most fundamental arguments pertaining to comparison. As his career progressed, he spent more and more time defending, elaborating, and updating the basic scientific assertions made in his earlier work. In the end, these defenses became such a prominent feature of his work that they effectively eclipsed the comparative creativity that characterized his earlier work.[38] This was an unfortunate trade-off, as Northrop's scientific defenses ultimately proved to be less than compelling to the scientific community and to his fellow comparativists.

The challenges were similar with respect to his cross-cultural expertise. Northrop made a number of strong claims about Eastern traditions in his early work and drew significantly on its contributions in the formation of his comparative synthesis. In his later work, by contrast, he focused largely on the goods of Western civilization—specifically, legal contractual democracy—despite his undiminished claims to be developing a genuinely cross-cultural comparative framework. Although it would be difficult—and foolish—to try to trace this development to a single cause, it likely had to do at least partially with the persistent critique of his interpretation on non-Western traditions by scholars representing those traditions (see Moore 1951; 1962, passim). While these scholars typically expressed great respect for Northrop and his comparative initiatives, they nonetheless made their concern clear, especially toward the end of his career, that his interpretation of their respective traditions was not entirely adequate to the roles he assigned them in his comparative framework.

In light of the challenges that Northrop faced, it is worth considering what should be required of the comparativist. On the one hand, the comparativist must have a credible and informed perspective on the traditions he or she would compare, which suggests that comparative philosophy is best undertaken by a consortium of "specialists" in each of the relevant disciplines and/or major philosophical traditions. On the other hand, the comparativist must also be able to recognize similarities and differences among traditions—both of which are often not what they seem—which suggests that comparative philosophy is best undertaken by a collection of "generalists" who have at least a basic understanding and appreciation of each discipline and/or tradition. In terms of its history, the early East-West Philosophers' Conferences seem to start with the former and work to cultivate the latter, and—understood in this light—Northrop can be considered one of its finest early products.

Most comparativists today realize that it is practically impossible for anyone to meet both of these demanding criteria. Certainly, scholars with unquestionable proficiency in multiple traditions do occasionally emerge— Francis Clooney is an oft-quoted example—but such scholars are notoriously rare, and their proficiency becomes increasingly questionable the more traditions they try to master. Understood against this backdrop, Northrop's failure to master the many disciplines and traditions is evident only because of his ambition to do so and by virtue of his near success in doing so. All things considered, perhaps he would have done better to have realized his own strengths and limited his contributions to those areas. He was a much better comparative generalist than he was a specialist in non-Western traditions and was at his best when he was surrounded by other specialists who could provide more informed testing of his cross-cultural hypotheses.[39] Perhaps his comparative work would have been improved if he had been better able to capitalize on the expertise of his many colleagues in the field.

If he were to restrict the sphere of his comparative work to the comprehensive oversight of a generalist, he would have had to incorporate a more substantive feedback mechanism in his method so that he could more critically assess the contributions provided by the specialists with whom he collaborated. As it stands, with Northrop filling the role of both specialist and generalist, it is unclear how any data running contrary to his comparative framework could be taken adequately into account. Reading his works, one often gets the sense that he found in cultural traditions precisely what he set out to find and that he validated these findings with reference to precisely those scholars whose work supported his own conclusions. It is perhaps for this reason that, despite the onslaught of criticisms of his work, Northrop seems to have seldom changed his positions; instead, he continued to defend his initial positions, updating them as any further supporting evidence became available.

In fairness to Northrop, it is not clear that his position proved ultimately indefensible but only that he was personally unable to adequately defend it on all fronts to the satisfaction of his colleagues from other disciplines and cultures. What becomes clear from this study of his work is that, if as broadly exposed and well-informed a scholar as Northrop had difficulty succeeding on all these fronts, it is probably too much for any comparativist. Northrop is perhaps as close an approximation to the comparative process as a whole that one may ever find, as noteworthy for his accomplishments in this respect as he is notorious for his own shortcomings. Contemporary comparativists should not judge Northrop too harshly for his shortcomings in this respect: at the middle of the twentieth century there was hardly a clear vision of what a full-fledged comparative method would look like, and Northrop's work—its inadequacies notwithstanding—filled a vacuum in comparative philosophy at the time. At the same time, we would also do well to learn from Northrop both the limits of the individual comparativist and also the demands of the comparative task. It remains for contemporary comparativists not to dismiss Northrop's work but rather to do still better what Northrop did first.

Cross-Cultural Sensitivity

Another distinctive feature of Northrop's approach is its characteristic cross-cultural sensitivity. He was concerned with providing not only an accurate description of other cultures (as indicated above) but also one in which each culture would be able to recognize itself. Northrop realized—to some extent in the *Meeting*, but more clearly in *Philosophical Anthropology*—that the truth of any culture, as recognized by that culture, is inextricably tied to its cultural context and that any description of a culture must take on the perspective of the culture it describes. Indeed, Northrop would say that a theory of comparison that ignores such cultural influences is not properly "cross-cultural" but is instead taking for granted the primacy of a single cultural context.[40]

This sensitivity was built into Northrop's work in three ways. First, he realized that the ideals of a given culture are not always exemplified fully in any particular concrete situation and may not even be fully understood in their own cultural context. In response, Northrop based his interpretation of those ideals on the way each culture represented itself at its best. This enabled him to resist seeing the best in cultures with which he was familiar and the worst in the rest by providing a consistent and readily available standard of comparison.

Second, Northrop knew that it would be difficult if not impossible to assess the ideals of any given culture without doing so on the basis of the ideals of another, something that would prove problematic for the construction of any cross-cultural synthesis of ideals. In response to this challenge, Northrop sought to look beyond the stated ideals of a culture to identify the insight(s) underlying each ideal. The insight(s), he contended, could be tested empirically against the available data and could therefore be used to assess the validity of the ideal itself. This, of course, is the exemplification of his theory of epistemic correlation, whereby any set of values could be correlated with a specific set of facts, the latter of which could be tested empirically. By pressing to the underlying ideals of a culture, he could arbitrate between the conflicting values of various cultures, providing a purportedly neutral ground (or, at least, *more* neutral ground) for determining the relative truth and falsity of those values.

Finally, and perhaps most importantly, Northrop knew that no culture would abandon its own ideology in favor of a cross-cultural synthesis unless it was able to see its own insights reflected in that broader synthesis. Any synthesis would have to be seen as an extension and improvement of its own ideology rather than a mere substitute. Accordingly, he made a point not only of highlighting the best in each culture but also of demonstrating how each culture contributed to the final synthesis. He did this not simply to appease these cultures (as if practical application compromises philosophical integrity) but because he realized that those insights are true at least to some extent and are thus better recognized and integrated than subsumed or ignored. His work can thus be read as a practical way of bringing all cultures together into a single, peaceful world civilization or as a philosophical way of recognizing and appreciating all that is true across the world's many diverse cultures, but it is best read as both simultaneously. The fact that Eastern and Western civilizations contribute what are purportedly equal shares to the final synthesis is at least as much cross-cultural diplomacy on Northrop's part as it is the result of his comparative investigation.

This cross-cultural sensitivity is in many respects an extension of his command of a variety of disciplines and cultures, as described in the previous section. Without a basic mastery of the cultures themselves, it would be impossible to provide accurate descriptions on even the most basic level. Without a mastery of the social and natural sciences—the former to identify a culture's values, and the latter to test them empirically—it would be difficult to present these descriptions and the resulting synthesis in a way that cultures would be likely to accept.[41] With his mastery of these diverse cultures and disciplines, however, Northrop was confident that he was able to provide the basis for a reliably cross-cultural synthesis of the world's insights.

His best intentions notwithstanding, however, Northrop ultimately fell victim to the strong influence of his own cultural commitments. While he expressed a genuine interest in non-Western cultures throughout his work, this interest ultimately proved to be subservient to the promotion of his own cultural interests. The result is an ultimately unbalanced reading of the world's cultures. Evidence for this can be garnered from even a cursory review of how other cultures are presented in his main comparative works. In the *Meeting*, for example, he committed a disproportionate amount of the text to Western traditions, giving Eastern traditions only the most general of glosses. Moreover, while he provided a properly critical reading of the traditions with which he was most familiar (i.e., English and American cultures), his reading of less familiar traditions (e.g., Russian communism and Eastern cultures) was surprisingly uncritical and irenic.

The lack of *equal* attention is perhaps forgivable, in that Northrop was likely speaking most to what he knew best; his lack of *critical* attention to other traditions, however, is less forgivable, as it ultimately proves ingenuine in his later texts. In *Philosophical Anthropology*, for example, his appreciation for Russian communism is subsumed by a determined argument for legal contractual democracy; likewise, his initial appreciation for aesthetics in Eastern cultures is overshadowed in this later work by a more straightforward promotion of theory from Western cultures as expressed in the natural sciences and economics. As Northrop progressed in his career, he becomes increasingly enthralled by the goods of Western society, and while he continued to wave the banner of non-Western contributions to a world order, this aspect of his work became increasingly marginalized and unconvincing over time.

In fairness to Northrop, there were a number of mitigating circumstances that no doubt contributed to this increasing shift toward non-Western traditions in his work. In his earlier works, the heavy emphasis on Western traditions can be attributed to his background and training; one writes most about what one knows best, so it is only natural that he would write more about Western traditions. By the same token, it is no less natural that he would be particularly gracious with respect to non-Western traditions, giving them the benefit of the doubt where his own familiarity was lacking.

In his later works, this emphasis can be attributed to the aforementioned need to continually defend his claims about the Western tradition within the context of perpetually developing disciplines. This would have been particularly true with respect to the rise of analytic philosophy in America: Northrop took great pains to defend his work to this emerging audience, so much so that it eclipsed the creativity of his later work. It is all the more unfortunate, then, that he proved unsuccessful in appeasing most analytic philosophers. No less unfortunate is the fact that he effectively had to forego substantive defense of his claims about non-Western traditions as a result; the prospect of taking on specialists in non-Western traditions seems to have appeared to Northrop either more foreboding or less rewarding than taking on his Western counterparts, and his later work reflects this choice.

Perhaps the most compelling—and telling—explanation for this shift pertains to an increasing appreciation for the comparative merits of constitutional democracy over the course of Northrop's career. While Northrop comes off as reasonably evenhanded in the *Meeting*, his appreciation for constitutional democracy becomes more evident in later works. This change makes sense in light of Northrop's context in the middle of the twentieth century, where the merits of democracy over fascism and—increasingly—communism were coming increasingly to the fore in the American mentality. Yet whether he was as appreciative early in his career, or whether that appreciation developed over time, it speaks to the difficulty of moving beyond the ideals that dominate one's own cultural context. One cannot overcome such biases simply because one works hard to do so, and of this Northrop is as good an example as any.

The saving grace for Northrop in all of this, something of which he was no doubt aware, is that cultural biases are not an all-or-nothing proposition. One can overcome one's biases to a greater or lesser extent, and it is therefore the comparativist's responsibility to try to overcome these biases to the greatest extent possible.[42] Moreover, by drawing attention to the insights underlying cultural ideals, he provided a means, however imperfect, for addressing the often conflicting ideals of diverse cultures. He knew that cross-cultural sensitivity is not just a feature of well-mannered comparative methods but also a necessary feature of any such methods that would be successful. Its failures notwithstanding, Northrop's notable attempts at achieving such cross-cultural sensitivity go a long way in bringing comparative philosophy closer to that end.

Comprehensive, Systematic Framework

The most distinctive feature of Northrop's method is the systematic way in which he links, relates, and unifies the world's diverse cultures in one comprehensive, systematic framework. The development of such a framework was one of the primary goals of the first East-West Philosophers' Conference, as evidenced by the opening lines of the conclusory essay written by Charles A. Moore as part of the collection of essays he edited in conjunction with the conference:

> The most fruitful view of the relationship of Eastern and Western philosophy . . . is that the one supplements the other, each providing or stressing the concepts which the other lacks or tends to minimize. This interpretation holds, further, that these two disparate sides of human thought can and should be brought together into a synthesis that would lead us closer to a world philosophy. . . . Neither East nor West is faultless in its perspective; both need the correctives that are not sufficiently forthcoming from within their own preju-diced perspectives. The wisdom of the East and the wisdom of the West must be merged to give man the advantage of the wisdom of mankind. (1944, 248)

The reader will notice that this is effectively a summary of the framework laid out by Northrop in his earlier essay in that collection, as well as developed more fully in the *Meeting*. If the collection of essays edited by Moore is any indication, Northrop was the only scholar to successfully lay out a framework like the one Moore described, with the result that he largely set the basic terms by which East and West were to be related in that conference (and several of the ones that would follow).[43]

As seen earlier, this framework was for Northrop a direct extension of his understanding of the fundamental unity of the sciences and the humanities: he believed it was possible to account for facts and values, the descriptive and normative sciences, aesthetic and theoretic concepts, and so on, all within the same framework. In the wake of the ideological conflicts pervading the Second World War, it was only natural for Northrop to extend this unifying framework cross-culturally as well. What made Northrop's framework distinc-tive was that it associated world cultures and broader civilizations with the types of concepts Northrop took to be most prominent in them. As Reck notes, for Northrop cultures are regarded as "overt, concrete embodiments of philosophical systems" (1968, 204). The result was a framework that or-ganized cultures and civilizations in the same ordered, systematic way that one would organize the sum total of possible concepts.[44]

The strengths attendant to such a framework are threefold. The first is the *clarity* it allows the comparativist in describing a diverse variety of traditions within the context of a single, common vocabulary. Without such a common framework, Northrop noted, one is left at the mercy of merely linguistic similarities:

[T]o learn from the expert linguist that the English literal equivalent of a certain Chinese or Sanskrit word is 'mind' does not tell
one very much that is significant for comparative philosophy. Such
a translation provides us with the denotative associations of the
common-sense symbol, but not with its technical philosophical,
contextual connotative meaning. That which is directly apprehended
is roughly the same in any philosophical system, but how it is analyzed and correlated with other factors, whether immediately given
or postulated, is different; *it is precisely these differences which concern
us in comparative philosophy* (1947, 80–81, emphasis mine)

Northrop's framework provides a means for understanding—in precise terms
that have bearing across traditions—how the directly apprehended features of
reality are analyzed and correlated in any given tradition, and thus provides
a framework for comparative philosophy itself.

The second strength of a comparative framework is its *comprehensiveness*
in being able to account for any aspect of a tradition. To those uncomfortable
with the idea of systematic philosophy, this may seem to indicate a severe
reductionism in interpretation, but in Northrop's case this is arguably not
so: because of his relentless commitment to remaining open to the novel
insights of all cultures, his framework is remarkably robust and capable of
accounting for aspects of a tradition in ways that typically ring true with
the traditions described. At the same time, however, because all of these
diverse facets are brought together in a single systematic framework, he is
able to compare not only individual facets of particular traditions but also
the traditions as a whole, a far more interesting and fruitful task, if notoriously more difficult.[45]

The third strength of the framework, finally, is its *coherence*, insofar
as it allows the comparativist to understand something of how all traditions fit together into a unified whole. By virtue of this framework, he can
identify—with a precision that can only come from drawing on a common
set of philosophical terms and categories—features that all cultures have in
common (e.g., a tendency to dismiss as illusory or evil what is different in
other cultures), as well as respects in which cultures differ (e.g., a focus on
the aesthetic or theoretic components of knowledge). Moreover, because
the framework takes its cue from all traditions, this coherence should be
capable of doing more than merely interpreting other traditions in light of
one particular tradition.

The point in outlining these goods is not to claim that they were
necessarily achieved by means of Northrop's framework; these were, however,
the goods that he sought to achieve in the construction of that framework
and that most of his contemporaries would have agreed he made great strides
in achieving.[46] Indeed, it was largely by virtue of the broad support for the

framework laid out at the first East-West Philosophers' Conference—and developed most fully in the *Meeting*—that Northrop distinguished himself as one of the foremost scholars, if not *the* foremost scholar, in postwar comparative philosophy.

This status had a significant impact on his involvement in the second East-West Philosophers' Conference (and to a lesser extent the third), as he became the sounding board for subsequent developments in the field. E. R. Hughes recognized this influence when he wrote that the second East-West Philosophers' Conference in 1949 was "the heir to the 1939 Conference and cannot but take into serious consideration the main thesis of *The Meeting of East and West*. It is undoubtedly the main contribution which has come from the East-West movement in comparative philosophy, and we are all indebted to Mr. Northrop for his trenchant defining of problems in this particularly blurred field" (Moore 1951, 65). There was certainly no uniform response to Northrop's approach: some scholars found it generally agreeable and took their own contributions to be improvements or elaborations of it (e.g., William Ray Dennes, Gunapala Piyasena Malalasekera, Wilmon Henry Sheldon, Y. P. Mei, Cornelius Krusé); other scholars found it misleading or problematic in some respects and founded their own contributions on its critique (e.g., E. R. Hughes, Dhirendra Mohan Datta, E. A. Burtt, P. T. Raju, John Wild). Yet almost every scholar who presented a paper at the conference found it necessary to refer—directly or indirectly—to Northrop's approach in the explication of his or her own ideas.[47]

The sustained interest in Northrop's approach at the second conference is of particular value to this study, as it provides privileged insight into the way that his approach was received by philosophers from a broad variety of traditions. Indeed, it presents an exceptional forum for critical reflection about his method, the results of which shed light on its weaknesses as perceived by his contemporaries. Significantly—although not surprisingly, given that this constitutes the most novel and distinctive feature of his approach—these critiques pertain almost exclusively to his use of a comprehensive framework for comparison. Although they were not provided with such systematic clarity in the conference itself, these critiques will be used to highlight the three primary weaknesses associated with that usage.

SOURCE OF THE CATEGORIES

If the first conference was characterized by a prevailing optimism regarding the prospects for cross-cultural understanding, the second was characterized by an increased awareness of the distinctiveness of terms and concepts arising out of other traditions and the consequent difficulty of translating those terms and concepts into other languages. Many of the attendees of this conference advocated keeping important cross-cultural terms in their original form, thus broadening the vocabulary of other traditions to include these terms and their distinctive meanings. In the context of such a shift, a framework like Northrop's—developed entirely out of terms garnered from the Western philosophical tradition—comes across as somewhat suspect in its apparent lack of interest in the terms and concepts of other cultures. The issue for Northrop was not that the terms he chose were English terms: if he were right, and his terms could find expression in any tradition, then one should be able to translate those terms into their representative equivalents in each tradition. The question at hand was rather whether there were, in fact, such equivalents in other traditions at all and, if so, whether they were the defining characteristics of those traditions.

This concern was raised most prominently at the conference by D. T. Suzuki, who initially argued that what Buddhists mean by "Nirvana" is unique to Buddhist philosophy. Northrop described his first meeting with Suzuki as follows:

> It was the first day of the second (1949) East-West Philosophers' Conference. Since I knew Suzuki only from his books, I called on him at his office near mine in the university. After mutually warm greetings he said: "I have read your *The Meeting of East and West* and have but one question to ask you. The answer which you give will tell me whether what you mean by 'the undifferentiated aesthetic continuum' is identical with what one who understands Buddhism means by 'Nirvana.'" His question was "Is the undifferentiated continuum an object other than one's subjective consciousness of it, or not?" "Obviously not," I replied. "Otherwise, there would be a dualism or difference between my differentiatable subjective consciousness and the undifferentiated aesthetic continuum. Then my subjective consciousness would not be undifferentiatedly identical with it." Instantly, Suzuki said: "Yes. That is Nirvana." (1962, 24–25)[48]

Northrop recounted a similar experience with respect to the Hindu notion of "the Atman that is Brahman without differences," arguing that this too is identical with his notion of the undifferentiated aesthetic continuum (1962, 21). Indeed, he argued throughout the first three conferences that his categories are relevant to non-Western traditions, and his arguments proved not entirely uncompelling for his fellow conference attendees.[49] In fact, his arguments are downright impressive, given that his primary expertise was not in non-Western traditions.

Yet the strength of his arguments depended not simply on his ability to account for the distinctive features of other traditions but also to do so in a manner consistent with the character of those traditions. Here the content of an idea runs up against its cultural context: does the fact that Northrop has presented a set of ideas that can be used to give expression to the main ideas of any tradition mean that he has identified a genuinely cross-traditional framework of ideas? If cultural context has a negligible influence on the content of an idea, then it should not matter what terms a cross-traditional framework uses to express its ideas; those terms should be interchangeable with the defining terms of any other tradition. If the influence is more acute than this, however, then it would not be possible to adequately represent the ideas of any tradition in terms garnered from another tradition.

The problem for Northrop was that, as Moore observed, the intellectual tide was slowly shifting from an emphasis on the content of ideas to their cultural context (1962, 4–5). Already at the second conference, some scholars started to draw attention to the cultural commitments of Northrop's framework and point out the consequent limitations of that framework. Edwin A. Burtt made this critique, for example, when he made the claim that "there is no precise equivalent in the language (or languages) of one culture for any philosophic category which has acquired its meaning in another" (Moore 1951, 119). Accordingly, he suggested that the distinctive terms of any tradition remain untranslated. Furthermore, he argued that frameworks like Northrop's should be suspended until comparativists are able to garner a better understanding of the many philosophical options and their cultural connections. Similarly, E. R. Hughes drew attention to the unspoken Platonist commitments of Northrop's framework (insofar as it identifies concepts by postulation primarily with mathematics and physics) and called for a revision of the framework in terms that more adequately reflect non-Western values.[50]

As the tide continued to shift over the next few decades, Northrop's framework looked less like the basis for genuinely cross-cultural understanding that he intended it to be and more like an unsuspecting vehicle for precisely the cultural imperialism he sought to avoid. In our own time, few comparativists pay any attention to Northrop—except perhaps as a passing historical interest—and the few who do take as their primary critique of his approach its evident debts to Western traditions.[51] These critiques are not entirely misplaced: they indicate an advance in comparative philosophy, at least insofar as it has become able to find inadequate what had previously seemed relatively adequate.

The task for contemporary comparativists, however, should be to develop a new, more adequate system of categories for comparison rather than to simply continue decrying the old ones. While the shift toward greater appreciation of the cultural location of philosophical ideas is surely not a meritless one, it would be a mistake to let this lead to cultural isolation.[52] Cross-cultural communication will continue to occur regardless, for better or for worse, and it is the comparativist's task to determine not only how such communication occurs but how to facilitate it in ways that are better and not worse. The truth of such communication must lie somewhere between perfect communication and complete isolation, and a sufficiently flexible comparative framework should be able to provide terms that aid such communication.

In short, whether comparativists pursue their task in Northrop's context or in our own—indeed, whatever the intellectual climate—a comprehensive, systematic framework can be a helpful tool for aiding cross-cultural understanding. Northrop's particular framework may have identifiable debts to Western philosophical traditions (how could it not?), but this does not render it completely useless for cross-cultural comparison. Rather, it provides the grounds for further improvement of the framework and thus the further improvement of cross-cultural understanding as well. If the limitations of Northrop's particular framework are definitive and well-documented, the weakness of this aspect of his method is only tentative. Indeed, it is only as weak as the traditions of philosophical comparison that continue to develop—or fail to develop—this aspect of Northrop's work.

APPLICATION OF THE CATEGORIES

As noted above, not all scholars at the conference were opposed to the use of Northrop's categories as the terms for a comparative framework. In fact, most scholars felt that the global spectrum of philosophical options exemplified distinctions like those he laid out and were willing to use these as provisional terms for comparative discussion.[53] What many *did* question, however, was the way that these distinctions were applied to particular traditions in light of the broader framework. That is, the question was not primarily whether the comparative categories suggested by Northrop were useful ones but rather whether they applied to traditions in the manner he described.

This critique was made primarily by scholars of non-Western traditions, who argued that their respective traditions did, in fact, develop concepts by postulation in important ways.[54] Dhirendra Mohan Datta, T. M. P. Mahadevan, and P. T. Raju all argued this with respect to Indian philosophy, while E. R. Hughes and Hu Shi did likewise for Chinese philosophy.[55] The most famous example of this critique, however, was raised outside of the context of the conference. In his landmark *Science and Civilization in China* (1954–2004), Needham took Northrop to task for his reading of science in China: he argued that "[t]here is no good reason for denying to the theories of *Yin* and *Yang*, or the Five Elements, the same status of proto-scientific hypotheses as can be claimed by the systems of the pre-Socratic and other Greek schools" (1956, 579).[56] Furthermore, he extended this argument to subsequent facets of Chinese thought, finding the culmination of scientific thought in China in Song dynasty Neo-Confucianism.[57]

In Northrop's defense, he never argued that concepts by intuition and concepts by postulation were the exclusive domain of Eastern and Western traditions, respectively; to the contrary, he not only acknowledged the presence of both types of concepts in each tradition but also argued that such presence was necessary if the types were to serve as effective comparative categories. The question for Northrop was not about presence but rather about emphasis: what type of concepts predominantly defines the character of a civilization? Moreover, when he argued for the prominence of a type of concept within a particular tradition, he defined that type in a precise sense that was persistently misunderstood by his critics. His responses reflect a frustration with this persistent misunderstanding, seeking to demonstrate that a more precise and accurate understanding of his terms would enable his critics to see the validity and applicability of his claims.[58]

At the same time, however, these critiques are not entirely unfounded. As impressive as the cross-cultural breadth of his knowledge was, Northrop was not a specialist in other traditions and did not know as much about Indian and Chinese traditions as many of his fellow conference participants. It is thus entirely possible that he failed to appreciate the full extent of the development of less prominent types of concepts in other traditions. It is also quite possible that his understanding of concepts by intuition and by postulation was not sufficiently cross-cultural (i.e., was too "Western-centric") and that it needed to be broadened in order to accurately account for all of the available data. In short, if his critics were correct, Northrop may have needed to adjust the application of his categories for comparison.

The first line of defense for Northrop here is, as in the previous consideration, a fallibilistic one: with more time and greater mutual understanding among Northrop and his critics, he may have been able to achieve a better application of his categories across traditions. By the same token, contemporary comparativists could (and should) continue his work and pursue a better application of his categories. To this extent, the weakness in question would again be less with Northrop's method than with his execution of it.

Yet, in this case, he should perhaps not be let off so easily. One should ask why he failed to alter the application of his categories in the manner I am suggesting. In the previous case, such a failure can be explained simply by pointing to the inevitable cultural biases to which any person is subject; in the current case, it is not immediately clear why the application of his categories should fail to hit the mark. Certainly, one explanation is that the critiques he encountered were, as he claimed, based on misunderstandings of his work, and this is undoubtedly true in at least some cases. Yet it is unlikely that this can account for all cases, especially given the number of such critiques concerned with this aspect of his work.

There is good reason to believe that, in at least some cases, Northrop inadvertently allowed the very structure of his comprehensive, systematic framework to unduly influence the application of its categories. The distinction he made between concepts by intuition and concepts by postulation conforms too neatly to the distinction between "East" and "West," such that the two seem intended to refer to a more basic, fundamental distinction among traditions. Finding a substantive example of concepts by postulation in Chinese history—to use Needham's example—would thus be akin to finding evidence of an Indo-European civilization in the middle of China.[59] To be fair, Northrop did mention some exceptions to these respective associations, but these pale in comparison to the persistence of his broader associations. The consistency of these associations and the vigor with which he defended them suggest that Northrop not only *described* what he found in philosophical traditions worldwide but that he also *essentialized* those traditions, such that each tradition *must* primarily represent the type of concept associated with its location in East or West.[60]

This drive to essentialize is understandable when one considers how much Northrop has invested in this dichotomy of concepts. His entire rationale for comparative philosophy lies in the claim that each philosophical tradition was deficient in some important sense and that it could therefore learn from other philosophical traditions even while it shared its own proficiencies. Making comparative philosophy work thus means recognizing the important contributions of each tradition and allowing them to approach the broader world philosophical conversation more or less as equals. Accordingly, it is of paramount importance for Northrop to maintain a basic parity among philosophical traditions and to ensure that each tradition has something important to learn even—and *especially*—from traditions furthest removed from it.

Here Needham's challenge becomes particularly dangerous for Northrop: what if Chinese philosophy *did* adequately develop both types of categories? Then it would already roughly approximate the cross-cultural synthesis he hoped to achieve through comparative philosophy. The Chinese would have little to gain from comparative philosophy (by Northrop's account), while all other philosophical traditions could do little better than approximate the Chinese tradition. In short, it would not only destroy Northrop's framework for the synthesis of world philosophies but also call into question his very justification for comparative philosophy (at least in China).

This is not to say that all of this was Northrop's intention. He seems as aware as any of his contemporaries of the radical diversity among the world's philosophical traditions and would have been the first to object to any oversimplification of those traditions. At the same time, however, it is unlikely that, in such a diverse world, there would be such a strong and consistent distinction in conceptual emphasis between East and West as the one maintained by Northrop, and yet he maintained this distinction almost right down the line. Indeed, it is unlikely that anything like the world's philosophical diversity could be adequately represented by a two-fold distinction in types of categories, yet this is the cornerstone to Northrop's entire comparative synthesis.

Were Northrop to address this shortcoming to his framework, he would likely have asked whether the framework he developed was nonetheless reasonably effective at enabling a better understanding of the world's philosophical and cultural traditions. Its shortcomings notwithstanding, it is fair to say that it was quite effective at its outset, although its effectiveness has waned as our understanding of the comparative context has continued to develop.[61] What Northrop's critics should have asked is what their critiques add to our understanding of the relation among the world's traditions. In a narrow sense, of course, any critique can be helpful insofar as it points out the limitations of the framework; yet, in a broader sense, such critiques are ultimately only destructive if they pick away at the available framework without pointing the way toward another, better one. To the extent that frameworks are helpful for structuring our understanding, a reasonably adequate framework is better than no framework at all, and the flurry of critiques of Northrop's work left comparative philosophers bereft of any clear alternative.[62]

The lesson to be learned from these considerations is just how easily the structure of our understanding can affect our interpretation of things—not only for the better, but also for the worse. Where this led Northrop astray was in his broader vision for comparative philosophy: his anticipation of a final synthesis, and his justification for comparative philosophy as a whole makes him vulnerable to misinterpretation of data in pursuit of these ends. What he lacked was a methodological feedback mechanism that would have kept his broader vision in check and ensured greater fidelity to the evidence at hand in each case. As it stands, comparative philosophy would have to wait another generation for a comparative method with such an integrated feedback mechanism.[63]

STRUCTURE OF THE CATEGORIES

The limitations inherent in Northrop's structure of categories have already been discussed to some extent in the section above, insofar as it may unduly influence the application of those categories to the world's philosophical traditions. In this section, consideration will be given to a different—but related—dimension of the structure of his categories, namely, its static nature. To the extent that he effectively associated the distinction between concepts by intuition and concepts by postulation with the distinction between "East" and "West," he rendered his framework dependent on the ongoing validity of the latter distinction. For Northrop, it was crucial that this remained a two-part relation, insofar as it provided the basis for an epistemic correlation between the two types of concepts and, at least metaphorically, between East and West itself.

The problem with this dependence on conceptual pairing becomes evident when one considers the possibility that the world's cultures are not best understood according to such broad dichotomies. As contemporary comparativists are aware, a simple distinction between East and West is now rightly considered naïve, as the diversity within East and West and their historical interpenetration seriously compromise the validity of the distinction. And yet, without reference to this distinction, much of the impetus for Northrop's framework—beholden as it is to two-part relations—is lost.

Unfortunately for Northrop, the trend over the three conferences was a gradual movement from a two-part distinction between East and West to a tripartite distinction among India, China, and the West.[64] By the third conference, this shift was so complete that Moore could proclaim that "at last we are now convinced that there is no simple or single 'East' or 'West'—and that even within each of the many cultures and philosophical traditions, East and West, there is wide variety as well as historical variation and that a failure to recognize this genuine diversity is tantamount to no genuine understanding whatsoever" (1962, 701). Although the conferences would still use "East-West" terminology to express their agenda, these terms took on a merely metaphorical status describing not the encounter of opposites but the encounter with difference in any form. Unfortunately for Northrop, this was an evolution of terminology that was not available for his framework, and it left him defending a basic conception of the world's cultures that his contemporaries had all but left behind.

Readers of a deconstructive bent are likely to applaud the demise of Northrop's framework, seeing in it the inherent tendency of any binary opposition to privilege one side over the other. Without conceding that this is a necessary or even generally applicable reading of dualisms, it is worth noting that this reading makes good sense of the available data in this case. Attention has already been paid to how the concepts by postulation associated with the West eventually took prominence over the concepts by intuition associated with the East. Similarly, despite arguing for their underlying parity through epistemic correlation, Northrop ultimately gave precedence to facts over values, arguing that while facts can be verified in their own right, values can only be verified insofar as they are epistemically correlated to their respective facts. Moreover, despite his best efforts to present both sides of each dualism in complete parity with one another, it is clear by Northrop's later works that the side of each dualism associated with his own tradition ultimately takes precedence over its corresponding alternative. In this case, what set out to be a culture-neutral framework for cross-cultural comparison ultimately becomes a vehicle for the self-promotion of its author's own cultural values.

It would perhaps have been possible for Northrop to fundamentally revise his approach to reflect this change ("epistemic tri-relation?"), but doing so would have undermined most of the claims he made by means of the framework set out in the *Meeting*. Indeed, revising the framework would have required that he more or less start from scratch again in his use of comparative terminology. There is a certain irony here that should not be lost on contemporary comparativists, namely, that the very structure that initially enabled such clarity and organization in cross-cultural understanding ultimately stood in the way of such understanding as it developed over time. If there is a lesson to be learned from this facet of Northrop's work, it is that comparative frameworks are like prescription lenses: they are extraordinarily helpful—indeed, necessary—for seeing things more clearly, yet, as one matures and one's eyes continue to develop, the old lenses eventually prove inadequate and must be replaced with new ones made specifically for the next context. As helpful as Northrop's framework was initially, it could never be a permanent solution, and—as helpful as it was initially—it would eventually have to be replaced by a new framework. It is left to subsequent comparativists to ensure that new frameworks continue to be made available as necessary and that they improve on the older frameworks in important respects.

CONCLUSION

Northrop lived most of his life in the context of ideological conflict on a global scale. His own education was interrupted by the First World War, and by the Second World War he had already made the failure of the League of Nations and the development of the United Nations among his foremost concerns. Indeed, the issues that would vex him most by the end of his career were those pertaining to the conflicting ideals of the United States and the Soviet Union as exemplified in the Cold War. Throughout his career, he sought to harness the resources of philosophy for the purpose of cultivating cross-cultural understanding, despite that—or perhaps because—his contributions were consistently marginalized in favor of the prevailing power politics of his time. Northrop died in 1992, not long after the effective end of the Cold War, and would have seen the space this opened up for a new model of international relations. It remains unclear whether we will embrace this opportunity or allow the challenges of global terrorism to drive us back to the power politics of our recent past, but it is fair to say that Northrop's work may provide renewed guidance for us as we chart our course moving forward.

Northrop's legacy is a complicated affair. He clearly initiated one of the most ambitious projects in midcentury comparative philosophy and propelled the discipline forward by his example. Not all of his contemporaries agreed with his conclusions, but all of them were aware that in his work they encountered one of the most carefully constructed and methodologically sophisticated approaches to comparison of their time. To this day, most of his major works are still in publication, and the *Meeting* is still relatively standard undergraduate reading.

At the same time, however, he left no clear heirs to his comparative method. While many would find his approach interesting and insightful, none felt it sufficiently compelling to take it up and develop it more fully on his oer her own. Indeed, if Northrop was a source of inspiration at the first conference and a subject of critique at the second, he was all but ignored at the third conference (at least relative to the attention he garnered at the previous ones). While he was still clearly respected as a senior scholar, his was the respect afforded to scholars whose prominence had passed and whose contributions were deemed passé.

Significantly, however, Northrop was not alone in his fate. In counterpoint with the rise of analytic philosophy in America, indigenous American philosophies went on the decline as did the comparative methods that developed out of them. Although there remained proponents of pragmatism, process philosophy, and naturalism, these figures failed to gain the public voice of their forebears and could not keep pace with the optimistic advance of the analytic tradition. Like Northrop, American philosophy was revered like an aged relative: important for the sake of heritage but hardly cutting edge. In fact, serious comparative philosophers in the pragmatist and process traditions would not arise until shortly before Northrop died (see, e.g., Hall 1982a, 1982b; Neville 1982). These comparativists have acknowledged their debts to earlier philosophers such as Hocking and Northrop, although they develop and transform their predecessors' contributions in bold new ways. It is to their works that we now turn.

CHAPTER THREE

DAVID HALL AND ROGER AMES

Comparative Philosophy as the Philosophy of Culture

the single greatest obstacle to understanding Chinese philosophy and culture has been the unannounced assumption that it is similar enough to our own tradition that we shall be able to employ interpretive categories resourced in our tradition to understand the lineaments of that culture. This assumption often seems justified when, by recourse to these categories, we seem to arrive at meanings strikingly similar to our own. But this is often the case only because the application of our most familiar interpretive concepts foreground certain content while concealing what, to us, would be the more exotic meanings.

—Hall and Ames, *Anticipating China*

The collaborative work of David Hall (1937–2001) and Roger Ames (1947–) constitutes one of the most extensive and original approaches to comparative philosophy at the turn of the twenty-first century. They have made a point of highlighting lesser-known alternative philosophical traditions for the purpose of revealing the assumptions, the limitations, and the contingency of the dominant tradition(s) of philosophy and thus aiding the development of a broader, richer, and more authentic understanding of philosophical traditions moving forward. By demonstrating the relevance of these alternative traditions and the inherent challenges of engaging them on their own terms, they have introduced a much-needed corrective to prevailing ways of translating philosophical texts, thinking about other cultures, and ultimately thinking about thinking itself.

One of the alternative traditions highlighted in their work is the Chinese philosophical tradition. Hall and Ames maintain that this tradition has been unduly cast aside in contemporary thought because it does not conform to the assumed contours of what constitutes "philosophy" properly conceived; yet, they maintain, the Chinese tradition is replete with ideas, texts, and methods that are nothing if not philosophical (Ames 2002, par. 15). One simply needs a less narrowly conceived understanding of philosophy to recognize their relevance. If philosophy is to be truly comparative—and Hall and Ames make clear their conviction that serious contemporary philosophy cannot be otherwise—then it must be prepared to call into question the very definition of what counts as philosophy in light of the insights of other cultures. Accordingly, one of the driving concerns in their work as comparative philosophers is to problematize this dismissal and bring the Chinese tradition back into the global philosophic conversation.

Another alternative tradition that is highlighted in their work is the American philosophical tradition. This tradition—as exemplified especially in the pragmatist and process traditions—bears important similarities with the classical Chinese tradition that enable it to serve as a cross-cultural "bridge" for better understanding that tradition (1987, 15). In fact, one can travel this bridge both ways, they maintain, such that a better understanding of classical Chinese philosophy can enable a better understanding of the possibilities for American philosophy (see, e.g., 2002, par. 13). Perhaps most significantly, the similarities among these traditions can reinforce each other insofar as they both offer a critique of and alternative to the dominant tradition of Western philosophy. While most of their collaborative work has taken classical Chinese philosophy as its primary subject matter, it has always been accompanied by a conscious appreciation of the relevance of American philosophy to their task.

Hall and Ames clearly cast a wide net in identifying resources for their constructive philosophical critiques, a net that most comparativists would find difficult to successfully draw in on their own. However, the task becomes more feasible when undertaken in the context of successful collaboration. The joint work of Hall and Ames is an outstanding example of such collaboration. Although each author has developed a broad proficiency in each of the areas of the larger project, each also brings to the task a distinctive skill set that, when coupled together, enable them collectively to address each aspect of the project with unquestionably high scholarship.

This joint project has its roots in the earlier work of David Hall. Hall was a professionally trained philosopher who specialized in the pragmatist and process traditions of American philosophy. His dissertation, written under the direction of Robert Brumbaugh, details a "Whiteheadian theory of culture," which he later revised and published under the title *Civilization of Experience: A Whiteheadian Theory of Culture* (1973). Here he characterizes Whitehead—much as he will later characterize himself—as "primarily a philosopher of culture" (1973, x). In this early work, he uses the term in a relatively innocuous way to mean that subfield of philosophy that asks the question: "What have been the significant human interests which have consistently led to public expression?" (8). The implications of this idea are that philosophy is not always primarily concerned with what is "true." As Whitehead noted, "it is more important that a proposition be interesting than that it be true. The importance of truth is that it adds to interest" (1929, 259), and it is the philosopher's task to elucidate and cultivate these cultural interests in as responsible a manner as possible.[1] Philosophy is thus seen to be a primarily descriptive rather than deductive discipline (1973, 8–10). On this basis, Whitehead becomes a point of entry for Hall's interest in an analogical alternative to the *ontologia generalis* and *scientia universalis* that characterizes the mainstay of Western philosophy, although this interest is not yet fully developed in this early work.[2]

The basic framework for Hall and Ames' collaborative work, however, is to be found in Hall's two subsequent books, *Eros and Irony: A Prelude to Philosophical Anarchism* (1982a) and *The Uncertain Phoenix: Adventures toward a Post-Cultural Sensibility* (1982b). It is here that his strong dissatisfaction with contemporary modes of Western philosophy is first given unapologetic expression. It is here that Hall first looks back to the roots of the Western tradition to question the stigma associated with such notions as chaos and plurality (1982b, 45-94). It is here that the key terms for his later collaborative work with Ames are first laid out ("first-" and "second problematic thinking," *mythos* and *logos*, etc.) and the notion of "philosophy of culture" developed into a more full-bodied philosophical alternative. Most significant for his subsequent work, it is here that he first undertakes—with some guidance from Roger Ames, among others (1982a, ix)—a substantive engagement with non-Western philosophical traditions (especially Chinese philosophy).[3]

Hall's interest in alternatives to and critiques of the dominant Western tradition continued through his life, especially as these are found within the various strands of American philosophy. Most significant, Hall published an excellent study on the neopragmatist Richard Rorty entitled *Richard Rorty: Poet and Prophet of the New Pragmatism* (1994). Until that time, Rorty had been given a secondary role and a lukewarm reception in Hall's thought (see, e.g., 1982a, 104–105; 144–45); when looking for "the pragmatic thrust of contemporary philosophy" (148), Hall tended to look instead to analytic philosophers such as W. V. O. Quine, Wilfrid Sellars, and Nelson Goodman.[4] Upon completion of his research on Rorty, however, Hall began to take Rorty as the philosophical touchstone for his pragmatist critique of the Western tradition in all subsequent work (see esp. Hall and Ames 1995).[5] Hall was also working on a more general book on American philosophy, which was interrupted by his untimely death in 2001.[6]

Roger Ames became interested in Hall's project when the latter published his first comparative essays in dialogue with the Chinese tradition (Hall 1978, 1980)—an area that was proving a productive ground for the application of Hall's project. Ames had been trained as a classical sinologist, but he also had a substantive background in philosophy; as he points out, his training as a sinologist rather than a philosopher stems in part from the near impossibility of studying Chinese philosophy in traditional departments of philosophy (Ames 2002, par. 6–9). He had become interested in Chinese philosophy as an alternative to Western philosophy and perhaps also as a corrective to it. In this connection, he was drawn to the work of Marcel Granet and—more recently—A. C. Graham, especially insofar as it interpreted Chinese philosophy in terms of "correlative thinking" (as opposed to the "causal thinking" of Western philosophy). When he read Hall's work, he "recognized a student of Chinese culture who was dealing with issues similar to those with which he was concerned, and in ways that he could happily endorse. Contact was made; discussions ensued. And the result has been a productive, and personally enjoyable collaboration" (Ames 2000, 167–68).[7]

What Ames brought to the collaboration was a ready familiarity with the Chinese language, philosophy, and culture that Hall—trained as a Western philosopher—did not possess (Ames 2002, par. 23). Moreover, he had already established for himself a solid reputation in the translation and interpretation of Chinese texts (see, e.g., Ames and Young 1977; Ames 1983), so he could lend an air of credibility to their cross-cultural work, something that greatly benefited the project given the controversy it would invoke. In fact, Ames would continue his dedicated sinological work throughout his association with Hall, often collaborating with other sinologists and comparative philosophers as well (see, e.g., Ames and Lau 1996, 1998; Ames and Rosemont 1998), thus increasing the influence and credibility of their project as a whole.

Hall's originality as a constructive philosopher is incontestable, although it is unlikely that he could have pursued the most fertile dimensions of his project—the cross-cultural dimensions—without the assistance of an enterprising yet well-grounded sinologist like Ames. Similarly, Ames is an unquestionably creative and well-informed student of Chinese culture, but it is questionable whether he could have broken with the established conventions of philology to the extent that he did without the encouragement of a philosophical anarchist like Hall. It is perhaps fair to say that both scholars challenged each other to engage their respective disciplines, as well as their intersection in comparative philosophy, in groundbreaking and original ways. The result—as will be seen below—is an approach that challenges, broadens, and ultimately improves the possibilities for comparative philosophy.

DESCRIPTION OF METHOD

Following Herbert Fingarette (1972), Hall and Ames describe their comparative method as a "problematic" one, meaning that it focuses on the identification of a philosophical problem in one tradition and then attempts to address—and, ideally, to remedy—that problem with resources from another tradition (1987, 5–6).[8] Hall and Ames employ this method on three levels simultaneously, consisting of historico-philological translation, the cultivation of cross-cultural understanding, and a revisioning of the Western tradition. While they never explicitly order these three levels as part of a broader, systematic method—something that is itself distinctive of their method— each level is present in their comparative work and receives self-conscious methodological development at various points. Perhaps more significantly, each level contributes to the "problematic" approach as described above. Accordingly, each level will be considered in detail here.

Philologico-Philosophical Translation

The first level identifies a methodological problem in the cross-cultural translation of philosophical texts.[9] The problem originates in an ethnocentric bias on the part of the Western philosophical tradition that manifests itself in a resistance to recognizing the philosophical traditions of other cultures *as* philosophical traditions. This bias is particularly pronounced in the case of Chinese philosophy, no doubt due to the fact that it is the tradition that seems to differ most substantively from the Western tradition (generally conceived). As a result, when Chinese philosophical texts have been translated, they have been translated primarily along philological lines, with inadequate concern for the integrity and coherence of the philosophical concepts expressed in the text. Historically, most of these texts were translated by Christian missionaries and sinologists, whose predominantly nonphilosophical concerns—religious and linguistic, respectively—have tended to obscure and even distort the philosophical dimensions present in the text.

Hall and Ames are appreciative of the work done by translators hitherto and do not intend to malign missionaries and sinologists as much as to impugn philosophers for failing to take the Chinese tradition more seriously (Ames 2002, par. 15). They also grant that, more recently, there has been growing dissatisfaction among comparative philosophers with the amount of attention—or, rather, the lack thereof—paid to philosophical concerns in translation. In this connection, they point to Wing-tsit Chan, D. C. Lau, and Wm. Theodore de Bary as noteworthy predecessors for maintaining a philosophical awareness in the translation of cross-cultural texts (1987, 2). Of these three, Lau has clearly been the strongest influence: Ames lauds him as "probably the most highly respected translator of Chinese philosophical classics" (Ames 2002, par. 9).[10] Lau supervised Ames' doctoral work at the University of London (1978) and imparted to him a strong appreciation for the historical and linguistic rootedness of philosophical concepts as well as the consequent importance of philosophically astute translations, which Ames brought to bear on his subsequent work with Hall.

The significant contributions of these predecessors notwithstanding, Hall and Ames maintain that current conditions in comparative philosophy require a further reconsideration and reformation of the way Chinese philosophical texts are translated. The first of these conditions is the fact that, at present, all of the most significant Chinese philosophical texts are readily available in translation—some in manifold versions—such that the cultivation of a responsible understanding of Chinese philosophy is served at least as well by revisiting these translations as it is by continuing to translate increasingly obscure ones. Western understanding of Chinese philosophy has already been shaped in large part by the terms set out in these translations, yet because of lack of adequate attention to the philosophical implications of these terms, they often convey meanings that are absent in or even contrary to the original text.[11] If such misunderstanding is to be rectified, these translations must be revisited and revised with more attention paid to the philosophical commitments of their authors (1987, 41–42). For this reason, Hall and Ames take great care to provide "philosophical translations" of such prominent texts as the *Zhongyong* (2001) and the *Dao De Jing* (2003).

A second condition pertains to the recent discoveries of new texts and new versions of existing texts in China; collectively, these provide an ideal opportunity for a more substantive reevaluation of existing translations. For example, their translation of the *Dao De Jing* (2003) is based on a version of the text recovered from a tomb in Guodian, China, in 1993, which is believed to be about 125 years older than the (otherwise) oldest existing version. Similarly, Ames and Rosemont recently published a new translation of the *Lunyu* (1998), based on a manuscript discovered in Dingzhou in 1973. In each case, careful attention is paid to ensure that the text is presented in a manner as consistent with its original intentions as possible.

As should be clear, Hall and Ames advocate an approach to translation that operates on two fronts. On the one hand, they maintain the traditional emphasis on historical and linguistic (i.e., philological) translation, although they pay increased attention to the meaning of Chinese characters in their original context before determining an acceptable English equivalent in order to avoid allowing inappropriate Western associations to corrupt the communicated meaning of those terms (1987, 1–2). This aspect of their work consists primarily of considering the relevance of characters similar to the one in question and of looking to the use of that character in other comparable texts (42–43). On the other hand, they also engage in conceptual analysis of the terms and ideas present in the text (i.e., philosophical translation) to ensure that there is an adequate level of coherence among them such that each term and idea has a meaningful place in the broader philosophic vision. Both dimensions are crucial for proper translation (1–2), and Hall and Ames are able to balance these well by virtue of their respective strengths.

It should be noted that, according to their stated method, philological analysis must always precede philosophical analysis. "To settle upon an English equivalent for each major concept and then pursue the analysis through the equivalent rather than the original term," they argue, "is unquestionably the most problematic methodological pitfall of Western interpreters of Chinese philosophy." By looking to philological analysis first, they maintain, it is possible to develop not only more philosophically sensitive linguistic equivalents but, once these equivalents have been established, a more accurate understanding of classical Chinese philosophy as well (41).

Hall and Ames are well aware that their approach to translation inherently entails a great deal of interpretation on their part and anticipate objections from those who disagree with their interpretive stance. On the one side, there are those who would limit the role that interpretation plays in translation. Despite that it is virtually common knowledge among contemporary comparative scholars that translation *is* interpretation (at least in part), many translators continue to resist emphasizing the interpretive side in the fear that it will compromise the integrity of the translation itself. Hall and Ames, by contrast, argue it is precisely the failure to bring the interpretive process to the fore that distorts the translation process. Interpretive categories will inform translation whether they are acknowledged or not, and therefore the better translations will be those that openly acknowledge and deliberately (and deliberatively) adjudicate their use.

On the other side, there are those who argue that translation is *nothing but* interpretation, such that it is impossible to translate across cultures. "One really does not quite know what to make of [these] arguments," they write. "They have a certain logical cogency. But their persuasiveness is of the type possessed by arguments to the effect that bumble bees cannot fly. We do after all make the effort to communicate across cultures. And we do seem, on pragmatic grounds, to have greater or lesser success in these endeavors, at least in the sense that there are often useful consequences attending our efforts" (1995, 174). Indeed, it is these pragmatic—or, rather, pragmatist—grounds that inform their stance on interpretation. Hall and Ames have little difficulty eschewing the extremes of universalism and relativism and are content to till the muddy grounds of uncertainty with the aim of cultivating some degree of increased clarity and understanding. "As pragmatists," they declare, "we are perfectly sanguine about the fact that we shall never 'get it right.' Our task, certainly less grandiose but assuredly more fitting, is rather to 'get on with it' in the most responsible manner possible" (119). Indeed, the better part of their collaborative work consists of drawing such linguistic and conceptual analysis into a hermeneutical relationship and thus slowly and carefully developing a novel—and, they would argue, more accurate—understanding of the philosophical cultures they examine.

In sum, for Hall and Ames, critical comparative work is no less relevant for translation than the latter is for the former, so it is only natural for them to bring the interpretive task of cross-cultural comparison back to the initial work translation. They accomplish this fusing of linguistic and conceptual concerns with methodological resources from the American pragmatist tradition, which frees them from the problem of starting points and allows them instead to pursue translations that are never perfect but always increasingly responsible to the comparative endeavor. Indeed, so central is translation to Hall and Ames' comparative work that it constitutes the larger part of their work together. It is, however, only the first of three levels of their comparative work.

Cross-Cultural Understanding

"Our ultimate purpose," write Hall and Ames, "is to create a context within which meaningful comparisons of Chinese and Western cultures may be made" (1995, 111). This is the foremost challenge of comparative philosophy (though not limited to Chinese and Western cultures), and it is the focus of the second level of Hall and Ames' method. The challenge lies precisely in coming to understand another culture without allowing one's understanding to be unduly informed—or, rather, misinformed—by the assumptions of one's own culture. The use of "unduly" here indicates that it is inevitable that one's cultural context will influence one's understanding: an American's understanding of Chinese culture, for example, will never be the same as a Chinese understanding of the same. While one's external cultural location may allow for the possibility of novel insights on that culture, it is far more often epistemologically hallucinogenic, causing one to see things in other cultures that are not really there or to see them in grossly distorted ways. The challenge for Hall and Ames is to enable an understanding of Chinese culture that is as authentically Chinese as possible.

This challenge, they maintain, has not been adequately met to date. The history of comparative philosophy is marked by intellectual ethnocentrism, with other cultures being (mis-)understood in terms often surreptitiously smuggled in from the West. The result is an understanding of other cultures as being endearingly simplistic simulacra of one's own culture, with perhaps a touch of reverential awe thrown in for the sake of political correctness. The problem with this is that such accounts typically leave out the most profound dimensions of these cultural dimensions, in short, precisely those dimensions that the Western tradition could learn from the most. If this shortcoming is to be overcome, they maintain, comparativists must develop a more sophisticated understanding of culture and its relation to philosophy. Accordingly, they make the development of such an understanding one of the foremost concerns of their collaborative work. Indeed, Hall and Ames often style themselves "philosophers of culture" to emphasize their distinctive approach and contribution to comparative philosophy.

"Philosophy of culture," as understood in Hall and Ames' collaborative work, is the product of a radical reassessment of the cultural role of philosophy undertaken in Hall's earlier work (esp. 1982a, 1982b), and a brief review of that earlier work is necessary in order to appreciate its application in their later work. Hall's main argument in those prior works was that philosophy is not primarily—nor even properly—concerned with questions of truth or falsity; to the contrary, "[p]hilosophy is the critic of posited value, or it is nothing worthwhile" (1982a, 41). That is, the philosopher should be concerned not with which theories are true but rather with which theories are worth having in a given cultural context. As indicated earlier, Hall takes Whitehead as his model par excellence for such philosophy:

> [A] speculative philosopher such as Whitehead is really a philosopher of culture who wishes to assess the relevance of any theoretical scheme to the important phases of human experience both as regards the question of the sources of evidence as well as in the application of the scheme. The ultimate test of a general speculative vision is its relevance to the width of civilized experience which contains the principal perspectives on the world provided by the various species of importance. Only if the philosopher seeks the widest possible relevance to the cultural matrix from which his scheme was born can he hope to promote the importance of his philosophic vision. (103–04)[12]

What makes a philosophic vision "important" (to use Whitehead's term) is thus not its truth-value (whether understood in terms of correspondence, coherence, or otherwise) but rather its capacity to engage the experiences of a given culture.[13] These experiences, as well as their perceived importances, are already roughly present in the content of a culture; what they lack—and what philosophy should provide—is a speculative vision that "integrates" and "enriches" the broadest array of such experiences within a particular cultural milieu (1982a, 104).

The philosophy of culture, in turn, seeks merely to identify and examine—but not to dialectically develop—the perceived importances of a given culture. By articulating the spectrum of cultural importances, the philosophy of culture promotes cultural self-understanding and thus maximizes the range of possible experiences within a culture. It also challenges speculative philosophy to integrate these importances into a more comprehensive philosophic vision, thus setting the standard for philosophy and ultimately enriching the experiences associable with those importances. In short, by "telling the story" of a cultural tradition, the philosophy of culture finally seeks to "heighten one's experience of the world" (1982b, 346; see also xii; 93 n. 32; 415–16).

As one might expect, telling the story of a cultural tradition necessitates a return to the origins and development of that culture; however, this return journey is not a simple review of well-known histories but a two-fold journey of critical examination and rediscovery. The first journey attempts to "retrace the adventures of those ideas that have dominated our cultural experience and expression since our beginnings, and will involve us in an attempt to advertise the fundamental presuppositions of our intellectual culture" (1982b, 46–47).[14] This should not only renew a culture's connection with the concrete bases of its abstract ideals (thus preventing alienation from its guiding insights) but also demonstrate the contingency of those ideals (thus preventing the absolute allegiance to those insights). Cultural ideals are important to the extent—and only to the extent—that they allow a culture to engage experience, and tracing the origins and development of the dominant strain of a cultural tradition allows philosophers of culture to account for the ideals most influential in a given culture.

The second journey, by contrast, seeks to identify novel insights in lesser-known alternative strains of the tradition (i.e., those ideas that have not had the "adventures" that they might otherwise have had). "As I conceive it," Hall writes, the philosophy of culture "must presume that the richness of resources provided by any relatively complex cultural circumstance is such as to provide important alternatives to posited ideas and norms which, though alternatives, are not necessarily engaged with the current dominant principles" (1982a, xiv). Because ideas are not so much "true" or "false" as they are "important" or "unimportant" for a given cultural milieu (according to Hall's reading of Whitehead), these alternatives remain potentially relevant to the cultures that engendered them; there is every reason to believe that yesterday's uninteresting asides are tomorrow's guiding insights. Thus, highlighting them broadens the range of possible experiences open to a given culture. For Hall, then, cultural history is a veritable "repository of models of cultural experience" (254 n. 4), which can be drawn on whenever cultural experience is in need of novel insights: when trying to prevent cultural hegemony, when entering periods of significant cultural change, or when encountering very different cultural traditions.

Although Hall only hinted at the cross-cultural dimensions of the philosophy of culture in his own work (e.g., 1982, 172–73), it would become a dominant feature of his collaborate work with Ames. As noted above, the primary difficulty in cross-cultural work lies in the pervasiveness of one's own cultural influences, which render other cultures incomprehensible, endearingly simplistic, or mere simulacrum of one's own culture. Hall and Ames hope to overcome this difficulty by exploiting the "cultural repository" of the West to find models of cultural experience that enable a more authentic understanding of other cultures. More specifically, they hope to identify lesser-known alternative philosophical traditions within the broader

Western tradition that have important features in common with both the dominant tradition of Western philosophy and the dominant tradition of classical Chinese philosophy.

Such an alternative tradition would thus be able to serve two important functions. First, it could serve as a check on the excessive influence of the dominant principles of Western culture. Journeying back to the origins of the Western tradition allows one to examine and reevaluate the philosophic choices made by the tradition. When these choices are seen to be arbitrary—as Hall and Ames insist that they are—one is faced with the radical contingency of Western culture. That is, one sees that the tradition could have been different and indeed has been different at certain points in time. Moreover, closer examination allows one to see more clearly the inherent assumptions and presumptions of the choices that were made, thus enabling one to more readily recognize the influence of the dominant Western tradition when it unduly influences one's cross-cultural work. In short, the presence of alternative traditions allows one to recognize the contingency of the dominant philosophic tradition and enables one to prevent the dominant tradition from becoming the default standard for all philosophy.

A second role that these lesser-known traditions play is that of a bridge between Western and non-Western philosophic traditions. When closer attention is paid to the philosophic alternatives within the Western tradition, there is an increased likelihood of identifying traditions that have more in common with non-Western philosophic traditions. When such alternatives are found, they not only lend to non-Western traditions the credibility of these alternatives *qua* alternatives, but also lend terms from the broader Western tradition that can be employed for a more authentic understanding of non-Western traditions. Of course, there is still significant work to be done in translating from an alternative Western philosophic tradition into a non-Western one, but such alternatives can nonetheless serve as a conceptual way station, easing the journey of ideas and norms across cultures and ensuring that more of them arrive at their destinations intact.

Identifying such a mediating tradition is surely a tall order, but Hall and Ames believe that they have found just such a tradition in early Greek philosophy. They point to the pre-Socratics (e.g., Thales, Anaximander, Anaximenes)—the *physiologoi*, as Aristotle called them (*Metaphysics* 983b6–984a4)—who, in rejecting the mythological explanations of their predecessors and contemporaries, argued that the explanatory principle(s) (*logos*) of nature (*physis*) is/are wholly immanent and natural. Yet, despite rejecting the supernatural, these early philosophers nonetheless maintained a strong sense of the arbitrariness and unpredictability of nature, allowing not only for plurality among their accounts of the world but also—among certain of them—within the accounts themselves. In short, for Hall and Ames, the *physiologoi* are significant for their development of cosmologies that affirmed the possibility of a potentially infinite number of worlds (*kosmoi*).

The *physiologoi* were succeeded in this respect by the Sophists, who interpreted the conflicting views of their predecessors as indications of an inherent irrationality in nature: their views conflict not because they are inaccurate but rather because they are merely conventional representations of an unpredictable and inharmonious set of *kosmoi*. Particular orders, patterns, or principles may exist at any given time, but they can only be coincidental and momentary; hence, all that remains for philosophy is "practical philosophy," which eschews the search for eternal principles in favor of a concern with immediate needs. In this view it is chaos that is creative and order that is destructive, and it is therefore the task of the philosopher to productively engage this chaos with the goal of creative and ever-novel transformation. Because this was the first known formulation of a philosophical problematic to emerge in early Greek thought, Hall and Ames refer to it as "first problematic thinking" (they also refer to it as "aesthetic," "correlative," or "analogical" thinking).

Plato and Aristotle, by contrast, argued for the existence of a single, ordered cosmos that operates on the basis of external principles and that it is the responsibility of philosophers—and to some degree all critical thinkers—to identify and comprehend these principles. They privileged order over chaos, rest over motion, and being over becoming and accounted for all instances of change in terms of static principles of causality. This account should sound more familiar to Westerners, as it is the account that has dominated Western history; however, the prior existence of first problematic thinking demonstrates that it is neither the only nor the first such account. To the contrary, the notion of a single-ordered cosmos is but an invention of Plato and Aristotle. For this reason, Hall and Ames refer to this line of thought as "second problematic thinking" (they also refer to it as "rational," "causal," or "logical" thinking).

Hall and Ames acknowledge that first problematic thinking failed to gain a foothold in Western philosophy and that second problematic thinking quickly established itself as the philosophical standard.[15] Yet, consistent with their position on the role of ideas within culture, they insist that this has nothing to with the philosophical viability of the alternative (1982a, 119).[16] Rather, it was eclipsed simply because first problematic was not adequately developed by the time of Plato and Aristotle; the tour de force accomplished by these two great philosophers quickly established second problematic thinking as philosophical orthodoxy.[17] This near-complete sublimation of first problematic thinking notwithstanding, Hall and Ames maintain that "[i]t remains nonetheless true that from a strictly philosophic perspective there are two dramatically contrasting claims providing the parameters of cosmological speculation for our subsequent philosophers and scientists" (115). That is, first problematic thinking can and should continue to be a viable alternative for Western philosophy, and Hall and Ames take it as part of their task to reconstruct first problematic thinking for contemporary use.[18]

More important, for comparative philosophy, first problematic thinking has proven itself a viable alternative in traditions outside of the West. As Hall and Ames note, "a form of first problematic thinking ... dominates classical Chinese culture" (1995, xviii), and therefore Western examples of first problematic thinking can serve as models for understanding the basic features of classical Chinese thought. This is certainly a controversial claim. They have taken a contrast—between first and second problematic thinking—that the classical Chinese have never explicitly entertained and argued that this allows for a more authentic understanding of classical Chinese philosophy. Indeed, the very character of first problematic thinking as described by Hall and Ames—influenced as it is by pragmatist and postmodern sensibilities—must span both cultural and temporal expanses to engage the classical Chinese.

Our authors are aware of these difficulties and indicate this by referring to their method as "cross-cultural anachronism" (1987, 7); however, these difficulties do not deter their confidence in the aptness of their approach. The problem of cross-cultural comparison, they are quick to remind their readers, is not the influence of one's cultural background on one's understanding of other cultures; such an influence, they acknowledge, is inevitable, and they do not claim to have eradicated or neutralized it (12). The problem, rather, is the *undue* influence of one's cultural background, where "undue" means uncritical, excessive, and/or distortional. Responsible thinking across cultures, therefore, relies on the judicious use of the resources of one's own tradition. In other words, the relevant question is not *whether* one's culture should influence one's understanding, but rather *which* facets of one's culture should be used to inform one's understanding of other cultures.

Hall and Ames are confident that they have identified in first problematic thinking a facet of the Western tradition that allows for a more authentic understanding of classical Chinese philosophy than has hitherto been the case. They are aware that the terms they employ for comparison are foreign to the classical Chinese cultural context and that a number of cultural differences will therefore remain to be addressed. The first problematic thinking of the early Greeks is not the same as that of the classical Chinese; thus, they are careful to claim only that "something like" first problematic thinking dominates classical Chinese culture (1995, 122; see also xix). However, they also maintain that, because first problematic thinking has more in common with classical Chinese thought than does the dominant tradition of Western thought, these differences will be both fewer in number and less substantial than presently exist in comparisons made from the dominant tradition. They write,

> We have no choice but to start with the most fruitful interpretive
> categories at our disposal, but we must be conscious of the fact that
> we are speaking from our own tradition. When we begin a direct
> exposition of classical Chinese thinking, it will be necessary, to the
> extent possible, to adjust these categories and distinctions to better
> suit the Chinese context. As pragmatists we are perfectly sanguine
> about the fact that we shall never 'get it right.' Our task, certainly
> less grandiose but assuredly more fitting, is rather to 'get on with
> it' in the most responsible manner possible. (119)

In short, they claim that their approach, while not eradicating cultural
barriers, does the most responsible job of mitigating those barriers and thus
enabling the most accurate Western understanding of classical Chinese
thought (1987, 7).

The distinction between "getting it right" and "getting on with it
responsibly" again draws attention to the strong pragmatist roots of Hall
and Ames' method. It is this influence that allows them to work productively with the resources at their disposal, rather than merely balking at
the formidable obstacles of cross-cultural comparison. Indeed, this is the
influence that allows them to value the incremental advances that can be
made in understanding other cultures, despite not having "broken the code"
of cross-cultural difference.

In this context, it is only natural that they adapted the central metaphor for their work from the early pragmatist John Dewey, describing their
comparative method as one of "clear[ing] away the useless lumber blocking the path to China" (1995, xx).[19] They note that Western interpretive
constructs, however helpful for understanding Western culture, often merely
stand in the way of an authentic understanding of non-Western cultures.
The task of the comparativist, therefore, is first to remove those interpretive constructs—that is, the "useless lumber"—that stand in the way, and
thus effectively to clear a path to China (xxiii). This path is no intellectual superhighway, allowing a free and easy interchange of ideas between
Western and classical Chinese philosophy; rather, it is merely a rough trail
strewn with rifts and ravines, and it therefore requires the use of some of
the old lumber—the least obstructive lumber—to bridge as many of the
rifts as possible (119). Upon completion of this path, ideas will be able to
survive the journey in only something roughly like the condition in which
they started. The quality of the path, however, lies not in the ultimate
condition of the ideas but rather in the improvement in their condition
after traveling other paths.

The extent to which Hall and Ames have succeeded in clearing a better
path to China—or even whether the path they have cleared is one that leads
to China—will be discussed later in this text. For the moment, it suffices to

note that, of the three levels of their broader method, this second level is clearly the most significant for comparative philosophy as such. It is this level that directly engages the difficulties of "doing comparison," insofar as this means seeking to understand the respects in which traditions are similar and those in which they are the same. It is also this level about which Hall and Ames are most often speaking when they reflect critically on their method. And it is their success on this level that will most cogently determine the success of their broader method for comparative philosophy.

Revisioning the Western Tradition

On this final level, Hall and Ames take the comparative work initiated on the second level and use it to revision their own—that is, the Western—philosophical tradition. Having contrasted first and second problematic thinking, they already have at hand the main contours of each mode of thought as well as a running commentary on their respective strengths and weaknesses. Because first problematic thinking has strengths and insights that second problematic thinking does not, they conclude that there is much to be gained by broadening the perspective of those who have hitherto taken second problematic thinking as the unquestioned norm of philosophic thought. In fact, they ultimately maintain that first problematic thinking provides a superior alternative for addressing the most pressing concerns of the contemporary Western cultural milieu. As a more general precept, however, they maintain that the West has always had much to learn from Chinese philosophy—lessons that could very well alter the very ways it thinks about things as basic as thinking itself.

Like the second level, this one also has its roots in the earlier work of David Hall. In *The Uncertain Phoenix* (1982b), he described the contemporary Western cultural milieu as one of uncertainty, confusion, and change. Western culture suffers not only from the "death of God" but also from the death of scientific orthodoxy; faith in the rational order of science was only grounded, after all, in the faith in a God who could create and maintain such a rational order. Indeed, "with the collapse of the belief in God came the failure of *all* absolutes" (4). The result of this change is the development of a culture plagued by doubt—not methodological doubt, which (supposedly) results in more certain knowledge, but rather a more fundamental, skeptical doubt that precludes the positive development of culture.

The solution to this problem is not, as many have done, to blindly and dogmatically embrace the set of beliefs most readily at hand. To do so would be to attempt to prolong something that has already had its cultural moment; belief in God and scientific orthodoxy have already had the ground pulled from beneath them, and for good reason according to Hall. Rather, a positive response to radical cultural change is best served by maintaining an openness to all manner of possible experiences. Along with radical cultural change comes an emergence of novel possibilities for experience: possibilities that had been hitherto suppressed by the dominant cultural paradigm and that may be instrumental in moving beyond the old paradigm. Hall writes that "cultures in transition do not survive by the strength of their convictions, nor by the productiveness of their intellectual activities, but by their ability to remain open to experience" (1982b, 9). In any period of cultural transition, it would be premature to predict which ideas or values will be of greatest importance for the newly emerging culture; fostering that emergence, and thus fostering the emergence of the richest, most fertile culture possible, therefore entails remaining open to all possible experiences in which those ideas and values can be expressed.

Hall argues that the "openness to experience" required in the current milieu is similar to the attitude found among the early Greeks. "The age of early Greek philosophy, the principal source of our Western cultural experience," he notes, "was a period in which certain questions were asked for the first time, a period in which the ideas and values that have dominated the entire subsequent history of tradition were first constructed" (1982b, 8). While they may not have suffered through the collapse of a prior culture, they nonetheless exemplify the questions that must be asked, experiences that must be had, and possibilities that must be considered in the formation of a new culture. Similarly, subsequent cultural transitions require that these questions, experiences, and possibilities be considered anew.

As noted above, one finds in the early Greek tradition a rich variety of philosophic visions. Some of these are consistent with the mainstay of the Western tradition (i.e., second problematic thinking), while others stand in contrast to it (i.e., first problematic thinking). Hall goes to great lengths to demonstrate that the latter are no less valid than the former as philosophic visions. He argues that the failure of these alternatives was due more to the exceptional brilliance and charisma of the early proponents of second problematic thinking than for any inherent inadequacy in first problematic thinking. Similarly, he points to the success of first problematic thinking—and the failure of second problematic thinking—in the Chinese tradition (especially in the Buddhist and Daoist traditions), thus demonstrating its viability and importance as a philosophic vision. These two moves are brought together to impress upon the reader the potential relevance of these alternatives as resources for the revisioning of the Western tradition.

It is not that Hall does not recognize the value of the second problematic thinking expressed in the Western tradition. He acknowledges the importance of the rational and moral emphases that it entails and notes that these have enabled the development of economic, scientific, technological, and other advances that have been beyond the pale of other civilizations. It is his responsibility as a philosopher of culture, however, to also draw attention to the way in which this narrow focus underlies the current crisis in Western culture:

> In his role as articulator of importances, the speculative philosopher confronts the condition of contemporary cultural existence and finds that some of the unexamined consequences of the dominance of the moral and scientific interests are deleterious in the extreme since they have led to the suppression of burgeoning interest in alternative modes of activity aimed at the realization of aesthetic and religious value. . . . Thus it is primarily the responsibility of the contemporary philosopher of culture to articulate the importance of aesthetic and religious interest, thus enriching our cultural expressions by enabling us to draw upon the width of civilized experience. (1982a, 41)

Accordingly, Hall, as philosopher of culture, draws the Western tradition's attention to the full range of alternatives present in the early Greek tradition and demonstrates that the aesthetic and religious are no less feasible as philosophic interests than the rational and moral. The resources for overcoming the current cultural crisis in the West, therefore, require that it take seriously the full range of possible experiences.

In Hall and Ames' collaborative work, this same contrast is developed more fully in a cross-cultural context: in place of the early Greek tradition, the classical Chinese tradition now stands in as the predominant exemplar of first problematic thinking. The primary purpose remains that of impressing upon the reader the relevance and viability of Chinese philosophy as an alternative to that of the West and of bringing the insights of that tradition to bear upon the further development of Western philosophy. As with Hall's work, the intent of this analysis is not to denigrate the second problematic thinking of the Western tradition. They recognize that it has a number of readily identifiable strengths (1987, 31) and also admit that the Confucian tradition has some significant challenges of its own (307–13).

The promises of the Western tradition notwithstanding, Hall and Ames maintain that there are nonetheless significant philosophical problems deeply engrained in the Western tradition, problems that, in the current cultural milieu, have only intensified and threaten to compromise the entire basis of Western philosophy. Distinctions between fact and value, theory and practice, reality and appearance, and so on, have proven increasingly problematic, and attempts to resolve them have largely resulted in fundamental challenges to traditionally Western ways of thinking (e.g., pragmatism, process philosophy, hermeneutics, postmodernism). Reliable foundations in universal principles, empirical methods, or logical deductions—long the hallmarks of Western thought—have proven increasingly difficult in the face of a rapidly intensifying pluralism. Western philosophers have long sought to address these difficulties but have been ultimately unable to move beyond them because it is the very biases underlying these distinctions that largely sustain their efforts. This being the case, Hall and Ames conclude, "it is doubtful whether the resources available within our own cultural tradition are adequate to resolve successfully the crucial dilemmas associated with attempting to think one's way through to a sufficiently novel understanding of thinking" (1987, 39).

If this Western dilemma is to be resolved successfully, they argue, the solution will most likely arise out of an alternative cultural milieu. Such a milieu can demonstrate the viability of an alternate way of thinking and can therefore indicate a way of moving beyond that distinction as necessary. As Hall and Ames take great pains to demonstrate, the Chinese tradition stands as an important contrast to Western philosophy: it focuses on the aesthetic where the West focuses on the rational, the analogical in contrast to the logical, and the correlative rather than the causal. In short, the Chinese tradition has a long history of productively engaging precisely the nonlinear, irreducible plurality that the West is increasingly forced to address.

This being the case, Western philosophy would do well to glean some of the insights of the Chinese tradition as a means of bolstering and enriching its own tradition.[20] "[W]e have presented the philosophy of Confucius," they write, "as a sophisticated complex of ideas which, once clarified in their own historical context, might serve us in the extension of our own tradition (1987, 308). Further, "Anglo-European culture is in need precisely of the sort of philosophic enterprise which Confucius' valuational thinking represents" (308, 328). Effectively, then, Hall and Ames propose to turn the tables on the challenges of the comparativist, turning the difficulties of cross-cultural understanding into the virtues of intracultural reformation.

The idea that the West has something important to learn from the East is no revolutionary hypothesis; it is even standard fare among comparativists, stemming back at least as far as Hocking and Northrop, if not further to Leibniz, Hegel, and Schopenhauer. Hall and Ames give further voice to this call and do so with eloquence and suasive force. Yet their hypothesis is much more radical than this: they argue that first problematic thinking is not only a valid alternative to second problematic thinking, but moreover that it is a superior alternative within the context of the contemporary cultural milieu.

This normative move is evident in Hall's early works, as he advocates not only the supplementation of the rational and practical with aesthetic and religious modes of understanding but also for the adoption of an "anarchistic" view of the world, one that eschews a single-ordered world in favor of a positive chaos that allows for the acceptance of both rational and practical *and* aesthetic and religious insights. The single-ordered view of the "cosmos," demanding as it does a transcendent *arche* (i.e., principle) according to which all things must conform, unnecessarily limits one's purview to that which can be rendered consistent with that principle; the typical result is the near exclusion of the aesthetic and the religious.

In its place, Hall argues for an "anarchistic" view of the world, which posits multiple *kosmoi* (i.e., orders) and thus allows for the appreciation of inexpressible, irreducible, and even conflicting experiences. Such an openness to the rich variety of possible experiences, he maintains, is precisely what Western culture needs during this period of cultural transition.[21] "Has the cultural context of Western thought altered sufficiently," he asks, "not only to allow for the introduction of an anarchist philosophy into the melting pot of ideas forming intellectual culture, but altered radically enough that one may sensibly make the claim that this form of philosophical anarchism provides the most viable interpretation of our emerging sensibility?" (1982a, 187–88). In his early works, Hall's answer is an unequivocal *yes*.

This argument is also carried through in Hall and Ames' collaborative work, although it is somewhat more difficult to decipher.[22] As noted above, they speak affirmatively with respect to both the Western and Chinese philosophical traditions. They are, of course, more critical of the Western tradition, but this is not sufficient to conclude a preference on their part for the Chinese tradition; it is perhaps simply a matter of rhetorical flair, included to encourage their readers to take the Chinese tradition seriously. The clue toward their preference comes instead from two distinct but related sources.

First, in their examination of both Western and Chinese intellectual history, they consistently embrace a cultural positivism that maintains that the final validation of ideas, thoughts, principles, and so on, can run no further than their cultural location; that is, ideas are not objective but are products of their cultural milieu. Although some contemporary Western subtraditions—namely, the pragmatist, process, and postmodern ones—have begun to arrive at the same conclusion, this has only been at the cost of a radical challenge to and revisioning of the broader Western tradition. Indeed, such a move runs counter to the very quest for certainty and objective knowledge that characterizes the larger part of the Western tradition. By contrast, this cultural positivism is entirely consistent with the classical Chinese philosophy that they elaborate throughout their work (e.g., 1987, 67–68). The inference that one must draw from this is that Hall and Ames are interested in commending the classical Chinese tradition not only as a corrective supplement to the Western tradition but also as a more radical corrective alternative (see, e.g., 331–32).

Second, they maintain that, while it is difficult—if not impossible—to synthesize first and second problematic thinking (1987, 135–36; 1995, 117–18), mutual appreciation between the two is possible "to the extent that one does not foreground the sort of abstractive procedure presupposed in her approach to a given subject matter. But it is precisely this sort of foregrounding that is required by resort to rational or causal analyses. In a consciously rational culture, the conflict of the logical and the aesthetic is unlikely to be overcome" (1987, 118). An aesthetically oriented culture, by contrast, is capable of incorporating not only its own aesthetic insights but also the rational insights of other cultures in such a way that does not necessarily foreground its own assumptions (137). Thus, they seem to suggest, cross-cultural appreciation—precisely the goal of comparative philosophy—is likely, if not possible, only in the context of a philosophy informed by first problematic thinking.

The presence of this third level in Hall and Ames' work is by no means an open and shut case. They make far more numerous and clear references to their interest in extending and enriching the Western (and Chinese) philosophic traditions than they do to their interest in fostering a radical repositioning of Western philosophy.[23] Indeed, the fact that there are only oblique references to the latter intent may make it appear to the uncritical reader that there is no such normative concern in their project whatsoever. However, one need only look to their strong reaction against traditional Western philosophy (e.g., 1987, 333–36)—its admitted goods notwithstanding (31)—to see that their ultimate interest is nearly as much about supplementing as it is about radically revisioning the very bases of the Western philosophic enterprise (see, e.g., 331). Furthermore, and most important, one finds in their work the persistent suggestion that, while contemporary Western philosophers are only recently learning to engage the plurality of possible views that characterizes the contemporary Western cultural milieu, the most promising basis for a philosophic vision most adequately reflective of such a milieu is to be found principally in the classical Chinese tradition (336).

Before concluding the third level, a word should be said about the character of the "normative" aims attributed to Hall and Ames in this chapter. The only normativity that could be ascribed to their work is a normativity vis-à-vis the present cultural milieu. That is, they *do* make claims pertaining to what is the best or most appropriate philosophic orientation for the current Western cultural context (hence, its milieu-specific normativity); however, they never make the claim—and vehemently guard against the insinuation of doing so—that the philosophic orientation they prescribe is the best or most appropriate for any cultural milieu. They write, "Our project is not at all to *tell it like it is*; we merely wish to present a narrative which is interesting enough and plausible enough to engage those inclined to join the conversation" (1995, xx, italics original; see also Hall 1982b, xv–xvi). In other words, their narrative will entail its own specific claims, but these will only be as normative as the narrative is compelling.

While their rhetoric would seem to suggest that there is no milieu in which second problematic thinking could prove itself a superior alternative to first problematic thinking, strict logical adherence (. . .) to their claims proscribes any such absolute normative conclusion. Indeed, their approach entails an implicit affirmation of the normativity of any narrative to the extent that it proves to be a compelling one. Thus, while Hall and Ames can be understood to make normative claims, these claims must be understood as only the most contingent and fleeting of claims (even if they are vociferously defended by their authors).

In summary, the third level of this approach identifies a problem with Western culture itself and seeks to resolve this problem by drawing attention to traditions (in this case, the classical Chinese tradition) that roughly correlate with alternative traditions in early Greek thought (namely, the *physiologoi* and—especially—the Sophistic traditions). According to Hall and Ames, what both of these broad traditions have in common—their first problematic thinking—is precisely what the contemporary Western tradition is in need of for its own reorientation, revitalization, and revisioning. Stated simply, the West has something to learn from the East, but not simply the standard fare of cross-cultural appreciation; the West must look to the East to reorient itself away from itself and toward a radically different way of thinking. Although this receives neither the sustained attention of their translational concerns nor the careful defense of their methodological concerns, this third level arguably constitutes the normative force driving their collaborative project. At the end of the day, Hall and Ames are not merely interested in providing better translations nor even of providing a more accurate understanding of Chinese culture; rather, they are ultimately interested in giving voice to the important insights they see within the Chinese tradition and trying to demonstrate their crucial relevance to the development of Western thought.

ANALYSIS AND APPRAISAL

That Hall and Ames have made a significant contribution to the comparative study of philosophy is beyond question; equally clear, however, is that their contributions have been consistently met with controversy within the academy. Such, perhaps, is the cost of making genuinely novel contributions to the field. As one might expect, then, the novel features that constitute the strength of their method are also closely associated with its weakness. To reflect this connection—which is especially strong in Hall and Ames' work—these strengths and weaknesses will be discussed in tandem according to its most distinctive features (as was done in the previous chapter). Four such features will be examined: its cross-cultural dimensions, its employment of "bridge traditions," its use of typological contrasts, and its emphasis on responsibility over and against truth.

The Cross-Disciplinary Dimensions of Comparative Research

The first and most readily apparent characteristic of Hall and Ames' comparative method is its careful integration of philological and philosophical perspectives. As noted above, their argument is that one cannot adequately understand the thought of another culture without taking into account both of these perspectives. This argument carries with it the strength of more than a century of hermeneutical investigation, by which contemporary philosophers have become aware of the dependence of thinking itself on the terms and concepts made available through language. Given this close relationship between language and thought, Hall and Ames' attempts to integrate philological and philosophical analysis have undoubtedly allowed for a more critically informed study of comparative philosophy. Indeed, the integration of these two fields has become a hallmark of their work, where seldom a chapter goes by without a subtle and detailed consideration of Chinese terms and concepts.

This contribution, however, has not been without its challenges. Their strong argument for the mutual relevance of these traditionally disparate fields notwithstanding, Hall and Ames are well aware that they face a formidable practical challenge in actually bringing these two fields together. In an anticipatory *apologia* to their first collaborative work (1987), they anticipate two critiques that will plague their project moving forward. On the one hand, professional sinologists "will be exercised by the apparent importation into the text of concepts and categories which, they believe, can only determine in advance (and therefore distort) the meanings of terms" (1987, 2). Hall and Ames have responded consistently with the claim that such concepts and categories will be imported in any instance of translation and that the most responsible reaction is to choose them deliberately and carefully from the broader milieu of the culture in question. Professional philosophers, in turn, "might . . . become impatient with certain of the etymological discussions. They want to 'get on with it,' believing after all . . . that since hermeneutical principles determine philological interpretations (so they would think), the philological work is superfluous at best and, at worst, represents a semantic smoke screen meant to dazzle the naive philosopher into believing that the meanings have in fact leapt full blown from the text itself" (3). Hall and Ames have responded to this critique by arguing that, while meanings cannot "leap from the text itself," they are nonetheless rooted in the words of the texts themselves. It is, after all, the words that make the text what it is rather than something else, so any careful consideration of the meaning of a text must begin with a careful consideration of its terms. As noted earlier, Hall and Ames argue that, in the translation of philosophical texts, philosophy and philology must develop by means of a hermeneutical circle: each must inform the other from the very outset and continue to inform the other even as it is informed in turn by the other. Thus, while there is no clear starting point, there is clearly development in both fields as each informs the other.

This argument is not entirely new; it is grounded in the last hundred years of hermeneutical research. Yet despite this, and despite having anticipated and responded to potential critiques from philologists and philosophers from the very outset of their work, it is these critiques that have nonetheless chilled the reception of their work. Sinologists have often questioned the philological integrity of their translations, while philosophers derided their work as question-begging smuggled within excessive concern with philological details. In short, the response to their work has been much like they anticipated, their anticipatory *apologia* having done little to quell that response.

This is a curious but not entirely surprising result. Disciplinary boundaries are what they are because they allow for a common focus and basis for evaluation within the discipline. From this perspective, bringing philological criteria to bear on philosophical investigations only blurs the focus of study and confuses the basis for evaluation. Thus, when Hall and Ames provide philologically informed resolution to longstanding interpretive problems in philosophy, they seem not only to skirt the philosophical issues altogether but also to isolate themselves from the critique of anyone without the combined philosophical and philological expertise that they muster collaboratively.

At the same time, however, scholars in both disciplines are becoming increasingly aware of the conventional and contingent nature of disciplinary divides, as well as the potential validity and productivity of transgressing these divides to take advantage of the insights of other disciplines. Hall and Ames bring the data from these two disciplines together because they maintain that a strong case can be made for their mutual relevance. From this perspective, it is entirely appropriate to press philosophers with philological data (or vice versa), so long as the case for relevance can be made. In fact, although they obviously respect the comparative work of dedicated sinologists and philosophers, Hall and Ames suggest again and again that comparative judgments are ultimately best left to those who—either individually or collaboratively—have expertise in both disciplines.[24]

Taken together, these two perspectives mark an academy in transition: one that recognizes and appreciates the distinctions among disciplines but that is also coming to realize that these distinctions are only as important as they are useful. Hall and Ames' work exemplifies the progressive arm of this shift, while their critics' response exemplifies the conservative response. There are few who would still argue that language and philosophy are not mutually relevant, especially when considered in a cross-cultural context; however, there are many whose understanding and appreciation for each of those fields has been shaped by traditional disciplinary boundaries and for whom the blurring of disciplinary boundaries obscures the means for evaluation of work relating to their respective fields.

Hall and Ames have noted that the challenge of their comparative work will be not only to satisfy philosophers and philologists individually but also to make what is important to one group intelligible to the other

(1987, 2–3). This is surely a Herculean task given the still-early development of cross-disciplinary comparative work, and thus it is not entirely surprising that their *apologia* failed to achieve its desired effect (i.e., to stem criticism from each discipline individually). There are simply too many scholars in each discipline whose perspectives have been too much shaped by traditional disciplinary divisions to expect a wide and ready acceptance of their cross-disciplinary initiatives. Stated simply, it laid the groundwork for a cross-disciplinary study of comparative philosophy but fell short of developing it sufficiently for those whose perspectives have been too much shaped by traditional disciplinary divisions to critically engage their work.

These challenges notwithstanding, however, Hall and Ames have made significant strides in laying the groundwork for cross-disciplinary study of cross-cultural comparison. Drawing on their respective areas of specialization, they have been able to fuse philosophical and philological insights with a subtlety and sophistication that is beyond most comparativists and thus pushes comparative philosophy to a level hitherto unachieved by their predecessors. Moreover, they have done so in a methodologically self-conscious way, which allows others not only to appreciate the insights undergirding their cross-disciplinary work but also to potentially employ these insights in new and additionally fruitful ways. While the fact that they have encountered a stifling resistance among more traditionally discipline-conscious scholars may be seen as a minor weakness in their approach, it is unquestionably overshadowed by the novel cross-disciplinary initiatives they have introduced in their work. Their insightful, challenging, and even controversial integration of these two disciplines stands as one of the notable strengths of their comparative method.

Moving forward, the hope for their approach—and for all who adopt it moving forward—is that it will continue to provide insights garnered from cross-disciplinary data but that it will also continue to provide critical and self-conscious defenses for the relevance of this data in order to persuade other comparativists of the validity and fruitfulness of cross-disciplinary research. If this proves to be the case, then Hall and Ames' work not only will represent an important cross-disciplinary subset within the study of comparative philosophy, but it can also lead the field as a whole to take advantages of the cross-disciplinary insights made available through their work.[25]

It should be noted in closing that, although they focus on the two disciplines of philosophy and philology in particular, there is nothing about their approach that necessarily limits cross-disciplinary comparative work to these two disciplines. A strong argument can be made that philosophy and philology are the disciplines most directly relevant to the sort of comparative work that Hall and Ames employ, but there is no reason to believe that they would not welcome the insights of other disciplines if a strong case could be made for their relevance. It is this pragmatist openness to all potentially relevant data that drives their cross-disciplinary initiatives: they want to provide a narrative that is "interesting and plausible" (1995, xx) but by no means claim that their narrative is exhaustive or complete. There is always more for the comparativist to learn, and, while Hall and Ames are exemplary for having integrated such a broad spectrum of relevant data, they would be the first to admit that it is but a subset of the potentially relevant data.

The "Bridge Tradition" in Cross-Cultural Comparison

Another of the distinctive features of Hall and Ames' method is their use of lesser-known alternative Western traditions to enable Western scholars to better understand Chinese philosophy. Cross-cultural understanding, they maintain, will always begin from the context of one's own cultural self-understanding, and although the goal of comparative philosophy is to enable one's understanding to become genuinely cross-cultural, an element of one's own cultural context will always inform that understanding. In the context of their own work, this means that any understanding of Chinese philosophy among Western scholars will be—at least initially, if not persistently—a Western understanding of Chinese philosophy.

This being the case, they maintain, the important question is not *whether* the Western tradition will inform that understanding, but rather *which aspects* of it should be employed to enable as authentically Chinese an understanding of Chinese philosophy as possible. Their selection of a particular set of alternative traditions in the West to serve as "bridge traditions" for comparative philosophy is thus predicated on the argument that these traditions have the most in common with the Chinese tradition and are therefore best suited to guide Western scholars in their pursuit of an authentically Chinese understanding of Chinese philosophy.

The strength of this move lies in the seriousness with which Hall and Ames take the hermeneutical problem of engaging other cultures. They are surely right with respect to the pervasive influence of one's own cultural tradition on one's interpretation of other cultures and are right to seek to stem its undue influence, even if that is by allowing alternative Western traditions to stand in their place. In fact, this is precisely the strength of their use of alternative traditions: it puts a check on the most pervasive of Western assumptions (insofar as these should critically inform one's understanding of another culture), while simultaneously allowing other less familiar Western perspectives to guide one's understanding (insofar as one must still broach the cultural divide on initially familiar grounds). In this way, their work walks the line between the familiar and unfamiliar, which is arguably where the best comparative work can take place.

Not all comparativists have been so critical with respect to their interpretive lenses. For example, G. W. F. Hegel, whose work might be considered one of the first sustained modern Western attempts at comparative philosophy, sought to incorporate data from all available religions into a broader conceptual scheme. While his intention to accurately interpret the full range of available data is clear—adjusting his interpretation as additional information was made available[26]—it is also clear that the interpretive lens he employed was reflective of only a very limited subset of the data (namely, that of nineteenth-century German idealism).[27]

A somewhat more sophisticated approach can be found at the turn of the twentieth century in the work of the leading figures of the Kyoto school—Nishida Kitarō, Tanabe Hajime, and Nishitani Keiji—each of whom sought to find ways of synthesizing the insights of the Eastern and Western traditions. These scholars clearly work with a broader array of comparative data than did Hegel and are more careful to prevent their understanding of one tradition from unduly coloring their interpretation of other traditions. Yet, while their comparative work clearly brought about creative developments in constructive philosophy, their interpretations of each tradition have nonetheless incited controversy for being too influenced one by the other.[28]

More recently, Cheng Chung-ying—a colleague of Ames' at the University of Hawaii—has also sought to interpret Eastern and Western philosophical traditions in light of one another, although he does so with the increased hermeneutical awareness that characterizes much of twentieth-century Western philosophy. His primary interest has been to bring the resources of the Chinese tradition to bear on contemporary philosophical concerns, which are taken currently to be dominated by Western philosophical conceptions; accordingly, his explication of the Chinese tradition takes place in terms very familiar to contemporary Western philosophers (see, e.g., Cheng, 1991). Although Cheng has made great strides in demonstrating the relevance of Chinese philosophy to contemporary philosophic concerns, there remains a lingering anxiety among some comparativists that Chinese philosophy may not be best understood in terms of contemporary and predominantly Western philosophic concerns.[29]

A number of other examples could be cited, but suffice it to say that there has been a growing appreciation throughout the development of comparative philosophy of the need for serious critical reflection about the hermeneutical challenges in interpreting traditions across cultures. This need would be felt with particular urgency if comparative philosophy were understood not as the attempt to find a creative ground among the various traditions for a constructive philosophical project (as do Hegel, the Kyoto school, and Cheng), but rather as the attempt to find a means for producing a more accurate description of each tradition as it stands. As exemplifications of the latter understanding, Hall and Ames take on the hermeneutical challenge with renewed vigor, plumbing the depths of each tradition to find the most effective "bridge" for understanding the other tradition. Their familiarity with the alternative traditions within the broader Western philosophical tradition enables them to provide descriptions of other traditions across cultures in terms that are more inherently consistent with the aims and concerns of those other traditions. Within the context of such a longstanding hermeneutical challenge in comparative philosophy, their initiative allows for greater subtlety and sophistication in the interpretation of other traditions; it is thus both a welcome development and a clear strength of their method.

The laudability of this strength notwithstanding, it is nonetheless important to ask from a methodological perspective whether this use of alternative "bridging" traditions does not obscure important facets of the tradition interpreted even as it reveals other facets. For instance, what interpretations of the classical Chinese tradition are precluded by the analogy with the first problematic thinking of the early Greek *physiologoi* and Sophists that would nonetheless be valid interpretations in their own right? The alternative, of course, is to attempt to approach the classical Chinese tradition on its own terms, altering one's interpretations as they prove consistent or inconsistent with the data available for that tradition. This is, as the reader will recall, the approach that Hocking employed, and while he did not have the full interpretive sophistication of later comparativists, he nonetheless demonstrated a remarkable understanding of the Chinese tradition for his time.

Yet understanding Chinese culture on its own terms is precisely what Hall and Ames are trying to do by finding bridging traditions between East and West. As noted above, they maintain that one's own tradition will inevitably inform one's interpretation of other traditions and that the challenge is to identify the features of one's tradition that will allow for the most accurate understanding of another tradition. That is, human beings learn in large part by analogies, and because analogies are inevitable, care should be taken to ensure that only the most revealing analogies are employed, and employed with the full realization that they are, in the end, only analogies. Thus, Hall and Ames write that "we cannot support any final dependence upon the specific content of ideas and doctrines developing from first problematic thinking in the West. Rather we shall argue that comparativists must, insofar as is possible, attempt to understand Chinese culture on its own terms. This means that we must take our cues from the manner in which the intellectual activity in classical Chinese *most analogous to* our first problematic has been articulated" (1995, xix). Their use of analogies is thus merely a starting point in their interpretive work, with every analogy employed only to the extent that it reveals more than it obscures about the tradition in question. By crafting these analogies for their audience, Hall and Ames enable an understanding of the classical Chinese tradition that is consistent with their own expertise, thus saving modern-day readers from having to reinvent the wheel and develop an understanding of the tradition from scratch.

Given that analogies are not only an inevitable feature of comparative understanding but also a variably beneficial one, a second question that must be raised about their work pertains to their particular choice of analogies. Does their use of first problematic thinking in the early Greek tradition as a bridge tradition reflect more about the classical Chinese tradition or about Hall and Ames' own philosophical commitments? As noted earlier, Hall and Ames demonstrate a clear preference for first problematic thinking over second problematic thinking—at the very least as a basis for comparative philosophy, although their arguments suggest a broader affinity—and it is at least possible that this preference unduly colors their interpretation of first problematic thinking in the early Greek tradition and/or the classical Chinese tradition.[30]

Obviously, it would be impossible to definitively identify the driving force in their interpretation; however, some insights can nonetheless be gained from certain features of their approach. One way of addressing the question is to look to the history of their interest in the analogy. Hall's initial interest was in the first problematic thinking of the early Greeks and its potential as a basis for a new philosophical program, although he quickly realized that this tradition seemed to bear significant similarities with certain facets of the Chinese tradition; from this perspective, it is possible that his reading of the Chinese tradition was unduly influenced by his constructive reading of the early Greeks. Ames' initial interest, by contrast, was in accurately interpreting the classical Chinese tradition, and he also saw significant affinities between Hall's account of the early Greeks and the classical Chinese tradition; it is possible that his reading of the early Greeks was unduly influenced by his reading of the classical Chinese tradition. Taken together, however, it is difficult to see how misreadings of one or the other tradition could have borne themselves out for very long in their close collaborative work, and thus there is good reason to believe that the analogy between the two is reasonably well founded.

Moreover, as consummate pragmatists, Hall and Ames have been generally willing to allow their analogies to be subject to correction. Although their main thesis has not substantively changed in the nearly two decades since *Thinking through Confucius*, if one looks to the details of their work one finds a number of ways in which they have allowed the available data not only to inform but also to temper and correct their conclusions. The most notable example of this is their acknowledgment that their analogy to first problematic thinking applies primarily to the classical Chinese tradition (and to Confucius in particular) and not necessarily to the Chinese tradition more broadly. They note that, beginning to some extent with Xunzi and increasing throughout the Han dynasty, there is a noticeable rise of second problematic thinking that ultimately becomes incorporated in much of subsequent Chinese thought (1995, 202–11, 239) All of this serves as further evidence that Hall and Ames are interested not primarily in the defense of their own philosophical commitments but rather in the most accurate possible rendering of the classical Chinese tradition.

In conclusion, Hall and Ames have used analogies to provide an account of the classical Chinese tradition not unlike what one would do were one to try to engage the that tradition on one's own from scratch. Methodologically, the process is identical: analogies are proposed (based on one's best understanding of the tradition), tested out with respect to relevant data (in Hall and Ames' case, the philosophical and philological data), and revised in light of their ability to account adequately for the data.[31] The obvious difference is that Hall and Ames are able to bring to their account all of the expertise they have in the relevant traditions. While it remains possible that their readings of these traditions are misleading because of the analogies employed, this would be an incidental rather than a methodological failure: even a mistaken analogy reveals something of its subject and only awaits further correction and revision from the broader community of scholars. Because Hall and Ames remain open to such correction as a basic feature of their method, there is nothing to their use of analogies that need necessarily limit their comparative project. To the contrary, given their expertise in the relevant traditions, there is every reason to look to their choices of analogies as at least guiding lights in the interpretation of classical Chinese culture.

The Typological Contrast as Organizing Principle for Comparison

Another distinctive feature of Hall and Ames' method is their use of typological contrasts to elucidate the differences between cultural traditions. This method is particularly amenable to their work since their comparisons pertain almost exclusively to two broad traditions, the classical Chinese and the contemporary Anglo-European. Responding in large part to the tendency to assume that cultures are interpreting the world in largely the same ways, Hall and Ames identify defining differences among these two traditions and use them to help their readers better understand the distinctive character of each tradition (or, more commonly, of the other tradition in contrast to their own). It is perhaps in this respect above all other that Hall and Ames—recalling their Deweyan metaphor—are most proactive in "clear[ing] away the useless lumber blocking the path to China" (1995, xx).

The most prominent contrast employed in their work is the one drawn between first and second problematic thinking (as detailed above), but this contrast is further specified in terms of the aesthetic and the rational, the correlative and the causal, the analogical and the logical, and immanence and transcendence. In each case, however, the same typological device is employed: each tradition is associated with one or the other side of the contrast, and the defining features of each tradition are thus seen in opposition to one another. This notion of "opposition" should not be overplayed.[32] Hall and Ames do not maintain that, whatever one tradition is, the other must not be (e.g., that if one tradition is "logical," the other must be "illogical"), nor do they maintain that traditions are so far removed from one another that they do not also share important commonalities. They have done too much painstaking work in linguistic translation to accommodate any such oversimplifications. Rather, in drawing these distinctions, they simply mean to give priority—albeit a strong priority—to the distinctiveness of the traditions they compare.[33] The point at issue here is the overall effect that such prioritizing has on the process of comparison.

The use of typologies to elucidate cultural and traditional contrasts has an established history in comparative philosophy, and Hall and Ames are not only conscious of this history but also appreciatively critical of that history in the development of their own method. This being the case, it is worth examining their treatment of this history in some detail as a means for understanding their own use of typologies.

As early as his first published text, Hall acknowledged the significance of Pepper, McKeon, and Brumbaugh for recognizing the sea change taking place in the understanding of the relationship among philosophical traditions (1973, 24, 55–56n. 1). According to Hall, the comparative work of these three marks "the progressive realization of the existence of competing philosophic systems as irreducible schemas of interpretation that apparently will not yield to refutation, reduction, or assimilation by alternate philosophic schemas." Their response to this realization, as seen earlier, was to seek to develop a "metaphilosophic" vision, one that allows diverse philosophic visions to be understood in contrast to one another in terms that do not privilege one tradition over the others. "This trend amounts to a progressive development in philosophy," he argues, "insofar as it does not repeat the same futile juggling of alternatives, the familiar substitution of the philosophy of Tweedledum for that of Tweedledee" (1982b, 17).

At the same time, however, he notes, this attempt to rise above particular philosophic traditions poses a certain problem. All three of these incorporate readily identifiable ideological commitments into their respective metaphilosophic frameworks: McKeon's system is grounded in the Aristotelian distinction between the four causes, Brumbaugh's is based on Plato's analogy of the divided line, and Pepper's is developed out of a Sophistic delineation of "root metaphors" (1982b, 17). Any such commitments are, from a metaphilosophic perspective, not only unwarranted but also entirely arbitrary; moreover, they inevitably skew the accounts of other traditions in favor of the tradition underlying the metaphilosophical schema. At the same time, however, he acknowledges that it is unclear whether there are any viable alternatives: a metaphilosophic framework by its very nature nullifies any possible criteria for characterizing philosophic systems (let alone choosing them). "Meta-mentality invites a kind of intellectual fascism which elicits commitment to values and ideals, not because they are true, but for the sake of law and order, the harmony of society, or 'the destiny of a people' " (18). From his preliminary reading of the metaphilosophers, then, it would seem that metaphilosophy constitutes an important step forward but one that is itself fatally flawed.[34]

This interest in the metaphilosophical approach persists in the collaborative work of Hall and Ames; however, because they now present their own comparative method, the character and focus of their interest shifts noticeably. Perhaps the most noticeable of these shifts is that of terminology: they speak less of "metaphilosophy" and more of "transculturalism." The latter term denotes an approach that seeks to look beyond the purview of any particular cultural tradition and thus cultivate a "single hermeneutical community which putatively includes every thinker of importance" (1987, 4). In general, Hall and Ames are sympathetic to the transculturalist goal of creating a single hermeneutical community for philosophic dialogue. Indeed, such a goal must at least be the long-term ambition of any comparative project. They are particularly appreciative of the fact that entrance into this community is not dependent on assent to any particular philosophic position. In short, they affirm the favorable reception of pluralism in the transcultrualist approach to comparison.

At the same time, however, they maintain that there is far more cross-cultural groundwork that must be done before any such transcultural framework can be employed without oversimplifying and distorting the traditions compared. They explain:

> We differ only in the sense that we are less sanguine than are these transculturalists as to the possibility of constituting such a community without considerably more work being done. That is, until we are capable of detailing certain fundamental presuppositions relevant to the understanding of alternative cultural contexts, this pursuit of a hermeneutical community will lead us inadvertently to foist upon an alternative culture a set of criteria drawn from our own tradition which are then chauvinistically presumed to characterize the determinants of philosophical thinking per se. (1987, 5)

As in Hall's previous work, they draw attention to the parochial commitments that inform the intertheoretical frameworks of Pepper, McKeon, and Brumbaugh—Sophism, Aristotelian, and Platonism, respectively. These commitments inevitably inform one's understanding of the traditions considered and thus obscure important differences in and among those traditions. This is not to say that typologies are inherently flawed and unhelpful, but rather that they can be dangerously misleading if sufficient attention is not paid to identifying and minimizing their biases.

A second but related shift in their collaborative reading of the transculturalists is their decreased attention to the work of Pepper, McKeon, and

Brumbaugh and their increased attention to that of Walter Watson (1985) and—most especially—David Dilworth (1989). Immediately following the work of the early transculturalists, a debate ensued among their followers over the proper role of typology in the consideration of divergent traditions: should it attempt to provide an exhaustive system of all possible ways of thinking, or should it merely attempt to organize some ways of thinking for the purposes of facilitating intertheoretic conversations? Watson and Dilworth are taken as exemplifications of the former position: although they maintain the early transculturalists' commitment to pluralism, they apply an arguably provisional taxonomic framework to diverse philosophical traditions as if it has a unique transcendental status. Accordingly, Hall and Ames term this reading of taxonomies "transcendental pluralism."

As with the earlier transculturalists, Hall and Ames laud the methodological commitment to pluralism inherent in Watson and Dilworth's work. Yet they maintain that this commitment is ultimately compromised by their attempt to delineate that pluralism within the context of a transcendental framework. That this framework is not transcendental, they maintain, can be seen in the inadequate and misleading readings of non-Western cultures that result from the application of this patently Western framework.[35] Indeed, whereas parochial influences were only noticeably present in the work of the earlier transculturalists, they are dangerously present in the transcendental pluralists precisely because they present methodologically limited and biased readings of other traditions as if they were at least fundamentally sound.[36]

It is in their response to the transcendental pluralists, however, that Hall and Ames give their clearest account of their use of typologies. In contrast to the transcendental pluralists, "interpretive pluralists"—the other side of the debate about transculturalism, with which they identify themselves—"promote open-ended typologies and celebrate the plurality of interpretive perspectives to which philosophic thinking has given rise as pragmatically useful devices for handling intertheoretical and intercultural conversations" (1995, 160). That is, they do not object to the use of typologies per se, but rather to the restrictive use of typologies to account for every philosophically important feature of any philosophic tradition.[37] "Obviously," they write, "we ourselves have taken taxonomic pluralism with some seriousness since . . . we went to some effort to demonstrate the manner in which the Platonic and Aristotelian fourfolds . . . have dominated the theoretical and practical activities of our cultural tradition almost from its beginnings" (162). Where they differ is in the adequacy of such a culturally conditioned taxonomy to adequately account for philosophic traditions outside of that cultural context.[38]

With the transculturalists, then, Hall and Ames acknowledge the value of taxonomies in delineating important points of contrast among diverse philosophic traditions, and they affirm the pluralism that these taxonomies allow. This is true even when—or rather, precisely when—those taxonomies derive from one's own cultural context. They admit that "[t]here is a certain pragmatic value to be realized in translating ideas from an exoteric culture into the standard idioms of one's own culture." After all, comparative study always begins from one's own cultural context. At the same time, however, they reject the transcendental pretense of the transcendental pluralists, arguing that this pretense feigns a necessary transcultural applicability that is ultimately—and dangerously—misleading.[39] Thus, while taxonomies can be helpful interpretive devices, they must not be considered anything more than devices and must be discarded when their interpretations fail to be compelling. In other words, while it is important for one to start compara-tive work from one's own cultural context, "it is equally important that one not accede to ending there" (1995, 164).

For all of their similarities with and appreciation for the transculturalist approach, their own work is actually far more akin to that of F. S. C. Northrop. Hall and Ames readily acknowledge Northrop as one of the founding fathers of comparative philosophy (1982b, 183) and comment constructively more on his method than any other. In contrast to the transculturalists, they characterize Northrop's approach as an "interculturalist" approach, indicat-ing its fundamental presupposition that there are "irrevocable differences" among cultural traditions, along with its understanding of the comparativist as one who "demonstrates what is distinctive about each cultural milieu in the broadest of theoretical strokes" (1987, 4). Following Northrop's lead, Hall and Ames employ typologies solely in the form of polar contrasts between the classical Chinese and Anglo-European traditions (their version of Northrop's "East and West"). Although they are sympathetic to the transculturalist goal of creating a "single hermeneutic community," their primary interests are ultimately more consistent with Northrop's goal of elucidating the important differences among philosophical traditions across cultures.

For example, while the transculturalists are importantly present in Hall's early work, it is Northrop whose method is taken there as the stan-dard for comparative philosophy. Hall demonstrates a broad familiarity with both Northrop's method and the debates surrounding its applicability (see, e.g., 1982a, 191, 1982b, 184–85, 193–95, 289). Moreover, it clearly has a defining influence on his own work, as his contrast between first and second problematic thinking strongly mirrors Northrop's own contrast between East and West. Not only does Hall use similar terms for his contrast (aesthetic and rational, as opposed to Northrop's aesthetic and theoretic), but he also frames the contrast in similar fashion—two ways of thinking, both of which ultimately prove to be relatively adequate ways of interpreting the world (1982a, 236–37).[40]

In his early work, however, Hall's most immediate interest in Northrop's comparative method was for its use as a foil for explicating a comparable method that he believed was implicit in Whitehead's *Science and the Modern World* (1925). Specifically, he argued that, while Whitehead's approach was closely related to Northrop's, it was ultimately a superior approach. Whereas

Northrop sought to identify the differences among the major world traditions and then, on this basis, to propose a means for synthesizing these different perspectives, Whitehead sought to develop a single philosophic vision that integrated the insights of the Western tradition along with novel insights that seek to address its oversights. The result was a vision that—despite Whitehead's relative ignorance of the connection—was surprisingly similar with the dominant features of Eastern thought.[41] Thus, Hall writes: "[I]n embryonic form, Whitehead's philosophic bridge between East and West is one that attempts to relate the particularity of concrete process with the efficacious generalizations of abstract speculation without disdaining either the particular or the universal aspects of experience" (Hall 1982b, 189). This is, he notes, much like what Northrop was trying to accomplish; yet the difference between Whitehead and Northrop in this respect is that, whereas Northrop maintains an almost Kantian distinction between intuition and postulation, Whitehead argues for their continuity.[42] This continuity allows for the presence of either foci (or both) in any cultural context, even if one of them was not adequately developed within that culture.[43]

Ultimately, in his collaborative work with Ames, Hall would leave aside this comparative use of Whitehead, but his interest in Northrop would continue to inform their subsequent work. Hall and Ames, from the very beginning, announce their intention to "remain sensitive to those contrasting cultural emphases that establish real alternative approaches to significant theoretical and practical concerns" (1987, 4–5)—a statement of intention that Northrop could just as well have penned himself. Even their use of typological contrasts resembles Northrop's work more closely than Hall's, as their focus on cross-cultural differences is more consistent with Northrop's comparative work than was Hall's work on philosophical anarchism.

A more substantive similarity is to be found in the precise terms they use to shape their cross-cultural contrasts. Working conjointly, Hall and Ames further specify Hall's earlier contrast between first and second problematic thinking in terms of immanence and transcendence, the aesthetic and the rational, the correlative and the causal, and the analogical and the logical. Northrop framed his contrasts in somewhat different terms, focusing on the distinction between concepts by intuition and concepts by postulation, the aesthetic and the theoretic, and particulars and universals. Yet, despite the differences in actual terms, the broad outlines of a distinction between a more open-ended and aesthetic way of thinking and a more rigidly comprehensive and theoretic way of thinking are evident in both sets of contrasts. Indeed, it is fair to say that in an important sense Hall and Ames give new life to Northrop's approach, developing and refining it in new and interesting ways.

Beyond these broad similarities with Northrop's approach, Hall and Ames also express a number of concerns with their predecessor's work and thus differentiate their approach in crucial and formative respects. The first concern—as anticipated in Hall's earlier work—pertains to the quasi-Kantian way that Northrop derives the terms for his categories. Northrop sought to arrive at a complete list of "possible concepts" by means of transcendental deduction (following Kant) and then to employ these terms to characterize any observed point of contrast among cultural traditions (1995, 118). While Hall and Ames readily acknowledge the power of Kantian deductions and the formative role they have played in the Western tradition, they are highly critical of the defining role it is given in Northrop's work. They maintain that the strength of a set of philosophical commitments within one cultural tradition should not automatically give it priority in cross-cultural comparative work; to the contrary, taking comparative work seriously requires that one question the very foundations of what philosophy is taken to be. That is, "it is illegitimate simply to assume the usefulness of interpretive constructs drawn from our own cultural milieu" (103; see also 212). Ultimately, then, Northrop's Kantian predisposition—especially when integrated uncritically—can only distort one's understanding of other cultures such as to make it look deceptively familiar (212).

Their second concern with Northrop's work pertains to the "heavy-handedness" of his contrasts (1987, 4). Although even a cursory review of his work will reveal that Northrop applied his contrasts with full awareness that the two sides of a contrast are seldom if ever mutually exclusive—see, for example his work on the cultural context of Mexico (1946, 15–65)—his use of Kantian language often suggests that this is not the case.[44] Even the fact that Northrop sought to bring the two sides together through "epistemic correlation" fails to mitigate this perception, since that correlation merely associated rather than synthesized. Indeed, his attempt at correlation only further solidified the quasi-Kantian division between the sides of his contrasts. Thus, however nuanced Northrop may have been (or intended to be) in his own understanding of the relation among the world's philosophic traditions, the net effect of his work—especially among those who employed his contrasts—has been an unduly rigid employment of those contrasts and a consequently facile understanding of that relationship (1987, 4–5).

In contrast to Northrop, Hall and Ames try to found their distinctions on a solely empirical basis, allowing only their understanding of the cultures observed to inform the terms by which they understand and compare them.[45] That is, one should observe one culture and seek to identify its defining characteristics, then observe another culture and do the same, and finally suggest contrasts that identify points on which the two traditions appear to differ. Obviously, there is a hermeneutical problem here, and Hall and Ames are well aware of it: "We cannot understand another culture until we have a language and a schema allowing translation into a cultural idiom appropriate to our understanding, but we cannot develop such a schema in a satisfactory form until we have sufficient understanding of the similarities and differences illustrated by the exoteric culture" (1982b, 182–83). Northrop ran afoul of this very problem, although he was entirely unaware of it: because all of the cultures he examined had already been translated into familiar cultural idioms for him (Northrop was not a cultural linguist), the Western-biased schema that Northrop developed appeared entirely appropriate to the data as it was presented to him. Hall and Ames would agree that Northrop made good use of the materials available to him; however, they would also maintain that his work is nonetheless compromised by the quality of his materials. To avoid his mistake, they make careful translation of the content of other cultures a central part of their own comparative method (as noted above).

Yet even this does not wholly resolve the hermeneutical problem described above, since one can only translate the content of other cultures within the framework of some particular schema. To address this double-bind, Hall and Ames again draw on the resources of the pragmatist tradition: "The only reasonable response to the difficulties that intercultural translations represent is to recognize that the development of a comparative methodology is an extended process of tentative pragmatic endeavors which only gradually may approach philosophic adequacy" (1982b, 183).[46] That is, they allow their translations of a culture to inform their understanding of that culture and its relation to other cultures and then use that understanding to allow for more cogent and informative translations, which then further inform their comparative framework, and so on. In short, translation and comparative understanding are brought together within the context of a hermeneutical circle, allowing each to inform and build on the other in ever-increasing adequacy of understanding.

What Hall and Ames have learned from their predecessors about the use of typological contrasts, then, is that they can be very helpful tools for cultivating an understanding of cultural differences, but one must remember that they are only tools—and imperfect tools at that. In their own employment of such contrasts, then, one must remember that, while they will strive ardently to eliminate any undue cultural biases or premature assumptions of cross-cultural similarity, they have no illusions about the complete adequacy of their contrasts. Their primary concern in the use of contrasts is with whether the contrasts enable a clearer and more accurate understanding of cultural traditions.

The primary evaluative question for Hall and Ames' use of typologies, therefore, must be whether their contrasts help or hinder the cultivation of cross-cultural understanding, or, rather, to identify the respects in which they help and those in which they hinder, since they have likely done both to some degree. Hall and Ames have already made their own case—and a strong case at that—for the ways that their contrasts facilitate such understanding; it remains to consider possible drawbacks and dangers to the use of comparative contrasts. There appear to be two primary drawbacks: the privileging of differences over similarities and/or incongruities and privileging features consistent with the contrast over its exceptions. There may be other relevant concerns to the use of contrasts, and this short list does not feign to be comprehensive; the two points examined here merely seek to identify and examine the most relevant and pressing concerns within the particular context of Hall and Ames' comparative work.

The first danger pertains broadly to the use of contrasts as a controlling lens for comparative studies. Comparative contrasts focus specifically on the differences among traditions and do not typically address instances of similarity or incongruity.[47] If differences are the only important feature of the comparative relation between two (or more) traditions, then this focus would be entirely adequate; however, to the extent that similarities and incongruities are also relevant and important to that relation, then a focus on differences alone can ultimately only provide a skewed perspective on their comparative relation.

For their part, it is clear that Hall and Ames have focused almost exclusively on the differences between traditions (in particular, the differences between the Anglo-European and classical Chinese traditions).[48] They have done so quite consciously, and for explicitly stated and defended reasons. They maintain that comparativists have historically been too eager to identify points of similarity among divergent traditions, thus skewing the general understanding of the relation between these traditions; indeed, these assertions have often been overzealous, misinformed, and even naïve, with the result that comparative understanding is not only unbalanced but also at least partially inaccurate. The task of contemporary comparativists, they argue, must therefore be to counter this trend both by identifying important points of difference among traditions and by being more critical with respect to any proposed points of similarity. Their use of contrasts as a central feature of their comparative method is thus one tool—perhaps the most prominent tool—that they employ to bring about this much-needed corrective.

Their use of this tool is not without merit: many of the assertions of early comparativists were, in fact, naïve and misplaced, and a correction in such cases—both to these figures, and to the comparative (mis)understandings that resulted—is clearly warranted. Methodologically, however, this positive use of comparative contrasts must be weighed over and against the ways that it obstructs or obfuscates comparative work. Insofar as they have very little to say about similarities and incongruities, their comparative appraisal of traditions—however good it is with respect to their differences—can only remain incomplete. It may be true that, "in the enterprise of comparative philosophy, difference is more interesting than similarity" (1987, 5), but difference is by no means the only relevant concern in comparative philosophy.

To those familiar with Hall and Ames' broader corpus, however, the use of "interesting" in the previous sentence reveals that they are not just focusing on difference for sake of their own amusement. Rather, they use the term in a manner similar to Whitehead, for whom—as the reader will recall—"it is more important that a proposition be interesting than that it be true. The importance of truth is that it adds to interest" (1929, 259). Following their reading of Whitehead, Hall and Ames maintain that the interest an idea generates is both formative for and reflective of the current cultural milieu. The fact that differences are the most "interesting" for them, then, has everything to do with the present context: namely, that differences among traditions have been insufficiently heeded by comparativists, and that what comparative philosophy is most in need of is not further speculation on similarities but rather increased criticism of proposed similarities and further consideration of important differences.

What is of utmost importance here is that there is nothing inherent in Hall and Ames' approach that specifically precludes consideration of similarities and incongruities. In a different cultural milieu, the prevailing interests might be quite different, and the application of the method would have to adapt accordingly. What remains constant in their method is not the particular focus of any particular milieu but rather the focus in each milieu on its particular comparative needs (i.e., interests). Indeed, the only limiting factor for consideration of differences, similarities, and incongruities is the amount of interest for these within a given cultural milieu.

Thus, an appraisal of Hall and Ames' method that focuses solely on the particular focus of their contrasts will miss out on the broader context of what they are trying to accomplish. They are not trying to produce an account of comparative relations that is objectively accurate and complete but are rather trying to cultivate a better understanding of those relations. Accordingly, they take into account not only the information pertaining to those relations but also the historical context of that information within comparative philosophy, making their distinctive contribution by providing a much-needed corrective, even if such a corrective does not, in itself, say everything there is to be said about comparative philosophy. Hall and Ames are surely aware that similarities and incongruities are an important part of the comparative relation among cultural traditions; they have simply determined that what is of utmost important for their cultural milieu is a clearer and more critical appreciation for the differences among cultural traditions.

Returning to the original question, then, do Hall and Ames fall victim to the danger of privileging the differences among traditions over the similarities and incongruities to such an extent that it skews their perspective on the comparative relations among cultural traditions? Supporters of and detractors from their approach would probably both agree that Hall and Ames had given the differences among traditions attention that is disproportionate to the ratio of similarities and differences actually present among traditions; they would disagree, however, on whether or not this lack of proportionality is merited by the cultural milieu. The interest of this study, however, is neither to give an account of the cultural milieu nor to suggest which responses to a given account of that milieu are warranted;

the interest here is solely methodological, and from that perspective there does not appear to be any inherent danger in focusing on the differences among traditions, even at the cost of ignoring potentially significant similarities and incongruities. Hall and Ames' method is based on a philosophy of culture, and by their reading of the current cultural milieu it is far more interesting and important to consider the differences among traditions; if the cultural milieu changed such that insufficient attention was being paid to the similarities and incongruities among cultures, their "interest"—and, consequently, attention—would change accordingly.

In conclusion, Hall and Ames' methodological use of comparative contrasts should not be read or evaluated on a first-order basis, to the effect that comparative philosophy—properly conceived—consists in the use of typological contrasts to highlight the important differences among cultural traditions. This *is* what Hall and Ames do, but their primary method is not to be found at this level. Rather, their method must be read on a second-order basis, whereby the primary concern is in addressing the needs—or, rather, interests—of the current cultural milieu; upon this reading, their use of contrasts is the result of their reading of this particular milieu, and it is effective only to the extent that it addresses the needs of this milieu effectively.[49]

A second danger in employing typological contrasts is that, because contrasts are used as defining features of the differences between two traditions, exceptions to those contrasts will be discounted or even ignored for the purposes of identifying, clarifying, and defending the contrasts. Traditions are broad, diverse entities, and while it can be helpful to locate traditions within the context of narrowly defined contrasts, one must also realize that it is unlikely that the entirety of a tradition will conform to one side of a contrast without exception. Contrasts are, after all, only generalizations, and every generalization has its exceptions. The usefulness of a contrast—like that of any generalization—is therefore dependent on the number of exceptions it allows and the relative significance of those exceptions. Thus, a contrast can only hold a definitive role in one's comparative work to the extent that its exceptions (i.e., those aspects of the traditions compared that do not conform to its assigned place in the contrast) can be shown to be relatively minor "aberrations"—that is, nonessential features for understanding the character of a tradition or its relation to other traditions.

An important question to ask of any employment of contrasts, then, is whether the contrast has fairly and accurately represented each of its traditions, that is, without overemphasizing their differences and/or underemphasizing important exceptions. This is a point that Neville raised about the use of contrasts in his foreword to first collaborative work: "[T]he controversial question" he writes, "will be whether the contrast does indeed catch the main drift of the cultural differences (1987, xii–xiv). A contrast will not "catch the main drift" if it avoids, obfuscates, or explains away its exceptions. Such a contrast only catches the select currents the author(s) would have readers believe are the relevant cultural differences; it does not account—or even try to account—for the whole picture. A fair and accurate representation of cultural differences would make use of a contrast to highlight important differences but will not overlook examples that do not conform or even run counter to the proposed contrast.[50] Although he did not state so directly in that context, Neville implied that some of their contrasts may be misplaced or overstated; that is, they may not have "caught the main drift" of the cultural differences between the classical Chinese and Anglo-European traditions.[51]

Hall and Ames respond to this point in the introduction to their next collaborative text, *Anticipating China* (1995).[52] They maintain that the most important question pertaining to the use of contrasts is not whether exceptions are present in the traditions compared (something that they seem willing to concede, at least implicitly), but rather whether those exceptions are "importantly present." They navigate the question of importance by means of their Principle of Mere Presence, which states, "*The mere presence of an idea or doctrine in a particular cultural matrix does not permit us to claim that the doctrine or idea is importantly present—that is, present in such a way that it significantly qualifies, defines, or otherwise shapes the culture*" (italics original). Hall and Ames are, first and foremost, philosophers of culture and are thus not primarily interested in providing an exhaustive account of things potentially relevant to comparison; rather, their interest lies in outlining the main contours of a given culture in order to ensure that its distinctive character is not lost when brought into comparative contrast with other cultures.[53] With this goal in mind, it makes good sense to consider something "importantly present" only if it has "contributed significantly to the shaping of a cultural milieu" (1995, xv).

An exception to a proposed contrast, then, can only be "importantly present" if it shapes its culture to anything like the extent of the contrast itself. Hall and Ames concede that exceptions may be "important" in their own right (e.g., as interesting variations within a particular culture) but maintain that such exceptions are seldom if ever as important as the broader contrasts within the context of cross-cultural understanding. They write,

> While attempting to maintain a real sensitivity to the nuances of the Chinese experience, we must not become lost in the details. As important as such details are when performing analyses of this or that aspect of a society or culture, comparativists will be prevented from making sense of a culture if they do not diligently avoid the Fallacy of the Counterexample. After all, generalizations concerning cultural importances are often vindicated, not falsified, by resort to counterexamples precisely to the extent that such examples suggest the relative absence of a particular belief or doctrine. (1995, xv)

Cross-cultural contrasts, by their very nature, identify the most definitive features of the cultures they compare, so it is difficult to conceive of an exception to those features that could be considered importantly present relative to the broader contours of the tradition in which it is found. Indeed, it seems that, for Hall and Ames, exceptions serve their most positive and productive role in comparison insofar as they function as the proverbial "exception that proves the rule," a designation that effectively quashes the relevance and integrity of the exception. For Hall and Ames, it seems that it is the comparative contrast that is of utmost importance in comparison, and "an employment of the Principle of Mere Presence, where relevant, [will allow] the comparativist to remain focused upon what is truly important in shaping cultural sensibilities" (1995, xv).

One can infer from the above remark that Hall and Ames are aware that their contrasts will admit of exceptions and that the employment of these contrasts in accordance with the Principle of Mere Presence may cause them to overlook exceptions that—however significant in their own right—are not as important to an accurate understanding of the comparative relations among cultures.[54] Yet this fact does not appear to unduly trouble them: having a particular focus is inevitable in any interpretive work, and having a particular focus requires that some things are excluded; as long as the choice of focus leads to a better—or, preferably, the best conceivable—understanding of the cultures that would be compared, Hall and Ames appear fully prepared to embrace that choice.

It is hard not to appreciate the very practical bent of this approach to comparative philosophy. Hall and Ames realize that no one can understand everything about all cultures and their comparative relation to one another all of the time, so the task of the comparativist should be to enable an accurate understanding of at least the most definitive features of cultural traditions and their relation to one another. Again, assuming that exceptions are merely that—exceptions—they run counter to the broader characteristics of the relation among cultures. Accordingly, if one can only understand something of that relation, one is better served by having a clear understanding of the contrast itself than of its exceptions. Given the ever-developing status of comparative philosophy, they contend, one must contend first with the most egregious errors before trying to cultivate a more subtle and extensive understanding of cross-cultural relations.

Hall and Ames are surely right with respect to the need to make difficult and even compromising choices in comparative work, and it is clearly a methodological strength that they allow practical considerations like these to play such a prominent role in their work. However, this same feature is also a weakness. To the extent that these choices are emphasized to the *exclusion* of other potentially interesting and important points (to use their Whiteheadian terminology), they present not only an incomplete account but moreover an at least partially distorted one. In their employment of contrasts, Hall and Ames have not merely chosen to focus on the contrasting features among different cultural milieus; they have also presented those contrasts as though—at least on a practical level—the exceptions to those contrasts do not exist.[55] As a result, they obscure the full richness and diversity both within and among cultural traditions and ultimately provide a misleading account of both.

How one discerns this combined strength and weakness will depend largely on how one understands the task of comparative philosophy. If the primary purpose of comparative philosophy is to define, as accurately and completely as possible, the complex nature of the relations among the world's many cultural traditions, then the omission of exceptions to any proposed contrast is both an unforgivable and a dangerous weakness in Hall and Ames' approach. By contrast, if the primary purpose is to provide a clearer and more accurate understanding of each of the world's philosophical traditions, then omission of exceptions can be justified in light of the generally more accurate understanding of traditions that result. The temptation from each side has been to accuse the other of what might best be described as the academic equivalent of gerrymandering (i.e., emphasizing some features to the exclusion of others in the service of one's own theoretical interests). The underlying problem in resolving this conflict is that there is no clear set of guidelines for determining how much each feature should be emphasized. To the extent that Hall and Ames' use of contrasts has been controversial, it has been precisely because it is the very understanding of comparative philosophy that is at stake.

Something of this tension can be seen in the ongoing debate surrounding their use of the distinction between immanence and transcendence. It is not only the most prominent of the contrasts they employ; it is also the most controversial. It is significant that Neville highlighted this distinction in particular in his comment in their foreword; he would subsequently provide a more developed account of this critique in his *Boston Confucianism* (2000, 47–50, 147–66). Other prominent comparativists would also call their position on transcendence into question, including Tu Weiming, Wm. Theodore de Bary, and Joseph Grange.[56] Suffice to say, the question of transcendence makes an appropriate test case in that nothing can be taken for granted on this point among comparativists.

For their part, Hall and Ames argue assiduously throughout their work that the concept of 'transcendence'—the notion that the world consists of entities that find their value, goals, and principles in a transcendent source—is not importantly present in and for all intents and purposes irrelevant to the interpretation of classical Chinese thought.[57] More precisely, they define "strict transcendence" as follows: "[A] principle, A, is transcendent with respect to that, B, which it serves as principle if the meaning or import of B cannot be fully analyzed and explained without recourse to A, but the reverse is not true" (1987, 13).[58] In the classical Chinese tradition, they argue, there is no such notion of transcendence; rather, the world is understood in terms of radical immanence, whereby events are interdependently linked within particular contexts, and whose values, goals, and principles are to be found in their interrelations.

Hall and Ames' primary concern in employing the distinction between transcendence and immanence is to enable Westerners to better understand classical Chinese culture on its own terms (or, as close to its own terms as possible). "One of the principal barriers precluding the Westerner from understanding China on its own terms," they write, "is the persistence in Western cultures of what Robert Solomon [1993] has so aptly termed the 'transcendental pretense'" (1995, xiv). This pretense consists of the belief among Western scholars that, because transcendence has played such a central role in Western traditions, it must also figure prominently into non-Western traditions. That belief, they maintain, is largely the result of insufficiently critical translations of non-Western terms and ideas: when translated into Western idiom, it is all too easy to allow Western biases to pervade these terms and ideas; whether this is done intentionally or unintentionally, it nonetheless distorts one's understanding of non-Western traditions.

As they have tried to make clear from their own careful translations of classical Chinese texts, it is not necessary for translations to lead to such a distorted view of other cultures. Rather, "[t]hese distortions arise from a failure to give adequate notice to contrasting assumptions that shape the cultural milieux of China and the West" (1995, xv). If one is to avoid these distortions—and thus to overcome this principal barrier to understanding China—then one must present an account of the Chinese tradition that stands in sharp contrast to the Western tradition insofar as it demonstrates the lack of any significant interest in transcendence (or any other characteristically Western concern) as a defining characteristic of classical Chinese culture.[59] Hall and Ames accomplish this by drawing attention toward what they believe to be the definitive characteristic of classical Chinese thought (i.e., its focus on immanence) and away from prevailing misconceptions (i.e., the "transcendental pretense").

Are Hall and Ames right in suppressing consideration of transcendence in classical Chinese philosophy? One might think that the answer to this question depends on whether or not transcendence is actually present in classical Chinese thought in more than trivial ways, and, to some extent, it is. From the perspective of methodological evaluation, however, the more relevant question is whether Hall and Ames should be primarily concerned with an accurate representation of classical Chinese philosophy. As noted above, this has everything to do with how one understands the task of comparative philosophy. Neville, for example, has been primarily concerned with defining, as accurately and completely as possible, the nature of the relations among the world's many cultural traditions and thus sees the omission of these exceptions as a weakness in their comparative method and a hindrance to comparative philosophy in general (2000). Hall and Ames, by contrast, are primarily concerned with providing a clearer and more accurate understanding of each of the world's philosophical traditions, so they are prepared to suppress considerations of potentially misleading features of a tradition if that means that the broader features of those traditions are more accurately understood.[60] Again, one arrives at the apparent deadlock of fundamental differences in the conception of comparative philosophy.

Yet, the example of transcendence sheds some additional light on the situation. If Neville is wrong about transcendence in the classical Chinese tradition (i.e., it is either not importantly present, or not present at all), then this should be able to be demonstrated through careful deliberation— deliberation that is aptly characterized by the ongoing scholarly debates in journals, conferences, and monographs. Such deliberation may include debate about the interpretation of data pertaining to the classical Chinese tradition, the proper character and role of the philosophy of culture, or both.[61] The crucial point is that there is nothing intrinsic to Neville's approach that militates against conceding the point to Hall and Ames if faced with sufficient evidence.

By contrast, if Hall and Ames are wrong (i.e., transcendence is both present and significant within the classical Chinese tradition),[62] it is unclear how this could be demonstrated to them in a compelling manner. They have constructed their contrasts in such a way that only those features that are so influential as to define a cultural tradition can be brought to bear on comparative philosophy. As the reader will recall, an idea is "important" for Hall and Ames only if it has "contributed significantly to the shaping of a cultural milieu" for a particular culture (1995, xv).[63] Thus, when faced with a potential exception, they appeal to their definition of the philosophy of culture and maintain that even if such exceptions exist they only distract the comparativist from the more important points of cross-cultural contrast. In effect, then, they define the exceptions out of existence (or, at least, out of relevance).

This is not to say that it is impossible for exceptions to be presented to them in such a way that they could concede their importance; Hall and Ames obviously discern among potential contrasts with great care, eliminating those that do not seem to do justice to the defining features of the cultural traditions compared. Nor is this to maintain that they have removed themselves from the ongoing debate: they participate in the same journals and conferences as their critics and have published substantive monographs that focus on the points in question above. It is also not to suggest that they manifest some obstinacy or incorrigibility that runs counter to their pragmatist commitments; they are no less committed to fallibilism than any of the figures discussed in this study, and their readiness to alter their conclusions in the face of compelling evidence has already been noted (especially with respect to issues of translation).

The point here is rather that, methodologically, they bear a significant potential blind spot. By employing contrasts that appeal to the defining features of each tradition, Hall and Ames are able to capture many of the distinctive features of each of the traditions they compare and also to make it more likely that those features are preserved in any instance of comparison. However, it also leaves them unable to address any features that are not definitive in any of these traditions but that may still be significant with respect to their comparative relation. In the case of transcendence, for example, it would be significant if all traditions were concerned with the concept of transcendence, even if not all traditions took this as a defining priority; the very existence of this concern in all traditions would reveal something very fundamental about the way human beings think about the world.

Hall and Ames do not argue directly that such unimportant (by their definition) features cannot nonetheless be significant for comparison; however, their arguments that such features are "unimportant" does militate against further consideration—both in their own work and in the work of others who would consider the possibility. This is confirmed by their arguments that any such consideration only further entrenches mistaken assumptions. The result is a set of features that may pertain to a cultural tradition that are marginalized from the outset as a matter of principle and never given the opportunity to demonstrate their relevance to comparative study.

The interesting exception to this is, of course, their use of first problematic thinking in the Western philosophical tradition. Drawing on the terms of their definition, it does not appear to have "contributed significantly to the shaping of [the Western] cultural milieu" (1995, xv). It might be argued that, while first problematic thinking did not "define" the Western philosophical tradition in the way that second problematic thinking did, it nonetheless "qualified" it in important ways; however, by such a loose definition of "qualifies," it is unclear what would not count as important.[64] This seems to introduce a contradiction within their work, whereby an idea that is by their own definition unimportant is nonetheless raised to penultimate importance in their comparative work, thus calling into question the "cash value" (to use James' term) of their concept of 'cultural importance' itself. Given that their comparative method is founded on a philosophy of culture, this seeming inconsistency further calls into question the means by which some facets of a culture are included in comparison while others are excluded.[65]

The point of highlighting this weakness is not to suggest that their method is fundamentally flawed. The methodological blindness described above is a notable weakness, but it is a weakness balanced by an equally notable strength (i.e., that of tailoring the results of comparison to the current needs of comparative philosophy). Moreover, it seems to be a choice among two alternative conceptions of the primary task of comparative philosophy. The pressing question here is whether the weakness can be mitigated without compromising its strength. The answer to this question, I think, is a resounding "yes." Hall and Ames' primary concern in suppressing consideration of the presence of transcendence in classical Chinese thought is to countermand the transcendental pretense that still pervades much of contemporary comparative philosophy. They have the sympathies of their critics in this concern, as most would agree that the case for transcendence in classical China has historically been overblown. The question one must ask, then, is why this objective cannot be accomplished by means of additional discretion with respect to how the question of transcendence is addressed within the academy?

A revised program for eliminating the transcendental pretense could be as follows: introductory books, basic journal articles, and general lectures on Chinese philosophy can take great care to differentiate that tradition from what would seem to be Western counterparts, to ensure that those just entering the field are appropriately dispossessed of their mistaken assumptions about the Chinese tradition; however, in more sophisticated venues such as professional conferences and more technical scholarly works, such issues can continue to be discussed critically and productively. This would allow Hall and Ames' concern with maintaining the distinctiveness of each tradition to be maintained, while also allowing for careful consideration of potential areas of commonality among more seasoned scholars.

There is good precedent in academic circles for such an approach, a prime example of which can be found in the history of comparative studies. Throughout the early development of comparative religion, a number of arguments were made for the superiority of Christianity as the most developed of all religions; this argument was made perhaps most famously by Immanuel Kant, Friedrich Schleiermacher, Ernst Troeltsch, and Rudolf Otto, but it was commonplace among pre-World War I scholars of religion.[66] It became increasingly clear through further research, however, that the very criteria established for the comparison of religions were biased in favor of Christianity. Moreover, it was not at all clear how criteria could be developed that would *not* be intrinsically biased in favor of some religions.

Rather than ceasing comparison altogether in light of these difficulties, however, subsequent scholars have addressed the situation productively on two fronts: first, they have remained doubly critical of any attempts to employ criteria that have traditionally favored Christianity (thus stemming the tide of unduly biased comparison); second, they have continued to pursue comparison among religions with an increased awareness of how the biases of their criteria influence their conclusions. In short, they have realized the biases are a significant concern in comparative study but that there is more to such study than the biases themselves and that it would therefore be a cumulative loss to cease comparison altogether.[67]

This is the way that the question of transcendence in classical China (and elsewhere) is, for the most part, already discussed. The problem with

Hall and Ames' approach is that they have effectively defined alternative positions with their definition of "importance," so they have rendered their position a conversation stopper. This is evident from the effective deadlock there is on the question of transcendence among Hall/Ames and their opponents. The conversation will continue either way, but it would be a richer conversation if it were able to continue incorporating the contributions of scholars such as Hall and Ames rather than simply being faced with the prospect of agreeing or disagreeing with their conclusions.

Opening up the lines of communication again would only require an adjustment of their definition of 'importance' to include more than what has proven to be definitive for a given culture. As I have tried to demonstrate, this need not countermand their contributions in highlighting the definitive features of each tradition; rather, it need only complement this with a careful and informed discussion of what is interesting and perhaps also important about the features of a tradition that are not so prominent as to define them. It would take a sober analysis of the state of comparative philosophy to determine whether such a broadening of the discussion is a wise choice, but there have to be at least some contexts in which such a careful and informed discussion can take place.

To some, this plea for disciplined middle ground may seem to be only slightly less naïve than the early belief that transcendence is present in China in the same way that it is present in the West. The strongest reading of Hall and Ames would suggest that the transcendental pretense is so strong that any such attempt to moderate the response can only fail to stem the tide. Such a reading, however, fails to take into account the fact that such a strong reaction against the transcendental pretense stifles creative work among those who take the point about transcendental pretense and would get on with a more sophisticated comparative study. A more moderate version of their approach would realize that it is possible to broaden their project without necessarily countermanding their basic concerns, thus enabling them to both prevent mistaken assumptions of similarity among cultural traditions and also allow for more careful and nuanced considerations of potential similarity.

Hall and Ames insist that their project "is not at all to *tell it like it is*; we merely wish to present a narrative which is interesting enough and plausible enough to engage those inclined to join the conversation" (1995, xix–xx, italics original). They have already produced a narrative that is interesting and plausible in many respects, and they have undoubtedly brought comparative philosophy a long way through their careful and discerning research. Yet there remain many who are inclined to join the conversation—and, indeed, many who have been involved in the conversation for some time—but whose potentially interesting and plausible contributions have been defined out of the conversation in advance. To the extent that they exclude these voices, Hall and Ames resort to "telling it like it is," something that not only compromises their contribution but also runs counter to their own aims. Because their contribution is strongest when it takes into account all of the potentially relevant information, it is the hope moving forward that they will be able not only to guard against mistaken assumptions but also to open up their understanding of "importance" to include the full range of ideas relevant to comparison.

Getting on with It Responsibly

One of the recurrent threads of this analysis and appraisal of Hall and Ames' method has been the provisional and largely narrative character of their philosophical work. Strictly speaking, by their own account they are not interested in arguing for the "truth" of any of the conclusions they reach in their research, but rather in presenting the most compelling, edifying narrative possible about the development of Western philosophy, the character of classical Chinese philosophy, and the nature of the relation between the two. They inherit this narrative approach from the pragmatist tradition—especially as it is read through the work of Richard Rorty[68]—and thus see their own constructive project not as the discovery of philosophic truth per se but rather as the contribution of novel ideas that are edifying to the current cultural milieu (1987, 316–17).

As should be apparent to anyone familiar with Rorty's work, however, Hall and Ames have a conflicted relationship with his philosophical commitments. On the one hand, they appreciate his strong critique of the Western philosophical tradition and the ground it clears for novel contributions—especially from non-Western traditions, which have historically been excluded from much of the Western philosophic conversation. To the extent that philosophical traditions are judged on the basis of their capacity for edification rather than their conformity to some prevailing norm, a pathway is cleared for a more open engagement of classical Chinese philosophical contributions. On the other hand, however, Hall and Ames do not seem prepared to do away altogether with claims to truth. Their modest demurrals notwithstanding, they do seem to want to "get it right," at least with respect to the interpretation of classical Chinese thought.[69] For example, they make repeated references to trying to arrive at "a more accurate picture of Confucius' thinking" and even "a truer account of Confucius" (1987, 7) if not also of the classical Chinese tradition more broadly. Indeed, their entire project is aimed at preventing misreadings of the Chinese tradition, whereas misreadings—and specifically "strong misreadings," as per Harold Bloom (1997)—are precisely what Rorty aims to encourage.[70]

For their own part, Hall and Ames have been explicit about their refusal to give up on the notion of truth altogether, but the notion of truth they espouse is distinctively Chinese in character. In contrast to what they characterize as a Western obsession with *episteme* (understood as a knowledge of the underlying reality of things), they argue—following Graham (1989)—that Chinese philosophy has traditionally been more concerned with the aesthetic quality of things in relation to one another (Hall 2001; Ames 2007). "Truth" for the Chinese, then, is not so much a matter of knowing what a thing *is* but rather of being able to relate to it appropriately *as* a particular convergence of relations: it is better to be a true friend and to have true friends than to be the one who knows the truth about friendship (as if there were some such abstract truth).

Part of the difficulty in assessing Hall and Ames' work in this respect is that it is not entirely clear what account of truth they espouse in their own philosophic work. At first glance, in the context of their commendation of classical Chinese philosophy as a promising alternative to the shortcomings of contemporary Western philosophy, it would seem that they adopt that alternative in their own work. Yet, as noted above, this does not seem to adequately account for their strong concern to represent classical Chinese philosophy accurately. What is it to be true to Chinese traditions of philosophy (to use their parlance) if not to get those traditions right?

A stronger account of truth would seem to be something that would take account of both Western and Chinese concepts. For example, just as it is ultimately more important to be a true friend than to know the truth about friendship, so it is difficult to be a true friend without knowing the truth about what a good friend is. Knowledge without action may be fruitless, but action without knowledge is aimless. In the short run, one might be willing to forego a working definition of friendship and simply maintain friendships with those who seem, for ungeneralizable reasons, to be "true friends."[71] This approach shows its limitations, however, when one encounters new experiences in friendship, has to make difficult decisions about how to treat a friend (or interpret how one has been treated), or—perhaps most tellingly—has to teach a child how to be a good friend.

One may be tempted, with Rorty, to take care of freedom and allow truth to take care of itself (1989a, 176), thus opening up the bounds of what friendship may be and trusting in the general competence and acuity of humankind to maintain true friendships if given adequate space. Hall and Ames, however, do not seem willing to allow this with respect to Chinese philosophy. They may not be interested in getting the Chinese tradition right, but they are very concerned with stopping others from getting it wrong, and at the end of the day this seems to amount to largely the same thing. The problem for Hall and Ames is that, eschewing the framework for "getting it right," it becomes difficult if not impossible for them to relay how others get it wrong.

Their standard means for addressing what they consider errant interpretations of Chinese philosophy is to suggest that such interpretations are "flat and uninteresting." This contrasts with their own, stated goal of providing interpretations that are "interesting enough and plausible enough to engage those inclined to join the conversation" (1995, xx). Yet it is difficult to see how a claim about what is flat and uninteresting could be defended outside of some more general theory of what Chinese philosophy has been concerned with and what about it should be interesting and important—in short, without a general framework like the one characteristic of Western concerns with *episteme*. Perhaps more problematic, with respect to comparative philosophy, is that a significant portion of the comparative conversation is thus rejected without any detailed justification.

The difficulties of this position become clear in cases where Hall and Ames must defend their approach against those who do not adhere to its narrative commitments.[72] Certainly, Hall and Ames take note of and respond to other comparative approaches, seeking to understand and appreciate the insights made possible in each method while also identifying and attempting to avoid their weakness; in fact, they are among the best of the comparativists at developing their own method in self-conscious, critical reflection vis-à-vis other methods. Yet, when confronted with the task of engaging other approaches on the level of specific points of interpretation, they have had greater difficulty fostering productive comparative reflection.

A good example of this can be found in their response to reviews of their first collaborative work by Gregor Paul and Michael Martin. Paul had written a general essay (1991) challenging the use of the term *logical* in the works of Donald Munro, A. C. Graham, and Hall and Ames (74). He dedicated most of his essay to a critique of the distinction between the "rational" and the "aesthetic" in Hall and Ames, suggesting that the way that these terms are used suggests a cultural divide among traditions that goes beyond anything that is possible—or, at least, comprehensible—in comparative philosophy (76–84). His conclusion amounted to a call for the use of more nuanced terminology to distinguish among cultural emphases, as well as for further consideration of important points about the classical Chinese tradition that seem to have been overlooked or underestimated (84).

Similarly, Martin had written what is by all accounts a standard book review of *Thinking through Confucius* (1987), which consists of a balance of both judicious appreciation and constructive criticism. He makes a number of well-thought-out points throughout the essay, ranging from the difficulty of distinguishing Hall and Ames' constructive project from their interpretation of Confucius (497) to the inherent difficulties of imaginative advances in a system where personal excellence is identified in accordance with traditional analogies (502). Significantly, however, he concludes with a point similar to Paul's, arguing that the distinctions drawn between cultures suggest a greater difference between ways of thinking than can really exist.

Paul and Martin both call Hall and Ames to task for the sharp distinction the latter make between the Anglo-European and classical Chinese traditions and thus call into question much of the impetus for their emerging project. Because of the salience of these critiques and their common focus, Hall and Ames respond to these critiques in a single response (1991, 345). They make a number of valid points in their response—pointing out, for example, the limited definition of logic in Paul's critique (333–36) or the underestimation in Martin's critique of the inherent hermeneutical difficulties of distinguishing one's interpretation of Confucius from Confucius himself (344). What is most interesting about their response, however, is that it consists more of an attack on the critiques themselves—and, to some extent, the critics as well—rather than a careful and sustained defense against them.

For example, in response to Paul's critique, they opt to refer Paul and other readers to their other works and to the works of others who have employed similar cultural contrasts (1991, 337). They conclude with the hope that "anyone puzzled by our arguments in *Thinking through Confucius*, beginning with Professor Paul, will scrutinize the alternative texts which discuss in even greater detail the categories and distinctions which we have, with appropriate revisions, found applicable to classical China" (339). There is certainly a virtue to not simply repeating one's arguments in response to serious critique; however, this leaves open the question of how otherwise to respond. By referring their critics to other texts that make largely the same point, Hall and Ames respond in a manner characteristic of the narrative approach: if a narrative is seen at first to be implausible or uninteresting, all that remains is to point to ways in which the story has been told that may add to its interest and plausibility. What is missing in their response, however, is any further defense of their position in light of these critiques. In short, it becomes unclear how their response moves the conversation forward.

The tenor of their response becomes still clearer in their response to Martin. They begin by reemphasizing the distinction between Western and Chinese philosophy—precisely the strong distinction Martin had previously called into question. They write,

> A duck-rabbit problem emerges which is most familiar in the analytic philosopher's critique of continental philosophy. Martin demands clarity, conciseness, rigor and certainty from a philosophical position that does not accept those premises which would make such conditions a signal of good philosophy or good interpretation. In this case of a comparative study, Professor Martin does not see the Cantonese Crispy Duck for the Kananchen Braten, and as a consequence, says repeatedly and often with exasperation, "This isn't rabbit!" And what can we say but "It's duck, Michael, it's duck." (1991, 343)

This is, in fact, the mainstay of their response to Martin: rather than explaining their position with greater care, in more detail, or on a simpler basis, they note their differences from him and merely insist on the accuracy—one wants to say "truth"—of their interpretation. Thus, in response to each of his critiques, they reply with a series of jabs, "What can we say? It's a duck, Michael." "Hey, Michael, it's you who ordered the rabbit!" "You know the refrain, Michael" (1991, passim). A similar example of this can be seen in their response to Paul's article when they conclude, "In this failure really to confront the difficulties of intercultural understanding, Paul reminds us of the American tourist who, never leaving his room at the Bangkok *Holiday Inn*, is pleased to discover how similar is Thailand to the good old U.S.A." (336).

Perhaps Hall and Ames' response was intended not as a sharp rejoinder but rather as a playful critique, as one might expect of a postmodern Sophist or Zhuangzian of sorts, who wittily chides his colleagues for being too attached to shifting foundations. Whatever the intention, the more important point is that it ultimately failed to demonstrate the "interest" and "plausibility" of their account and thus failed to "engage those inclined to join the conversation" (1995, xix–xx) in any constructive way. Rather, their response communicated that, if at first persuasion fails, derision follows closely behind; that plurality is paramount, as long as it does not include positions that one finds unplausible or uninteresting; and that the narrative approach is such that only one narrative can prevail, all other narratives (whether self-understood in this sense or not) being berated out of the conversation. This sentiment is summed up when they conclude that "as harsh as this may seem, we believe that unless Professors Paul and Martin gain a somewhat broader understanding of both the Chinese and Anglo-European philosophic traditions, and until each is willing to reflect in a more serious manner on the specific requirements of comparative philosophy, productive communication with them on the issues each has raised seems unlikely" (345). The implications for comparative philosophy are significant: if one fails to accept the basic tenets of a particular approach to comparative philosophy, one is to be excluded from the conversation.[73] This is effectively comparative philosophy eschewing its own comparative commitments on the basis of method. If comparative philosophy is worth anything at all, it must be able to negotiate difference without simply eliminating it out of hand. Indeed, given Hall and Ames' response, one can hardly imagine Paul and Martin being inclined to continue in the conversation.

Not surprisingly, this is precisely what happens. Martin opens his rejoinder by noting his dismay at the querulous tone of Hall and Ames' response: "Since I went out of my way to praise aspects of their book," he notes, "I was taken aback by the hostility of Hall and Ames' response and their reluctance to consider seriously the various views I tried to express. Readers can judge for themselves the tone, the ad hominem remarks, cat calls and other disturbing features of Hall and Ames' response" (1991, 489). His critique of their response drives straight to the heart of the narrative approach and is worth quoting at length here:

Some interpretations are better than others. Therefore, a responsible modern commentator will be careful to defend his interpretation against others. How the defense is set forth and justified is a
complicated matter involving questions of (say) clarity, cohesion,
history, philology, explanatory power and any number of further
parameters—all themselves standing not on an immutable foundation but subject to challenge and discussion at any time. The
very nature of interpretation and the related question of how
one can argue for one interpretation over another are themselves
philosophical questions which Hall and Ames should consider
carefully. . . . However worthy Hall and Ames' views may be, they
will prove of very limited application if Hall and Ames can preach
only to the converted. Instead of lecturing Gregor Paul and myself
on the shortcomings of our education and the narrowness of our
philosophical perspective, could I be so forward as to suggest that
Hall and Ames, who so champion the idea of "appropriateness" in
their interpretation of Confucius, reflect a little more on what is
appropriate for serious academic writing and what is appropriate
to say to others who took the time to read their book, reflect upon
it and write at some length about it? (489, 493)

Paul, for his part, is much more short and to the point, although he makes
essentially the same point: in his rejoinder—"Against Wanton Distortion"—he concludes, "Generally speaking, Hall/Ames distort my views, and
attribute to me positions I have never held. This notwithstanding, I don't
mind reflecting 'in a more serious manner on the specific requirements of
comparative philosophy,' as long as they do not imply that I must do it their
way. But since Hall/Ames eschew dogmatism, they would certainly never
make such a demand" (1992, 121). Both of these responses draw attention
to the apparent contradiction in Hall and Ames' response, namely, that an
approach that takes fallibilism, pluralism, and narrative as its guiding commitments nonetheless became eminently dogmatic when faced with differing
perspectives. This is not to say that Hall and Ames inevitably and necessarily
turn to dogmatism when pressed—neither Paul nor Martin seem to suggest
this—but it is nonetheless disconcerting that their open, nonfoundational
approach so easily seemed to morph into its opposite.[74]

It is possible that the strong reaction evident in Hall and Ames' response is more the reflection of a certain defensiveness on their part than
of any inherent dogmatism in their method. Although Hall and Ames had
each published prior works, *Thinking through Confucius*—the text in question
in these reviews—was not only their most controversial work to date but
also the inaugural text in what they hoped would become—and what would
indeed become—a productive collaborative effort. Yet the approach they
commended was of such originality that it was called into question by a

number of scholars, and they may have felt their situation to be one of *Hall et Ames contra mundi*. Thus, they may have felt compelled to respond with particular vigor to these critiques that seemed to call into question the very validity of their approach.[75]

If one looks at more recent responses to critiques, one finds a much more patient and irenic temper and a much more open and fair consideration of alternative perspectives. A fine example of this can be found in Ames' recent response to a relatively strong critique from Eske Møllegaard. Møllegaard charged Hall and Ames with introducing into the interpretation of Chinese thought a "notion of philosophy that . . . is too narrow to do justice to the wide range of styles and concerns of Chinese thinkers. Therefore, this philosophy cannot claim any special status in the study of Chinese thought—in fact it hampers productive research in this area" (2005, 321). In fact, he went so far as to accuse them of logocentrism (330)—the very logocentrism they had, in other works, sought to critique and move beyond (Hall 1982b; Hall and Ames 1995).

Despite the strong tenor of Møllegaard's critique, Ames' response is nothing if not exemplary: it is as irenic in temperament as it is careful to address resolutely the points raised in the critique. He acknowledges the legitimacy of many of the basic concerns that his critic raises but demonstrates that they are not concerns that he and Hall have unconsciously elided but rather concerns that they have consistently sought to address throughout their work. He is careful to point out that the Continental reading is not the only valid reading of the Chinese tradition, and that the pragmatist tradition Møllegaard so easily dismisses also has important contributions to make to the task of interpretation. He concludes, "It is our position that the best philosophical readings—analytic, American, and indeed Continental—add to our interpretations of these texts rather than detract from them. I am grateful for Møllegaard's critique of exclusively 'philosophical readings,' but as one philosopher to another, I would enlist his help in making philosophy a part of a more comprehensive appreciation of the Chinese philosophical tradition" (2005, 152). There is perhaps no better contrast to the earlier response to their critics, as this response exemplifies the attempt to "present a narrative which is interesting enough and plausible enough to engage those inclined to join the conversation" (1995, xx).[76]

It would be a mistake, however, to attribute the apparent dogmatism of their earlier response merely to the "errors of youth," as the tendency inherent in that response finds expression in other facets of their work as well. Interestingly, it is none other than Eske Møllegaard—in the same critique mentioned above (2005)—who appears to have crafted the most compelling account of this dogmatism in their published works.[77] He notes that there is a "considerable gap between the posture of modesty in regard to truth claims and the ambitious schemes and narratives that constitute [their] argument[s]" (2005, 328). On the one hand, Hall and Ames repeatedly insist that they are not interested in establishing any "final truth" in the interpretation of Chinese culture; yet, on the other hand, they appear very interested in unseating prevalent "untruths" in such interpretation and thus do appear to be arguing for objective truths in some form or another. Møllegaard notes, "It is as if Hall and Ames have not quite decided if they should act as modest cultural critics, who just take part in the conversation among interpreters of China as best as they can, or if they should act as 'philosopher' and try to root out naïve opinion and raise the consciousness of those, 'by far the majority,' who are living in the darkness of 'ideological biases' " (329).[78] That is, Hall and Ames are not satisfied to simply identify the ideological biases of other comparativists; they also want to dispossess them of the mistaken readings of the Chinese tradition that result. That is, they *do* seem to want to "get it right," at least to the extent that this means "not allowing others to get it wrong."

A third and final example of this tendency toward dogmatism can be seen in their patent dismissiveness of those who disagree with them on the issue of transcendence.[79] For instance, despite that their definition of transcendence (1987, 13) is sufficiently narrow as to exclude some of the most original and creative interpretations of that term, they nonetheless apply their conclusions to all interpretations of transcendence.[80] Similarly, when they note the waning of the concept of transcendence in the West (e.g., 1998, 212–18), they fail to acknowledge the existence of any interpretations of transcendence that take seriously the challenges facing the concept and yet make strong arguments that they are not susceptible to those challenges (e.g., Neville 1992a). As a result, when the question of transcendence in the Chinese tradition is raised by dissenting voices, they are suppressed to such an extent as should disquiet one committed to encouraging the diversity and plurality of perspectives.

The point here is not simply that Hall and Ames manifest a certain dogmatism at points (most philosophers do), but that they do so despite having a methodological commitment of not doing so. In theory, their self-professed commitments to a Rortian-style pragmatism would seem to allow for the possibility of all manner of narratives—including "strong misreadings," which do not necessarily "get it right" but nonetheless enable new insights for a particular cultural milieu—but in practice they seem less willing to allow for such divergent narratives. It would seem that, however much it facilitates some features of their project, their commitment to a Rortian style of pragmatism ultimately runs contrary to other important features of their project. In the end, then, it only compromises the project as a whole.[81]

The question to ask of Hall and Ames, then, is why they feel the Rortian facet of their project to be an important one—sufficiently important to merit the difficulties it introduces into their work (because they are surely aware of the difficulties it presents). The answer, I think, lies in the careful attention that Rorty has paid to hermeneutic developments within the Continental tradition, especially as they are expressed in terms of postmodernism and poststructuralism.[82] Of the main proponents of the pragmatist tradition, he has arguably taken their insights the most seriously. He is steadfastly cognizant of the ways that one's cultural context informs every aspect of one's life—including one's philosophical activities—and that such influence is unavoidable. Moreover, he acknowledges that any attempt to assess a culture, a philosophical position, or anything else for that matter can only be done from the context of a particular cultural location.[83]

As should be readily apparent, this poses serious challenges for philosophy as it is traditionally conceived, as it becomes difficult if not impossible to distinguish philosophical truth from cultural bias; indeed, if Rorty is correct then there is no such thing as "philosophic truth," since nothing escapes the long arm of cultural influence. Rorty's solution to these challenges is to understand philosophy not in terms of dialectic (as it has traditionally been understood in the West) but rather in terms of poetry. That is, one should construct a narrative that interprets all of the facets of one's culture that one finds important from the perspective of one's own particular cultural location.[84] The purpose of such a narrative is similar to the originally conceived purpose of philosophy (i.e., to enable one to better understand and engage the world), but its goals are much more modest: rather than seeking to be "true," a narrative should seek to be "edifying" (Rorty 1979; see also 1989a, 1998, and 1999).

The advantage of narrative over the more traditional dialectical discourses is that it allows for the possibility of inconsistencies and even contradictions among competing narratives without requiring—or even allowing—that they be resolved. In this respect, they can be powerfully liberating to anyone who feels the prevailing account to be oppressive, mistaken, or otherwise out of place, as appears to be increasingly the case in the contemporary philosophic milieu. Hall notes his appreciation for Rorty's work in this respect when he writes that

> Rorty's measures, desperate as they may seem, are hardly out of place in our desperate times. One wonders how any reasonably sensitive, self-conscious, engaged thinker could believe that the perpetuation of the same tired strategies of logical analysis or dialectic which generate "truths" about the character of the world will improve our state. Rational appeals based upon stipulated meanings of evidence, argument, reason, and so forth, at variance with other theoretically stipulated sense, are broadly *irrational*. (1994, 53)

According to Hall, the real strength of the American philosophical tradition is its longstanding struggle with the implications of pluralism, and he sees Rorty's narrative approach as one of the most recent and perhaps most compelling of the positive responses to pluralism.

The problem with narratives, however, is that they are very good at breaking down supposedly nonnarrative accounts (deconstruction) but not terribly effective at providing a compelling narrative in its stead (reconstruction). As a result, while narratives about narrative philosophy have been widely popular and influential, narratives about anything else have been little more than amusing stories. Evidence of this can be seen in the fact that, while his followers make a great deal of hay from Rorty's deconstructive jabs, far less is made of his particular reading of Enlightenment modernism.[85] This is the case, as Hall notes, even for Rorty himself: "[H]olding our particular historical and cultural present in thought will require that we wield the sword not only to dub the noblest knights of intellectual culture, Sir Philosopher, but, as well, to cut down the villains who do not yet, no longer, nor ever shall deserve that honorific. This negative task is fully as important as the positive and, given the nature of the times, it is the one in which Rorty is perhaps most actively involved" (1994, 14). The negative task, however, cannot be separated from the positive one: at the end of the day, Rorty wants to assert that, in some way that is important for the practice of philosophy, these honorifics really do apply. That is, while he does not expect any consensus on the issues, he nonetheless seeks to be *persuasive* in his narrative accounts.[86] Yet, because he has already removed any possible ground for validation of these claims, it is unclear how he expects these claims to gather any credence.[87]

The result is a persistent tension between his philosophical commitments (i.e., for philosophy as narrative, for the cessation of nonnarrative philosophy, for the pertinence of his particular narrative, etc.) and his claims that his work is merely a narrative (that it is not universal, that it need not inspire consensus, that it need not justify itself vis-à-vis other narratives, etc.). Hall registers this tension at the close of his study on Rorty:

> One can become very frustrated with the attempt to discover whether Rorty is primarily a poet or a philosopher, whether he is more inclined toward the production of novel metaphors or their consumption on behalf of the aims of public praxis. As a metathinker and critic of alternative philosophies he is clearly performing the philosophic task as he defines it. But his "strong misreadings" of his predecessors, his creative juxtaposition of philosophic and/or literary texts, and his belief in the importance of self-creation, all point to a poetic disposition. (1994, 235)

This tension is like that described by Møllegaard (2005, 329) with respect to Hall and Ames: whereas the question for Rorty is whether he is a poet or a philosopher, the question for Hall and Ames is whether they are "modest cultural critics" or philosophers. The answer, of course, is that they are both; the problem is that the two are at least awkward if not impossible positions to hold simultaneously.

While Hall and Ames face a tension similar to that of Rorty, they seem to differ ultimately in the side of the tension they favor. As Hall suggests in his study of Rorty, this "poet and prophet of the new Pragmatism" ultimately favors the poetic over the philosophic. He notes that, in his more recent works, Rorty has "turned away from his role as the arch internal critic of the philosophic tradition and has moved through the looking glass. Standing now behind the mirror of nature, he is seen by many of his philosophical colleagues to be . . . beyond the pale" (1994, 3, ellipsis original). A self-described "lonely provincial" (1991a, 30), he still needs to express himself to others but neither needs nor expects others to find his narrative compelling. Thus, Hall concludes, "Rorty's idiosyncratic narratives are charming, disarming, and often most profound. But when all is said and (little) done, one realizes that his self-encapsulating strategies privatize his language to the extent that what he provides us is broadly irrelevant to interactive public discourse. What we are finally offered are obiter dicta . . . Richard Rorty's tabletalk" (1994, 236).[88] Hall and Ames, by contrast, seem to aspire to more than "tabletalk" in their own work. Not only do they want to challenge the legitimacy of the prevailing discourse of Western philosophy, but they also want to alter and improve it. They believe that the classical Chinese tradition *really has been* misunderstood by the West and that the interpretation they provide *really is* better than the prevailing one. Moreover, they often provide reasons for their interpretation, reasons that are meant to be subjected to public scrutiny and subjected to correction if found inadequate or inaccurate. Hall and Ames may include occasional demurrals to the effect that their interpretation is but one narrative of the relation between modern West and classical China, but the broader impetus driving their work suggests an interpretation that aspires to something more than mere telling of stories.

This difference from Rorty is a significant one, although it is not overtly advertised in their work. It is unclear whether this is because the issue was never seen as particularly pertinent to the philosophical task at hand, because the nature of their project changed over time, or because the precise nature of their relationship with Rorty was never fully worked out. Regardless of the reason, the consequence is that Hall and Ames seem to borrow a great deal more from Rorty in rhetoric than they do in practice. That is, the narrative philosophy described in Rorty's works does not appear to adequately describe the nature of Hall and Ames' work. As a result, not only do Hall and Ames sometimes appear to be more dogmatic than their Rortian rhetoric would allow, but they also end up becoming more dogmatic than even their own philosophic commitments would allow.

In conclusion, it is clear that the Rortian narrative approach Hall and Ames have employed has brought with it both strengths and weaknesses. On the one hand, it has provided them with a basis for critique of many of the prevailing assumptions in comparative philosophy and has allowed them to make novel and often controversial claims in the form of modest narratives. This has been particularly important when challenging the assumptions of the Western philosophical traditions that still prevail in comparative philosophy. On the other hand, however, it has prevented them from making the strong claims they want to make regarding the classical Chinese tradition, which has created a great deal of confusion with respect to the status of their claims and ultimately resulted in an unanticipated tendency toward dogmatism that runs counter to their stated intentions. This does not necessarily mean that a narrative approach is incompatible with comparative philosophy, but it does suggest that embracing narrative philosophy carries with it certain consequences that are not entirely consistent with Hall and Ames' interest in comparative philosophy.[89]

This tension is a salient point for the further development of comparative philosophy. Of the four methods considered in this text, the one pursued by Hall and Ames is the most noticeably non-Western in its orientation. Hall and Ames may not have fully escaped the Western concern with *episteme*, but they have drawn attention to its limitations and its limitability. In fact, in the same way that this study draws attention to their occasional return to *episteme*-centered philosophy, so their work implicitly critiques this study for its own emphasis on *episteme*. If this study is to be truly comparative and not dismissive of significant difference, it must be able to bring all methods into the conversation, including those with no compunction for *episteme*. This is a challenge that neither Hall and Ames nor the present study has adequately overcome, but it is hopefully one that becomes somewhat more capable of being overcome in light of this methodological consideration of Hall and Ames' experience. In the meantime, it should suffice to say—in light of what has been learned—that the proper role of *episteme* in comparative philosophy should currently be the subject of conversation rather than something presumed at its outset.

CONCLUSION

At the beginning of his own comparative work, Hall made the following observation: "Though comparative philosophy is still in its infancy, we are beginning to make some progress in articulating the relationships of Oriental and Western thought and culture. And though we should not claim too much for our comparative endeavors, since they still have the crudeness of mere first attempts, we are apparently at least beginning to see where the real issues lie" (1982b, 183). With comparative philosophy now in what might be best described as the awkward throes of its preadolescent years, it is clear that some significant progress has been made in articulating those relations, and this is due in no small part to Hall and Ames' distinctive contributions. For all of the strengths and weaknesses of their particular method, it is beyond question that these two scholars have been instrumental in helping philosophers, sinologists, and comparativists be better able to "see where the real issues lie."

In this study, attention has been given to the cross-disciplinary, cross-cultural, typological, and narrative dimensions of Hall and Ames' method. In each case, a prominent concern pertained to the preservation of difference in comparative study. In the cross-disciplinary dimension, both philosophy and philology were brought to bear on the translation and interpretation of Chinese texts in an attempt to preserve the original meaning of the text from assimilation into a misplaced context. Likewise, "bridge traditions" were employed between widely divergent traditions as an intermediate means of loosening one's own cultural assumptions in cross-cultural engagement. In addition, the typologies they employed were constructed precisely in order to highlight the points at which two cultures differ so that cross-cultural understanding does not become cross-cultural hegemony. Finally, even their comparative conclusions are posed as mere narratives, in the recognition that the subjects of their study can never be entirely reduced to how they are rendered in any comparative study. In short, Hall and Ames seek to provide tools for dealing productively with difference, even though they realize that difference neither can nor should be ultimately overcome.

By contrast, they provide little in the way of identifying or interpreting instances of similarity among cultural traditions. They state good reasons for this avoidance in their work (namely, that undue consideration of similarity can only jeopardize an appreciation for difference in this cultural milieu), but for the comparative philosopher the question must still stand as to whether consideration of similarity should also be an integral part of the comparative endeavor. For the moment, suffice it to say that, if a comparativist is primarily interested in better understanding each of the cultural traditions involved in comparison and their differences from one another, then one would be hard pressed to find a better set of methodological tools than those developed by Hall and Ames.

It is difficult to really conclude a study of "Hall and Ames' method," because their collaborative project has concluded in one sense and yet still continues in another. With David Hall's untimely passing in 2001, a significant source of the inspiration and development for the project was lost. Undoubtedly, much of the approach will be carried forward in Ames' subsequent work, but precisely what and how much is difficult to say. There is good reason to believe that Ames will seek out further collaborative work, as he has in the past, but it will be difficult to find as long-lasting or as mutually stimulating a collaboration as he had with Hall. At the same time, due in large part to Ames' influence as a teacher and an administrator, there is a thriving community of inquirers centered around the University of Hawaii who will surely draw on his work with Hall, develop it further, and take it in new directions of their own. Of the methods examined in this study, theirs remains the most influential, so there is little chance that it will fade from the conversation anytime soon. How it develops moving forward is anyone's guess, but there is good reason to expect many novel contributions from those who take this method as their own.

CHAPTER FOUR

ROBERT C. NEVILLE

Comparative Philosophy as Systematic Philosophy

> The heart of our conception of the comparative enterprise is that it is an ongoing process, always proceeding from comparative assumptions, formulating comparisons as hypotheses, making the hypotheses vulnerable to correction and modification until they seem steady and properly qualified, and then presenting them for further correction while accepting them as the new comparative assumptions.
>
> Neville, *The Human Condition*

Each of the figures examined in this study has demonstrated a distinctive and defining reason for his involvement in comparative philosophy, and in this respect Neville (1939–) is no different from the others (namely, in being different from them all).[1] In his case, the interest in things comparative stems from his commitment to a pragmatist-inspired form of Scotistic realism. This commitment, cultivated within the context of an increasing awareness of and interest in other philosophical and religious traditions, has led—and continues to lead—to the development of a philosophy of cross-cultural engagement that is as readily (yet critically) receptive to non-Western traditions as it is (at least initially) indebted to the Western tradition.[2]

For Neville, as for Duns Scotus, there is a real world that serves as the measure for any interpretations that claim to be true. Of course, the question of truth has become somewhat more complicated since the thirteenth century, and Neville draws heavily on the pragmatist tradition—and on the work of Charles Sanders Peirce in particular—to rework Scotistic realism for the modern world (see esp. 1989). This task defines the core of all of Neville's philosophical work, which in itself does not necessarily lead to an interest in comparison; however, it does have significant implications for comparative philosophy that Neville would soon realize and develop.

The most significant implication of this realism is that, if there is a real world that can serve as the measure for any interpretation, then that measure should be applicable for anyone regardless of their cultural location. Moreover, if the measure is the same, then a true idea in one tradition should theoretically be capable of finding expression in any tradition that aspires to achieve a comprehensive interpretation of the world. Neville recognizes this explicitly when, in his first major publication, God the Creator (1992a [1968]), he suggests that "our speculative categories can interpret other religious traditions as well" (187; see also 196).[3] This acknowledgement hardly makes God the Creator a comparative text; quite the contrary, the argument for the theory of creation ex nihilo laid out there (that God creates all things determinate, including God's character as creator) is drawn exclusively from Western and predominantly Christian sources, and it pertains to a philosophical concern that is identifiably Western in its orientation. Yet it nonetheless demonstrates that a concern for comparative philosophy—however embryonic—was a part of Neville's broader philosophic project from the very beginning.

This concern would be cultivated over the course of his career, nourished by an increasing exposure to the texts, communities, and scholars of non-Western traditions. At the time that God the Creator was published, Neville had had only minor exposure to such traditions: his university training at Yale focused on traditionally Western philosophical concerns, and there were no philosophers there besides Northrop who maintained any sustained interest in comparative philosophy.[4] Yet all of this would begin to change for Neville when he accepted his first academic position at Fordham University in 1965. There he would meet Thomas Berry, who would quickly become for him a "mentor in world philosophy" (2000, v; see also 1982, xiv). While Berry was—reminiscent of Northrop—virtually alone at Fordham in his interest in non-Western traditions, he was forthright in challenging Neville to take these traditions seriously and was integrally involved in enabling him to do so. In fact, it was Berry who first invited him to teach a course in Indian and Chinese philosophy, which he did (with some coaching from Berry). In similar fashion, Berry would prove to be one of Neville's most important early resources in comparative philosophy, both at Fordham and thereafter.[5]

Neville had further opportunity to teach courses in non-Western traditions when he accepted a position at the State University of New York at Purchase in 1971. By that time, many of his students, influenced by the countercultural movement of the late nineteen sixties, expressed a strong interest in learning about non-Western—and especially Indian—traditions, and this allowed him to expand departmental offerings in that direction

(Neville, interview by Robert Smid, July 17, 2006).[6] He took time to learn some Chinese and Sanskrit and even had the opportunity to teach introductory Sanskrit courses for a number of years.[7] He soon realized that he would probably never have enough time to gain reliable control of these languages, but he also determined that—because his interests were primarily philosophical rather than philological—this was not *necessarily* prohibitive to his participation in comparative philosophy.[8]

The influence of this increasing exposure to non-Western traditions is readily apparent in some of Neville's essays written throughout the 1970s. The most important of these is "A Metaphysical Argument for Wholly Empirical Theology" (1973), in which he follows up on the comparative task first introduced in *God the Creator* by putting its hypothesis about God to the test against the empirical data of non-Western traditions.[9] That he calls it "a *metaphysical* argument" is significant, because it underscores his commitment to the centrality of speculative hypotheses for cross-cultural encounter; that it moves toward a "wholly *empirical* theology" highlights his contention that all such hypotheses must be ultimately grounded in empirical evidence. Taken together, the title announces an approach to comparative philosophy that seeks to find the terms for comparison at the highest levels of abstraction and that tests those terms at every level of the concrete.[10]

This dual emphasis on the epistemological status of philosophical claims as speculative hypotheses and on the importance of empirical evidence for deciding among these claims is derived, of course, from the American pragmatist tradition. The first emphasis is derived from Neville's study of Charles Sanders Peirce, who had played an important but by no means central role in *God the Creator*.[11] Since that time, Neville had been reading Peirce with increasing interest, such that Peirce would soon come to be the foremost pragmatist influence in his subsequent work. The second emphasis is due to the influence of Neville's principal mentor, John E. Smith, a leading interpreter of American pragmatism and a pragmatist in his own right (see, e.g., 1978, 1983, and 1992). Smith had written a number of influential texts focusing on the nature of experience (see, e.g., 1961, 1968, 1970, and 1973), so it was only natural that this theme would find expression in Neville's own work.[12]

Of these two influences, Peirce ultimately proves the most pervasive and definitive for Neville's comparative method. This can be seen from the centrality in his work of a key concept in Peircean semiotics, namely, that of the "vague" hypothesis. For Peirce, "A sign that is objectively indeterminate in any respect is objectively *vague* in so far as it reserves further determination to be made in some other conceivable sign, or at least does not appoint the interpreter as its deputy in this office" (Peirce 1998, 2:351, italics original). That is, a sign is vague if it is capable of further specification in multiple ways, all of which are not necessarily compatible with one another; Peirce contrasts this with a "general" sign, which is specified in the same way in every instance. The strength of this concept is that it allows for the creation of signs that are not wholly determined by the original context of their creation.

Recognizing its immense potential not just for traditional semiotics but also for comparative study, Neville quickly adopted the concept of 'vagueness' into his own thought and began to work out its implications for comparative philosophy. "A Metaphysical Argument" is a crucial text for tracing this adoption: in its original version, the essay only spoke in terms of general hypotheses; by the time it was revised and republished (1982),[13] however, all references to generality had been replaced with references to vagueness. The consequences of this shift cannot be underestimated.

The claim of "A Metaphysical Argument" is that the basic hypothesis of *God the Creator*—that God is the creator of all things determinate, including God's character as the creator—can be expressed in sufficiently vague terminology that it can find specification in any one of the world's philosophical and/or religious traditions, even when those specifications contradict one another or otherwise fail to exemplify the same general characteristics. "Minimally," he writes, "I hope to show that the main claims of the various religions are special instances of the vague hypothesis; although the religions' claims may conflict with each other, they all illustrate the vague hypothesis. Maximally, I hope to show that the vague hypothesis illuminates the religious claims themselves, particularly, that it resolves conflicts between claims by showing that on a higher lever [sic] they are either compatible or identical" (1982, 112–13). This statement reads almost exactly as it did in the original (1973, 217), except that it refers to vague hypotheses rather than general hypotheses. Of course, Neville seems to have *meant* the same thing in the original, but it was less clear why it would be possible for so many different traditions to be instances of the same hypothesis. The introduction of the word *vagueness*, which must have happened sometime between the two editions (in the mid- to late seventies), allows Neville to make that distinction. As will be seen, it is this lithe notion adopted—or, rather, *adapted*—from Peirce that Neville will rely on to do the "heavy lifting" in comparative analysis.

At first glance, it should strike the critical reader as suspect that so Western a concept as a monotheistic 'creator God' is used to express what is held in common among all religious traditions. After all, many traditions have multiple gods (e.g., Hinduism), some have no god at all (e.g., most forms of Buddhism), and some seem to lack even a conception of ontological creation—*ex nihilo* or otherwise (e.g., Chinese Daoism and Confucianism). However, to make such an objection is—in terms of Neville's revised language—to mistake a vague category for a general one. Although the Christian notion of a creator God is one possible specification of the vague category, it is not necessarily the only one, and since it is a vague category, the other specifications need not be the same as, or even compatible with, the Christian one.

To understand how the speculative hypothesis about God can apply to other traditions as well, it is necessary to understand the terms through which the hypothesis is expressed with adequate vagueness. As noted above, the basic hypothesis of *God the Creator* is that God is the creator of all determinate things, including God's character as the creator. More precisely, it states that, insofar as all existing things are determinate (i.e., determinately different from other things), they are ontologically dependent on (i.e., "created by") an indeterminate ground that is of ultimate religious importance (i.e., "God") and whose character is derived entirely from the determinacy of its relationship to all other determinate things (1982, 113).[14] Thus, to demonstrate the adequacy of his vague category of "God as creator," Neville need only demonstrate that every tradition addresses questions about the nature of the world (metaphysics) and the things in it (cosmology) and then to argue that these inevitably address the relationship of determinate things to some ultimate, indeterminate source.

There is not adequate space to rehearse the details of that demonstration here; for that, I refer the reader to the essay itself (preferably in its revised form). It is worth noting, however, that Neville casts a wide net, examining the empirical data of most of the world's major traditions.[15] He does not shy away from considering the traditions that, at first glance, would seem to be exceptions to the proposed hypothesis and is up front about which traditions are most difficult to account for in terms of the proposed hypothesis (see, e.g., 1982, 121). Yet it is not sufficient that a hypothesis merely be able to account for the data of religious experience; as he notes, "[w]hether the hypothesis is *true* depends on whether it interprets experience well" (1982, 125, italics original). The question of whether Neville's hypotheses interpret experience well must be postponed for the moment, since it is best judged with respect to his most recent work; for now, it is sufficient to note that—by virtue of his methodological openness to any and all empirical data—Neville is well-positioned to make a strong claim for the truth of those hypotheses.

For all of the opportunities that Neville had at Fordham and SUNY Purchase to lay out the foundations of his comparative approach, he had still more opportunities to refine this approach with his move to the State University of New York at Stony Brook in 1977. Thomas J. J. Althizer, who had been introduced to the study of Buddhism by the comparativist and process philosopher John Cobb, fostered the development of a faculty at Stony Brook that was deeply interested in issues of comparison. For example, the faculty already included the comparative philosophy of Walter Watson and the nipponologist/comparativist David Dilworth, and Neville soon expanded this interest by hiring such scholars as the comparativist/Buddhologist Sung Bae Park.

This broadened exposure had two noticeable effects on the development of Neville's comparative approach. The first is the cultivation of a more critical appreciation for the role of categories in comparative analysis. While at Stony Brook, Neville was confronted with two opposing views of the role of categories in comparison. On the one hand, he was in continual conversation with his colleagues in the philosophy department, Watson and Dilworth, both of whom were working on their own texts on comparative method during his tenure there. They advocated an architectonic approach to comparison based on the work of Richard McKeon, who adapted Aristotle's categories into a typology for describing philosophical traditions.[16] Watson was the first to develop this typology in detail (1985), but his typology was restricted primarily to Western philosophical traditions; Dilworth's (1989) followed soon thereafter, expanding Watson's work to include non-Western traditions as well. For both Watson and Dilworth, categories are heuristic devices that are determined at the outset of comparison for the sake of elucidating the traditions compared.[17]

On the other hand, he was also in increasing contact with the process philosopher-turned-philosophical anarchist, David Hall, who was also beginning to write on comparative philosophy (soon in conjunction with Roger Ames).[18] Hall, as the reader will recall, maintains that categories are precisely the problem in comparison, as they are inevitably indicative of a parochial and culturally misleading form of philosophy. Hall was thus, for Neville, the effective counterweight to the influence of Watson and Dilworth, for whom the categories are central to comparison.

This dual influence is not to be underestimated, as Neville's own thought about cross-cultural categories was still in its early stages of development. One can see this quite clearly if one looks to *Soldier, Sage, Saint*, one of his earliest attempts at comparison. He writes there that

> the models of soldier, sage, and saint are a combination of historical generalizations of spiritual types with a philosophical construct regarding those aspects of life to which the models might be applicable [i.e., Plato's tripartite division of the soul]. The philosophical construct is responsible for the demarcations of the models. I shall not attempt here to develop the construct in a fully responsible philosophic sense. . . . The construct is needed only for heuristic purposes, to provide a blueprint for drawing out the historically important features of the three models. The philosophical target here is those dimensions of experience illuminated by the models, not the justification of the construct according to which the models are elucidated. (1978, 5)

Granted, the primary purpose of *Soldier, Sage, Saint* was not to lay out and defend a set of comparative categories, but the later Neville would be much more critical of their use in this text. For example, he would point out that the "demarcation of the models" described above is not such an innocent affair but one that is inherently shaped by one's choice of categories.[19] While Watson, Dilworth, and Hall would influence his thought about categories, however, he would not develop a well-formed critique of their positions until much later (see, e.g., Neville 2000).

The second effect the broadened exposure at Stony Brook had on Neville's thought was an increased readiness to engage in direct cross-cultural comparison on his own. This is no doubt due in part to the cross-cultural understanding he had been cultivating since his time at SUNY Purchase, but it was also facilitated and expanded by his contacts at Stony Brook. Moreover, his colleague Dilworth also introduced him to Wm. Theodore de Bary's Neoconfucian Seminar at Columbia University, which further stimulated and cultivated his interest in Chinese philosophy. As will be seen below, Neville would become profoundly influenced by Chinese Confucianism and would make his own contributions as well in return.

This increased readiness to engage in cross-cultural comparison is best seen in *The Puritan Smile* (1987), the last of Neville's books published before he left Stony Brook. In this book, he argues that the Liberal tradition—the dominant tradition in the Western world (at that time)—had exhausted its resources for moral reflection and thus stands in need of a new, or at least supplementary, set of resources for such reflection. In response, he advocates looking to the Puritan and Confucian traditions, each of which has its own shortcomings but which can nonetheless make important contributions to contemporary culture.[20] The final vision he offers, then, is a Liberalism enriched by its encounters with Puritanism and Confucian, and indeed partially Puritan and Confucian in its orientation as a result.

In the process of making this argument, however, Neville must take for granted three controversial claims. The first is that it is possible to extract features (concepts, values, etc.) from a tradition such as Puritanism or Confucianism without thereby distorting those features. The second is that it is possible to bring those features together even when the broader traditions from which they are drawn are contradictory in several other respects (as are Liberalism, Puritanism, and Confucianism). The third is that this "cutting and pasting" of features can lead to the development of a coherent tradition in its own right, rather than a mere collection of disparate parts. These three claims are left undefended in *The Puritan Smile*, because—as he notes in his preface—the text at hand "is not a metaphysics book. . . . It rather is a book in the genre of criticism, taking as its subject matter the need of culture for moral reflection, and the traditions and categories serving as resources for that reflection" (1987, viii). Naturally, the text draws on the metaphysical foundations laid out in his previous works and even indulges in a modicum of metaphysical reflection of its own; yet the project undertaken in *The Puritan Smile* cries out for a metaphysical defense equal to its enterprising comparative claims.

Such a defense was not long in coming. In fact, it had already been initiated with his publication of *The Reconstruction of Thinking* (1981), the first volume in his Axiology of Thinking series (hereafter, "the Axiology"). However, this project would only be completed after 1987, when Neville left Stony Brook for Boston University. Soon thereafter, he published *Recovery of the Measure* (1989) and *Normative Cultures* (1995), the second and third volumes of the Axiology, respectively. These three volumes, taken together, lay out a robust theory of interpretation that would inform all of his subsequent work in comparative philosophy. Although he would further refine this method in his more mature works, the Axiology provides the clearest and most complete exposition of his method. Accordingly, we now turn to a more detailed consideration of these works.

DESCRIPTION OF METHOD

The Axiology of Thinking

According to Neville, the Axiology is intended to provide "a systematic philosophic examination and reconsideration of conceptions of thinking"; indeed, it lays out and defends a new hypothesis about the nature of thought itself. As its name suggests, the main thesis of the Axiology of Thinking is that "valuing . . . is at the heart of thinking" (1981, x). In this way, it challenges all those traditions—and especially the dominant traditions in the West—that distinguish too sharply between facts and values and that typically give priority to the former at the expense of the latter. According to Neville, "thinking is always some kind of valuing," although its axiological dimensions are often suppressed or ignored; conversely, "nearly all kinds of valuing" are interpreted as some kind of thinking, although its cognitive dimensions often remain undeveloped and thus unappreciated (1995, x).[21] In the interest of highlighting and developing these connections, Neville provides a systematic examination of four aspects of thinking (imagination, interpretation, theory, and the pursuit of responsibility) along with the guiding value of each aspect (beauty, truth, unity, and goodness, respectively).[22]

Of the four aspects of thinking/valuing discussed in the Axiology, it is the third of these—theory, as measured by the value of unity—that has the most direct bearing on Neville's comparative method (although a somewhat extended foray into his work on theory is necessary to understand its implications on comparison).[23] Theory, according to Neville, is "that kind of thinking, a family of cognitive activities, that pursues the value of a synoptic vision, both for the theoretical purpose of understanding things in the subject matter together and for the practical normative purpose of orientation" (1995, 30). Consistent with the Greek roots of the term, theory is involved any time that one seeks to see things in connection with one another (syn-optic) or, perhaps more accurately, to "think things together."

Theory brings together one's many interpretations of reality into a coherent whole, proposing relationships among those interpretations that are not reducible to the interpretations themselves.

The guiding value of theory, according to Neville, is importance (1995, 6).[24] 'Importance' is, of course, an axiological term, and a relative one at that: a thing is only considered important if someone deems it to be so, and one only designates something as important relative to other, less important things. The fact that the determination of importance has a subjective element does not, however, mean that it is *merely* subjective. As he argued in *Recovery of the Measure*, value is a real feature of things, interpretations of the value of things are only true to the extent that they recognize that value; hence, he defined truth there as "the properly qualified carryover of the value of a thing . . . into interpreting experiences of that thing" (1989, 65).[25]

What importance adds to the interpretive experience is an assessment of the value of things relative to each other. Interpretations are never isolated to a single object of experience but are rather of the full diversity of objects in one's experience at any given time. Importance allows one to ascribe relative value to these objects and thus to navigate between the diversity of the things interpreted and the desired unity of interpretation (1995, 6). As with individual interpretations, one can interpret the importance of things more or less truly; acting effectively—and thus living well, and ultimately living responsibly—requires learning to interpret importances accurately. Theory is that by which one represents the relative importances of things, and which—at least when done well—allows one to maximize the amount of value that can be realized in any experience.

Of course, Neville is well aware that theory is currently held suspect by many of his contemporaries and that any attempt to exonerate it will run against the grain of most contemporary scholarship. Critics of theory argue that, insofar as theories represent the values of a particular group, they privilege those values over other possible values; consequently, insofar as that theory is applied, its values are imposed on others at the expense of the latter's values. Such axiological imperialism not only marginalizes the values of the less powerful, but at the same time ignores otherwise valid and insightful perspectives.[26] Seeing this as the inevitably result of theory, these critics call for an end to theory in the hope that this will encourage the flourishing of the full plurality of possible perspectives.

Neville is entirely sympathetic to the concerns of these critics but is critical of their proposed solution to these concerns. With his critics, he affirms the now-commonplace claim that all theory is value-laden and that any theory will necessarily impose its values insofar as it is applied. At the same time, however, he maintains that theory is a crucial and inevitable dimension of thinking itself and as such cannot be eliminated without bringing thinking itself to a halt. One cannot "think things together"—that is, understand things in relation to one another—except by selecting certain features among them by which to understand their togetherness; such selection, in turn, cannot occur except according to a particular commitment to the value of those features relative to other features. It is theory that provides our orientation toward the world and ultimately enables us to act responsibly in the world. In short, from the moment we begin trying to make sense of our experience, we theorize, and we bring our values with us.

The proper solution to concerns about theory should not be to feign the evasion of theory altogether; rather, it should be to allow for the improvement of theory itself so that it can represent the value of its objects as completely as possible. Toward this end, Neville proposes the development of a "theory of theories"—an overarching theory that would seek to do for theories what those theories do for their interpretations: assess them in their diversity and seek to bring them together into an integrated whole. The desired result of this theory of theories would be a clearer and more critically informed understanding of theory itself that could inform the further development and improvement of all theories (including itself).

"The challenge for a contemporary theory of theories," he writes, "is to make the case for the possibility of non-reductive theories. Non-reductiveness has been the ideal from the beginning. What is synoptic vision if not a non-reductive view of the whole?" (1995, 21). Nonreductive theories were originally championed by Plato and were distinguished from reductive theories by their commitment to represent the objects of experience as completely and accurately as possible. A nonreductive theory "attend[s] first to aspects of the phenomena that might not be registered within the preliminary theory and make[s] the theory broad enough to recognize them" (4).[27] A better nonreductive theory, then, is one that registers as much of the available phenomena as possible. The charge that theories marginalize the perspectives of the less powerful and distort the reality they represent thus applies most directly to theories that do not remain open to the perspectives they may have overlooked (i.e., reductive theories). Conversely, the best way to address these concerns is through the pursuit of nonreductive theories.[28]

Looking to Plato's account of theory in the *Republic,* and complementing and updating it with reference to A. N. Whitehead, Charles Peirce, and the Confucian tradition, Neville identifies a number of defining qualities and concerns for nonreductive theories. The first is a commitment to *dialectic* as a guiding virtue for the development of theories. To be dialectical, a theory must attend to its own principles at every level of abstraction. Plato did this by pressing his interlocutors to consider the implications and restrictions entailed by their theoretical commitments, to test these against their experience, and to adjust their theory as necessary. More recently, Whitehead posed a fourfold set of criteria for evaluating theories: at the lower, more concrete levels, its principles must be "applicable" and "adequate" to account for the available data; at higher levels of abstraction, its principles must remain "consistent" and "coherent" with one another. Moreover, changes on one level should bring about changes on the other, thus bringing about a hermeneutical circle between the more abstract and more concrete levels of interpretation. For Neville, as for Plato and Whitehead, attending to theories at every level of abstraction helps to ensure that they do not fail to address important aspects of reality that are relevant to their theoretical purview.

A second quality of nonreductive theories is a commitment to *fallibilism*. In the *Republic*, Plato tested a number of different theories of justice, holding each until it was proven inadequate and then adjusting it to address the newly identified need; indeed, by the end of the text, Plato has still not told his audience what justice is (definitively), which Neville would say is precisely the point. More recently, Peirce developed the notion of fallibilism explicitly by describing theories as hypotheses, emphasizing that theories should only be held provisionally and rendered perpetually open to further correction. For Neville, as for Plato and Peirce, a thoroughgoing fallibilism helps to ensure that, if anything of importance has been left out of one's theoretical account, there is always the possibility—if not probability, in the infinite long run—that this synoptic oversight will be amended.

As far as Plato and the subsequent Western tradition can bring the development of a theory of theories, Neville observes that there are two problems for theorizing in the contemporary context that have received only scant attention in that tradition: "the comparison of fundamentally different cultures and the appreciation of the inter-resonance but incommensurateness of overlaid metaphors" (1995, 5). To address these problems, Neville finds and develops resources from the Chinese Confucian tradition, which he notes was addressing these problems as early as the time of Plato.[29]

It is the first of these problems—that of cross-cultural comparison—that is the primary interest of this study. During the Warring States Period (475–221 BCE), the early Confucians had unique experience of realizing that they may be watching their own high culture slip back into a prolonged barbarism. This experience made them realize that their own culture was merely conventional but that it was precisely these conventions that served a civilizing function for them. In *Normative Cultures*, Neville characterizes their position as follows: "Culture is something added to nature in the sense that it provides rule-governed, symbolically meaningful behaviors that overlie, enrich, and complicate natural behaviors, and it is in these additions that human life takes on the excellences of civilization. They called the symbolically shaped behaviors *rituals*. . . . When the Confucians feared the dissolution of civil society and a return to barbarous nature, what they had in mind was the loss of practiced ritual habits" (1995, 14–15). This understanding of ritualized culture shaped the Chinese sense of cultural identity and informed their interactions with all other cultures. For the Chinese, the measure of another culture was not its conformity to Chinese customs but rather the extent to which its own rituals were able to perform a civilizing function for that culture.

Yet herein lies the basic problem: on what basis does one assess the civilizing function for cultures that are fundamentally different from one's own? More broadly, how does one compare any two cultures with such different perspectives, commitments, and means of self-expression? Although the Confucians are important for having considered problems of this sort, they also did not answer the question completely; as with Plato, Neville maintains that their insights must be updated in a contemporary theory of theories.

The second problem addressed by the Confucians is the problem of metaphoric overlay: in Neville's words, "theory needs to be able to recognize the *theoretical* implications of the ways metaphors, symbol systems, and even pluralities of theories pile up on one another in layers" (1995, 17). Due to the irreducible singularity of things, ways of describing things will not always be commensurate with other ways of describing them; in fact, in some cases this is precisely the point, reflective of the difficulty of capturing the singularity of things in words. The Confucians were particularly attuned to this problem, as they were faced with the challenge of integrating their own insights with those of the Daoists and Buddhists, who were often less inclined to express their insights in theoretical forms similar to those of the Confucians. Not all insights relevant to theory will be expressed in readily accessible theoretical forms, but a genuinely nonreductive theory must have the means of appreciating and integrating these insights in their own terms nonetheless.

It is with these four qualities of and concerns for a nonreductive theory of theories that Neville develops his own theory of comparison, which is best understood as a theory of theories applied in the broadest possible purview. This theory of comparison is concerned primarily with the identification, vetting, and improvement of cross-cultural categories for comparison.[30] These categories are intended to constitute corollaries to the "Forms" Plato used for his own theory construction, revised and updated by Neville with respect to the aforementioned Confucian concerns (1995, 74). As will be seen below, these three stages in pursuit of comparative categories incorporate the four qualities and concerns for a theory of theories as described above.[31]

The first step is the identification of possible categories for comparison. Categories, like the theories that give voice to them, must always be selective, and selection always entails loss with respect to the things that are not selected. A nonreductive theory of comparison must therefore work to ensure that the things that are selected are the things that are deemed important in the cultures compared. In order to accomplish this, the comparativist must strive to remain open to the full range of possible sites of importance in the theories compared, no matter their theoretical form or relation to other theories. Neville refers to this as the "representation of integrities" (1995, 56) and utilizes it as a check in the comparative process to ensure that the similarities and differences among things compared are actually similarities and differences that are important to the things compared. What distinguishes this use of comparative categories from most others is that the categories are not determined prior to the comparison but arise directly from the things that are compared; to simply impose categories on the comparison from the outset, according to Neville, would not be to compare them but rather to give expression to one particular theory.[32]

The second stage, the vetting of comparative categories, consists of the attempt to coordinate the sites of importance observed in various cultures in such a way that one can identify common categories by which to compare those cultures. Since there is such diversity among cultures, it would be difficult if not impossible to identify general categories that would represent sites of importance in each culture in the same way with any integrity. As noted earlier, Neville draws on the concept of vagueness developed by Peirce to move beyond this seeming impasse (1995, 62). The phenomena characterized by a vague category do need to specify that category, but they do not need to specify it in the same way. Vague categories can thus represent not only both commensurate and incommensurate specifications, but even contradictory specifications. Such divergence within a vague category does not compromise the category but instead enhances it by increasing the number of ways in which a category can be understood, ways that are not mutually exclusive, but rather represent the multiple sites of importance through which the category can be engaged.

Comparative understanding, then, arises at least initially by translating the features of a given culture into the terms of a broader vague category that is capable of registering the importance of those features for that culture; that culture can then be understood in contrast to other cultures by identifying the other ways in which that category can be specified for other cultures and learning how these relate to the importances expressed in one's own cultural context.

The third stage in the formation of comparative categories arises because this process of forming categories is usually not so straightforward. Often, comparative categories need to be made still more vague to encompass anything important in other cultures, and sometimes the categories must be made so vague that it almost represents nothing meaningful in a culture at all; conversely, further investigation is often required to see if a given culture provides specification of a proposed category, and sometimes this investigation shows that the category has no such specification in that culture. For a nonreductive theory of comparison, there should exist a dialectic between the vague categories and the terms of their specification whereby greater understanding is garnered about each culture not only from the information collected from each culture but also from what the categories themselves reveal about those cultures. Moreover, this dialectic should be understood as an ongoing *process* (1995, 81–82), because comparison is always incomplete—and thus subject to further correction—so long as there remain potentially relevant categories unidentified and specifications not understood in light of their respective categories.

The theory of comparison outlined in *Normative Cultures* constitutes the basic contours of Neville's comparative method. Appropriate to the context of its exposition, the method is well developed in its theoretical underpinnings but less developed with respect to its application in actual comparisons. Granted, his incorporation of Confucian insights into his account of theory is already comparative in an important way, but it constitutes no major advance beyond his earlier works that attempt similar feats. Likewise, while he does undertake minor comparisons in the course of *Normative Cultures*, these comparisons are always only for the purpose of clarifying the theory of comparison itself and are never the primary intent of the study. Rather, Neville's primary purpose in this study was to develop a theory of comparison, a theory that he notes is sorely needed in such fields as comparative religions (1995, 80). *Normative Cultures* proposed a new theory of comparison, organized with the purpose of providing more adequate comparative categories. What remained was the need to apply this theory in the context of sustained, critical, empirical study to identify new candidate categories and thus to provide both validation for theory and further comparative insight.

The Comparative Religious Ideas Project

The theory of comparison laid out by Neville in *Normative Cultures* did not have to wait long for its application: immediately after its publication, Neville was awarded multiple grants to subject his new theory to empirical testing within the context of comparative religions and thus to see whether or not a community of religious studies scholars could arrive at a set of defensible, vague categories that could further inform both the categories and the religions themselves. This project, the Comparative Religious Ideas Project (hereafter, CRIP), consisted of a diverse range of mostly Boston-area scholars, who worked together over the course of four years to investigate potential categories for comparison. The result was the publication of three separate volumes detailing the results of their investigation with respect to each of three categories: *The Human Condition* (2001a), *Religious Truth* (2001b), and *Ultimate Realities* (2001c).

This project made a great deal of sense in light of Neville's context. As the Dean of Boston University's School of Theology, he had the resources to organize a project as extensive as CRIP. Furthermore, in the Boston area, which is home to several world-class universities, he had access to some of the leading scholars in religious studies and related disciplines. There are few other contexts in which a project of CRIP's magnitude could have taken place successfully, and it thus stands at the leading edge of what can be accomplished through collaboration in the comparative study of religions.

There are several intentional limitations to CRIP that must be acknowledged at the outset. The first is that it presents itself as a comparison of *religious* ideas, not of religions considered in the broader sense. The group decided early on that the term *religion* did not constitute an adequate term for cross-cultural comparison, mired as it was in the Western, and predominantly Judeo-Christian, tradition. By contrast, the group had less difficulty—for reasons that are not entirely clear—with the adjective *religious*, so it remained possible to talk about "things religious" if not "religions" per se.

Second, CRIP is presented as a comparison of religious *ideas* rather than of liturgies, practices, experiences, hagiographies, and so on. As it frames its vision, CRIP is surely not opposed to investigations of that sort (i.e., it is not that religious ideas are somehow more important, true, or comparable than any other "things religious"); it is rather that they constitute a manageable starting point supported by a wealth of textual data in each of the traditions compared. True to its fallibilistic form, CRIP seeks not to start in the "right" place but rather to start where it is and then approach a better place through perpetual correction. For better or for worse, the study of religions has long been dominated by textual study and consideration of the ideas represented in those texts and therefore constituted a natural starting point for the project. But, again, the point of CRIP is that it is not where you start but where you end up that matters most.

Finally, CRIP is not intended to represent the final word on the categories proposed. Any one of the categories proposed may turn out to need revision in light of new information or correction of inaccurate or biased interpretations; indeed, the categories may prove to do more harm than good in the interpretation of things religious and may therefore need to be discarded at some later date. The volumes of CRIP are published not because they are complete but rather to make the intermediary results available to the broader body of scholars and thus subject to their further correction. Likewise, there is no suggestion that the three categories proposed by CRIP are in any way exhaustive of the possible categories for comparison; to the contrary, there is every expectation that further categories will be identified by other, similar investigations. Again, the volumes of CRIP are published as models (though not necessarily paragons) of an improved comparative method, one that will hopefully be adopted—and, indeed, *adapted* through further corrections—by subsequent bodies of scholars.

With these limitations understood, it is possible to return to the comparative method laid out in CRIP. At its most basic, the project should be understood as the embodiment of the comparative philosophical vision laid out in *Normative Cultures*. As Neville wrote in the preface to that work, "Examining things from as many angles as possible is the best informal definition of system in philosophy. A good system has built-in requirements for shifting perspectives, for trying to be as complete in examining things as we can imagine, and for repeatedly disconcerting its conceptions of what an adequate array of angles of vision might be. As Paul Weiss says, system is the best guard against dogmatism" (1995, xii). For Neville, it is as necessary to avoid dogmatism in comparative philosophy as it is in philosophy more broadly, and consequently the comparative method he laid out in that text had an intentionally systematic character.

Likewise, the method employed in CRIP—which was largely based on the one laid out in *Normative Cultures*—is also intentionally systematic, with built-in opportunities for "shifting perspectives, for trying to be as complete in examining things as we can imagine, and for repeatedly disconcerting its conceptions of what an adequate array of angles of vision might be" (1995, xii). In CRIP, however, this systematicity was expressed in terms of an on-going *process*, as exemplified in the following statement: "The heart of our conception of the comparative enterprise is that it is an ongoing process, always proceeding from comparative assumptions, formulating comparisons as hypotheses, making the hypotheses vulnerable to correction and modification until they seem steady and properly qualified, and then presenting them for further correction while accepting them as the new comparative assumptions" (2001a, xxii).[33] That is, comparisons are not determined in advance and then backed up with empirical evidence; rather, the comparisons themselves are the results of the process of comparison. Referring to comparison as a process highlights the hermeneutical circle that exists between the formation of hypotheses and the interpretation of empirical evidence: each informs the other as the process of comparison continues. It is this ongoing process that continually develops the categories for comparison, ensuring that they continue to be considered from as many perspectives as possible and thus preventing any hypotheses from becoming too calcified and contrary to the empirical data. In a successful productive process of comparative investigation, the categories that inform comparison at its beginning should almost never inform it at its end (at least not in the same way).

The process of comparison as exemplified by CRIP can be understood as having taken place in seven stages. First, the process required a general theory of comparison on the basis of which to proceed with the comparison. As noted above, for CRIP this consisted primarily of the theory laid out by Neville in *Normative Cultures*. Such a starting point was both necessary and dispensable. It was necessary because it would have been futile to have brought such diverse scholars together in the hope that undirected empirical research would bring forth theoretical goals; while it may be empirical evidence that first inspires comparison, the pump of actual comparison must always be primed with theory. Yet, while necessary, this theoretical starting point was ultimately dispensable: although CRIP would begin with the theory laid out in *Normative Cultures*, it would adapt and revise this theory throughout the comparative process on the basis of critical contributions from other members of the project—something that was welcomed and encouraged by Neville himself. Thus, while Neville had a strong influence on the founding and subsequent direction of the project, it would be inaccurate to say that it was merely an outworking of his own comparative vision.[34]

The second stage in the development of CRIP was the selection of participants on the basis of the needs as laid out by the underlying theory. The organizers of the project decided that it should consist of four groups of scholars. The first group consisted of generalists, whose expertise in subfields of religious studies and related disciplines could direct the broader process of comparison and provide integration for the project as a whole.[35] The second group was made up of specialists in each of six major world traditions, whose primary responsibility was researching the potential relevance of each proposed comparative category in their respective tradition and for ensuring that the integrity of that tradition was not lost in simplistic comparisons undertaken on the basis of their research.[36] A third group consisted of graduate students, each of whom was assigned to one of the specialists to ease his or her research workload; their involvement is particularly interesting insofar as it highlights the collaborative nature of the project, not only among contemporary scholars but also with future generations (2001b, 274).[37] Finally, the fourth group was made up of a number of senior advisors who did not meet regularly with the group but nonetheless reviewed the project at points and offered their guidance; they brought the perspective of a broader community of scholars to the work throughout its formation.[38]

Once the participants had been selected for the project, the third stage was to propose a set of categories for comparison. Since these occur at the very beginning of the process of inquiry, they can only be "best guesses." Neville and Wildman refer to these as "stable hypotheses": stable not because they are no longer subject to correction but rather because there is good reason to believe that they will not completely fall apart when subjected to increased scrutiny (and, likely, correction). In their words, "an hypothesis is stable if many exceptions to it are noted and yet on balance the comparative point holds" (Neville 2001a, 13). Stable hypotheses, then, are meant to be destabilized through further scrutinization but are considered stable to begin with only because it is believed—correctly or incorrectly, as empirical testing will show—that they will be able to survive the destabilization process and emerge more stable as a result. For CRIP itself, six topics were initially proposed (in the original grants), only three of which were explored in further detail—one for each of the first three years of the project, corresponding to the titles of the three published volumes.[39]

Following the proposal of a comparative category, the specialists then departed to research the possible relevance of that category in their respective tradition. Over the course of the next year, in what constitutes the fourth stage of the development of CRIP, the participants would meet six more times to hear the results of each of the specialists. During the first three meetings, each of the specialists would present on some of the ways the category in question might find exemplification and further specification in his or her tradition of expertise. Over the subsequent three meetings, each specialist would follow up on his or her previous presentation with suggestions about how the possible specifications identified in his or her tradition of expertise might—or might not—relate to specifications identified in the presentations of other specialists. This stage constitutes the moment of "destabilization" described above: as applied to any particular tradition, it is hardly to be expected that the category will apply to that tradition in every possible way, much less that it will apply in ways similar to or even consistent with its application to other traditions. Yet, because the category is intentionally vague (as per Neville's *Normative Cultures*), what is of greatest importance is precisely *how*—if at all—the category will find application and what this suggests both about the category under consideration and about the tradition itself.

Once all of the specialists had presented their findings, the participants convened for an eighth and final time, during which attention was directed by both specialists and generalists toward the implications of these findings for the proposed category itself. If the category was found not to have specification in each of the traditions examined, or to have specification that is only trivial, then the category was rejected; subsequently, a new category—stable yet vague—would have to be proposed and tested in the same manner as the previous one (though hopefully with more positive results). If the category *was* found to have specification in each of the traditions, then it was tentatively reaffirmed as a stable category, and the attempt was made to determine the subcategories and specifications of that category in light of the specialists' presentations.[40]

In the sixth stage, the generalists—armed with the vague category and its attendant subcategories and specifications—attempted to provide some reflection on the significance of the category for comparison. While these reflections were based in large part on the research and discussions pertaining to the formation of the categories, they also sought to move the categories from those discussions to a potentially broader application in comparative religion. It was these results that would constitute the final conclusions of the project and that would serve as the founding assumptions—as always, subject to further corrections—for any subsequent investigation.

The third through the sixth stages constituted the mainstay of the project and were cycled through three times over the course of the project. It was only when the process was completed for the third category—thus completing the original proposal for the project (and the funding approved in the original grants)—that the project entered the seventh and last stage. When all of the manuscripts were drafted, the participants held a conference in which several distinguished scholars were invited to reflect, along with the original members of the project, on the project in both its whole and its parts. These outside scholars—each well established in the study of world religions—had only marginal involvement with the project as it developed and thus were able to provide fresh yet informed perspective on the results of the project (Neville 2001a, xv). It was only after this final conference—this final opening of the categories to critical analysis and correction—that the results of the project were published and thus made available for any subsequent work comparing religious ideas.

All things considered, this rigid division of the development of CRIP into seven stages is—while accurate—somewhat beside the point. The core of the project is the dialectic that exists between the determination of comparative categories and the interpretation of the empirical data, as represented by the generalists and specialists (respectively) who participated in the project. While this dialectic was formalized in the actual administration of the project, the two sides of the dialectic increasingly interpenetrated; indeed, one might say that CRIP was at its best when both sides of the dialectic were applied simultaneously. In this sense, CRIP was truly an ongoing process in the organic rather than rigid artificial sense.

What, then, is the method of CRIP? In Neville's own words, "[c]omparative method is a process of framing stable hypotheses, destabilizing them in properly empirical fashion, amending them and recovering stability where possible, and scrapping the hypothesis in favor of a new idea when the time comes" (2001a, 14). In terms of his earlier *Normative Cultures*, this is to say that the best type of theories—nonreductive theories—should always be accepted only tentatively and should always be concerned most with what is obscured in their perspective. For Neville, as for CRIP in general, it is possible to identify valid categories for comparison; the key to identifying them, however, is a carefully crafted, multiperspectival, self-critical, and perpetually fallibilistic method for determining just what those categories are.

ANALYSIS AND APPRAISAL

In what follows, I will highlight the two features of Neville's comparative method that I believe to be the most distinctive: its close association with classical pragmatism and its commitment to broad collaborative investigation. As I will demonstrate, each of these provides clear advantages for his method but is not without its attendant costs. As was the case in the previous two chapters, therefore, the strengths and weaknesses of each feature will be considered in conjunction with one another rather than in separate sections (as was done in the first chapter).

Close Association with Classical Pragmatism

One of the great strengths of Neville's comparative method is its ability to capitalize on the insights of the classical pragmatists—especially Charles

Peirce and, to a lesser extent, John Dewey—by updating, refining, and apply-ing them to the contemporary context of cross-cultural comparison. Neville jokingly refers to himself as a "paleopragmatist" to emphasize his differences from "neopragmatists" such as Rorty and others, whose (re)interpretations of pragmatism run counter to his own. Specifically, while Rorty also draws on the classical pragmatists—Dewey, and to a lesser extent William James—he rejects the metaphysical dimensions of their thought in favor of a radical his-toricism and relativism; Neville, by contrast, maintains that the metaphysical contributions of the classical pragmatists are among their most important and that they provide a powerful alternative to the broader tradition of modern philosophy that avoids the late modern critique (1992b, 13–18).[41] Thus, while many of the features of Neville's comparative method may seem to resonate with neopragmatist commitments, their character and significance are always informed by his commitment to metaphysical realism.

Of the many characteristics of classical pragmatism that are developed and exemplified in Neville's comparative philosophy, there are two that are particularly relevant to his comparative method: fallibilism and fidelity to the empirical data. Both have been introduced in the previous section; each will be highlighted here with respect to the strengths they lend to his comparative method. This will be followed by a more general critique of classical pragmatist contributions to comparative philosophy, focusing on the shortcomings of fallibilism and the relevance for nonpragmatists of a comparative method founded on pragmatist commitments.

VULNERABILITY TO CORRECTION

The pragmatist commitment to fallibilism, as the reader will recall, requires that one treat all theories as mere hypotheses. As hypotheses, they can function in the same way as theories in the more general sense, being used as ways of understanding, rules for action, and so on; the only difference is that they are held only tentatively, being rendered perpetually vulnerable to correction—or even rejection—as new evidence arises. The strength of this commitment is that it allows one's theories to be perpetually improved, whether with respect to something as simple as its further development or as profound as its fundamental reconsideration. In every case, it is the compatability of new empirical data with an existing theory that determines the extent of the change.

As applied to the practice of comparative philosophy, this commit-ment has a number of advantages. The first is that it removes the pressure of trying to start the process of comparison from the "right" place. As em-phasized in the introduction to this book, there is no "right" place to begin; there is only the place where one is. As John Berthrong writes, "One must start somewhere in the task of making comparisons and, if we are honest, we will confess that we start from where we ourselves are" (Neville 2001b,

243). The great strength of fallibilism is that, by allowing for correction and thus improvement where that starting point is inadequate, it allows for the development of an ever more adequate process of making comparisons.

In the context of the Comparative Religious Ideas Project, this allowed the organizers of the project to limit the scope of the project to those aspects to which they believed it could make a significant contribution. A large part of the preface that precedes each volume details the many facets of comparative religion that the project would be unable to consider. Of course, they acknowledge, each of these facets is entirely relevant to the broader comparative vision of CRIP and should rightfully be included in any comparative analysis of religious traditions; however, one can only make so many contributions, and the project appeals to its commitment to fallibilism to address these other possible contributions in the long run:

> The only way to make progress in comparison . . . is to have steady and well-formulated hypotheses to criticize. Does the hermeneutics of suspicion overturn these comparisons? Supplement them by comparisons on behalf of women and the marginalized? Reconstruct the intellectual causal boundaries? To respond Yes to any of these questions and to justify the affirmative answer would be to make solid and important progress. Our comparisons are aimed to be in a form vulnerable to precisely these corrections. (2001a, xxv)

To the extent that it left important concerns unaddressed, it appeals to its readers and critics to address those aspects of comparison that it was unable to address and thus aid in the further realization of its comparative vision.

The second advantage of fallibilism is that it does not limit the value of contributions in comparative philosophy to the ultimate accuracy of those contributions; rather, it grants those contributions the status of works in progress, subject to further correction by the broader body of scholars. One of the prevailing problems in comparative philosophy—indeed, in all philosophy, though magnified in comparison—is that one simply cannot know enough to make accurate and reliable claims about much of anything on one's own. The more novel and extensive the claim, the more likely one is to have gotten things wrong. Fallibilism relieves this pressure by opening up the process of inquiry to the insights of anyone who has a contribution to make, thus allowing an inquiry to incorporate the full range of available expertise on the issue. Thus, Neville can modestly write of comparative philosophy, "The best we can do individually is to make a series of runs at comparative topics prepared by what we know something about, hoping that our friends will fill in what we miss and gently reprove us . . . for the stupidities and wrong directions caused by our thousand lakes of ignorance" (1991, ix). It is nothing new for philosophical traditions to allow for the correction and improvement of positions over time; what makes the fallibilism espoused by the classical pragmatists different is that this openness to correction is built into the theory of inquiry itself. It is welcomed, sought after—expected, even. Accordingly, the strength of a contribution is judged not in terms of whether it is complete and accurate in its own right but rather whether it is able to correct and improve current processes of inquiry. In this way, a fallibilist theory of inquiry not only subsists on its own insights but also feeds on the insights of its most able critics.

Of course, in both aspects of fallibilism, there is no mitigation of the responsibility of scholars to make well-grounded and critically informed contributions. While one's starting point and contributions can be amended and corrected by the broader body of scholars, the value of one's contributions is ultimately measurable by the extent to which it allows for the further improvement of philosophical claims as a whole. What a commitment to fallibilism adds is the confidence that one's own insight, however incomplete and imperfect in its own right, can nonetheless make a positive contribution to the development of comparative philosophy more generally.

FIDELITY TO EMPIRICAL DATA

The commitment to fallibilism is not the only feature of classical pragmatism that Neville brings to bear on comparative philosophy; another equal important feature is fidelity to the empirical data of its subject matter. One of the persistent weaknesses of comparative philosophy over its relatively short history has been its tendency to stray from the empirical data and thus to reach conclusions that are more expressions of the comparativist's own ideological commitments than they are reflections of the traditions compared. The result of this tendency has been a distrust of comparative philosophy and a suspicion that comparison can only be an expression of the power and self-interest of the one comparing. Reflective of his commitment to the empirical data, Neville insists that even this fundamental concern about comparison should be understood as an empirical question to be addressed in the process of comparative inquiry. That is, rather than deciding in advance whether comparison is possible or not, one should pursue it under the best possible circumstances and use the results to help determine whether or not legitimate comparison is possible.[42]

In his own work, he tried to accomplish this by laying out a theory of comparison that takes fidelity to empirical data as one of its basic features in the formation of its basic categories and then offering it to the broader community of scholars for testing (see esp. Neville 1995). This was followed up and expanded in CRIP, where such fidelity was preserved by the involvement in the comparative process of dedicated specialists who could ensure that the comparative generalists did not stray too far from the empirical data. Moreover, the generalists themselves kept careful watch over the development of the project, looking to determine whether and to what extent the hypothesis about the possibility of faithful comparison was confirmed. To this end, Wildman is able to conclude after the first year's completion, "We had improved over the impression-of-similarity approach to comparison because we had detailed descriptions at our disposal that were capable of refuting initial impressions of similarity as more details were drawn into the interpretive picture. We had succeeded in making our comparisons vulnerable to correction by amassing details that comparisons, thought of as interpretative tools, needed to take properly into account" (Neville 2001a, 279). It is precisely because of their reliance on the empirical data, he explains, that the group was able to assess their comparative categories, rejecting those that proved unable to account for the available data, affirm those who prove able to do so, and revise appropriately those that fall in between.

The clearest exemplification of this commitment to empirical accountability, however, is found in one of the hallmark features of CRIP, namely, its refusal to provide specification for its vague categories until the end of inquiry. Broad definition of the category in question would be given at the beginning of inquiry for the purpose of focusing the inquiry itself, but even these broad definitions would be subject to change throughout the process of inquiry.[43] Any significant specification of the categories, however, was resisted until all of the empirical data had been presented; such specification was then pursued on the basis of that data. This arguably reinforced the integrity of those categories with respect to the data from which they arise.

All things considered, the pragmatist commitments adopted, adapted, and exemplified in Neville's approach to comparison come together to create a formidable method for comparison. It is difficult to argue with an approach in which any oversight is a further contribution waiting to be offered, and any mistake is a correction waiting to be made. It is even more difficult when the method seeks to remain open to the full array of possible empirical data. In fact, I would go so far as to say that, if Neville's assessment of pragmatism is correct, then—at least as judged with respect to the infinite long run—there can be no better method for comparison. Indeed, it would seem that any method that would improve on his method could only do so in a manner entirely consistently with his method.

This does not mean, however, that Neville's method is impervious to critique; it simply means that any critiques should have less to do with any shortcomings exemplified in the method's application (since improving on these is a part of the method itself) than with inherent and intractable weaknesses in the method itself (since these may not be subject to improvement). Thus, in what follows I look to the underlying commitments of his method, rooted as they are within the American pragmatist tradition, and offer two critiques of that tradition as it applies to Neville's comparative method. The first calls into question the extent to which a theoretical commitment to fallibilism actually translates into practice when applied to ideas conceived at the highest levels of abstraction and the extent to which it can actually realize all of the aforementioned virtues associated with a perpetual vulnerability to correction. The second questions the extent to which a method rooted in the pragmatist tradition—or, perhaps still worse, in a very particular reading of that tradition—can really serve as a basis for comparative philosophy in a broader sense (as Neville believes it can). Both of these critiques are focused on the theoretical basis of his method but, as will be seen, have a direct and practical bearing on its application.

THE CHALLENGES OF FALLIBLISM AT THE HIGHEST LEVELS OF ABSTRACTION

The first critique questions the extent to which a pragmatist commitment to fallibilism can be a commitment not only of word but also of deed. As noted above, this commitment goes a long way in relieving the pressure of "getting it right" straight from the beginning: it allows one to start from the best conceivable starting point and simply requires that one modestly seek improvement from there through perpetual vulnerability to correction. To state it this way makes it sound simple—easy, even—unless one takes seriously the term *modestly*, which is crucial to the pragmatist account. Here, modest means neither "limited" nor "moderate" but rather something between "humble" and "earnest," where the emphasis is placed on a relentless pursuit of correction despite one's own pretensions or preferences. Understood in this respect, such modesty is anything but simple or easy.

My concern here is that the fallibilism professed by pragmatists is sufficiently difficult as to prove effectively impracticable, at least if one is interested in anything at the highest levels of abstraction and more proximate than the infinite long run. It is crucial to note that the concern here is not simply that fallibilism is difficult as such; of course it is, and no good pragmatist would claim to maintain that commitment without fail. The pragmatist response to this lesser concern is simple: do the best you can (which is the best that can be done, in any event), and trust that such fallibilism as you can muster will strengthen and validate the results of your inquiry to that extent. Given that Neville has made fallibilism such a consistent, central, and explicit feature of his method, it is fair to say that he has been as humble and earnest as any pragmatist in upholding this commitment.

The concern I am raising, however, seeks to assess the viability of fallibilism at a more basic level. One of the distinctive features of Neville's method is its readiness to extend inquiry not only to the most concrete and immediate but also to the highest levels of abstraction. My concern is that fallibilism becomes less and less relevant and applicable as one climbs the ladders of abstraction, insofar as it becomes increasingly difficult to subject such ideas to correction. The empirical data against which abstract ideas would be tested becomes more and more remote from those ideas, resulting in a wider and wider array of ways in which that data can be interpreted.

As the link between theory and empirical data loosens, the otherwise potentially corrective function of empirical data is weakened, and theory is left to stand as it will. At the highest level of abstraction, it is unclear whether fallibilism can have any realistic application at all.

If this assessment of fallibilism is accurate, then a professed commitment to it at the highest levels of abstraction does not simply become an empty gesture; insofar as it promises a check on the results of inquiry—and thus a claim to its reliability—that it cannot deliver, it also becomes a *deceptive*, even *self-deceptive*, gesture. A good fallibilistic theory, even at the highest level of abstraction, may *seem* to account for the empirical evidence (because this is precisely what it is designed to do) even when it cannot actually do so (because of the excessive distance between the idea and the relevant empirical data). Indeed, it can become a protective umbrella under which to pursue a philosophical project that is ultimately unsubstantiable, all the while untrammeled by the objections of those who would rain down their objections along the way. In this way, it can serve—however unwittingly—as a shield from the very vulnerability to correction that fallibilism was intended to provide.

I raise this question because one would expect a thorough-going fallibilist of the sort described above to have a career marked by an ongoing alteration of his or her philosophical positions. Neville's career, by contrast, is marked by a remarkable constancy in his basic philosophical position. Certainly, he has amended his position in a variety of ways over time, but these amendments have primarily been elaborations of positions already suggested in his earlier works. His comparative method is a case in point: embryonic in his earliest work, it has been developed significantly over the course of his career along what appears to be a largely linear trajectory. By contrast, there have been relatively few cases—especially at the most abstract level—where he has found ideas to be erroneous, rejected them, and changed course along the way.

Consider, for example, the concept of 'creation *ex nihilo.*' Neville first defended this idea in his doctoral dissertation (see notes on *God the Creator* above) and has continued to defend this idea over the course of the last forty years. Granted, it is a powerful argument in its own right, and I am unaware of any compelling refutation of it. At the same time, however, it has failed to gain broad acceptance within the academy; to the contrary, when it has been engaged seriously it has typically been met with opposition, especially when employed as a basis for cross-cultural comparison. Despite this relative lack of success, he has continued to argue for its relevance to and importance for philosophy at every level.[44]

This lack of broad acceptance should not be mere aside for a committed pragmatist, especially one of a paleopragmatist ilk. Vulnerability to correction was, for the classical pragmatists, a fundamentally democratic virtue: one of its most important dimensions consists of subjecting the results of one's inquiry to critique by anyone willing and able to take the inquiry seriously. Closely tied to this is the expectation that any failure of those results to gain broad acceptance should signal some failure in the results themselves. If one follows Neville and takes seriously Peirce's definition of truth—"the opinion which is fated to ultimately be agreed to by all who investigate" (1998, 1:139)—one should be prepared to fundamentally reconsider any idea that fails to achieve broad acceptance.[45]

There are a number of explanations that can be given for Neville's constancy despite the limited acceptance of his ideas. The easiest explanation is that he is simply correct about creation *ex nihilo* and that the broader community of inquirers just has not realized it yet. Yet no self-respecting pragmatist—Neville included—would ever claim to have "gotten it right" in any final sense; fallibilism itself is based on a strong recognition of human fallibility. Thus, one should still expect to find at least some significant corrections to Neville's position over the course of his career, changes in course, in addition to any amendments or further developments.

Another possible explanation is that the community of inquirers for Neville's work has simply been too small to provide much critical feedback: despite being a prolific writer, his texts are not read very widely in the academy. Change can hardly be expected if good reasons for change are not forthcoming. Yet this explanation also falls short, as there is always the possibility—and, indeed, responsibility—of unremitting self-critique. Indeed, the lack of broader interest in his work should itself be a critique, at least if Whitehead and Hall are right about the relationship between "interest" and truth.

The most compelling explanation, however, pertains to the extent to which fallibilism is relevant to ideas conceived at the highest levels of abstraction. In this respect, creation *ex nihilo* provides an excellent test case for the question at hand. It is the most abstract of all of Neville's ideas, going to the very root of his metaphysics; in going to the root, of course, it informs all of his philosophical work. It is also the aspect of his work that has proven the least compelling, despite his careful and sustained attention to its defense. The fact that he continues to defend the idea, its lack of success notwithstanding, is a good indication that something has gone wrong in the application of fallibilism—either in the ability of true ideas to convince the broader community of inquirers or in the capacity of mistaken ideas (at least when held by committed fallibilists) to be corrected by that community.

Both of these possibilities bespeak the challenge of rendering abstract ideas vulnerable to correction. The first possibility suggests that Neville is right—or, at least, relatively right—about creation *ex nihilo* but that the idea is so abstract that it is unclear what data is relevant to assessing it and how that data should be interpreted. The second possibility suggests the opposite, that the idea is wrong but is so abstract that reasons for its inaccuracy are equally not forthcoming. Whatever the case, a committed fallibilist such as Neville would take refuge in the infinite long run, pointing out that even the most abstract of ideas will eventually have its day or reckoning; it may just take some time for that day to arrive.

Abstract ideas, however, are not innocent with respect to time: it matters now whether the idea of creation *ex nihilo* is true, especially when that idea is considered in the context of comparative philosophy. One of the things made eminently clear in Neville's ongoing conversation with Hall and Ames is that one's understanding of the philosophical relevance and importance of the notion of transcendence—central to the idea of creation *ex nihilo*—has a significant impact on how one interprets Chinese philosophy at the most fundamental level. Ideas that can only defer their validation to the infinite long run are of only questionable use—and, indeed, validity—in such cases, yet the question of transcendence cannot remain unanswered.

Neville knows as well as anyone the relevance of the most abstract ideas for the interpretation of even the most concrete of experiences and is also well aware of the difficulties in subjecting abstract ideas to empirical testing. His response has been to argue that the most abstract ideas should be treated no differently than less abstract ones, namely, that they should be treated as tentative hypotheses and tested according to the available evidence. For the most abstract ideas—what he calls "speculative systematic hypotheses"—the criteria for evaluation consist of their ability to interpret well the full breadth of possible experience while also satisfying the conditions of logical consistency and coherence.[46] It may be difficult to evaluate such abstract ideas, but one cannot avoid acceding to one hypothesis or another; it is therefore incumbent upon the community of inquirers to get on with the hard work of figuring out which one is most likely true.

For Neville, then, even the most abstract ideas should be the subject of philosophic discussion, since even those ideas are vulnerable to evaluation—and thus, presumably, to correction as well. Here again, however, his ongoing conversation with Hall and Ames proves instructive: despite over twenty years of discussion, they are still at an almost complete impasse regarding the relevance and importance of transcendence for philosophy in general and for Chinese philosophy in particular. Their arguments for their positions have, of course, changed over this period, becoming both more nuanced and more informed as a result of the conversation, but their basic positions have remained unchanged. If so little progress can be made within even this most accomplished subset of the community of inquirers, one must wonder what hope there is for the broader community. Indeed, one must wonder whether such abstract ideas are really vulnerable to correction in any realistic and practicable way.

The question here is not whether Neville's account of the evaluation of speculative systematic hypotheses is valid, or even whether it is applicable in the infinite long run; in both cases, I think, he is on solid ground. The question is rather whether or not this account has any practical bearing on the most pressing and immediate questions in comparative philosophy, questions that cannot defer to the infinite long run for their resolution. Chinese philosophy will be understood more or less by Western philosophers, depending on which basic assumptions they bring to that understanding, and one important assumption will be concerning the philosophical relevance and importance of transcendence. More broadly, Chinese culture will also be understood more or less by Westerners, dependent in large part on the same set of assumptions. Actions will be interpreted, moral characters assessed, policy decisions made—all based on these assumptions—and these choices will not wait on the infinite long run. Making these choices responsibly requires a fair and balanced assessment of such assumptions in the immediate short run.

In sum, however vulnerable to correction the most abstract of ideas may be in the infinite long run, that vulnerability is all but irrelevant in the immediately foreseeable short run. In fact, to the extent that a defense of the most abstract ideas claims validity in the short run on the basis of its vulnerability to correction, it is also inherently deceptive insofar as it claims a virtue in its defense on which it cannot deliver. Whatever the criteria may be for philosophical questions requiring answers in the immediately foreseeable short run, vulnerability to correction in the infinite long run cannot be the primary or only criterion.

Perhaps a short anecdote will help clarify this point. When I was a graduate student at Boston University, I had the good fortune to walk in on a discussion between Neville and Wildman that exemplifies the point at hand. They were discussing whether it is theoretically possible to render ultimate reality in defensible, philosophical language (Neville's position) or whether it must in the final analysis remain apophatic (Wildman's position). The metaphor they used was that of paintings hanging in a museum, each representing various conceptions of ultimate reality. Both welcomed the diversity of representations and acknowledged that such diversity enriched the possibilities for understanding ultimate reality. Where they differed, however, was on the extent to which progress could be made in determining which of the paintings was the best representation in light of the available evidence.

Looking back on that interaction, I find their metaphor to be instructive for the issue at hand. While I am inclined to agree with Neville that, given enough time and discussion, it would be possible to determine which painting was best, I am not at all convinced that such a determination could be made in any reasonable period of time (e.g., the course of a lifetime, or even several). Moreover, this is not how paintings—or conceptions of reality, for that matter—function: most people judge them within a reasonably short period of time and then get on with the business of their lives. Certainly, they may have the opportunity to reconsider these evaluations, but these opportunities are both rare and fleeting while their results are nebulous and incomplete. It is only a very small subset of the population that has the luxury of more extensive consideration, and even their results make only questionable advances over their peers.

The point here is not that there are some levels of abstraction at which no evaluations can be made at all. To continue with the metaphor above, the existence of museums of fine art—as well as museums of bad art—are a testament to the fact that at least some evaluations can be made at any level of abstraction. The point is rather that informed evaluations made at the highest levels of abstraction are much more difficult to come by than a claim to fallibilism would suggest and all but impossible to come by without lifetimes of critical consideration. This being the case, it is unclear that claiming the virtues of fallibilism for such evaluation—or, to return to philosophy, the most abstract of ideas—adds anything to their merit in the immediately foreseeable short run.

For those familiar not only with Neville's written works but also with his approach to philosophic discourse, it should not be difficult to recognize a consequent tension in his work. While he consistently extols the virtues of fallibilism and never claims to make of even his most abstract ideas anything more than a strong tentative hypothesis, one also gets the sense that he is not ultimately content to have those ideas be rendered nothing more than one painting among many in an exhibit. As an equally strong advocate of "public philosophy," Neville is well aware that it matters which ideas we adopt in the short run and that it is therefore important to adopt—as well as to develop and defend—the most compelling ideas possible (see esp. 1992; also 2000, 127–28). He maintains that his argument is the strongest he has encountered and challenges others to find fault with it, correct it, and/or improve it. The sticking point, however, has always been these most abstract of ideas, which Neville at the same time wants to hold tentatively and also to argue for in the public sphere. The problem with all of this for fallibilism, again, is that the most abstract hypotheses both demand an answer in the short run and yet cannot provide reliable evidence outside of the infinite long run.

If the problem with fallibilism and the most abstract ideas is a problem of degree, then the final question must be whether the problem can be mitigated and, if so, how. In other words, how can the infinite long run be brought to bear more directly on the immediate short run? If one takes Peirce at his word, this should entail an intensification of the degree to which the most abstract ideas are considered critically and a maximization of the community of inquirers willing and able to do so. In this respect, CRIP should represent a better test case for fallibilism than Neville's single-authored works, insofar as it brings a dedicated community of inquirers working together over the course of four years to consider some of the most abstract of religious ideas (i.e., the human condition, ultimate realities, and religious truth).

When one looks to CRIP, one does, in fact, see fallibilism in action to a much greater degree than one does in Neville's single-authored works. Part of this can be attributed to the genre: CRIP was designed to display the process of comparative inquiry, whereas Neville's texts follow the more traditional format of presenting only the polished results of inquiry. For example, reference is made at various points in CRIP to comparative categories that were considered seriously, tested, and eventually rejected in the course of inquiry (e.g., 2001a, 279). One would expect that a similar process is undertaken by Neville in his own works, even if it is not reported in its entirety in his published works.

This caveat notwithstanding, however, there is also good reason to believe that CRIP was able to change in more substantive ways by virtue of the intensification of the process of inquiry. For example, Neville and Wildman note how, in the original vision for the project, specialists were more clearly distinguished from generalists: the former specifying the data, and the latter conforming it to broader comparative categories. By the final year, however, the specialists themselves had become sufficiently attuned to the process of comparison to make comparisons of their own, leaving generalists largely to summarize and reflect on the specialists' own comparative conclusions (2001a, xvii). The capacity of the project to adjust for this change suggests that it was not simply the forceful outworking of one person's original vision but rather the careful working out of a collaborative and responsive vision for comparison.

Moreover, CRIP recorded changes over the course of its development that ran counter to some of the fundamental convictions of its main organizer. Especially in the first volume, Neville was committed to the idea that comparative categories should be specified not only in some broad sense for each tradition but also more intricately according to a more precise set of subcategories.[47] The extraneousness of this requirement for the majority of CRIP participants meant that the burden fell on Neville (and, to a lesser extent, Wildman) to try to organize the results of inquiry in that manner after the fact. So burdensome and foreign to the work of the specialists was this task that Neville—at least somewhat reluctantly—abandoned this commitment in the subsequent volumes (2001a, 282–86; 2001b, 5–6). As awkward and uncomfortable as this transition was, it demonstrates the capacity of a committed community of inquirers to alter even some of the most basic commitments of some of its members—alterations that, in this case, would not have been likely to have changed if the inquiry were undertaken by Neville alone.

CRIP did improve on Neville's work in a number of significant ways, and at least some of the improvements came at the cost of corrections to deeply held commitments. What is important to remember about CRIP, however, is that its improvements in this respect—especially as exemplifications of a commitment to fallibilism—are only improvements in degree and not improvements in kind. It was simply not possible to test all ideas completely, and some ideas likely slipped into the process without adequate testing. It is significant, for example, that intimations of transcendence make their way into CRIP (2001b, 274–78), although there was surely not consensus about its relevance to or character in each of the traditions represented.

Still more significant is the fact that CRIP now faces many of the same challenges as Neville's own works: despite the unquestionable qualifications of its participants, the exceptional care undertaken in the construction of its method, and the relentless rigor of its application, CRIP has received surprisingly little critical attention by the broader academy. If the fallibilism at the heart of the project is all that it claims to be, one must wonder why it has not become a methodological landmark for the burgeoning field of comparative religions.

In the final analysis, it is this lack of broader acceptance of the results of inquiry that remains most problematic for methods that appeal to fallibilism. Perhaps no one else on the contemporary philosophical scene has done more than Neville to champion the virtues of fallibilism, and there is surely no comparative method that has better exemplified a commitment to fallibilism than has CRIP. The underwhelming response by the academy to both of these is deeply problematic for any appeal to fallibilism. The only possible respite is an insistence that the academy take seriously the results of inquiry and become the community of inquirers that can critically assess them. Short of this being realized, however, the strength of fallibilism is weakened considerably and—insofar as one takes the broader academy's disinterest in appeals to fallibilism seriously—a sharp rejoinder to any claims of its strength, at least at the highest levels of abstraction. Indeed, short of this, it is difficult if not impossible to distinguish accounts that genuinely intend to be fallibilistic from those that are actually able to be fallibilistic all the way down and perhaps the whole lot of these from accounts that merely feign fallibilism.

The Challenge of the Broader Applicability of a Pragmatic Method

The second critique of the close association with classical pragmatism pertains to its relevance for comparativists who are not classical pragmatists. Again, at first glance, it would seem hard to argue with a method that takes perpetual openness to correction and improvement as guided by the interpretation of all of the available empirical data. Indeed, no matter how errant a claim is, it is always also partially right, and if it remains open to further correction it can always be (or become) a step in the right direction. Yet, as appealing as such a position may appear, it depends on a number of philosophical commitments that many comparativists do not share. Consider, for example, the following extended citation from Neville and Wildman pertaining to CRIP:

> Our judgment about the prospects for successful comparison of re-
> ligious ideas can be summarized in a triply conditional statement,
> as follows. If the category vaguely considered is indeed a common
> respect for comparison, if the specifications are made *with pains to
> avoid* imposing biases, and if the point of comparison is legitimate,
> then the translations of the specifications into the language of the
> category can allow for genuine comparisons. It must be stressed that
> even this conditional judgment is a *provisional, empirical result and
> not somehow guaranteed* in the abstract by some theory of how much
> human beings can know about religious matters. . . . Our comparative
> method does not guarantee that the three conditions can be met;
> it only optimizes the process of comparison. It is our *experience*, not
> our philosophical commitments, that suggests that the three condi-
> tions can be met, sometimes, and so that genuine comparisons can
> sometimes be made. (Neville 2001a, 16, emphases added)

This statement has all the hallmarks of classical pragmatism: a commitment to fallibilism, empiricism, and experientialism. Indeed, it is a passage that, in his moments of more lucid prose, Dewey himself might have written. Neville and Wildman claim that it is their "experience, not [their] philosophical commitments" that brings them to their conclusions about the prospects for comparison, but it is arguably their philosophical commitments that lead them to interpret their experience as they do and to give it such weight over and against other possible interpretations. What, then, are nonpragmatists—or pragmatists of a different stripe (neopragmatists)—to make of this claim?

More specifically, one might consider one of the more questionable philosophical commitments underlying both Neville's work and that of CRIP, namely, the philosophical realism espoused by Peirce.[48] In his essay "The Fixation of Belief," he characterized this commitment as the belief that: "[T]here are real things, whose characters are entirely independent of our opinions about them; those realities affect our senses according to regular laws, and, though our sensations are as different as our relations to the objects, yet, by taking advantage of the laws of perception, we can ascertain by reasoning how things really are, and any man, if he have sufficient experience and reason enough about it, will be led to the one true conclusion" (Peirce 1998, 1:120). Because the position elaborated by Peirce sounds so similar to the naïve realism that dominates most noncritical discourse outside of the academy, it is easy to forget that philosophical realism is by no means a foregone conclusion. At least after Hume and Kant—if not after the medieval Scholastics—it is no longer clear whether the world is in any way how we perceive it to be. Peirce and many of his fellow prag-matists are notable for having enabled a new realism after Kant, based on fallibilism and fidelity to the empirical data (as noted above). Neville and Wildman make this point explicit in their own way in the introduction to *The Human Condition*:

> As Ricoeur and others have pointed out, realism requires the ac-quisition of a "second naiveté." By paying attention to criticisms, insisting that doubts be based on as much concrete evidence as positive assertions, and disciplined engagement with the real subject matter under discussion rather than merely generalized rumors about it, a legitimate route is open to substantive "critical commonsen-sist" embrace of the subject matter. From that embrace comes new knowledge that is, at the very least, an improvement over both what is claimed in the "first naiveté" and what is left after its skeptical rejection. (2001a, 4)

Certainly, "critical commonsensism"—Peirce's description of his own philo-sophical position—is one possible answer to Kant, but it is only one, and it is not the only one. What are those who answer Kant differently to do with Neville's comparative method?

Neville has tried to address this problem in a number of different ways. Philosophically, he has tried to defend his position by giving defini-tion to the criteria by which all positions should be judged. This has already been seen in *Normative Cultures*, where it was argued that the best theory is a nonreductive theory, which seeks to incorporate all of reality into its purview (and to choose judiciously when forced to choose among apparent contradictories). At other points (e.g., *Behind the Masks of God*), he has argued that the best theory is the one that can account for all other theo-ries. Both of these are different forms of the underlying criteria that Neville has carried throughout his work from the very beginning: namely, that the ultimate goal of philosophic theory is to address the problem of the One and the Many, and that the best theory will be the one that best resolves this problem—both in its content and in its form.[49]

As noted earlier, Neville has long maintained that the theory of creation *ex nihilo* provides the best possible solution to that problem. As Wildman has noted, Neville may very well be right about this, as his argu-ment is an unquestionably powerful one; yet it is by no means clear that the identification of this particular criterion for judging theories is anything but an arbitrary one (Yong and Heltzel 2004, 8–12). That is, if one accedes to this criterion, Neville's argument will likely carry the day, but it is unclear why one should agree to do so in the first place. Moreover, if this criterion is in question even within the Western tradition, it is even more so when considered in the context of comparative philosophy, where many traditions have given this problem only minor attention if any attention at all.[50]

A secondary strategy on Neville's part has been to simply try to provide a compelling account of his theory for the sake of convincing others to utilize it. Again, he is able to provide a very convincing defense of his theory, so this is hardly a futile endeavor. It appears to have been sufficient, at least, to carry along CRIP, which was made up of religious studies scholars of no small stature: most of these would not have considered themselves pragmatists—let alone paleopragmatists—but nonetheless found Neville's framework a sufficiently compelling one to organize the project.[51] At the same time, most of those involved in CRIP were religionists rather than philosophers, and Neville has found it more challenging to convince his fellow philosophers. Of course, he can more than hold his own among philosophical colleagues, but when it comes to philosophical disagreements about such fundamental commitments it is difficult to see what can hold sway besides rhetoric.[52]

In the end, whether it is by defining the criteria for good theories or by convincing colleagues more generally, it is difficult to see why one should find Neville's approach to comparison compelling *unless one happens to do so*—that is to say, if one agrees with the underlying commitments of his position, then he makes a very convincing case. Or, if one does not yet agree with his method, it seems to be the power of rhetoric above all else that determines whether or not one will find his method compelling. Yet Neville appears to want more than this. For example, in *Behind the Masks of God*, he writes that, while it is hardly new to compare different traditions or even to reformulate one's own tradition in the context of cross-cultural encounter, "[w]hat may well be new is the attempt to do theology that is normative and comparative and that also takes its audience to be anyone interested in the issue, including theological thinkers in all relevant religious and secular traditions. . . . [M]y aim here is also to do world theology whose worth should be judged from all critical perspectives." Neville takes the global public as his audience not only in theology but also in philosophy and its related fields. Accordingly, the comparative method he lays out in *Normative Cultures* and in CRIP is not intended to be merely a method for classical pragmatists; it is meant to be a method to be taken seriously by "anyone interested in the issue . . . [and] whose worth should be judged from all critical perspectives" (1991, 4).

If this ambitious goal is a weakness in Neville's comparative method, it is because it is a goal that cannot likely be achieved, at least not in a manner consistent with its commitments. While Neville is also an accomplished preacher, he would not want to cede that the strength of his philosophical arguments ultimately lies in rhetoric. Indeed, this is precisely what differentiates his brand of pragmatism from neopragmatism. The problem is that, when one gets down to the most basic commitments driving a philosophical vision, those commitments do not typically translate well across competing visions.[53] This is presumably why there are many who maintain the commitments of the classical pragmatists, and still more who do not. Certainly, comparative philosophy does not require that everyone agree—quite to the contrary, it relies on the fact that they do not!—but the diversity of these commitments, as well as their persistence, pose deep-rooted problems for a comparative method that would seek application across philosophical traditions.

It should be noted that, in his desire to be taken seriously across philosophical traditions, Neville is entirely consistent with the character of comparative philosophy. If the comparative task is a valid one at all, then something of the strength of his method should be able to be translated into the language of other philosophical traditions, and the more careful and concerted the endeavor, the more that should be capable of being translated. This is not to say that translating the strengths of his method into other philosophical traditions should result in its acceptance; Neville's commitments to fallibilistic inquiry run deeper than his commitments to his own arguments. If it can be translated, he would maintain, it can be evaluated, and the prospects for philosophy more broadly should improve no matter what the outcome for what is translated.

Understood in this light, if Neville's attempts at arguing for the broader acceptance of his paleopragmatic method remain inconclusive, it is perhaps only because comparative philosophy itself is still at such an early stage of development. If so, only time will tell whether this effort is ahead of its time, at the cutting edge, or hopelessly optimistic concerning the prospects for comparative philosophy. In the meantime, it is difficult to see what a comparativist with Neville's commitments should do except continue arguing for the method that exemplifies them, on the conviction that this is not only the best exemplification of those commitments but also the best exemplification of comparative philosophy in practice.

Commitment to Broad Collaborative Investigation

As noted above, collaboration is one of the key features of the pragmatist commitment to fallibilism. It has typically been difficult to realize the communal dimensions of that commitment, as research and scholarship in the humanities have traditionally been considered individual affairs. Within the confines of this understanding of the humanities, Neville has sought no less than the classical pragmatists to make his work subject to correction by the broader body of scholars; yet this has had to be a methodological afterthought rather than integrated feature: one develops and publishes one's insights and only then renders them subject to correction.[54] The result, as seen above, is a muted capacity and/or readiness to remain subject to correction and a consequent hindrance of improvement and advance in scholarly research.

As noted in the previous chapter, this limitation was mitigated significantly for Hall and Ames by virtue of their longstanding collaborative work. Yet, if Hall and Ames' approach is impressive for its skill in bringing the insights of two very different scholars to bear on the task of comparison, the Comparative Religious Ideas Project was even more remarkable: it was the collaborative enterprise par excellence. Not only did it allow the classical pragmatist method Neville developed in his earlier works to find exemplification in a broader community scholars, but it also allows that method to be tested and subject to correction within that community. As Wildman notes in his appendix to the first volume, "The project was designed on the assumption that it is not possible to implement and evaluate a cooperative, self-correcting methodology for the comparison of religious ideas without also creating a community of scholars to serve as medium and laboratory" (2001a, 267; see also 2001c, 234–35). CRIP was ambitious enough in its own right, though no more so than in its collaborative dimensions. It is clear from the published work of CRIP that this collaboration was as challenging as it was rewarding, but it effectively confirmed the merits of collaborative work by magnifying it on a scale rarely seen in comparative studies.

As noted earlier, this commitment to collaborative inquiry is modeled on the paradigm for research in the natural sciences. In the natural sciences, it is assumed that there is a real world in which events take place and that this world is the same world for all who would interpret these events; thus, while interpretations may vary, there is nonetheless a common reference point whereby those interpretations can be communicated, tested, and evaluated profitably. The classical pragmatists, who drew on the natural sciences for much of their inspiration, recognized this as well and built collaborative inquiry into their basic method; thus, it is no surprise to see this connection in the work of their heirs. It is largely this commitment to the "method of science" (Peirce 1998, 1:120)—interpreted in subtly different ways by each of them—that the classical pragmatist sought, in the wake of Kant, to reconstruct philosophy in the manner of a science.

Though not a pragmatist himself, Peter Berger highlights this connection when he draws attention to what is at stake in CRIP, namely, the possibility of scientific knowledge in religious studies. He writes that "if there is no conceivable 'natural reason' on the basis of which different ideas can be compared and assessed, there can be no such thing as 'science'" (Neville 2001a, xiv), and if there is no such thing as "science" in religious studies there can be no such thing as comparative religions as undertaken by CRIP.[55] Of course, religious studies is not as susceptible to controlled and repeatable experiments as the natural sciences, but it is nonetheless susceptible to constructive critique and enhancement from fellow scholars and thus can arguably benefit no less from collaborative inquiry. Indeed, it is the possibility of such communication among scholars that stands as the basis not only of CRIP's collaborative method but also of the possibility of comparison itself. Thus, the project's commitment to such inquiry should be seen not only as a natural extension of its commitment to the possibility of scientific knowledge in religious studies (if it can be known scientifically, it can be shared) but also as a bold litmus test for the possibility of their own comparative project (if it can be shared, it can be compared).

This simultaneous commitment and litmus test is made all the more profound methodologically by the intentional transparency of the project. In addition to the descriptions of the vague category investigated in each volume and the many chapters specifying that category in the different traditions compared, the volumes of CRIP also provide multiple chapters of intricately detailed and self-consciously critical reflection on the philosophical method employed over the course of the project. It also includes a number of insightful forewords and later chapters written by generalists and senior advisors providing additional detail and critical relief with respect to a number of facets of the project.[56] Equally important is the fact that the changes and developments that the project experienced over the course of its tenure were deliberately preserved in the three volumes that corresponded to it; as a result, readers can get a sense for what the process of comparison actually entailed for its participants.

With respect to transparency, however, the most insightful resource in the texts of CRIP is undoubtedly the three appendices penned by Wesley Wildman. Each appendix—one for each volume—tracks the development of the project for that year with remarkable openness, honesty, and candor. This stands in stark opposition to what readers usually receive in comparative texts: an exquisitely finished product, airbrushed to conceal any potential flaws and streamlined to obscure any trace of the process that lead to its completion. By contrast, the appendices draw their readers into the process of the project itself, not merely to witness it but also to experience it (albeit vicariously), to provide additional corrections for it, and to continue it in new venues.[57] Large-scale collaborative ventures such as CRIP are all too infrequent, though justifiably so in light of the practical challenges such ventures entail; by recording all of these challenges and reflecting on their attempted solutions, Wildman effectively speeds up the learning curve for future comparativists and thus makes it more likely that further ventures like CRIP will not only be attempted but also undertaken successfully.

By including these appendices, CRIP holds true to its commitment to comparison not only as an *ongoing* process but also as one that can be communicated profitably (even if not completely) to anyone interested in contributing to the project, even among those not originally involved in it. Perhaps the ultimate test for the project, then, is not merely the success it had among its own participants, but moreover the success it has among future generations (cf. 2001b, 274). If comparison is truly a scientific endeavor, then the process of CRIP—no less than its results—should be able to continue to inform future generations of comparativists.

Unfortunately, this commitment to collaboration does not come without a price, and it is a price that CRIP had to pay throughout the process of its development. What makes collaboration valuable is the diversity of perspectives that it can bring to the discussion; at the same time, however, it is precisely such diversity that often stands in the way of the success of a collaborative effort. Anyone who has participated in collaborative efforts knows that it is wishful thinking to expect that success can be realized without compromise, and compromise always entails loss. Yield to the lowest common denominator, and the collaboration will be too facile to have any real bearing; sacrifice the goal of coherent conclusions, and the collaboration will be too diffuse to make any identifiable contribution. Since both aspects of collaboration are important for success, there must be a "sweet spot" somewhere between these competing aims that balances the two goods. The questions at hand are thus what that middle ground is and the extent to which CRIP was able to adequately approximated it.

It is clear that the organizers were concerned with addressing both aspects of collaborative work (see, e.g., 2001a, xviii). This is seen best in the way that the project was structured to consist of both specialists and generalists, each of which had different and often conflicting concerns with respect to the process of comparison. On the one hand, specialists brought the diversity of the world's most prominent religious traditions to bear on the process of comparison, and each had an interest—both personal and professional—in ensuring that the integrity of the tradition they represented was not compromised by overly simplistic comparisons. On the other hand, the generalists brought to the project a background in comparison and an interest—no less personal and professional—to see what, if any, the commonalities among these traditions are.[58] Certainly, each group was interested enough in what the others brought to the project to take part in it collaboratively, but this hardly mitigated the tension between their respective concerns.[59]

In those cases in CRIP where perspectives among participants conflicted, they are typically presented by Neville and Wildman—who penned most of the chapters describing the method—as a healthy, productive, and even intentional tension, designed to balance the competing goods of the project and thus provide multiple points of potential correction for it.[60] Neville and Wildman are surely right that such tensions can serve a productive role; however, they can also prove to be frustrating impediments, if not outright stalemates. The question, again, is which it was for CRIP and why.

There is certainly ample evidence that there were elements of healthy, productive tension throughout the project. For example, even though the project was organized around a prevailing tension between generalists and specialists, the specialists soon found themselves making comparisons of their own, and the generalists found themselves making contributions from their own areas of specialization. As Neville observes,

> We are pleased to find now that all of us engage in comparison, each in ways reflecting our beginning tendencies *but even more what we have learned from one another in the collaboration.* Moreover, as the group became conscious of itself as having an integrated identity, with habits of language and thought developed through time invested together, we came to think of our project in terms of the *comparisons to which we all contribute* rather than merely the comparisons each of us makes as influenced by the others. (2001a, xvii, emphasis mine)

As Neville was quick to add, this process was "by no means complete" (xvii), but it is sufficient to demonstrate that the tension put in place between generalists and specialists was capable of producing mutually enriching and productive results (2001a, 177). Thus, Neville is able to conclude at the end of the first volume that "we hope . . . to have shown that our collaborative discussion has made real progress in identifying how religions, at least in the branches we studied, do have vague comparative elements in common and specifying them differently in something like the ways we suggest" (264).[61] Consistent with this, Neville and Wildman would track the course of this development over the course of the three volumes of CRIP, concluding in the end that the relative success of the collaborative dimensions of the project had indeed confirmed the feasibility of their broader comparative method (see, e.g., 2001b, 270; 2001c, 221).

Yet tensions between the scholarly expertise and commitments of the participants did not always manifest themselves in such a productive manner. As Neville notes, "There have been some discouraging times when we realized just how hard it is to learn to think together without dropping to a lowest common denominator, or giving in to pressures for consensus, or quickly agreeing to disagree without pushing the arguments as far as possible" (2001a, xviii). While these challenges differed over the course of the project's development, they can all be understood within the context of coming to terms with the conflicting goods of diversity and coherence.

During the first year of the project, these challenges pertained primarily to understanding and appreciating the diversity of the insights and concerns of the group's participants in context of the drive to arrive at consensus conclusions. Above all, this was true of the tension between the generalists and specialists. On the one hand, specialists had difficulty comprehending the complex philosophical method underlying the project. For example, participants were asked to read the chapter on comparison from Neville's *Normative Cultures* for the group's first meeting, and their difficulty in understanding and appreciating it was clear from what Wildman characterizes as the group's "first blank look" (2001a, 274). Granted, Neville's work is demanding and its language highly specialized, but his method was one of the major contributions he stood to make to the project, one that was made all the more challenging by the diversity of the participants' backgrounds. As Wildman recalls, "I was half convinced that the whole project was impossible, that the group was too diverse to achieve anything, that the method was impossible to test, and that we would never become sufficiently comfortable with each other to speak up when we didn't get it. And I doubt that I was the only one with such thoughts." He insists that "it could only get better in those respects" (275), and it appears from the volumes that follow that it did to some extent, but it is also clear that at least at this point the very diversity of the group could prove prohibitive (see, e.g., 2001c, 222).

On the other hand, the generalists had difficulty understanding and appreciating the concerns of the specialists with respect to the way that they could represent the traditions for which they were responsible. This can be seen, for example, in the ongoing debate between Neville and Paula Fredriksen (the specialist in Christianity) regarding the possibility of anachronism in philosophy.[62] Fredriksen was concerned with the perpetual attempt in comparison to use the data of particular figures, texts, and movements to characterize broader traditions; philosophy, she pointed out, had no corollary to the critique of anachronism, and insofar as comparison is guided by philosophers (as CRIP, for the most part, was) this jeopardizes the feasibility of the comparisons themselves. Consistent with his philosophical commitments, Neville argued that such a corollary could be found in at least some philosophical traditions, including the one elaborated in CRIP and that it should therefore be able to be detected as part of the comparative method itself.

Wildman writes of this encounter that "this was a moment of genuine intellectual excitement: archetypal historian meets archetypal philosopher in a critical dialogue. It's just as good as historian meets phenomenologist, or tradition-specialist meets comparative-generalist" (2001a, 282). However exciting the encounter, however, it also represented a methodological impasse, with Fredriksen unable to convince Neville of the validity and relevance of her concerns despite his method, and he unable to convince her of his method's capacity to address those concerns. In short, it is another example where the tension of opposing goods brought by diversity acted not as a productive tension but rather as an impediment to more productive inquiry.[63]

The net result of this mutual failure was a conclusion to the first year's project that was noticeably disconnected from the year's collaborative inquiry. Due to their discomfort with the underlying method, specialists remained skittish about making cross-cultural comparisons of their own and thus effectively left that task to Neville and Wildman after the first year's conclusion.[64] Neville and Wildman, in turn, were primarily concerned with making such comparisons, yet because their comparisons were informed by the very method that remained somewhat foreign to the specialists, their results proved largely unrecognizable to the rest of the group. In the end, this result left all of the participants dissatisfied (2001a, 282–86; 2001b, 3–6) and convinced that "there had to be a better way" (2001a, 285).

In light of this general dissatisfaction, the group decided to "give up the goal of fully cooperative comparisons for the first volume and allow the generalists to say what they wanted in the conclusions, so long as it was accurate, while the specialists would be content to take responsibility for their own chapters only" (2001a, 285). Both Neville (2001c, 223) and Wildman (Neville 2001a, 285) acknowledge that, while this relieved many of the participants' immediate concerns, it also represented a partial failure in collaboration, one that produced a partial rift between the contributions of the generalists and specialists. While this rift would be mended to some extent over the course of the next two years (2001a, 286), as Wildman notes, "we never completely achieved the goal of cooperative work that took us *as a group* all the way from data to consensus conclusions" (2001a, 286, emphasis mine; see also 2001b, 262).

The challenges of the second year were of a different sort. It was clear that specialists had gradually become more comfortable making comparisons of their own, but they were also more explicit about their methodological objections and concerns; likewise, the generalists became more willing to loosen the method and allow for a greater plurality in the findings of the specialists but also more focused on encouraging the specialists to drive toward comparative conclusions. In short, the group seemed to have learned from its shortcomings in the first year and was prepared to move forward with better habits of collaboration in the second (2001b, 262).

The way that the group sought to move forward was by making a virtue of its pluralism. As Clooney noted, given all of the seemingly irresolvable diversity among the project's participants, the group "might as well make some good come out of it. That is, these volumes are interesting in part because people like you [presumably, Neville] and people like me are both contributing to them, such that we are claiming that different ways of writing and thinking can come together" (2001b, 154). Consistent with this sentiment, the participants decided to remain responsible only for their own contributions to the project—and indeed free each other from remaining bound by the contributions of others—but also to increase the critical dialogue shaping each participant's contributions.

The problem with this way forward is that, while it avoided the sharp and unexpected disjunctions of the first year, it not only finalized the failure to arrive at consensus conclusions about its comparisons, but it also magnified the inconclusiveness—indeed, the inconclusability—of the project. One of the consequences of specialists taking more explicit exception to the underlying method meant that more of that method had to be called into question than previously necessary. Now, holding one's hypotheses only ever tentatively is a high virtue in pragmatist theories of inquiry, but it is also maintained that one cannot call into question too many of one's assumptions at any given time; one needs those assumptions to test the other assumptions in question. What I am arguing here is that, by opening itself up to the objections of its specialists at such a fundamental level, the method has been rendered susceptible to such question as to be of only questionable utility.[65]

Perhaps the best example of this is found in Eckel's chapter on Buddhism in the second volume (2001b, 125–50). There, he points out that Buddhism often constitutes the "knotty exception" in the comparison of religious traditions and suggests that it might serve a similar role in the philosophy of comparison as well. Specifically, the Mādhyamaka tradition of Buddhist philosophy pursues the question of ultimate reality in a way that not only is different than other traditions but that moreover challenges the very notion of an ultimate reality. He writes,

> If our procedure is to identify "vague" concepts (concepts with broad reference) that allow further "specification" (narrow reference), the Mādhyamaka approach to reference presents a serious barrier. Mādhyamikas simply do not use words this way. If our intention is to identify comparative concepts in a way that Mādhyamikas would recognize as productive, it would be better . . . to look for interpretive principles or orientations that govern the traditions approach to ultimacy rather than for descriptive terms that name a fixed reality. One way to do this would be to pursue the Madhyamaka suggestion that the ultimate is rational, requires a distinction between ultimate and conventional, and yields no stable foundation or resting place. . . . Another productive way . . . might be to put the microscope on the "breaking" of symbols as explained in *The Truth of Broken Symbols.* . . . Mādhyamikas speak of their terms as "metaphors" (*upacāra*), but in a way that constantly suggests instability of reference. They would not say that there is any stable process of analysis that can determine what a metaphor definitively "means," if by "meaning" we expect to find the object or reality that the word finally names. (2001b, 127)

In short, Eckel finds that the Madhyamaka tradition not only does not conform very easily to the categories posed for comparison, but it also challenges the very way that the categories are compared. It drives to the heart of the compative method that Neville brings to the project—its commitment to philosophical realism—and asks whether a nominalist commitment is not also welcome in the process of comparison.[66] If a comparative method is to take seriously the traditions it compares, it must also take seriously the philosophical commitments of those traditions—not just seriously enough to try to represent them well in the comparison, but also enough to allow for the validity of their insights.

Neville and Wildman's response is an interesting one: on the one hand, they maintain a ready sensitivity to these concerns, shifting their terminology away from the more realist tone of the first volume to allow for the possibility of nominalism in the second volume. For example, in their introduction, they write that "[u]ltimate realities, in the plural, refers to ontological ultimate reality (which may itself be plural) on the one hand and anthropological ultimate reality (which also may itself be plural) on the other" (2001b, 2). Similarly, they note, "We try hard in this volume not to assume that we know what the ultimate realities are and then cite which aspect this or that text or tradition reveals. That is made easier by the fact that we (the entire group) are in severe disagreement among ourselves on that question as well as on the question about whether we can know much about ultimate realities anyway" (2001b, 3). On the other hand, however, they continue to defend the realist commitments of the method and their importance for the method and take pains in *Ultimate Realities* to rehearse their arguments in light of the data presented by Eckel and others.[67]

The reason why the mediating position Neville and Wildman take is such an interesting one is that it preserves the dual goods of the project: it remains open to the diversity of the empirical data, while also maintaining the methodological structure necessary to make comparisons. If the nominalistic alternative commended by Eckel was not incorporated into the underlying method, it was only because doing so would have rendered it unable to make any meaningful comparisons: just as there is no neutral position from which one can compare all traditions, so a method that is open to all possible commitments becomes no coherent method at all. While pragmatist methods of inquiry have long affirmed rendering all commitments subject to further inquiry, they have also recognized that one can only inquire into so many commitments at a time (one needs to maintain at least some commitments to pursue the inquiries at hand). Accordingly, the *modus operendi* of CRIP has been to start with a promising set of commitments and work from there.[68] At the same time, it incorporates Eckel's contributions and thus makes them available for further inquiry by future scholars, thus preserving another potential site for further correction that could not be explored adequately at present. In this way, it provides what is arguably the possible balance between the competing goods of diversity and coherence that was possible under the circumstances.

In the third year, the project seems to have hit its stride, having productively resolved those tensions that it could and remaining susceptible to those that it had been unable to resolve. On the positive side, there was not only a greater sense among the group of how the categories operate in the context of comparison but also a better sense of what categories and subcategories would be relevant to the vague category at hand, all based in large part on the experience garnered through the previous work of the group (2001c, 229–30). Moreover, there was also a naturalness that accompanied the specification of those categories that, because it was no less faithful to the empirical data, was a strong testament to the collaborative success of the group. At the same time, however, the group remained unable to arrive at consensus conclusions, although this failure had now become such an accepted limitation to the project that it no longer hindered its execution, and, in fact, seems to have aided it in the added freedom it allowed its participants to pursue their own comparative conclusions. All things considered, the project seems to have been at its best over the course of its third year of inquiry and thus stands as the best evidence of what the project could achieve *qua* collaborative venture (see, e.g., 2001c, 221).

From a classical pragmatist perspective, this makes a great deal of sense. If truth is as Peirce described it—as "the opinion which is fated to be ultimately agreed to by all who investigate" (1998, 1:238)—then unrelentingly fallibilist inquiries such as CRIP should improve over time. This is one of the underlying commitments of the project and presumably why it sought to pursue its inquiry over the course of its four years. Indeed, it is its very longevity that sets it apart from almost every other comparative inquiry.

In this sense, time is no less a part of CRIP's comparative method than is the community of inquirers itself. The diversity of its participants may have slowed down the inquiry, but this brings with it a greater possibility for mutual correction that the organizers of CRIP deemed well worth the extra time.[69] If there is one thing that all of the participants could agree on, it would seem to be that the project was better for having pursued its inquiry over so many years (certainly, it would have been a questionable success if it had restricted its inquiry to a single year). It was arguably these corrections—affecting even the method of the project itself—that constitute the mainstay of the project's contributions.

If all of this lauding of the methodological importance of time is true, however, the project would presumably have been even more successful if it had extended its inquiry over an even longer period of time, so it is worth asking why the project opted to end where it did. According to Wildman's account, Neville decided not to apply for additional funding for the continuation of the project for two reasons: on the one hand, it seemed that enough inquiry had been undertaken to evaluate the comparative method employed; on the other hand, the identification, specification, and refinement of comparative categories was a task without end, and it seemed best for this particular group of participants to bring the inquiry to a close at that point rather than later (2001c, 228–29). This is an interesting conclusion for a committed pragmatist to draw: all things being equal, more inquiry is always better, especially when it is so extraordinarily collaborative, and all of the basic conditions for the continuation of the project seem as though they could have been met. Clearly, there must have been something else at play in the development of the project.

What that "something else" seems to have been is something that is pivotal to but often unacknowledged in pragmatist theories of inquiry: the finitude of its inquirers. For one, the participants seem to have simply become exhausted by the enormity of demands of such a large-scale project (2001c, 228–99; 234). At the same time, the inability and/or unwillingness of participants to take the necessary steps to further improve the collaborative dimensions of the project suggested that the project had exhausted its capacity to further develop the underlying method (222–24). Certainly, in a perfect world, additional time would have continued to allow for further improvements; in this work, however, both time and the ability to work together are limited by human finitude, with the result that even the most ambitious projects often fail to achieve their aims, at least in part, if not in their entirety.

Of course, the fact of human finitude was not something unknown to the pragmatists, and it is something about which CRIP was also well aware. Rather, both maintained that, even if inquiry could not be pursued under perfect conditions, it is still best pursued by a community of inquirers over time since this allows for the greatest vulnerability to correction. Ultimately, improvement is not a guaranteed result of inquiry, but something that can be achieved to a greater or lesser extent dependent largely on how the inquiry was executed. For their part, the organizers spent a great deal of time considering how to maximize the potential of their admittedly finite process of inquiry.

At first glance, then, it would seem hardly interesting—let alone helpful—to point out that CRIP was limited by its own finitude. Yet, at a deeper level, I would suggest that this is something for which the project did not take adequate account, and which therefore at least in some cases worked against it. If finitude can limit the outcome of inquiry, then all such possible limitations need to be considered at the outset of inquiry—and in a fallibilistic inquiry, throughout it as well. Yet, in the context of planning and carrying out a collaborative inquiry, there are important limitations that the organizers of CRIP seem not to have adequately considered.

The overlooked limitation most relevant to this study is the impact of the group's diversity on the possible efficacy of the inquiry. Certainly, the project's organizers consistently express their awareness of the challenges that such diversity brings with it, but they consistently frame this not in terms of its negative potential to compromise the project but rather in its positive potential to provide additional sites of correction to it.[70] This orientation toward the challenges is evident in Wildman's comment, "The behind-the-scenes story of the project is how the CRIP scholars came together to forge an effective working group—despite profound disagreements that were introduced by design in order to strengthen the group's ability to make persuasive comparisons through juxtaposing points of view and types of expertise" (2001b, 261; see also 2001c, 227). The organizers of CRIP are arguably right about the possibility and importance of forging such a community, especially when understood in the context of producing results that are to be offered to the broader academy. In discussing all of this, however, they never give serious consideration to the possibility that the challenges of forming such a diverse working group could prove too much for the fledgling method underlying it to support; rather, they take the project for what it was and appeal instead to what such diversity could possibly contribute to the project.

Consider, for example, the objection raised by Eckel with respect to the realist commitments of the project: he argued that those commitments ran counter to the tenor of Mādhyamaka Buddhist philosophy, which compromised the method's ability to represent that tradition. Neville, for his part, provided a philosophical defense of those commitments, while also insisting that they were—like the entire method—always subject to correction. Yet that was as far as the objection was able to go in the context of the project's discussions. Neville writes of the specialists,

> They bumped against the theory hard enough to see its sharp edges and hence to recoil in favor of narrative, for instance, or swinging attacks on metaphysics. But they did not get into the philosophy enough to go the next step, to see how the theory acknowledges and attempts to answer those criticisms, and to engage more thoroughly on those levels. Objections were often left at the level of merely citing alternatives, saying that the alternatives seem more congenial to some specific texts or traditions without exploring how the theory would respond at the level of theory. (2001c, 222)

Neville attributes this failure to an unwillingness on the part of the specialists to master the necessary philosophical language to debate this question, but I think it has more to do with inability than unwillingness. The objection raised is a serious one, and it is difficult even for trained philosophers to navigate the question clearly, let alone religious studies specialists-become-philosophers. Even for participants with a background in philosophy, there does not seem to have been adequate space within the project to give careful consideration to these questions. In other words, in this context I think it is the diversity of CRIP itself that has gotten in the way of the project's progress.

That there can be too much diversity is an idea that is hardly new to the organizers of CRIP. The prefaces to each volume list in detail the many topics for comparison that were excluded from the project for sake of sheer practicality. For example, Neville and Wildman write,

We focus on the old-fashioned approaches of textual studies, literary analysis, historical research, philosophy, and methodology itself. This was a deliberate choice on our part in order to work our effective collaboration. If collaboration has seemed difficult and occasionally baffling to us, think what it would have been if it had to include the vast array of other approaches to religious studies. That we do not include them does not mean that we reject them nor deprecate their importance. Rather, it means that our approach to the religious ideas of the traditions we cover is fragmentary. The strength of our approach in their matter, however, is precisely here: we are clear about the limits of what our literary methods can do, and it will be a great advance when our comparisons are corrected by what arises from outside those limits. (2001a, xxiv)

Given this awareness, it is curious that they do not give any substantive consideration to the possibility that the project in its current form still encompassed too much diversity. This may have been a purely practical consideration, as the project could hardly adjust the scope of its participants midstream, and it would have been counterproductive to rue the diversity under those circumstances; yet, given the thorough-going self-assessment of the project and the importance of the consideration for the method itself, it is surprising that this is not even discussed in the closing of the third volume.

Instead, Neville and Wildman address the open-endedness of the project in a variety of ways. For his part, Neville mulls over what might have been done differently to encourage greater coherence and integration of the project's conclusions (2001c, 224). Alternately, in a coauthored passage that seems to bear more of Wildman's imprint, they express hope that the apparent chaos of diverse voices "will in time yield to something more like the organized frenzy of the natural and social sciences" (2001b, 232; see also 2001c, 213). What both of these responses overlook is that the level of diversity in the project itself may be behind the failure to arrive at more coherent and integrated solutions.

There seems to be an assumption among the organizers of the project that any level of diversity in the project will, in time, make a constructive contribution to the project. What I am suggesting here is that there can be too much diversity within a finite project and that such excess diversity can actually work against it—not only making coherent and integrated conclusions more difficult in the short run but also making them less possible entirely. At its worst, excessive diversity can even compromise otherwise promising insights by making them seem too unclear to present viable collaborative conclusions, thus shutting off any further consideration.

All of this is not to suggest that diversity is somehow antithetical to successful collaboration; to the contrary, as noted at the very beginning of this section, diversity is crucial for such success, understood in the broadest possible sense. Rather, in the context of finitude, diversity can both help and hinder a collaborative project, and in any finite project it will likely do some of both. It is a good that brings with it its own challenges, and collaboration is more successful when it only incorporates as much diversity as it can profitably digest.

In sum, it is without doubt one of the distinctive and invaluable contributions of CRIP to have pursued and largely realized a thoroughly collaborative process of inquiry, which draws together an exceptional diversity of participants who are nonetheless able to work together with remarkable productivity. The collaborative character of the project not only magnifies what the group is able to accomplish but also strengthens its results by virtue of the many sites of potential correction. Moreover, it is made all the more distinctive and valuable by the self-conscious and critical documentation of that process along the way, which by virtue of its apparent success and ready transparency can serve as a model for future processes of inquiry.

At the same time, it is not an unqualified success, as the challenges of collaboration also proved to limit the possibilities of the project in significant ways. Without doubt, CRIP is one of the most—if not *the* most—ambitious cross-cultural comparative projects of our time, and it should come as no surprise that it may have been a bit too ambitious in certain respects (as noted here, with respect to the diversity of its collaboration). All things considered, though, the positive aspects of its commitment to broad collaboration easily outweigh the negative ones, such that—even if not an unqualified success—CRIP arguably represents a model for collaborative inquiry that future undertakings could do worse than emulate. In fact, it is the hope of this author that projects that even approach the collaborative success of CRIP are not long in coming.

In closing, it is important to point out the important parallel that exists between collaboration and the comparative task more broadly. Recall Wildman's comment, cited at the beginning of this section, that "[t]he project was designed on the assumption that it is not possible to implement and evaluate a cooperative, self-correcting methodology for the comparison of religious ideas without also creating a community of scholars to serve as medium and laboratory" (2001a, 267). If it is not possible for a diverse community of scholars to communicate effectively in the process of inquiry, then one could hardly expect the traditions they represent to be brought together comparatively in any meaningful way.[71] In this light, the remarkable success of CRIP in the former testifies to the validity of its success in the latter.

Moreover, if the collaboration was not an unqualified success, this too arguably reflects the nature of comparison itself. Collaboration, like comparison itself, is arguably not such a neat and tidy endeavor, as CRIP found out in its second year of inquiry. One takes one's best guess in advance, but one never knows where the collaborations or comparisons will lead. Indeed, they often lead in multiple directions, rendering it unclear which path is the right one or even whether there is only one right path (e.g., the difference in vision between Neville and Eckel). What is needed in both collaboration and comparison is a certain allowance for messiness (cf. 2001b, 7), a messiness that is sufficient to clear space for creativity but not so much as to devolve into absolute chaos. Coupled with a methodological commitment to fallibilism, this provides the grounds for creative advance, which is both the sole claim and great achievement of CRIP.

CONCLUSION

The comparative method developed in Neville's works and exemplified in CRIP is, all things considered, a robust and formidable approach to comparative philosophy. While it has shortcomings, these pertain mostly to small oversights or potential problems that may yet be able to be resolved. By contrast, its strengths are manifold, having been developed in careful detail on a theoretical level and exemplified on a practical level at an exceptional scale. Yet, at the same time, the full potential of this method has hardly been realized.

As immense and monumental as CRIP was, Neville's ambitions are even more so: at the end of the project, he expresses not only his satisfaction with the fact the project was able to make discernable progress in the identification of comparative categories but also his disappointment that it proved unable to test the finer points of his method as laid out in *Normative Cultures*. Moreover, CRIP itself—as it readily acknowledges throughout its published volumes—has only scratched the surface in the identification, specification, and refinement of categories for cross-cultural comparison. The project is thus hardly finished but rather remains temporarily suspended, awaiting another group of willing and able comparativists and religious studies scholars to resume its task. The beauty of the project—and of the comparative method underneath it—is that it is never only as good as it is but rather only as good as future generations will make it.

Yet herein seems to lie the problem for CRIP, if not for Neville's comparative method more generally. For all of the careful detail in planning and execution of CRIP, for the powerful method underlying it, and for the overall stature of its participants within the broader academy, one would have expected it to have made more of a noticeable impact on the comparative study of religions. Indeed, given its bold claim of providing empirically grounded categories for comparison to not fall victim to excessive ideological bias, one would have expected more of the academy to have taken notice. CRIP participants, for their part, were concerned throughout with the radical claims the project was making (2001b, 269–70), concerned that their involvement in some areas might even compromise their reputations.

And yet, there has only been a hushed reception of its results. There have been only a few book reviews of the published volumes, most of which merely summarize the project and fail to make any critical rejoinders. Similarly, there have been no major publications addressing—positively *or* negatively—the results of the project. Certainly, the project has received some attention, but nowhere near what one would expect for such an extensive research project. There are a plethora of possible reasons for this: perhaps its results were not so controversial after all, and its results were simply received as common knowledge; alternately, perhaps everyone so disagreed with the results of the project as to reject them out of hand. Perhaps the length and intensity of the three volumes of CRIP were simply prohibitive given the dearth of time most academics have to indulge their interests. Perhaps the project was merely seen as the pet project of a particular group of Boston-area scholars, not directly relevant to those who do not share its interests and commitments. Arguably, none of these explanations finds their mark: a research project so extensive and so carefully executed should demand the attention of any scholars interested in comparison.

A more compelling reason can be found in the two critiques raised above. To begin with, the method underlying the project is developed in such rich detail that it is difficult if not impossible to understand it—let alone to appreciate it—without a major investment of time and mental energy.[72] It was Neville's ambition for CRIP that it should test that method by putting it into practice so that its empirical results could be assessed. For the participants of the project, however, it proved difficult enough to understand the method in all of its subtlety, let alone to put it into practice in its entirety, with the result that Neville ultimately has to conclude that his theory of comparison was not able to be fully tested by the group. If even CRIP participants have difficulty understanding and appreciating the method, how much more difficult must it be for readers who do not have the advantage of years of dialogue with its author?

At the same time, it is difficult to see in advance why one should make such a major investment of time and energy if one's philosophical commitments are different from those informing his comparative method. As Neville himself recognizes, his claims are very controversial and not of the avant-garde variety that draws broad readership despite its merits; it is rather controversial in what might be called an "*arrière-garde*" variety, which looks back to older schools of thought for its guiding insights (1995, 218). Nonetheless, he maintains that his argument should be judged not on the basis of its intellectual "sex-appeal" but rather on its validity. Combined with the immense complexity of his argument, however, this is a tall order that many scholars seem unwilling to fill.

Thus, in the end, it may be the very complexity of Neville's comparative vision (i.e., its detailed, systematic rigor) that works against him. Even CRIP, which ultimately failed to realize this vision in its entirety, is sufficiently complex as to be prohibitive. Whatever the shortcomings of the method itself or its exemplification in CRIP, its most stunning disappointment—and hence, arguably, its greatest weakness—is probably its failure to gain broader acceptance within the academy.

Still, Neville may yet have the last word. If his comparative method is as robust as it appears to be (at least on the basis of this study), then it should ultimately find its mark. That is, no matter how daunting his method may appear at first glance, if it is found to have merit by those who do take the necessary time and energy to understand it, then its influence can only spread over time. Most things worth believing are the products of long and difficult struggles (cf., 2001a, 277), and there is little reason to think that Neville's comparative method should be an exception to that.

Fortunately, irrespective of the level of accession to his work, Neville continues to develop his comparative vision. If collaborative work has the advantage of creating an increased propensity for self-correction (as suggested earlier), individual work has the advantage of being much easier to complete: over the course of his tenure at Boston University, Neville has continued to write on the topic of comparative philosophy. I have had to overlook many of those texts in this study—most notably, *Behind the Masks of God* (1991), which was published soon after his arrival at the university.

One text that should not be overlooked, however, is his *Boston Confucianism* (2000), which provides a masterful defense of the mutual relevance of the world's philosophical traditions for one another. Appropriately, the book is dedicated to Thomas Berry, whose influence on Neville at Fordham has been duly noted: like Berry, Neville argues that responsible philosophical work in the contemporary context of increasing global interconnection requires engagement with not only Western but non-Western sources as well (2000, xxxv).

Taking Confucianism as his test case, he demonstrates that understanding a non-Western tradition requires nothing inherently beyond what is required to understand the ancient Greek tradition: both require a linguistic and cultural translation of their ideas, but when this is accomplished, the underlying tradition can have an enriching influence on contemporary culture. Confucianism is finally at the point where most of its major texts have been translated in critical editions and its cultural context explicated, so, it is the responsibility of contemporary Western philosophers to draw on these resources to enrich to contemporary discussion. In this way, they can make the ongoing discussion a world philosophical dialogue rather than a merely parochial Western one.

If this sounds reminiscent of Hocking's comparative method, it should. For Neville, comparative philosophy should not be restricted to laying out a systematized method for comparison (although he does this at length in his Axiology) nor to identifying respects in which traditions are similar and different (although he also does this at length by means of CRIP); it should also be a tool for the critical engagement of other philosophical traditions for the purpose of enriching all of the traditions involved. It is because

Hocking exemplified this aspect of comparative philosophy before anyone else that Neville recognizes him as in a sense "the first Boston Confucian" (Lachs and Hester 2004, 367).

Having been brought full circle, this is perhaps as good a place to end as any. The complexity of Neville's method is beyond what can adequately be represented in this chapter, and there is seemingly no end to the facets of his approach that could have been discussed (many interesting facets have had to be eliminated here). Moreover, any conclusion for Neville's work can only be provisional, because he continues to write prolifically, and there is good reason to believe that he is not finished with comparative philosophy yet.

CHAPTER FIVE

REVISITING THE TWAIN

We ought not, of course, to yield to the Kipling fallacy. . . . Neither should
we claim that any single comparative methodology . . . is adequate to highlight the full range of similarities and differences patterning the relations
of Oriental and Anglo-European cultures. The only reasonable response to
the difficulties that intercultural translations represent is to recognize that
the development of a comparative methodology is an extended process
of tentative and pragmatic endeavors which only gradually may approach
philosophic adequacy.

—Hall, *The Unceretain Phoenix*

The purpose of this chapter is to pull together the results of the previous
four chapters and to utilize them for the basis of reflection on the nature of
comparative philosophy, at least as it has been undertaken in the American
pragmatist and process philosophical traditions. In the process, it will seek to
identify similarities and differences among the methods previously examined
and thus to shed additional light on each of them by virtue of their relation
to the others. This consists of an examination of their historical connections to one another (thus reinforcing the philosophical lineage highlighted
in this text), followed by a four-part examination of their methodological
connections.[1] Finally, it will conclude with some more general reflections
about comparative philosophy, based on the process of having undertaken
this investigation. While the scholars examined in the previous four chapters
might not agree with all, or any, of these reflections, they would all probably
agree that reflections of this type are of utmost importance in the further
development of comparative methodology.

HISTORICAL CONNECTIONS

One of the important dimensions of this project has been highlighting the
historical dimensions of the ongoing conversation within American traditions of philosophy about the nature of comparison. Although the figures

193

examined in this text are not the only advocates of comparative methodology in American philosophy, they do stand out as among the most influential of its proponents and thus provide a reasonable cross-section for study (reasonable, at the very least, for what can be included in a book-length account). While some of the historical connections among these figures have been mentioned in passing in the previous chapters, these facets have yet to be pulled together into a cohesive and telling narrative. It is the purpose of this section to do just that.

The first thing that stands out about the historical connections among these figures is their strongly biographical character. They are each an intellectual ancestor, heir, or contemporary of the others and can thus be seen to contribute to a single, ongoing conversation about comparative philosophy. In the broadest sense, the conversation started with Hocking at Harvard, moved to Yale with Northrop, and then spread throughout the United States with Hall at the University of Texas, Ames at the University of Hawaii, and Neville at Boston University. The many students of these three most recent comparativists—now spread even more broadly throughout the United States and beyond—are heirs to the cross-cultural philosophical interest initially expressed at Harvard by James, Royce, and others and cultivated by those participating in the conversation highlighted in this text.

What makes this ongoing conversation all the more interesting and significant is that its participants have been all too well aware of their participation in it. For example, Northrop could hardly forget his debts to his mentor, Hocking, especially given that it was the latter that arranged his initial involvement in comparative philosophy at the first East-West Philosophers' Conference (see, e.g., 1962, 10–11). Similarly, Hall, Ames, and Neville all discuss Northrop's approach to comparison in their own works and thus indicate their intellectual debts to him (Hall 1982a, 191; 1982b, 183–95; Hall and Ames 1987, 4; 1995, 118; Neville 2000, 49; 2006, xix). Finally, Hall and Ames have been in an ongoing conversation with Neville about their methodological differences with him, as can be seen not only from their respective texts (see esp. Hall and Ames 1987, xii–xiv, 323–25; Neville 2000, 47–50, 147–51; Chinn and Rosemont 2005, 21–34; Chapman and Frankenberry 271–88, 324–27), but also from the acknowledgments in those texts (see esp. Hall 1982a, ix; 1982b, vi; Neville 2000, xxxiv). While these debates have often involved sharp critiques, they have also been undertaken in the spirit of constructive criticism, mutual respect, and often good fun (e.g., Hall and Ames 1995, 278; Neville 1991, 73, 195; Chapman and Frankenberry 1999, 287).

A second thing to note is the strong connection of each figure with his own particular, historical context, as well as the similarities among the ways that these connections were forged. One good example of this is the significance of cross-cultural strife as an impetus for comparative philosophy. For example, Hocking's interest in cross-cultural comparison was inaugurated in the wake of the First World War, which came about relatively late in his career. This "war to end all wars" inspired him to expand the purview of his philosophical vision to include all of the world's traditions. For Hocking, this was expressed first and foremost in the context of Christian missions but soon extended to what he would call "world philosophy." By the Second World War, Hocking's comparative vision had reached its apex, but not before he had published his excellent essay on Zhu Xi (1936) and his signature essay in comparative method (1944b) for the first East-West Philosophers' Conference (1939). One can only wonder what Hocking would have done in comparative philosophy had the historical nudge to expand his philosophical purview come earlier in his career.

Representing the next generation of scholars after Hocking, Northrop's interest in comparison largely picked up where Hocking's left off: with the onslaught of the Second World War. As noted in the second chapter, Northrop expressed no significant interest in comparison prior to the start of the war but published his greatest comparative work immediately thereafter (1946). Indeed, he noted the significance of that war when he argued that it was arguably the first "world war" insofar as it was the first to bring East and West into "a single world movement" (1946, 1–4). Moreover, as Hocking's student, he carried on much of the work that his teacher began, especially within the context of the subsequent East-West Philosophers' Conferences: in the same way that Hocking was originally intended to anchor the representation of the Western traditions at the first conference, so Northrop was arguably the foremost comparativist among Western philosophers at the second and third conferences (if not also the first).

Finally, both Hall and Neville were students in the philosophy department at Yale, while Northrop was writing some of his most influential texts linking philosophy and international law. While neither would study extensively with him during his graduate education, each would remain well aware of his influence on the field and on his own development in comparative philosophy.[2] If there was a war that inspired the respective comparative work of Hall and Neville, it would undoubtedly have been the war in Vietnam.[3] Prior to the midseventies, neither Hall nor Neville made comparative philosophy a significant feature of his own philosophical work; yet, soon thereafter, both began publishing texts in comparative philosophy, and both were focusing on Asian traditions. Moreover, both have sought to cultivate an understanding of these traditions that avoids intellectual imperialism, consistent with the antiwar sentiment that ultimately dominated the American attitude toward the Vietnam War.[4] The war may not have been a conscious and explicit catalyst for either Hall or Neville, but it is too closely connected to their emergence as comparative philosophers to have been merely chance association.

The story is somewhat different for Roger Ames, who was raised in Canada (which was not directly engaged in the conflict in Vietnam), although his interest in comparative philosophy can also be traced to these geopolitical tensions. Ames completed all of his higher education during and in the wake of the conflict in Vietnam. He first went to Hong Kong in 1966—when the United States' ground offensive in Vietnam was well underway—and describes the impression left on him by such influential Chinese philosophers as Tang Junyi and Mou Zongsan concerning the negative effects of Western imperialism in China (Ames 2002, par. 3). Commenting on this imperialism as applied to intellectual culture, he writes, "The usually tacit assumption is that cultures beyond [the] Anglo-European sphere are not interested in the pursuit of wisdom. Having lived and studied in Hong Kong, I found this premise parochial and unworthy, and with the passage of the years, I became increasingly committed to challenging a Western philosophical tradition guilty of a profound ethnocentrism" (2002, par. 5). Especially since his collaborative work with David Hall, Ames has worked assiduously to challenge this ethnocentrism and to cultivate a more appreciative understanding of the insights of other cultural traditions. Thus, while Ames' interest in comparative philosophy can hardly be linked directly to any given cross-cultural conflict, its indirect connections to such conflicts have shaped it in substantive ways.

Hocking and Northrop may have been much more explicit than their successors about the connection of their work to the cross-cultural conflicts of their time, but all of the comparativists considered in this study have been all too well aware of these connections. They have also been well aware of the potential of comparative philosophy to cultivate a greater degree of understanding among cultures and thus to serve as a preventative to any such conflicts. In this respect, they would each oppose any suggestion that there are any intractable differences among such cultures, let alone that a "clash of civilizations" (Huntington 1996) is the only realistic possibility for their interaction. War may not be the only concern of comparative philosophy, but it is one of the most directly practical and pressing applications of the subfield in conflict-laden times.

In one sense, then, it is hardly surprising that comparative philosophers over the course of the twentieth century could be linked with some cross-cultural war or another: Northrop was right in seeing an inescapably global dimension to all further conflicts (1946, 6), and the last century has witnessed no shortage of such conflicts. Indeed, there has been at least one major international conflict among sharply contrasting cultures for each generation of American philosophers since the First World War. At the same time, however, this is precisely the point: the rise of comparative philosophy in America has everything to do with the increasing stakes of cross-cultural understanding, and thus it should come as no surprise that major developments in comparative philosophy accompany the events that most clearly indicate the need for—and the lack of—such understanding.

In the current context, this connection can be seen in the groundswell of interest among philosophy and religion departments in hiring scholars of Islam; new positions are being created for this specialty across the country, even in the midst of an otherwise very difficult job market. While the larger part of comparative philosophy has been developed in conversation with traditionally South Asian and (as examined most closely in this study) East Asian traditions, there is good reason to hope—and perhaps also to expect—that the field will be further developed by virtue of the contributions of these new scholars of Islam as well. If these emerging scholars are able to integrate themselves into the ongoing conversation alluded to in this project, there is good reason to believe that this hope is not misplaced.

METHODOLOGICAL CONNECTIONS

While this study has maintained an ongoing interest in the historical dimensions of comparative philosophy in America, its primary focus has been on the methodological features of some of that subfeild's most prominent representatives. At this point, then, it is appropriate to consider some of the more telling similarities and differences among their respective methods, not only to provide a stronger sense of cohesion among the previous chapters but also to cull some further methodological insights for comparative philosophy by virtue of their contrasts. In what follows, I examine four loci of methodological difference: their historical location, the structure of their comparative framework, their willingness to allow for transcultural inquiry, and their commitment to collaborative inquiry. In each case, some methods will stand together in contrast to other methods, but these alliances are always only limited to the particular locus of difference in question. Irrespective of which methods are paired with which, it is typically the differences themselves that are most able to inform comparative philosophy moving forward.

By Historical Location

The most obvious way to parse the approaches examined in this study is with respect to historical location. Something of this was suggested in the section above; here, however, the concern has less to do with the personal dimensions of their historical connection and more to do with its methodological implications of that connection. Hocking and Northrop share the dubious distinction of standing at the outset of comparative philosophy, not only for the pragmatist and process traditions but also for its flourishing across traditions. This afforded them unusual license in fashioning their respective comparative visions, and each of them seized the opportunity with remarkable creativity. For example, Hocking's willingness and ability to engage Chinese Confucianism on its own terms was well ahead of his time; if we take him at his word, "[w]ith the outstanding exception of Schopenhauer, no Western philosopher of the first rank has incorporated major Oriental ideas into his system of thought" (1944b, 1). Hocking took on this challenge, in however small a way, with interesting and insightful results.

Likewise, the comparative framework laid out by Northrop was similarly unprecedented, including an attention to detail and an appreciation for non-Western traditions that was rare among other traditions (and, unfortunately, largely remains so). While other philosophers would seek to integrate other traditions into their own philosophical system (e.g., Hegel), Northrop was arguably the first to devise a system solely for the purpose of organizing and thus understanding such diverse traditions with respect to one another. In short, by taking advantage of the emerging possibilities for cross-cultural comparison, both Hocking and Northrop were able to make creative and largely unprecedented contributions to the field.

The reason why this distinction is a "dubious" one, as suggested above, is that their work lacked the rigor that would characterize later studies in comparative philosophy. While Hocking's grasp of Chinese Confucianism was surprising given his lack of formal training in that tradition (as noted in chapter 1), it was still not a thorough and unquestionable mastery; however novel and creative his insights, later sinologists would be right to question his understanding of that tradition on its finer points. Similarly, while Northrop's grasp of non-Western traditions was affirmed in a variety of venues (as noted in chapter 2), his mastery of these would eventually be called into question by specialists who grew increasingly concerned with the extent to which the distinctive features of their respective traditions were being subsumed in the drive for synthesis characteristic of early comparative philosophy. Hocking and Northrop can hardly be blamed for not having mastery over the finer dimensions of such a fledgling subfield, but it nonetheless marks a shortcoming they share as early comparativists.[5]

Hall/Ames and Neville, by contrast, have a much greater sensitivity to preserving the distinctiveness of the traditions they compare. This is due in part to the flourishing of area studies since the time of Hocking and Northrop, which has provided a greater breadth and depth of information about these traditions to which comparativists are now—appropriately—held responsible. It is also due to an accompanying frustration with comparisons like those of Hocking and Northrop that, in light of this new information, often seemed to oversimplify and misrepresent this information (although, as noted in chapter 2, this was manifested primarily in the work of their less able contemporaries).

Hall and Ames, for their part, have made this concern with maintaining the distinctiveness of each tradition a defining feature of their comparative method. While there may be similarities among traditions, these similarities should be exploited not for their own sakes but rather for the purposes of helping to clarify the differences (i.e., similar aspects should serve as "bridges" among otherwise very different traditions). Ultimately, for Hall and Ames, to compare traditions is to understand just how different they are from one another.

Neville also maintains this concern but is less ready to shift the primary focus of comparative philosophy to the elucidation of its differences. The increased sensitivity to the distinctiveness of each tradition is represented in his conscious effort to ensure that the differences are recognized no less than the similarities among traditions; in his view, however, they should be emphasized no *more* than the similarities either. For Neville, to compare traditions is to provide an accurate rendering of the respects in which they are both different and similar (see, e.g., 2001a, 264).

Neville is perhaps more vulnerable to critique from specialists in his comparisons than are Hall and Ames, given that the latter count a trained sinologist among them. If Hall and Ames are right, this renders Neville susceptible to the same oversimplification and tendency to overemphasize similarities as plagued the work of the earlier comparativists (see, e.g., Chapman and Frankenberry 1999, 271–88; cf. 247–69). Yet, as Neville has argued in *Boston Confucianism* (2000), there is currently enough of the Chinese Confucian tradition—and, by implication, most other major world traditions—that it is also possible for nonspecialists to understand its similarities *and* differences with reasonable adequacy. Accordingly, Neville has been much more willing to assert instances of similarities and opportunities for synthesis as he sees them.

The character of our own historical moment is unclear. Certainly, Hall and Ames have been more conscious about trying to "hold their time in thought" (to use Hegel's phrase), at least in the sense championed by Rorty (1989a, 55; also 2006, 84–85; cf. Hall 1994, 11–64). CRIP, by means of Wildman's commentary, gives voice to this concern as well when it quips that "we do not need any more opinions about similarities." Yet Wildman then proceeds to argue, as Neville would as well, that CRIP had developed a method that could go a long way in avoiding the facile assertions of similarity trafficked in the past (Wildman 2001, 279). It will remain for comparativists now and in the future to determine which approach most adequately addresses the most pressing needs of their time.

By Structure of Comparative Framework

Another way to parse these approaches is with respect to the structure of their comparative frameworks. Most notably, Hall and Ames share with Northrop a conception of world traditions that focuses on the differences between them, while Neville and Hocking share a conception of them that is more continuous. For all four types, philosophical traditions have something to learn from one another; the difference lies in whether what is learned is taken to be an alternative to what one's own tradition has to offer or something that is—at least at the most basic level—consistent with it.

On the one hand, Northrop shares with Hall and Ames the belief that philosophic traditions can be characterized by one of two possible emphases.[6] For Northrop, this duality was an intentional and explicit feature of his comparative methods. As explained in chapter 2, he argued that philosophical traditions tend to emphasize one of two types of concepts: concepts by intuition and concepts by postulation. Historically, Eastern traditions have tended to emphasize the former and Western traditions the latter. For Northrop, however, these were only emphases, so one should expect to find exceptions within each of these broad traditions. This is important, because it suggests—insofar as they are part of the same broad tradition and develop out of each other—that these tendencies are not mutually exclusive. In fact, for Northrop, the ideal philosophical tradition would be the one that integrates both concepts by intuition and concepts by postulation into its purview.

Hall and Ames' comparative method also rests on a prevailing duality among philosophical traditions, although they choose to frame it in terms of first and second problematic thinking. With Hall and Ames, however, it is less clear that this duality persists among all philosophical traditions: they restrict their work to a comparison of classical Chinese and Western traditions and do not comment about the possible relevance of their framework to other traditions. It should be noted that this duality is so strongly emphasized in their work in both traditions that it seems a natural inference to extend this framework to other traditions as well; however, they do note that Northrop's distinction was "heavy-handed" (1987, 4), indicating their reticence to apply it more broadly. In the interest of being true to Hall and Ames' work as it stands, this study will limit itself to the classical Chinese and Western traditions.

In any event, like Northrop, Hall and Ames maintain that the dominant traditions of Chinese and Western philosophy are characterized by first and second problematic thinking, respectively. In fact, their distinction—expressed in terms of the aesthetic and the rational, respectively—is remarkably similar to Northrop's distinction as expressed in terms of the aesthetic and theoretic.[7] Also like Northrop, they maintain that these are merely emphases and not exhaustive alternatives, so they also expect to find evidence of each emphasis in both cultures.[8] In contrast to Northrop, however, they argue that these two emphases are not complementary but fundamentally alternative: they entail conflicting commitments that can only be embraced at the exclusion of the other. The ideal philosophy, then, is not the one that brings these commitments together but rather the one that identifies the commitments most adequately suited to its particular cultural context. Thus, it is possible for cultures to switch emphases, but not possible for them to merge emphases.

There are two important similarities between these two approaches that deserve some further examination. The first is that, while both approaches focus on the dominant characteristics of each tradition, both give priority to the exceptions within each tradition. For his part, Northrop continually sought to identify aesthetic, intuitive dimensions in Western philosophy and theoretical, postulative dimensions in Eastern traditions. For example, he lauded his mentor, W. E. Hocking, as being one of the foremost exceptions to the dominant tradition of Western philosophy. He wrote: "[Hocking's] post-Kantian idealistic influence has taken an aesthetic and intuitive turn . . . which renders [his] final position nearer in many respects to that of the Orient than to that of the traditional, orthodox Kantians and post-Kantians. This is a very important development because it provides a factor, indigenous in our own thought and culture, which is necessary for the basic task of our time of merging of Oriental and Western civilizations" (1946, 150). It is clear that, for Northrop, Hocking's philosophy provided an important resource for the improvement of philosophy. If his mentor was instructional in this respect, however, Northrop arguably saw himself as a veritable exemplar for comparative philosophy: not only could he understand and appreciate the insights of his own Western tradition, but he could do so for Oriental traditions as well.[9] Moreover, he could see these insights in conjunction within the context of his comparative framework and could thus envision the synthesis of these insights that constitutes the ideal philosophy. In short, insofar as he positioned himself as representing the exceptions in his own tradition, Northrop could position himself as maintaining an ideal perspective for comparative philosophical work.[10]

Likewise, although Hall and Ames readily concede that the Western tradition is dominated by the second problematic thinking of Plato, Aristotle, and their heirs, they choose to focus on the first problematic thinking of the pre-Socratics and Sophists, seeing in them a way to both better understand classical Chinese traditions and reorient contemporary Western philosophy. Similarly, they look to the work of contemporary philosophers in the postmodern and neopragmatist traditions as exemplars of first problematic thinking (e.g., Foucault, Derrida, and Rorty). Above all, however, Hall and Ames ultimately take themselves to stand as exemplars of comparative philosophy, because they understand not only the merits of the dominant Western tradition but also the merits of its exceptions. Specifically, they understand the importance of what they believe to be the most promising exception—first problematic thinking—for contemporary Western culture and are prepared to articulate that importance for it (1982a, 41). Ultimately, then, insofar as they represent the exception to their own culture, Hall and Ames—like Northrop—see themselves to hold an ideal position for the future development of philosophy.[11]

The second noteworthy similarity among these two approaches is the fact that both of them are represented by their progenitors as exercises in the "philosophy of culture."[12] For Northrop, philosophers should pay close attention to culture because it both reflects and informs the "goods" emphasized in its philosophical traditions. Only when these goods are understood in the context of a broader, transcultural framework can a culture's philosophic vision be broadened and improved through their interaction with other cultures. It is the task of the philosopher to develop this framework and thus bring cultures together while improving each one (Northrop 1949, iii).

As with Northrop, the philosophy of culture for Hall and Ames is intended to indicate the relative nature of the "goods" of any given culture; the latter, however, mean this in a much more profound sense, where these goods are *only* relative and can only *ever* be relative goods. In any given cultural context, it will better to value one set of supposed "goods" over others; in another context, it might be better to value another set. For Hall and Ames, it is the task of the philosopher of culture to be aware of the variety of goods that might be valued and to suggest which set might be most appropriate for their own cultural context.

Certainly, these two methods are not entirely alike, but they do both represent a duality among the world's traditions that goes a long way in shaping the role and character of comparative philosophy. In both approaches, one learns about other traditions because learning only about one's own leaves out important possibilities in philosophy. Culture is emphasized in each approach because it stands as a marker for the prevailing differences among traditions. While they may disagree on the precise relation of these traditions, comparative philosophy is defined in each case by the differences among traditions rather than their similarities.

For Northrop as well as Hall and Ames, then, there is an underlying duality to the traditions in question, and comparative philosophy should be concerned above all else with successfully navigating that duality; the difference between the two lies in what constitutes "success" in navigation for each. By contrast, for Hocking and Neville, comparative philosophy is defined primarily in terms of a commonality underlying all philosophical traditions. While both are aware that there are many significant and often profound differences among these traditions, both maintain that comparative philosophy should be concerned above all else with underlying continuity among all traditions.[13]

Hocking, for his part was quite vocal in his support of this continuity. As he wrote, "[t]he basic categories both of being and of value are the same everywhere. If it were not so, there would be no hope of an international understanding nor of international order. Nor could scholars write about these differences articles which would be understood in both hemispheres" (1944b, 3). By virtue of this continuity, it is possible to learn from other traditions in light of both their similarities and their differences: in both cases, one can "lend" to other traditions the best insights of one's own tradition and "borrow" the insights of others that improve upon one's own. The continuity among traditions, then, refers not to what traditions actually maintain but rather to what they all aspire toward. It is the "truth which is above race and nation" (1) that Hocking believed can, should, and hopefully will be the basis of the "emerging world-culture" (1932, 19).

Neville's emphasis on the continuity among traditions is much more subtle, but it is nonetheless present in his works. Whereas Hocking would be more inclined to talk about synthesis among traditions, Neville speaks in terms of the drive toward synoptic vision that is incumbent on any nonreductive theory. As the reader will recall, while reductive theories have their place, he gives priority to nonreductive theories insofar as they enable one to most effectively engage the world in all of its diversity (1995, 21). Significantly, for Neville the world is fundamentally the same world for all interpreters, even if they interpret it differently; thus, it is at least possible—if not probable—that continual inquiry can lead to the improvement of each tradition, especially when that inquiry includes data taken from other traditions. In short, for Neville, as for Hocking, there is a continuity to philosophic traditions that enables them to enrich one another, whether on the basis of similarities (which reinforce them) or differences (which augment them).

The key feature of this commonality, for both, is that it is not characterized by any identifiable structure (such as the duality emphasized by Northrop and Hall/Ames); rather, it is simply what it is: a mass of interconnected insights that are related to one another only be being about the same world. The task for the comparativist, then, is to penetrate this flurry of insights and distill from it key insights from one tradition that can improve other traditions.

The nature of this task reveals an interesting point of connection between the methods of Hocking and Neville: both rely on the capacity of comparativists to produce comparisons that arise not out of any acknowledged structure about the world's traditions, but rather by sheer force of insight on the part of the comparativist. As Hocking noted, philosophy is not a simple deductive science, but rather "primarily a matter of *what a person sees*, and then of his capacity to make a rational connection between what he sees and what he otherwise knows; his premises are his original observations about the world" (1944b, 7, italics original). Likewise, Neville puts a premium on the defensibility of any comparative claims but is less clear about the original impetus for the investigation of any specific claims. In both cases, the origins for comparative inquiry seem to be grounded in sheer imaginative insight, which is as productive for creative contributions as it is inscrutable for fundamental disagreement.[14]

In the end, in the same way that Northrop and Hall/Ames set themselves up as the exemplars for comparative study by virtue of their ability to understand and appreciate both of the prevailing tendencies among world traditions, so Hocking and Neville lift themselves up as exemplars insofar as they are able to penetrate the flurry of diverse traditions and emerge with constructive insights about the common philosophic quest.[15] This difference would prove definitive in debates among the two groups: Northrop would likely have suggested that Hocking's comparative vision was inadequately developed insofar as he never specified the differences that exist among traditions, but it is unclear that Hocking would have thought Northrop's framework to be necessary, accurate, or even ultimately helpful. This is certainly the case in the debate between Hall/Ames and Neville: Hall and Ames continually allege that Neville's understanding of first problematic thinking—especially in the Chinese tradition—is inadequate and argue that they offer a better conception of comparative philosophy because they understand both sides (see, e.g., Chapman and Frankenberry 1999, 271–88). Neville, by contrast, consistently argues that the distinction suggested by Hall and Ames between first and second problematic thinking is both unnecessary and misleading and that a better understanding of traditions would be one that allows engagement across cultural lines (see, e.g., Neville 2000, passim).

It would seem that setting oneself up as an exemplar for comparative philosophy is not limited to any particular approach to comparison but is rather endemic to the task of comparative philosophy itself. It is perhaps nothing other than a manifestation of the conviction that the way one is doing comparison is the best way, expressed within the context of a subfield that has not yet developed itself fully enough to navigate more productively among these competing claims.[16] Short of such development, it is to be expected that the subfield will be populated with only those who have the courage of their convictions—empirically, methodologically, and otherwise.

To conclude, one of the defining features of the comparativists examined in this study is whether they understand philosophic traditions as exemplifying one of two possible emphases (Northrop and Hall/Ames) or embodying a common quest for philosophic truth (Hocking and Neville). Stated simply, it is the difference between focusing on the differences among traditions or focusing on their underlying commonalities. All four methods take seriously the similarities and differences among traditions; what distinguishes them is their methodological starting point, and this starting point defines the very nature of the comparative task for each.

By Willingness to Allow for Transcultural Inquiry

A third way third way to parse the methods considered in this study is with respect to their willingness to pursue "philosophy" as a discipline that is common to most if not all traditions.[17] For some of the figures considered in this study, the radical diversity of philosophical traditions belies any suggestion that there is anything like "philosophy in general," while others insist that all traditions are accountable to the same underlying reality such that the claims of any tradition can be tested against that reality. At stake in the debate is the very nature of philosophy, which ironically informs the practice of comparative philosophy as much as it may be informed by the results of comparative philosophical inquiry.

What is interesting about this way of parsing the methods is that, while Hall and Ames clearly differ from Neville on this issue, Hocking and Northrop can be seen as occupying both sides of the debate, depending on the context of its application. The divergence between Hall/Ames and Neville on this issue should be clear at this point. For their part, Hall and Ames are primarily concerned with cultivating an understanding of classical Chinese philosophy that is accurate and not unduly biased by philosophic orientations that are foreign to it. While they are willing to draw on particular subsets of the Western tradition, they are only willing to do so insofar as those subsets can serve as a "bridge" for Westerners to understand classical Chinese philosophy.[18] This, for Hall and Ames, is seen as one of the primary functions of comparative philosophy.

It should be noted that they have been willing to take the further step of suggesting that one philosophical tradition or another may be better suited to a contemporary cultural milieu, but this has always been premised on the availability of an accurate articulation of the importances of those traditions and has thus been considered a merely secondary function of comparative philosophy.[19] In the end, for Hall and Ames, philosophy is not something in and of itself, but rather the total of culturally created practices from various traditions that, if only for practical purposes, can be loosely termed "philosophical."

Neville would agree that it is of vital importance for comparative philosophy that we cultivate a reasonably accurate understanding of philosophical traditions. Yet, while he takes this task with utmost seriousness, he understands this as a merely preparatory step for the primary task of comparative philosophy: namely, the cultivation of a better philosophical position—better precisely because it has been able to test the various hypotheses of the world's philosophical traditions against one another and thus to replace weaker tenets with stronger ones that can account more fully for a wider array of the available empirical data. Cultivating such a position requires serious engagement of any and all philosophical traditions, and its possibility assumes—and, Neville would argue, confirms by its practice—an underlying commonality to all philosophical traditions. It is this underlying commonality that gives philosophy its universality and that lends such rich possibilities to comparative philosophy.

Given this rendering of the differences between Hall/Ames and Neville on the nature of comparative philosophy, Hocking and Northrop can be seen to agree with both sides, which is at the same time instructive and problematic. On the one hand, they would seem to agree with Neville in that all of the world's traditions should be engaged philosophically. For example, Northrop has quoted Hocking approvingly as stating, "Everything is grist for the philosopher's mill" (Northrop 1962, 11), meaning that there is nothing that one should not engage for the purposes of cultivating one's philosophic vision. Hall and Ames would respond that this is fine so long as it is understood that, just as there are different philosophers and philosophical traditions, so there are different ways of milling.

Yet Hocking and Northrop seem to have meant something far more general by the "philosopher's mill." Neville's traditional response to Hall and Ames is instructive here: he would respond that the question of "different ways of milling" should be made an empirical question, leaving it to empirical research to determine whether these different ways are different and, if so, just how different they are. Similarly, Northrop claimed to have learned from Hocking that "one must not prejudge the result of any investigation. If one knows the answer, there is no point in initiating the study; and if one doesn't know, then only the investigation can give a trustworthy answer" (1962, 11). In other words, everything unknown should be subject to investigation, including any possible points of connection within comparative philosophy.

This commitment runs directly counter to Hall and Ames' concern to suppress investigations into the possible concern with transcendence among classical Chinese philosophers, on the conviction that these will mislead those who seek to understand that tradition long before it is able to prove itself misguided. This is what they intend when they write of "Saving Confucius from the Confucians" (1984) or of "Saving Neville's Project from Neville," for that matter (Chapman and Frankenberry 1999, 271–88). For Hall and Ames, it is far more responsible in the current cultural milieu to abandon all such inquiries and seek instead to understand traditions on their own terms.

Understood in this respect, Hocking and Northrop would seem to be most closely associated with Neville, insofar as the deferral to a common basis of empirical testing would seem to suggest an underlying commonality to all philosophical traditions. At the same time, however, there are clearly points at which Hocking and Northrop would seem to defer to Hall and Ames, running counter to Neville's comparative philosophical vision. For example, Northrop points out that

> no one in either the East or the West has yet shown how it is possible to convert Oriental people to the Christian religion without at the same time destroying the intuitive aesthetic unique cultural values of the East. . . . What must be realized is that nothing in any culture is more dangerous and destructive than the acceptance of new philosophical and religious beliefs, no matter how true and valuable, at the cost of the rejection of native beliefs which may be equally true and valuable. (1946, 430–31)

Consistent with this, he points to Hocking's experience to the same end in the context of Christian missions.[20] Apparently, not *all* is grist for the philosopher's mill, at least with respect to comparative philosophy; here, Hocking and Northrop seem to advocate a segregation of traditions, at least to the extent that one is in danger of being overcome by another, which is precisely the case that Hall and Ames make for the study of Ancient Chinese philosophy in the West.

Neville, of course, would admit that it is entirely possible for comparative philosophical inquiry to subsume the traditions it studies. Such would be comparative philosophy at its worst, and it is incumbent upon all philosophers to strive to avoid such subsumption in their comparative work. However, philosophers are also responsible to understand other traditions, and one can only understand by comparing. All things considered, then, the foremost responsibility for comparativists is to compare things well, and one can only compare well by not artificially obstructing the process of comparison. Yet Hocking and Northrop seem to advocate just such obstructions at least to some extent in their attempt to preserve the distinctive character of all traditions.

The best explanation for this apparent vacillation on the part of Hocking and Northrop is that, at such an early stage in the development of comparative philosophy, there was not yet any reliable means to compare traditions while also preserving their distinctiveness. To this end, Northrop wrote

> This is why the problem of determining the relation between the aesthetic component in things upon which the Oriental religion are based, and the theoretic component of things upon which the theistic Western religions rest . . . is so important. Until this problem is solved and the conception of the good and the divine in morality and religion is brought into accord with the solution, Western missionary activity for all its undeniable merits will continue to be a very dangerous and destructive thing for the Oriental people, unless those people are content to see their own culture lose most of its own unique values and individuality and turn into a mere second-rate imitation of the West; also, informed Orientals, who understand the philosophical foundations of culture are going to be wary of Western influences. (1946, 341–42)

Clearly, Northrop saw the development of his framework as the necessary means for balancing comparative inquiry with preservation of each tradition's integrity. Holding aside for the moment whether Northrop was successful in this respect, it is clear that no such structure existed during Hocking's time. More important, given the ongoing debate between Hall/Ames and Neville, it would seem unclear whether such a structure for preserving the integrity of traditions in dialogue exists even now.

What this says about contemporary comparative philosophy is that one of its most important tasks is the determination of whether or not such a structure exists and what would need to occur to bring one about if it does not. For their part, Hall and Ames have acknowledged their willingness to

> search for a single hermeneutical community serving as the context of viable philosophic dialogue. We differ only in the sense that we are less sanguine . . . as to the possibility of constituting such a community without considerably more work being done. That is, until we are capable of detailing certain fundamental presuppositions relevant to the understanding of alternative cultural contexts, this pursuit of a hermeneutical community will lead us inadvertently to foist upon an alternative culture a set of criteria drawn from our own tradition which are then chauvinistically presumed to characterize the determinants of philosophical thinking per se. (1987, 5)

Neville, by contrast, maintains that enough of the texts and traditions of Chinese philosophy have been translated into English that it is entirely possible for the careful scholar to engage these traditions responsibly and incorporate them into the broader global philosophic conversation (2000, 42).

The problem with the impasse is that neither side provides a feasible way to move beyond it. Hall and Ames can provide no clear indication—aside from their own cultural approximation—of when the "necessary presuppositions" (1987, 5) will have been detailed, so it remains unclear how long or even why one should observe their prohibition. Conversely, Neville can only advocate pursuing the sort of inquiry Hall and Ames warn against to see if the empirical data confirms their claims; however, if the latter are right about the dangers of this move the damage will have already been done, which renders this strategy questionable at best. What comparativists are left with is a difficult challenge: no side seems clearly more compelling than the other, both choices carries with them the danger of significant repercussions, and yet a choice between the two must be made. Indeed, not to make a choice is still to make a choice, and typically such choices are the worst insofar as they are the least critical and informed.

I do not have a solution to this problem, but the point of this study is not to promote or reject one method or another. From the perspective of methodological oversight, however, I can suggest what I think is the most likely and most promising resolution to the problem. That resolution is precisely the ongoing conversation that has been documented in this study. In all likelihood, Neville will remain unconvinced that the state of cross-cultural understanding is so unstable that any attempts at cross-cultural synthesis should be postponed; from his perspective, this would be to postpone the practice of philosophy itself. Likewise, Ames—carrying on the legacy of his work with Hall—will likely remain unconvinced that such syntheses can be undertaken without seriously distorting the traditions thus brought together; from his perspective, this would be to inadvertently take for granted the assumptions of one of the synthesized traditions. Effectively, then, Ames will continue to hold Neville accountable for his renditions of the Chinese tradition, and Neville will continue to make his case for and pursue constructive philosophy with resources drawn from any and all philosophical traditions.

Ultimately, Ames and Neville will keep each other accountable to the empirical evidence, thus mitigating the damage caused by any excessive restriction or expansion of comparative philosophy. Just as the character of the relationships among the world's philosophical traditions is clearer now than it was in Hocking's and Northrop's time, perhaps it will be clearer after another generation of scholarship. Until then, Ames and Neville will continue to provide the empirical data by which this problem may ultimately be assessed by that next generation. In short, as both Ames and Neville would agree, this is not a problem that should be resolved by means of theory alone; it will remain for those who inherit their conversation—*as they inherit it*—to determine for themselves the most appropriate course of action for comparative philosophy.

By Commitment to Collaborative Work

The fourth and final means of parsing the comparativists examined in this study is terms of their willingness to embrace collaborative work as a central part of their comparative method. At first glance, this is a relatively unremarkable consideration, as all of them have incorporated a significant degree of collaborative effort into their comparative work. Certainly, this has been more developed in some of them than in others, but it is fair to say that the commitment in principle, and in varying degrees of practice, pervades all their work. In this respect, they all belong in the same grouping, which—however important it is for underscoring the importance of collaborative work, as well as the longstanding perception of its importance in the development of comparative philosophy—is hardly surprising given the prominent place of the community of inquirers in the pragmatist tradition (and, to a lesser extent, that of process philosophy).

What is remarkable, however, is the variety of roles it has played in each figure's comparative career and the varying degree of success it has brought them in the development of their own work. For example, Hocking's involvement in collaborative inquiry began with what was arguably his first comparative venture: namely, his involvement with the Commission of Appraisal for the Laymen's Foreign Missions Inquiry, the fifteen-member committee that together published *Re-Thinking Missions* (1932). As noted in chapter 1, Hocking was the chairman of that committee and guided its research on missionary efforts in India, Burma, China, and Japan. Naturally, this provided him with a great deal of experience in collaborative ventures; it was probably not his first, but it was undoubtedly his most extensive. At the same time, however, it should be remembered that, while the committee was collaborative in the broadest sense, it was ultimately Hocking alone who was left—or perhaps self-selected—to write the four introductory and theoretical chapters to the inquiry.[21]

However formative his experience with the Commission of Appraisal, the overwhelming majority of Hocking's subsequent work would nevertheless consist of single-authored publications. That this is true is invariably due to the greater ease of single authorship coupled with academic traditions that favor and even expect such authorship. His experience with *Re-Thinking Missions*, however, may have informed his interest in the first East-West Philosophers' Conference, especially given his relative lack of expertise in non-Western traditions and the heavy educational emphasis of that conference.[22] There is good reason to expect that his participation in that collaborative venture would have further stimulated his comparative work, and every reason to regret that he was ultimately unable to attend.

As noted, however, Northrop was able to attend that conference, and it served not only as his point of entry into the comparative conversation but also as his introduction to collaborative philosophical work. He would attend at least the first three conferences and play a leading role in each of them. It is worth noting, however, that this role consisted primarily of defending the adequacy of the comparative framework that he laid out in the first conference and later developed in his *Meeting of East and West* (1946); while he benefited from the contributions of those at the conference who were convinced by his account, it is unclear whether the ongoing collaboration had any significant effect on the development of his comparative method.

This is a pattern that would be perpetuated in his later works as well. Northrop organized other loosely collaborative ventures in philosophy, which consisted primarily of collections of essays that he edited and published (Northrop 1949; Northrop and Livingston 1964). What made these collections collaborative is that they were all oriented toward the empirical elaboration and defense of some common idea, typically one that Northrop had suggested and attempted to defend on his own in earlier works. While this is collaborative in a very general sense, it sidesteps some of the most important dimensions of collaborative inquiry—most notably, the vulnerability to correction championed in American pragmatism.[23] Thus, while Northrop clearly recognized the value of collaborative inquiry for comparative philosophy, that recognition was at best only partial and incomplete. It would be left to later comparativists to develop more substantive accounts and practices of collaboration.

Hall and Ames have been centrally involved in the East-West Philosophers' Conferences, not least because of Ames' academic appointment

at the University of Hawaii and his subsequent role in facilitating the conferences. It goes without saying that this involvement has enabled them to
incorporate additional collaborative dimensions into their projects, although
the precise nature of this influence has been difficult to track.[24] Their greatest collaborative work has clearly been with one another. However much
it has sacrificed in terms of broader collaboration, their work together has
been among the most longstanding and intensive collaborative ventures in
comparative philosophy.[25] Hall and Ames have both profited immeasurably
from their association, and the exceptional quality and creativity of their
work together is a testament to the virtues of collaborative work. Indeed,
they have helped to challenge prevailing notions about the practical feasibility of thoroughgoing collaboration and its amenability to substantive
academic work. Unfortunately, however, it continues to be the exception
rather than the norm, as most comparative work continues to privilege
single authorship.

Finally, one may not have initially expected a great deal of collaboration from Neville: while he was also involved in many of the East-West
Philosophers' Conferences and takes very seriously the pragmatist emphasis
on the community of inquirers, almost all of his published texts through the
first thirty years of his career were single-authored texts. This all changed,
however, when he launched the Comparative Religious Ideas Project, which
constitutes one of the most significant, large-scale, collaborative projects in
the history of comparative philosophy. This project was remarkable enough
for the depth of its collaborative dimension, but it is the sheer breadth of
the group that is most remarkable. This was perhaps the best localized approximation of Peirce's "community of inquirers" that could realistically be
expected and thus constituted an ideal test case for collaborative inquiry.
As noted in chapter 4, the project's participants learned a great deal from
the experience, not only about religious ideas but also about collaborative
inquiry; at the same time, however, the success of the project was measured
most noticeably by the fact that the generalists were often left to craft the
comparative conclusions on their own.[26] Unfortunately, it proved only a
moderate success: the group was unable to come to any substantive comparative conclusions and was unable to develop these in the context of any
broader philosophic vision. It was left largely to Neville to harness these
conclusions, with the result that it made progress in its conclusions for the
most part only insofar as it broke away from the collaborative dimensions
of the project.

What is most remarkable about all of these examples of collaborative
work is that, with the exception of Hall and Ames, each of them did his
most substantive comparative work not in collaboration but in his own,
single-authored works. At the same time, however, these definitive comparative works seem to have been inspired in large part by their earlier
collaborative ventures. In Hocking's case, the main tenets of his comparative

method were laid out in *Re-Thinking Missions* (1932) but were developed in his two essays on comparative philosophy with much greater depth and precision. Likewise, Northrop's magnum opus, *The Meeting of East and West* (1946), was written immediately after the first East-West Philosophers' Conference, and while it incorporates many of the insights of conference participants, it has the focus and direction that only a single scholar could give it. Even Neville, who wrote the theoretical touchstone for CRIP prior to its initiation (i.e., Normative Cultures, 1995), wrote what is arguably his best comparative work to date (*Boston Confucianism*, 2000) over the course of CRIP's development. Moreover, his subsequent comparative works have achieved an additional depth and sophistication that are clearly informed by his experience in CRIP.

This is not to say that collaborative work was not helpful for these figures; it undoubtedly was, as evidenced by their ongoing willingness to continue participating in collaborative ventures. It is rather to point out that the benefits of such collaboration appear to be most effectively harnessed after the fact, by virtue of the focus and continuity that perhaps only single-authored works can provide. Thus, perhaps the most appropriate statement that can be made concerning collaborative work in comparative philosophy—at least from this small cross-section—is that it is daunting in its challenges, catalytic in its practice, and most productive in its longterm effects. Or, stated more simply, collaborative work is not a clearly superior alternative to single-authored works, but rather a constructive complement to them.

Again, Hall and Ames are the obvious exceptions to all of this. While they both made significant academic contributions outside of their collaborative work, their work together stands far and away as the best that either has yet accomplished. Perhaps this is because their collaboration was sufficiently restricted that its focus was not overcome by its diversity, as has been the case with so many larger projects. Perhaps it is because their personalities were peculiarly conducive to collaborative work, such that they succeeded where most others would have failed. Perhaps their collaboration occurred at just the right moment, when the need among Western philosophers and sinologists for one anothers' insights was felt most strongly. My guess is that it was probably a combination of all of these factors and perhaps some others as well. In the final analysis, however, what must be said of their work is that, as exceptional as it is in its quality, it is at least as exceptional in its collaborativity.

The rarity of successful collaborative work at the level achieved by Hall and Ames, of course, should not discourage other comparativists from trying to achieve it as well. It simply reinforces the previous point about the mixed results of collaborative work. Such work has the potential to generate insights that few if any comparativists are capable of garnering on their own—something that is perhaps no more important than in comparative philosophy, which spans so many different intellectual traditions. At the same time, it can fall victim to the challenges of mutual understanding

and productive interpersonal encounter, features that are themselves instructive for comparative inquiry but that can also inhibit the inquiry on a very
concrete and practical level. However future comparativists decide to pursue
their task, their work will be invariably better when they know both the
promises and the perils of collaborative work, and as George Santayana is
famous for pointing out, there is no better place to learn such things than
from our own—in this case, disciplinary—history.[27]

WHAT IS COMPARISON?

Given the many points of similarity and difference among the comparative
methods examined in this study, it stands to question what comparison is. In
one sense, this is to return to the question raised initially in the introduction,
armed with the information gleaned from the intervening four chapters. In
another sense, however, it is to ask a new set of questions: in what should
comparison consist, what is central to the process of comparison, and which
comparative method is the best of those examined? Since the purpose of
this study is not to propose its own vision for comparative philosophy but
rather to seek greater understanding of that subfield by means of already
existing methods, these questions are best answered by looking directly to
these methods to see how they have answered them and to consider what
this says about comparative philosophy as a whole.

To begin with, the question of what comparison should consist in is
naturally best answered by looking at that in which methods have actually
consisted. Each method will have its own concerns—some of which are
invariably shared with some other methods but probably not with all other
methods—and those concerns can perhaps be assessed with respect to the
strengths and weaknesses that accompany them. Hocking's method, for example, is primarily concerned with trying to "take seriously" the relevance
of non-Western philosophical traditions for Western philosophy and to encourage others to do so as well (Hocking 1944b, 1). Hocking accomplished
this at the very outset of comparative philosophy in America by bringing
the Chinese Confucian tradition to bear on modern Western science. If
the purpose of comparative philosophy is to bring diverse traditions into
conversation with one another, then Hocking's method of direct engagement—which is inherently interesting and mostly true—is an excellent way
to inaugurate that conversation.[28]

The inherent weakness of this approach is that any attempt to inaugurate further study by mere example (i.e. without some theoretic overlay) is,
even if successful, destined to prove inadequate relative to the very further
study it is intended to inspire. As noted in chapter 1, this proved only a
minor problem for Hocking (arguably because of his exceptional talent as a
philosopher), but because the problem is entirely structural this can only be
a difference of degree and not of kind. In other words, Hocking's method

can hardly get a free pass by virtue of his own philosophical prowess in its application, and one should expect that this problem will be more pronounced among less able philosophers.

By contrast, Northrop was able to assume that his audience is already interested in comparison; the very title of the Meeting (1946) advertises that interest, and the text's subsequent popularity attests to its success in that respect. The purpose of his method is thus different: it is to provide a framework of concepts and a vocabulary by means of which to understand philosophical traditions with respect to one another. Toward this end, his method proved very helpful at the outset of comparison, as evident from the extent to which it framed the discussions at the first and second East-West Philosophers' Conferences. Indeed, it became suspect only as the practice of comparative philosophy reached a level of sophistication beyond which the terms of his framework could still prove helpful.

This is the inherent weakness of Northrop's method: the terms offered at any given moment in the history of comparison can only represent the state of comparative philosophy at that moment. It always calls for fresh insight and imagination in vocabulary and conceptual framework, which simultaneously dates the terms and concepts currently in use and yet also calls for new exemplifications of the way in which those terms and concepts were originally formed. Ultimately, then, this is both a weakness and a validation of Northrop's method, although the validation can only be bittersweet for one who has put so much effort into constructing a particular set of terms and concepts.

This would have been particularly bittersweet for Northrop, given the lingering idealism he inherited from Hocking. It is clear that Northrop thought his terms and concepts for comparison remained relevant and continued to fight for them even when his fellow comparativists had moved on. From the perspective of a pragmatist appreciation for fallibilism, this is a trivial concern at best, although such recurrent change in the basic ways in which traditions are understood to relate to one another does lend a certain instability to comparative discourse. That is, while such instability is seen as a strength from the perspective of fallibilism, it ceases to be a strength when terms and concept become so unstable as to be unable to give comparative discourse any reliable definition, or, worse, such that comparative terms and concepts come to be seen as precisely the problem.

Hall and Ames' method is a response to precisely these changes that have taken place in comparative philosophy since Northrop, as exemplified in the failure of such frameworks to keep pace with improvements in area studies in non-Western traditions. The purpose of their method is to cultivate a better understanding of these traditions and thus to guard against oversimplification in the comparative process. In fact, they are so concerned with the potential for oversimplification that they effectively advocate a moratorium on cross-cultural comparisons except insofar as they elucidate the differences among those traditions. They may not have succeeded in achieving this moratorium, but they have undoubtedly made important contributions not only to comparative philosophy but to the study of Chinese philosophy as well, and their critiques of Northrop and his comparative method have undoubtedly had a strong effect on the practice of comparative philosophy.

The inherent weakness of their method is its tendency to overstate the case against continuity with other traditions. Often, rending the interpretation of another tradition from the moorings of one's own tradition requires a certain rhetorical flair, which can easily be mistaken for a straightforward statement of opinion. In the case of Hall and Ames, their argument against the importance of transcendence for the Chinese tradition has been extended to the absolute absence of it in the areas of the tradition they have studied and even to the suggestion that it is diametrically opposed.[29] It is unlikely that there are no resources at all in the classical Chinese tradition that are amenable to the idea of transcendence, and thus it is more than likely that the rhetorical point obscures certain features of that tradition.

The calculation that Hall and Ames seem to have made is that the potential ill effects for the understanding of Chinese philosophy brought about by entertaining such possibilities outweigh the potential benefits of doing so, such that a more accurate understanding of Chinese philosophy is best cultivated by consistently opposing such suggestions. Hall seems to suggest as much when he writes, "While I have tried to avoid romanticizing the 'otherness' of Chinese thought, I do admit that I have been more concerned to guard against any sort of easygoing assumption that the Chinese think pretty much as we do, only are not yet so sophisticated in their theoretical constructions" (Chapman and Frankenberry 1999, 272). They have been particularly vehement about this in their arguments against Neville, who has been keen to investigate such possibilities; I am not sure that they would express their point with equal vigor among philosophers less predisposed to look for references to transcendence.

Like Hall and Ames' method, Neville's is also a response to the changes since Northrop, although its purpose runs directly counter to theirs. Neville seeks to continue the task of identifying similarities and differences among traditions but to do so in a way that builds in enough safeguards to respect the integrity of the traditions compared. One of the most evident ways he has done this is by embracing a commitment to fallibilism, which accepts the changes in terms and concepts that ultimately rendered Northrop's framework obsolete. It is also reflected in Neville's resistance to setting up any rigid framework in the construction of his categories.[30] In this respect, he also effectively revitalizes the purpose of Hocking's method—promoting cross-cultural engagement—as a corrective to the current, arguably anticomparative attempt to simply allow traditions to speak for themselves.[31]

The weakness of Neville's approach is that its deep mooring in specific traditions of Western thought perpetually threatens to bias his comparative conclusions. For his part, Neville claims to be able to address any such bias in the long run by virtue of a thoroughgoing fallibilism, but it is unclear whether the effects of this fallibilism are sufficiently forthcoming to make a noticeable difference in practice (as noted in chapter 4). Moreover, it may be that these biases continue to inform his interpretations even when undetected. Ultimately, it is irrelevant whether the bias is detected or undetected, since the effect on the interpretations is the same. Neville's calculation is that biases will inform any interpretation and that interpretations must continue to be made; accordingly, the best interpretations are not the ones that try to do away with biases by eliminating creative interpretations but rather the ones that proceed with such interpretations while trying stringently to minimize such biases.

In each of these cases, the advocates of the method in question see the weaknesses in their method as only trivial relative to the potential gains, and thus well worth taking on relative to what might otherwise be lost. In other words, they value the concern addressed in their approach and value it more highly than the weaknesses that attend it. What is common to all of them, however, is that they are all pursuing comparative philosophy, albeit in different ways and with different ends in sight. As to the question of what is central to comparative philosophy, one finds that there is very little aside from trivial comments that can be made in light of the diversity of methods. Comparative philosophy can be defined generally as the attempt to better understand each of the world's philosophical traditions by understanding them relative to one another. What comparative philosophy consists of beyond this—that is, *how* better understanding is to be achieved—differs significantly from method to method.

As to the related question of what comparison should consist of, it should consist of all of the concerns represented by these four methods. Comparative philosophy may be more developed than it was for Hocking's generation, but it is still in need of inviting those who are locked into their own traditions to join the comparative philosophical conversation. What is needed, then, are comparisons that are interesting and plausible enough to entice others to join and thus enrich the conversation; Neville's comparisons in *Boston Confucianism* (2000) are an excellent example of this.

Likewise, while the terminology of Northrop's framework may have ultimately proven somewhat questionable, comparativists are still in need of a vocabulary to express the relationships that exist—both in terms of similarities and differences—among philosophical traditions. More recent examples of this can be found in Hall and Ames' distinction between first and second problematic thinking and also in the results of the Comparative Religious Ideas Project.

Finally, no matter how soon comparativists are able to learn to resist the urge to entertain facile assertions of similarity among traditions, they will always need to be reminded of the dangers of this temptation. The profound differences among traditions remain important, and comparative philosophy will always be in need of comparativists like Hall and Ames with the conviction and expertise to maintain the differences. At the same time, however, there are also important similarities among traditions, and these need to be understood. Neville has provided a sophisticated way of identifying these similarities by means of vague categories that is anything but facile and that is equally sensitive to differences. Both the distinctiveness of traditions and their commonality need to be considered carefully in comparative philosophy, and—however much they may be critical of each other's method—Hall/Ames and Neville balance each other well in this respect.

Which comparative method is the best, then? This question seems to be entirely beside the point. Given that they each pursue different ends, the answer to that question depends on how one evaluates the ends themselves. Moreover, insofar as all of these ends have a certain value, the best method would be the one that is best able to attend to as many of the ends as possible. Given that, as demonstrated above, some ends seem opposed to other ends (at least on a practical level), it seems unlikely that any method would be able to attend to all of the ends simultaneously. Perhaps more to the point, it would be impossible to determine which method most adequately balanced these ends, since such a determination would inevitably reflect one's own evaluation of the relative importance of the possible ends.[32] At least at this point in its development, comparative philosophers would do well to understand which ends each method serves and to employ each method consciously in pursuit of the end toward which it is oriented. Cultivating such an awareness has been the primary purpose of this study.

I say "at this point in its development," however, because the long-term prospects for comparative philosophy should be more than this. Comparative philosophy seems still at a sufficiently early stage that it progresses in fits and starts, and it is probably fair to say that the field is still finding out what it can and cannot—and perhaps should and should not—accomplish methodologically. Perhaps as comparative philosophy continues to develop, it will become clearer how to more successfully balance these many concerns. The best comparativists can do at this point is to be aware of these developments, seek to contribute constructively to them through both improvements and augmentations, and anticipate a time when the full task of philosophical comparison is rendered more clear and complete.

In closing, it is important to note that it is not only the comparative methods examined here that are continuous with the American pragmatist and process traditions but also the way in which those methods have been compared here. Each chapter in this book has sought to identify the particular problem in comparison addressed by its respective figure, and this problem was found to be largely specific to each figure (as suggested in this chapter). Moreover, each chapter ended with a consideration of the strengths and weaknesses of each approach, looking at what might be done to improve it. This is arguably how these traditions improve. In pragmatism, the emphasis on each method's concern with a problem at hand should be readily appreciated but could also be expressed in the process tradition in terms of its adequacy and applicability; likewise, in both traditions, theories are rendered perpetually subject to correction, with such correction initiated by critique. In a similar way, each of these four approaches looks to its heirs and asks that it be reexamined, reworked, and revitalized, something that is arguably due to each of these approaches insofar as it has shown the problem with which it has been concerned to be of any merit. It has been the concern of this text—and of the present chapter in particular—to demonstrate the importance of each of these concerns.

THE COMPARISON OF COMPARATIVE METHODS

It is in the summary considerations of the nature of comparison detailed above that the self-referential aspect of this project most comes to the fore. There has been a great deal of careful consideration of the methods employed in each approach to comparison, but not much mention of the approach undertaken in this comparison of those comparisons. This being the case, it is perhaps worth considering these issues for a moment to see if this sheds any further light on comparative philosophy or on the project at hand.

In light of the understanding of these methods garnered throughout this study, it should be clear that the method employed in this study is most like Hocking's. Like Hocking, I stand at the outset of a comparative project that has very little precedent: as noted in the introduction, there has simply not been a great deal of self-conscious critical consideration of available comparative philosophical methods—that is, no comparison of comparisons. There has only been the ongoing conversation among comparativists, which has been comparative in terms of methodology only occasionally and in passing (see esp. Hall and Ames 1987 and Neville 2000). In light of this context, this study seeks—much like Hocking did—to offer a comparison that is at least mostly right and interesting enough to inspire others to take up the task as well. If successful on both of these fronts, it should be capable of being improved and augmented by subsequent scholars. This may seem a modest goal, but comparison must always start somewhere, and one could do far worse than seek to live up to Hocking's example.

At the same time, this study has the advantage of looking over the longer course of development of comparative methodology and can thus see how these methods have developed over time. Certainly, it is not the same to compare comparative methods as it is to compare philosophical traditions more generally, but there are enough similarities to provide some guidance for this project. Accordingly, this study has been able to incorporate many of these developments into its own method.

Northrop's *Meeting of East and West* is a particularly good example. Similar to his work, this study has sought not only to provide detailed descriptions of each method (chapters 1 through 4) but also to use these descriptions to bring the methods together in the context of a broader comparative framework (in the current chapter). Attempts at such a framework can be seen in the distinction between those methods that assert an underlying duality among traditions and those that assert an underlying unity, or in the loose typology of methods based on their intended purpose. This has not been achieved on anything like the scale and precision of Northrop's framework, and it is clear that more could have been done here.

It stands to question, however, whether a more precise framework or vocabulary is really needed. The methods compared are not as diverse as the philosophical traditions that Northrop compared, and there is less of a need to bring them together into a common vision. A unified method that did all of the things that each individual method sought to do would be a magnificent accomplishment in itself, but as noted above it is not clear that such an "übermethod" would be manageable, let alone desirable. This being the case, it is perhaps sufficient to have provided a description and a loose framework for comparison of those methods.

Similarly, this project's method has adopted something of Hall and Ames' method. Specifically, it has sought to provide accurate renderings of alternative methods on their own terms, referring to other methods only insofar as this helps to elucidate the method in question (in this project, this has been done primarily on a historical basis). To aid in this process, the project has avoided taking a normative stance on the nature of comparison, since this would be most likely to foster the evaluation of one method on the terms of another; while strengths and weaknesses have been considered, these have been considered for the most part in connection with each method's stated goals. Hopefully, the rendering of each method in accordance with its suitability for a particular methodological—if not cultural—need demonstrates that the method employed in this project is not entirely alien to that employed by Hall and Ames.

At the same time, however, this project has not been as concerned with maintaining the integrity of each method as Hall and Ames have been, for example, with respect to the classical Chinese tradition. Certainly, it has sought to represent each method accurately and to avoid representing any method through the lens of another method (e.g., Hall and Ames' method as a "bad" version of Neville's), but there is probably more that could have been done here. Hall and Ames, however, were responding to a long history of misinterpretation of the Chinese tradition, and it remains to be seen whether I have so misrepresented any of these comparative methods that such vigilant corrective measures are necessary. If anything, I am battling a long history of ignorance about these methods, so what is most important is cultivating an awareness and appreciation for them.

Finally, like Neville's comparative method, I have sought to be as precise as possible about exactly what similarities and differences exist among the various methods examined. In one sense, this is much simpler for a project like the one at hand, because the things compared are inherently more similar to one another; this has surely been facilitated by my ability to narrow the scope to only comparativists in the American philosophical traditions. Hence, I have not needed to develop categories at a very high level of abstraction from the things compared. Yet something of this can be seen in the choice of terms used in the cross-methodological comparison of methods.

What is missing is an intricately developed, systematic account of what constitutes comparison, akin to what Neville produced in *Normative Cultures* (1995). Again, it stands to question whether such a systematic account is really merited for a comparison of comparisons; the point of comparing comparisons is simply to enable us to make better comparisons. One does not compare simply for comparison's sake, and the returns on comparison decrease as one gets increasingly distanced from the original subjects of comparison. While it is arguably worthwhile to compare comparisons, it would be of only questionable merit to compare comparisons of comparisons and still less worthwhile to compare on yet a further metalevel.

All things considered, if this project were to be developed in any further way, it would be in the direction of a new comparative method that was able to benefit from a clearer understanding of the methods that came before it. This is arguably the natural outgrowth of a project like this, which has been undertaken solely in the interest of better understanding, critiquing, and ultimately improving those comparisons. It is a distinctly separate project from this one, however, and can only begin when this one is complete. As was the case for Hocking, this project—no matter how incomplete and inadequate it may be in its own right—can be considered a success if it is able to inspire and inform the development of such further projects.

RETROSPECTIVE ANALYSIS

This project was originally conceived in response to my own frustration in trying to enter into the ongoing conversation among comparative philosophers. While I had access to as many first-rate comparativists as a graduate student in Boston as anyone might have a right to expect, gaining entry into the broader discussion was nonetheless a surprisingly formidable task. Certainly, it was possible to identify the definitive texts of the last few decades and easy enough to find out about the most interesting articles and essays recently published; indeed, most of the conversation among comparativists in the Boston area pertained to the most recent developments in the subfield of comparative philosophy.

It was more difficult, however, to determine the history and definitive texts of this subfield. In other words, one could see comparative philosophy in action but could less easily find out about its history. If one studies Continental philosophy, one knows at least to read Husserl, Heidegger, Merleau-Ponty, Adorno, Marcuse, Levinas, Gadamer, Habermas, Lyotard, Foucault, and Derrida. Similarly, if one specializes in analytic philosophy, one knows to read Frege, Moore, Russell, Carnap, Wittgenstein, Austin, Ryle, Searle, Quine, Ayer, Strawson, and Davidson. Who does one read when one decides to become a comparativist?

This last question is not without its answers. These answers, however, are typically more suggestions than anything else, and there seem to be as many suggestions as there are people suggesting them. The problem is even worse with respect to the study of comparison itself (as distinct from the area studies of specific traditions that might be compared), where there are few if any suggestions. While there have been a number of important generalists who have written on comparison, their work is seldom mentioned in the literature of comparison. Occasionally, comparativists will draw on the approach laid out by a single philosopher of comparison—usually a local, parochial favorite—as though that figure was the only worthwhile alternative. More commonly, however, comparativists tend to forego consideration of the philosophical dimensions of comparison altogether, as if "what comparison is" is sufficient simple and obvious as to require no additional consideration.

As I have tried to point out throughout this work, comparison is not such a simple matter, and there is a remarkable variety of conceptions of what it is and how it is best undertaken. In an important sense, this study is intended to serve as a resource for those seeking to enter into the comparative discussion by laying out at least a small subsection of the definitive texts in the philosophy of comparison and emphasizing the need for serious consideration about what comparison should entail. In this respect, it may even serve as a resource to those already engaged in the conversation.

In the interest of further facilitating the development of this conversation, it seems fitting at the end of this study to reflect on lessons learned throughout its development that may facilitate the further development of the field.

The Relevance of Historical Context

The first, of course, is that there is a rich history here that deserves to be uncovered. Within the confines of this study, I have only been able to focus on a select few figures and have had to eliminate a number of figures that I would have otherwise liked to have examined more closely. Some of the more notable figures include E. A. Burtt and Troy Organ, both of whom exemplify strong links with the American pragmatist and process traditions; I believe that still more figures could be identified by looking further into the American naturalist tradition. Similarly, as noted earlier, there is a strong architectonic tradition among American philosophers that runs through Stephen Pepper, Richard McKeon, Robert Brumbaugh, Walter Watson, and David Dilworth, that also had an important influence on the development of comparative philosophy in America. Although some consideration has been given to their contributions—see, for example, Berthrong (1998), Hall (1973; 1982b), Hall and Ames (1987) and Neville (2000)—there has been no definitive methodological study of these important alternatives. There is still a great deal that could be done to develop this still-emerging subfield of philosophy.[33]

A second lesson learned is the strong role that historical context plays in the prospects for comparative philosophy.[34] While the argument could be made that the ideas developed within comparative philosophy are sound ideas and thus should have been developed in any event, it is remarkable how closely they are connected to—and how very much they seem to be spurred by—their historical context. Without suggesting that ideas are *merely* historically contingent (as per Rorty), I would nonetheless advocate the general pragmatist conviction that the perceived "use" or "advantage" of an idea, as defined by its context, is closely related to its perceived truth and that a better understanding of the ideas prevalent in contemporary comparative philosophy can be cultivated by maintaining a more heightened awareness of the close relationship between the development of ideas and historical context.

For example, comparative philosophers—like comparative religionists and anthropologists—are often quick to forget that their subfield has some of its deepest roots in Christian missions. Hocking's example is instructive because it is a relatively clear case of how involvement in concerns over missions led an otherwise Western philosopher to cultivate an interest in non-Western traditions and to develop a method for comparing them. This would have been true not only for Hocking but for many of his contemporaries as well: the most prevalent and highly regarded translations of Chinese texts at that time were those penned by the former missionary to China, James Legge, and Christian missions was still the primary point of contact between Western and non-Western traditions.[35]

This historical connection is more than a mere aside—more, for example, than a historical accident that no longer informs the practice of comparative philosophy (however much contemporary practitioners would like to think themselves freed from its influence). While cultural traditions throughout the world have long found it both necessary and often beneficial to engage the other traditions around them, the global extent of this engagement has only been made possible within the context of exploration and expansion of Western powers over the last five hundred years. Moreover, for most of that time—from the *Patronado/Padroado* of the sixteenth century to the "Christian Century" that was supposed to be the twentieth—the vanguard of Western intellectual engagement with non-Western traditions has been Christian missions. It is thus no mere accident that Hocking gets his impetus for comparative philosophy from Christian missions and perhaps also no accident that so many of the debates within comparative philosophy seem to trace traditionally religious concerns (e.g., the debate between Hall/Ames and Neville about the relevance of transcendence for Chinese philosophy).

Certainly, the influence of Christian missions has not been a wholly positive one; in fact, there are some who would suggest that it has been wholly negative. My own sense is that the truth is probably somewhere in between, it having provided the impetus for this important subfield, but having also oriented it in ways that are perhaps more theologically focused than philosophically so (if Western philosophy and theology are so easily separated). Whatever the influence, however, it would be naïve to think that it has been undone in the span of the last seventy years—a short span in the life of a discipline—so comparative philosophers would do well to maintain a more critical awareness of the influence of this history on their own practice.

A similar lesson can be learned from Northrop's example. For Northrop, it was not so much the extended history of the field that influenced his work but the immediate history of his own geopolitical situation. His best work was done during the Second World War, when the problem of cross-cultural understanding was at its most poignant. By contrast, when the United States entered the Cold War in the 1950s, cross-cultural relations became more about superiority and dominance and less about understanding. The result was that Northrop's vision had less and less a voice, and he was forced to pursue his comparative vision in other venues. Consistent with the nature of Cold War competition, this meant an emphasis on mathematics and the natural sciences, which were seen as more useful, reliable, and conducive to the technological superiority so desperately sought throughout the middle part of the last century (especially after the U.S.S.R.'s launch of *Sputnik* in 1957); in philosophy, this was represented in the rise of analytic philosophy (which was built on an appreciation for precision and certainty) and the consequent decline of most indigenous American philosophical traditions.

Fortunately for Northrop, he had some substantial background in mathematics and the natural sciences, so he could express his insights in terms more amenable to analytic philosophers, which came to dominate philosophy departments throughout the country, just as it did Northrop's department at Yale. Yet, as noted in chapter 2, Northrop was not an analytic philosopher, and his attempt to render himself one distanced himself from most of his potential audience: his work was seen as too imprecise by analytic philosophers and too concerned with the definition of terms by nonanalytics. As a whole, his later works failed to exemplify the imaginative insight and natural creativity that characterized his earlier works.[36]

The point here is not that analytic philosophy is somehow inimical to comparative philosophy; the flourishing tradition of comparative philosophy within the analytic tradition testifies that this is not the case. It is rather to suggest that Northrop's changing historical milieu had a clear influence on the development of his comparative philosophy and that this influence was not entirely positive (if positive at all). While it is unclear how much Northrop was cognizant and intentional about these changes in his work—or even whether he could have continued to pursue his initial vision with any greater success—it nonetheless stands that he may have been able to engage these changes more productively if he sought to be more critically aware of them and what they entailed for the practice of comparative philosophy.

If comparative philosophy is influenced by its own immediate historical milieu, what does this mean for contemporary practitioners of comparative philosophy? This is more difficult to say, since history is typically best judged after it has been history for some time.[37] Moreover, because this has not been the primary focus of the text at hand, I can offer only suggestions in light of my research. Nonetheless, I find it instructive how much the context of World War II framed most of the early debate about comparative philosophy: there was an awareness before, during, and even after the war that East Asian cultures were more than distant European backwaters; they were serious, profound, and formidable civilizations that may be able to prove their supremacy over the Western world.[38] This, I think, engendered a spirit of respect across these traditions that encouraged serious engagement on all sides. By contrast, today's wars are fought against predominantly Muslim countries, which have a centuries-long history of having been dismissed by Western powers as precisely the cultural backwaters suggested earlier.[39] It is clear that these wars—like the wars before them—have also engendered an increased interest in cross-cultural comparison (as evidenced by the many job new openings for Islam scholars), and this revitalized interest will increasingly influence the study of comparative philosophy. This being the case, it is worth considering the extent to which the historically diminished respect for Muslim culture will influence the development of the field. We may not be any more able than Northrop to change the historical milieu of our own times, but we are not powerless to check its influence and should at least question the character of its influence at any given time.

The Prospects for Comparative Philosophy

In *The Rise of American Philosophy* (1977), Bruce Kuklick describes what he calls "the professionalization of philosophy," a gradual development over the course of the twentieth century during which philosophy came to be seen not as a vocation or calling, which might have amateur parallels, but rather as a traditional job defined by university status and driven by competition for promotion. As a result of this development, whereas philosophers through

the early twentieth century developed systems of thought that tended to
strongly reflect their own personality and broader social concerns, those writing since the middle of that century have tended to forego the construction
of philosophic systems and have instead sought to make technical advances
within already established and dominant modes of thought.

Kuklick is, I think, for the most part correct about his assessment of
philosophy in general. What is interesting to note, however, is that he is
less accurate insofar as this applies to comparative philosophy. Comparative
philosophy, by its very nature, requires that its practitioners break out of
narrowly defined fields of specialization. Chinese logic, for example, cannot
be understood outside of its context within the broader purview of Chinese
philosophy and cannot be compared to Western logic except insofar as the
latter is also understood in its own, broader context. Certainly, some thinkers attempt to circumvent this process, but the results can only be facile
and misleading. What makes comparative philosophy so challenging is that
the contexts are so very different, such that even when things look similar
those apparent similarities often rest on more substantive differences. What
is required are new ways of thinking that can incorporate the insights of
diverse traditions with as little reduction as possible, and this need runs
counter to any predefined specialization within a tradition.

As one might expect, then, those who engage in comparative philosophy have a much greater propensity to form broad philosophical views that
enable their own personalities and broader social concerns to shine through.
This has certainly been the case for the figures examined in this study,
and they are arguably representative of the broader body of philosophers
of comparison in this respect. As one might also expect, these figures have
been somewhat controversial within the study of philosophy for this reason.
Hocking completed his work early enough that this did not adversely affect
him in any significant way. By contrast, Northrop—as noted earlier—faced
this professionalization head-on in the wake of the rise of analytic philosophy
(which has arguably championed such professionalization more than any
other tradition in philosophy); it proved impossible for him to incorporate
the broad philosophical vision of *The Meeting of East and West* into terms
sufficiently defined to meet the demands of his later contemporaries. One
might consider his early work as an expression of preprofessionalized philosophy and his later work of a more professionalized variety.

The contrast between professionalized philosophy and comparative
philosophy is even clearer in the work of Hall/Ames and Neville. Hall and
Ames, for their part, have consistently run into challenges in trying to appease philosophers on the one hand and sinologists on the other (as noted
in chapter 3). Certainly, they have done an admirable job in addressing these
challenges, but it is arguably the breadth of their vision that has engendered
the challenges in the first place—something that can be seen particularly
in their "philosophic translations" of Chinese texts. By current philosophic

standards, they are not sufficiently precise in their concepts and terminology to adequately represent the philosophy and are too focused on philosophical ideas to give an accurate rendering of the text itself.[40]

Similarly, Neville has seldom been considered a traditional philosopher—or, at least one who is easily classed with others—and despite voluminous publications and important contributions has not achieved the broader success that would normally accompany such contributions. The reason for this, I think, is that he also addresses very broad philosophical notions (e.g., the nature of being, time, truth, etc.), which does not translate very well into the values of professionalized philosophy. While Neville often addresses the work of others, none of his works can be considered a narrowly defined technical advance on someone else's position.

What does this say about the nature of comparative philosophy? It suggests that this subfield rests on a conception of philosophy that is not currently very popular in the broader field of philosophy and that it rests on this conception not by choice but by necessity. It is arguably for this reason that comparative philosophy has flourished only at the margins of the broader discipline. For example, the Society for Asian and Comparative Philosophy, which "seeks to provide the same sort of professional outlet for philosophers doing work in non-Western and comparative areas of philosophy as the American Philosophical Association (APA) provides for their counterparts in Western thought," has had to meet as much in conjunction with the American Academy of Religion (AAR) and the Association for Asian Studies (AAS) as with the American Philosophical Association.[41]

It is also for this reason that comparative philosophers have had difficulty publishing their work in traditional philosophical journals, having to look instead to area studies journals (e.g., the *Journal of Chinese Philosophy* or the *Journal of Indian Philosophy*). As Bryan Van Norden pointed out in his "Letter to the Editor" (1996) of the *Proceedings and Addresses of the American Philosophical Association*, the reasons for this segregation are unfounded and are detrimental to both comparative philosophy and to philosophy more generally. I would add that this state of affairs is derivative of the disjunction between the desire to make comparative philosophy another narrow specialization within philosophy and its inability to be just that. Fortunately, journals such as *Philosophy East and West* and *Dao: A Journal of Comparative Philosophy* have arisen to help address this problem, but the disjuncture still remains.

The implications for contemporary comparative philosophy are troubling. To be done well, comparative philosophy requires mastery of a broad range of material, which prohibits the possibility of any meaningful expertise in some narrowly defined specialization; indeed, it is as much as most comparativists can do to gain a general mastery of the traditions in question. Yet such broad grasp is inimical to the professional practice of philosophy, as that discipline is currently understood. It seems clear that there must be some change in the broader conception of philosophy if comparative philosophers are to find their place in the discipline.

Yet there is some cause for optimism. As evidenced by the growing number of professional associations of comparativists—the Society for Asian and Comparative Philosophy (SACP), the International Society for Chinese Philosophy (ISCP), and the International Society for Comparative Studies of Chinese and Western Philosophy (ISCWP)—the subfield is growing at a rapid pace. As this influence continues to grow, it will be increasingly difficult to maintain the integrity of Western traditions of philosophy without also making reference to non-Western traditions. While it is unclear exactly how the discipline of philosophy would have to change if it were to incorporate comparative philosophy more fully, it is worth considering these changes sooner rather than later. Van Norden ended his letter to the editor with the Stoic adage, "The fates drag those who do not come willingly" (1996, 163), and it seems to this observer that their thread has only been spun further in the ten years since his letter.

The Role of Theory in Comparison

Of all the many aspects of comparative philosophy considered in this study, the role of theory seems to be the most problematic sticking point of all. On the one hand, there are those, like Neville, who develop a robust conception of theory but who are consistently called to account for developing that conception in a manner too consistent with one particular tradition (as seen in chapter 4). On the other hand, there are those like Hall and Ames, who try to develop their approach without reference to any particular theory but who either incorporate theory surreptitiously or falter in its absence (as seen in chapter 3). Indeed, it would seem that the only ones who can eschew theory altogether are those, like Richard Rorty, who are willing to eschew comparative philosophy altogether.[42] And yet, it remains unclear how theory is to be incorporated into comparison without unduly biasing the results.

The debate about theory is not restricted to the debate between Hall/Ames and Neville. It can also be seen in Northrop's distinction between concepts by postulation and concepts by intuition: the former represented a more theoretical way of thinking, while the latter represented a more aesthetic way. This distinction, as noted, is quite similar to the distinction observed by Hall and Ames and addresses the problem of theory quite well in itself. Northrop claims to represent both sides—and indeed spent the better part of his methodological considerations trying to figure out how to bring the two sides together—but in the end presents a primarily theoretical account (his many visual aids notwithstanding). The debate can also be seen in the important suggestions and objections raised by Eckel in the context of the Comparative Religious Ideas Project. In contrast to Neville's more theoretical orientation to the project, Eckel proposed a more narrative set of categories and suggested that the philosophically realist categories otherwise suggested did not—could not—adequately represent the Buddhists' more nominalist perspective.

The distinction between realism and nominalism is probably the best way to conceive of the difference; these are the terms used not only by Eckel and Neville to describe their debate but by Hall/Ames and Neville more broadly.[43] The problem with this distinction, however, is that they cannot be brought together into a higher unity; rather, they express mutually exclusive interpretations of the nature of things. Of course, from a Nevillian perspective, I have just provided a vague category by which to bring them together, but this is hardly instructive in the case at hand. The problem is that it seems unavoidable that comparative methods will be either realistic or nominalistic in their orientation and that this will then influence their rendering of the traditions compared.

The implications of this are significant. At stake is the very question of whether or not philosophical traditions can be compared. In short, the very definition of comparative philosophy is at issue, and there appears to be very little beyond this to which one can appeal in making one's case. This, I think, is why the disagreements between Hall/Ames and Neville have been so seemingly intractable: each has arguments to make against the other, but these usually consist of reasons that only those who already agree with them would accept. To my mind, this persistent failure constitutes one of the most troubling shortcomings of comparative philosophy.

If comparative philosophy is possible, it must be able to account for both realistic traditions and nominalistic ones. Such accounting cannot be merely accounting for their existence (i.e., as mistakes or "bad philosophy"); rather, it must be able to appreciate the insights of those traditions, as well as why they would find it so worthwhile to maintain their commitment even when confronted with other traditions. Hitherto, comparative philosophers have been unable to accomplish this, each merely arguing that the other is wrong (and usually for reasons that only those who already agree would agree to), and it arguably stands as one of the most troubling failures of the subfield.

It is also, unfortunately, a failure for which I have no remedy. Having encountered it throughout the figures addressed in this text, I have not seen any completely feasible way of resolving the difference. Yet I believe that this will prove to be one of the most pressing problems for comparative philosophy over the course of the next few generations. Surely the realism/nominalism divide is not the only example of a seemingly intractable difference, but any comparative method that claims to improve on those represented here should make some headway on this issue. It has been beyond the purview of this study to propose any such comparative method, but by highlighting challenges like these it can provide the impetus for further creative work in this important and growing subfield. The challenge has never been more difficult, but neither has it ever been surrounded by such a wealth of scholarly resources. I look with some urgency and yet with a guarded optimism about what the current generation of comparativists will accomplish methodologically, both in "meeting the twain" of diverse philosophical traditions and also in remembering how perhaps rightly elusive that twain shall ever be.

NOTES

NOTES TO INTRODUCTION

1. See Squarcini (2005, 14–16) for more on the etymological roots of 'tradition.'

2. This distinction between method and methodology is crucial for the current project: "method" consists in how something is to be done, while methodology consists in the study of methods themselves (it is the logos of methods). All of the philosophers examined in this text engage in methodological considerations in their own right but take the development and application of their own method as their primary task. My intent, by contrast, is to make methodology the primary focus of this study.

3. I am aware that this move to compare comparative methods introduces new challenges, such as what method one should use when the content of one's comparisons is precisely comparative methods. See "In Defense of Meta-Comparative Philosophy," anon.

4. These traditions are typically classed—along with American naturalism—under the broader heading "American philosophy," thus denoting their primary contextual location in the United States. I will be observing this nomenclature but will refer to American traditions (in the plural) to preserve a sense of the diversity among these traditions.

5. See, e.g., Emerson's 1841 essay on the Over-soul (1940, 293–311); see Leidecker (1951) for more on Emerson's Indian influences. See also James (1985 [1902]).

6. Hall and Ames were hardly the first to recognize the potential fruitfulness of process philosophy for understanding Far Eastern cultures and ideas, but they were among the first—along with Neville—to employ it in the service of comparative methodology.

7. Hocking was scheduled to attend in first (1939) but was prevented from doing so at the last moment. Northrop attended at least the first three (1939, 1949, and 1959). Hall attended the sixth (1989) and seventh (1995), conferences, while Ames attended the last four (1989, 1995, 2000, 2005). Neville attended the sixth (1989), seventh (1995) and ninth (2005). It was my privilege to attend the ninth conference with Ames and Neville.

8. This break was also due to changes in leadership and difficulty with funding, but these are arguably related to the challenges of the broader intellectual climate.

9. I will occasionally use "Hall/Ames" to refer to the collaborative work of Hall and Ames, primarily when an additional "and" would obstruct grammatical

flow. In doing so, I am following their example as laid out in their first collaborative work (1987).

10. The most notable exclusions are the history of religions school and the phenomenology of religions school, both of which have been integrally involved in cross-cultural comparison. Taken together, they account for the vast majority of comparative literature in religious studies. The reason for their exclusion is that, while both have been noticeably self-conscious and critical about methodology vis-à-vis religious studies, neither has expressed much self-conscious or critical interest in the methodology of comparison itself (Jonathan Z. Smith is a notable exception to this generalization). Because the primary concern of this text is the methodology of comparison, these schools—however prolific—do not provide the most fertile resources for further study.

11. One challenge that will not be considered here is whether comparative philosophy is even a viable subdiscipline (see, e.g., Rorty 1989b). While an important consideration, it is not the topic of this text; this text will take for granted the viability of comparative philosophy and focus on ways to improve the comparative process.

12. I am using the word *insight* to serve as a reasonably tradition-neutral term for the conclusions reached by any given tradition, since a more specific term (especially one pertaining to truth) would seem to give advantage to some traditions over others. It is not meant to represent a mystical "a-ha!" moment, but rather the product of sustained, critical work. See Royce (1977 [1912], 5–6), for a rough approximation of what is intended.

13. This would be akin to trying to determine, at the end of a comparative philosophical inquiry, which philosophical tradition is the best overall. Not only has this distorted and discredited comparative philosophy in just about every case, but it is also entirely beside the point of the comparative philosophical enterprise.

CHAPTER 1

1. See Riepe (1970) for more on the influence of Indian philosophy in particular on Hocking's predecessors.

2. Hocking's eventual dissertation, "The Elementary Experiences of Other Conscious Beings in Relation to the Elementary Experiences of Physical and Reflexive Objects" (1904), would meld these two interests: while it was directed by Royce, it is ultimately a study in philosophical psychology with clear debts to James.

3. See Richard Gilman, "Bibliography of William Ernest Hocking from 1898–1964" (Rouner 1966, 465–504), for a complete list of Hocking's publications.

4. This camp was part of the Plattsburgh System, a designed to encourage college students to receive training in military history, tactics, and policies (Gruber 1975).

5. Hocking had studied to be an engineer prior to attending Harvard.

6. In this role, Hocking published a study on the psychology of troop morale—"Morale and Its Enemies" (1918)—that he intended to have used as a handbook by the military. See Gruber (1975) for more information on the nature of these courses and their relation to political positioning and patriotic sentiment in anticipation of the First World War.

7. As Gruber notes (1975), political philosophy in and around the war was as impoverished in critical evaluation as it was intense in national commitment, and Kuklick (1977, 446) extends this assessment to Hocking in particular. Yet Kuklick misses the mark when he suggests that the latter's political activism was merely the result of the social strain of the war and not "a lasting commitment to the affairs of men extending from religious and moral questions to political ones" (447). Hocking's many subsequent—and more sophisticated—works on political philosophy demonstrate that this was, in fact, a serious and lasting concern for Hocking.

8. Unfortunately, by this time, James had recently passed away and Santayana retired.

9. See Reck's essay, "Hocking's Place in American Metaphysics" (Rouner 1966) for a detailed account of Hocking's relation to Peirce, James, Dewey, and Whitehead. According to Randall Auxier (2005), it is Hocking who was primarily responsible for luring Whitehead to Harvard in 1925 to cultivate the latter's philosophical interests.

10. Readers may be surprised to find that Hocking held such prestige in the academy, as his place in the history of philosophy has been all but forgotten. The implications of this for his contemporary relevance will be considered at the close of this chapter.

11. For more on the place of Hocking and the Inquiry in the broader context of debates about Christian missions, see Hogg (1952; 1980) and Yates (1994).

12. Thus, while I will refer to "the Commission" or "the report" for sake of bibliographic accuracy, the reader may infer that these references pertain no less to Hocking himself.

13. Throughout the eighteenth and nineteenth centuries, it was commonplace to compare religions without differentiating between a religion and its cultural context (e.g., Christianity is better than Hinduism because Hindus burn their widows). It was also common to find the best of Christianity contrasted with the worst in other religions. As both internal and external critics of Western Christianity arose in the late nineteenth century, both of these tendencies were quickly called into question.

14. Hocking often referred to humankind in the masculine plural, although this seems to be more a reflection of prevailing conventions than any overt patriarchalism on his part. Interested readers will find in his "Philosophy—the Business of Everyman" (1937) a surprisingly progressive perspective on gender relations.

15. This confidence makes sense in light of Hocking's philosophical idealism: the truth of religion is its religious ideas—what Hocking often referred to as "religious intuitions"—and those ideas persist as true ideas even when their context changes.

16. Hocking's essentialism was not a naïve essentialism: the commission recognized that religions are sufficiently complex as to defy any simplistic reduction to a statement of essence and furthermore acknowledged that the essence of any particular religion also changes as it develops. Accordingly, the report remained consistently vague with respect to the essence of (any) religion. However, it also remained committed to the idea that religion is something in particular (however difficult it is to define what that is) and that each religion is *itself* something particular (though, again, difficult to define). See Slater's essay, "Religious Diversity and

Religious Reconception" (Rouner 1966) for a fine reading of Hocking's nuanced use of the terminology of essences.

17. Taken from C. B. Olds, "A Venture in Understanding" (precise citation not given).

18. This concern with "the emergence of a world-culture" in *Re-Thinking Missions* would pervade many of Hocking's subsequent works, coming to its culmination in one of his last major works, *The Coming World Civilization* (1956).

19. See Kuehl and Dunn (1997) for more on the internationalist movement in America.

20. See Rouner (1969) for more on Hocking's commitment to internationalism.

21. In other words, they pertained to the first four chapters written primarily by Hocking; see Horton's essay in Rouner (1966, 230) for more information.

22. This protest was most vehemently expressed by the New Testament scholar J. Gresham Machen. Hocking's primary debate partner in mission circles, however, was Hendrik Kraemer, who argued for a "subversive fulfillment" theory whereby other religions could prepare the way for Christianity, but that Christianity—the most complete religious truth—ultimately had to supplant those other religions (Rouner 1966, 229).

23. A good example of this can be seen in the strong role of Christian mission in the development of the internationalist movement; see Robert (2002) for more information.

24. See Hocking (1940) for more on the distinction between philosophy and religion.

25. Hocking employed the Wade-Giles system of transliteration, as was the norm at his time; in all direct quotations from his work, I will preserve these transliterations for sake of easy reference. In my own use of Chinese terms, however, I will employ the Pinyin system that is currently the norm. Thus, for example, while Hocking writes about Chu Hsi, I will write about Zhu Xi.

26. This is not to say that Hocking was consistently accurate in his accounts of Chinese philosophy. Even sympathetic critiques have taken issue with some of the finer points of his accounts (see, e.g., Lachs and Hester 2004, 371). He was remarkably accurate, however, and bore the respect of most of his colleagues in Western and Chinese philosophy alike, although exceptions such as Shryock (1936) also exist. Neville probably said it best when he wrote that "Hocking had an understanding of Confucianism . . . that was extraordinary for his time and entirely respectable now" (368).

27. Neville argues that Hocking saw his role as a philosopher in terms of what we would now call a "public intellectual": he took it as his responsibility to be wise and informed on issues generally and to be in communication with other people who were wise and informed. Accordingly, Hocking had close friends and contacts in most of the world's great philosophical traditions and "took responsible understanding of the cultures of his friends and fellow philosophers to be a part of the philosophic life" (Lachs and Hester 2004, 368). This approach to philosophy stands in contrast to the "professionalization" of philosophy that has taken place since Hocking's time, where philosophical questions are believed to be of interest primarily for philosophers and their answers capable of being adequately understood and properly judged only by one's academic philosophical peers (Kuklick 1977, 451–80). This will be discussed in more detail in the final chapter.

28. "Sensitivity" is Hocking's term, although he also used "receptivity," "sensitization," and "adjustment" to describe the same idea. All of these refer to the capacity of the knower to register or "pick up on" the reality of the thing in question.

29. For a more extensive discussion of Hocking's view of nature, see Hocking (1944a).

30. Hocking noted that "this is the essential consideration accounting for much of the characteristic tenor of the theory of knowledge in Oriental thought" (109) but maintained that it is particularly well developed in the philosophical work of Zhu Xi (111).

31. Neville characterizes Hocking as the first of the "Boston Confucians," noting an important line of continuity between the latter's approach to comparison and his own. Neville notes this continuity more directly at the end of his essay, where he writes that "I have followed up modestly on Hocking's axiological program with my three-volume *Axiology of Thinking*" (Lachs and Hester 2004, 380 n. 16).

32. Sinclair hoped that Radhakrishnan would do likewise from an Eastern perspective.

33. Although the conference ended in 1939, the war postponed publication until 1944.

34. This chapter will take Hocking's distinctions between "East and West" and "Orient and Occident" for granted. These were the prevailing distinctions of his day, and the only thing remarkable about his use of them was his readiness to do away with them. See Hocking (1952, 99–100) for a surprisingly progressive account of these distinctions as poetic starting points for inquiry rather than definitive sets of metaphysical categories. These distinctions will be discussed in more detail in the chapter on Northrop, since it was over the course of his career that they ceased to be the norm.

35. The mention of Schopenhauer is likely due to Royce's influence, who was particularly impressed with the resonance between Schopenhauer's thought and Indian and Buddhist philosophy (Riepe 1967, 127–28). He might have also mentioned Leibniz, among others.

36. This distinction anticipates one that will be made famous by one of Hocking's best students, F. S. C. Northrop; his use of that distinction will be examined in the next chapter.

37. Contemporary philosophers might not want to go so far as to maintain that "the categories both of being and of value are the same everywhere" (1944b, 3), but his point about the necessity of some underlying commonality is nonetheless well taken.

38. Returning to the question of philosophical superiority, Hocking pointed out that one of the more compelling measures is the "durability" of a tradition: its ability to survive over time and to stand as the underlying framework for the greatest number of people. Such a measure, he noted, would clearly favor Eastern traditions of philosophy (1944b, 7).

39. Hocking used the term *supplementation* in this essay to address the potential relationship among different traditions. In essays that deal with the change within one tradition as a result of its encounter with another tradition, he used the word *reconception* (e.g., 1940). The basic idea is the same; the difference in terms seems to reflect whether the focus of the essay is cross-traditional or intratraditional.

40. For Hocking, idealism—by which he means Absolute idealism—is the conviction "that all reality is the same stuff that ideas are made or, that 'whatever is is rational' . . . that everything is known to one absolute Knower, whose being is thought, or Idea . . . [and that] the Absolute of Idealism [is] identical with the God of religion" (1912, vi). The consequence of this idealism is the conviction that "the universe has a meaning (or a system of meanings); a meaning which is objective, in the sense that it is there whether or not you or I discover it, but which can be discerned by us" (1959, 436). It is this commitment to a single universe of meaning that inspired Hocking's interest in comparative philosophy: if philosophy seeks the fullest possible interpretation of the universe, then any and all interpretations are useful toward that end. Indeed, this same commitment has inspired the cross-cultural interests of idealists from Hegel to Royce.

41. See James (1975 [1907], 21) for a good example of James' critique of idealism, with which Hocking would have been largely sympathetic (see, e.g., Hocking 1912, x, 184).

42. For more information on this fusion, see Reck's essay in Rouner (1966). See also Hocking (1912, v–xix, 157–62).

43. This idea is developed in conscious opposition to James' pragmatism; see James (1975 [1907], 97) for his contrasting theory of truth. While Hocking's negative pragmatism enabled him more flexibility in asserting the truth of things without direct verification (it can only show when ideas are *not* true), it also made him prone to make conclusions about truth and falsity where they are not warranted. For example, in *Science and the Idea of God* (1944a), he argued that atheism is likely false because the sciences have consistently failed to do without some idea of God. James' theory of truth is arguably the stronger of the two, perhaps because it is not saddled with both idealist and pragmatist commitments simultaneously.

44. This is something like Peirce's "infinite long run" read in reverse.

45. See, e.g., Flew's now-famous dismissal of all non-Western philosophy (1971, 36).

46. This is a significant assumption and one that will be questioned seriously by David Hall and Roger Ames in their assessment of comparative philosophy (see chapter 3).

47. Gilman's annotated bibliography in Rouner (1966) lists his numerous related works.

48. There are interesting similarities between Hocking's experience and that of early Protestant missionaries. See, e.g., Carey (1988 [1792]); see also Robert (2005).

49. See Moore (1951, 1) for one good example of how subsequent comparativists have taken up this task (in language that seems eerily reminiscent of Hocking).

50. See, e.g., Reck (1964), Rouner (1969), and Kuklick (1977). Rouner notes that similar critiques were made in Hocking's own time by James Wood and Charles Hartshorne (1969, 312–13; see also Rouner's essay in Lachs and Hester 2004, 280–89).

51. See John Stuhr's essay in Lachs and Hester (2005, 318–34) for a more detailed account of the causes for Hocking's contemporary obscurity.

52. More informally, his prominence is perhaps attested to in the comment made by the philosopher W. T. Stace upon hearing of the festschrift that was to be

published in Hocking's honor: "I am sure that there is no one in our profession who would not wish to be associated with any project in his honor" (Rouner 1966, vii).

53. It is significant that one of the few current philosophers to take Hocking's philosophical contributions serious is Neville, who shares with Hocking the commitment to treat all philosophers as intellectual peers. As will be seen in chapter 4, Neville disagrees with Hocking on several methodological points, but taking the time to develop one's disagreements is perhaps the best example of taking someone's contributions seriously.

CHAPTER 2

1. As noted in chapter 1, the strong distinction between East and West observed by Northrop will be called into question later in this chapter.

2. In a sense, it is surprising that the conference took place at all. As originally planned, it was to have a significant representation among Japanese scholars, including D. T. Suzuki and Junjirō Takakusu, none of whom would have been able to attend just a few years later. Indeed, most would not be able to attend if the conference was held much later.

3. There is a historical irony in the development of Northrop's prewar cross-cultural interests and those that developed as a result of the war: the attack on Pearl Harbor (December 7, 1941), which instigated American involvement in the war, took place less than ten miles from where the first East-West Philosophers' Conference took place.

4. Northrop studied under Hocking at Harvard, graduating with a Ph.D. in philosophy in 1924.

5. Although Hocking did not begin publishing anything in comparative philosophy until after Northrop graduated, his burgeoning interests in cross-cultural comparison would already have been apparent and influential for a close student like Northrop.

6. This conference constituted something of a "passing of the baton" from Hocking to Northrop with respect to comparative philosophy: whereas Hocking's involvement in the conference marked the near culmination of his comparative interests, it marked the inauguration of such interests for Northrop.

7. Adolf Grünbaum, for example, recalls that the *New York Times Book Review* rated it the most important intellectual event of 1946 (Seddon 1995, viii). The book's influence was reflected and magnified by its role in inspiring Robert Pirsig's novel, *Zen and the Art of Motorcycle Maintenance* (1974); see Pirsig (1974, 123–24; 1999, 97).

8. Although published a year after the *Meeting*, it consists primarily of essays written throughout the preceding decade. These essays will be considered collectively here.

9. The strong similarities of Northrop's argument in the *Logic* with Hocking's roughly contemporary essay, "Chu Hsi's Theory of Knowledge" (1936), only reinforces the earlier claim that Hocking's work continued to influence Northrop after his graduation.

10. It may seem that Northrop is endorsing a sharp distinction between facts and values, which would seem to run counter to the tendency in American

philosophy; as will be seen further *anon*, however, these two are epistemically cor-related in the final analysis.

11. Acknowledging the difficulty of separating oneself from such theoretical overlay, Northrop notes that, while important, this can only be a momentary step; as soon as one tries to communicate one's observations, one has moved to the next method (1947, 36).

12. The essay was originally titled "The Complementary Emphases of Eastern Intuitive and Western Scientific Philosophy" and was published in Moore (1944, 168–234).

13. David Hall and Roger Ames will make a similar case about translation (1987), although their proposed solution is quite different (see chapter 3 for more details).

14. Although published in 1946, the book was actually written during the war (1946, xi).

15. See Northrop's essay in Northrop (1949, 407–28) for his argument that ideology, like other moral and mental features of reality, is no less "real" than bio-logical ones. He defended this on the basis of epistemic correlation, which will be examined further anon.

16. Northrop provided a long list of such conflicts (1946, ix), which is made all the more poignant by the fact that all of them remain sites of conflict in the contemporary world.

17. Note the similarities between this and what his mentor, W. E. Hocking, referred to as "the coming world civilization." Their programs for achieving this were similar as well.

18. As this list indicates, Northrop's examination was heavily weighted toward the West. He committed six chapters to different facets of the Western tradition and only one, the longest of them all, to Eastern culture in general.

19. This readiness to identify the "meaning" of a culture or civilization constituted an important break with his teacher, W. E. Hocking. As the reader will recall, Hocking also used the terminology of "meaning," but remained consistently and methodologically vague with respect to what the meaning of any tradition actually was.

20. Northrop, of course, was writing prior to the rise of Eastern countries as economic powerhouses in the global marketplace. He would have been intrigued by more recent arguments that this rise has occurred not *despite* their cultural heritage but *because* of it.

21. Northrop claimed in Moore (1962, 525–32) that sinologists such as Joseph Needham and others misinterpreted his work by claiming that Chinese thought also entails postulation. His argument was not that there is no postulation (which is attendant to any scientific theory), but rather that there has been little in the way of "concepts by postulation" (which refers to imageless constructs that inform symbolic logic, pure mathematics, and mathematical physics). See Northrop (1962, 13–14) for more information.

22. It is significant that, in connection with his argument for epistemic cor-relation, Northrop explicitly rejected Whitehead's theory of abstraction. Whitehead was right to have rejected the modern dualism between mental and material sub-stance, he argued, but should not have also rejected the distinction between sensed

time and space and theoretically postulated time and space. This led Whitehead to maintain that "all scientific concepts are derived from [nature, the 'terminus of sense awareness'] by 'extensive abstraction' " (1946, 441), in other words, that theoretical constructs were nothing other than abstractions from sensory experience. This assimilation of sensed and mathematically designated time and space runs counter to prevailing scientific theories, he argued; these theories require a distinction between the two (he points to the theories of Max Planck and Albert Einstein as examples). In fact, he noted, Whitehead's theory of abstraction actually exemplifies the Western tendency to subsume aesthetic immediacy into its theoretical postulates (as simply the raw materials for theory construction). The best solution, he argued, is not to explain away one side of the distinction but rather to revalorize the underdeveloped side and show that the two sides can be brought together.

23. Northrop used the example of the color "blue" (perhaps reminiscent of Hume): it has both an aesthetic component (the color actually observed) and a theoretic component (its place on a color chart, the wavelength of blue light, etc.). One who has never seen the color can understand what the color theoretically represents but does not have a full sense of how that representation actually plays itself out in the particular. By contrast, one who has seen the color has knowledge of the blueness in its immediacy but cannot understand it in relation to anything else except by means of a broader theoretical framework. Both the aesthetic and theoretic components are called "blue," a fact that, as he noted, only obscures the full meaning of the term; but "blueness" cannot be fully understood except with reference to both components (1946, 448).

24. "Actually," Northrop admitted, "the relationship is more complicated than this" (1946, 451). He developed the theory further with respect to one-one, many-one, and one-many relations, but this does not significantly impact his theory of comparison and is therefore left aside in this study (see 451–54 for more information).

25. Although Northrop made his primary case with respect to the relation of East and West, he maintained that his theory of knowledge is capable of resolving cultural conflicts within East and West as well.

26. Northrop wrote in the *Logic*, "The important thing to note about the analysis of the problem in *The Meeting of East and West* is that as the analysis guided one to the relevant factual information necessary to clearly understand the problem, the initial question, which appeared first as a question of value to which scientific methods did not seem to apply, became transformed over, as the statement of the basic difficulty became more evident and precise, into a specific question of fact which scientific methods and scientific evidence could and did answer" (1947, 32).

27. Kluckhohn seems to have meant by "primitive postulates" what Northrop meant by concepts more generally.

28. The dissertation sought to consider this problem in biology from the perspective of Aristotelian logic. Reflective of his cross-disciplinary interests, he had a dissertation advisor in both philosophy (Hocking) and the natural sciences (L. J. Henderson).

29. Northrop originally studied with Whitehead while he was in London in the early 1920's, and he credited Whitehead with having "directed my philosophical analysis of the theory and method of 20th-century mathematical physics" (Northrop 1962, 15; see also 175). Northrop would maintain this close relationship

with Whitehead when the latter accepted a position at Harvard (largely due to the influence of Northrop's teacher, Hocking), during which time Whitehead wrote his own most influential philosophical works. Northrop was instrumental in promoting these works, in part by means of the anthology of Whitehead's works that he published in conjunction with Mason Gross (1953). See Reck (1968, 198–99) for more on this historical connection.

30. Northrop met with Einstein in Berlin in 1927 to discuss some of the problems he saw with Einstein's covariant chronogeometrical tensor equation (more on this anon). As with Whitehead, Northrop strengthened his relationship with Einstein when the latter accepted a position in the United States: the two met on an annual basis at Einstein's home in Princeton to continue discussing issues in the philosophy of science (1962, 20).

31. Northrop noted that, when he met with Einstein in 1927, the latter admitted that the tensor in his equation "permits two alternative solutions" (Northrop 1931, x), namely, his own and the one proposed by Northrop.

32. Like Northrop, Whitehead also noted similar problems in Einstein's theory. In fact, Whitehead had previously developed and published his own theory of relativity as an alternative to that of Einstein (Whitehead 1922). Yet even Whitehead noted that, other than his own solution, Northrop's macroscopic atomic theory seemed the only way of resolving the problems with Einstein's theory (1929, 333).

33. See Joyotpaul Chaudhuri and Norman Riise's bibliography of Northrop's works in Seddon (1995, 229–52), for a more extensive list of Northrop's related publications.

34. Again, see Chaudhuri and Riise's bibliography for more on his related works.

35. In addition to philosophy, Northrop earned degrees in history and economics.

36. See Northrop (1962, 11) for a poignant defense of his cross-disciplinary commitments.

37. This can also be seen with respect to his references to aesthetics and law. Aesthetics featured prominently in Northrop's earlier work (e.g., the Meeting), but it fades almost entirely into the background in his later work (e.g., Philosophical Anthropology). By contrast, international legal issues are one of the driving concerns of his later work, whereas they had been only a passing concern in earlier works. This transition naturally had to do at least in part with his increased involvement in the Yale law school over the intervening years as a result of his dual appointment; stated simply, he spoke most to the things with which he was most involved at the time. It also appears to reflect the tension between the many disciplines from which he wanted to address cross-cultural concerns and those few fields from which he could credibly do so.

38. This is seen nowhere better than in the difference between the Meeting and Philosophical Anthropology: while the first is truly remarkable for its imaginative insight, the second, while certainly more precise in its terminology and detailed in its defenses, is much less inspiring and arguably less insightful.

39. See Northrop (1949) and Northrop and Livingston (1964) for the most prominent examples of collaborative texts in comparative philosophy edited by Northrop.

40. In this respect, Hocking serves as a perfect contrast: whereas he brought Zhu Xi into direct conversation with the modern natural sciences, Northrop would

maintain that the differences between them run so deep as to preclude any such conversation.

41. See Northrop (1949, iii) for a poignant defense of the urgent need for more peaceful world order as well as the role of all disciplines for bringing this about.

42. Even if Northrop proved only moderately successful at overcoming his cultural biases, this suggests that he could have done better (or for that matter, worse). Northrop was aware that his framework would be reworked by others over time, so it might be said that he leaves it to his philosophical heirs to do better at overcoming their cultural biases.

43. Evidence of this influence can be seen in a number of the essays included in this collection, with explicit reference to his terminology in the essays by Wing-tsit Chan (Moore 1944, 147, 159, 165) and Charles Moore (1944, 282–85, 287–88, 303, 320, 289n).

44 Perhaps the best point of contrast in this respect is Northrop's own teacher, W. E. Hocking. While Hocking agreed that it is the differences among traditions that provide the richest ground for cross-cultural comparison, he remained skeptical of any strict rendering of the interactions among traditions (the reader will recall the discussion of Hocking's modified essentialism in the previous chapter); Northrop, by contrast, made such a rendering the crowning achievement of his comparative method.

45. The most prominent example of Northrop's comparison of traditions as a whole is his observation that Western thought is dominated by the theoretic while Eastern thought is dominated by the aesthetic. This is a more fruitful comparative observation than any of the more specific comparisons made throughout his work, because it is precisely these broad-scale comparisons that allow him to deduce his practical proposals (e.g., that the West could learn about aesthetic sensitivity from the East, while the East should learn scientific mastery and economic innovation from the West).

46. The framework garnered the support of most scholars at the first conference, and a number of those at subsequent conferences. A good example of this is Wing-tsit Chan's effective endorsement in his essay for the first conference (Moore 1944, 137–67).

47. In the collection of essays published in conjunction with the conference (Moore 1951), Northrop is mentioned more times and in more essays than any other conference member, more times, in fact, than any other figure alive at the time.

48. The story of this encounter is obviously too brief and quaint to provide much support for an actual identity among the terms discussed, but the issue at hand is not whether Northrop's claims are true in every respect but whether they represent a potentially fruitful method. Here, Suzuki's assent provides some support for this; see Suzuki's essay in Moore (1951, 42) for more evidence of his support for Northrop's distinctions (but note also his concern that the association will be misunderstood by others).

49. See Northrop's account of having convinced Junjirō Takakusu of the identity between Nirvana and the undifferentiated aesthetic continuum (1962, 21–24); see also Y. P Mei's likening of the Dao to the same (Moore 1951, 310). Unfortunately, due in large part to the very precise and specific terminology he employed, Northrop appears to have been perpetually misunderstood by his contemporaries. Many of those who accused him of mining his terms only from Western concepts often failed to appreciate the subtlety of their application to non-Western traditions (see, e.g., John

Wild's essay in Moore 1951, 249–70), while those who applied his terminology to non-Western traditions (including Suzuki and Mei) often appear to have done so without appreciating the full extent of what Northrop meant by those terms.

50. It should be noted that E. R. Hughes made a case, similar to the more famous one made by Joseph Needham, that Northrop had short-changed the Chinese tradition in his suggestion that it had not developed concepts by postulation in any significant manner; in contrast to Needham, however, Hughes argued more on the basis of epistemology and ethics than the natural sciences for the presence of such concepts in the Chinese tradition.

51. David Hall and Roger Ames (the subjects of the next chapter) make this critique (1995, 118), but differ from most others insofar as they also acknowledge their intellectual debts to his comparative method (1987, 4–5).

52. Something of the limitations of this shift can be seen in the irony of its justification: what do you do with the fact that a cultural change introduces the idea that ideas are dependent on the cultures out of which they arise? The very validity of this claim relies on its applicability across cultures, and even across the various changes within which the idea of the importance of cultural location eventually arose. This suggests that this most recent development in comparative philosophy, while an important corrective for the understanding of philosophical ideas, is less a definitive move than a temporary shift in emphasis, much like the swing of a pendulum. Once it has served its purpose, it will likely be corrected as well by a renewed—though revised—appreciation for cross-cultural translation, and the dialectical process of cross-cultural hermeneutics will continue accordingly.

53. See especially Moore's remark to this effect (1951, 5); even Hughes (Moore 1951, 64) and Burtt (119), while critical of Northrop's approach, express their admiration and appreciation for it.

54. It is interesting to note that a similar concern was not voiced among Western scholars for the significance of concepts by intuition in their tradition.

55. All of these critiques can be found in Moore (1949) except one; for Hu Shi's critique, see Moore (1959).

56. The reader is directed to vol. 2, *The History of Scientific Thought* (1956) for his critique of Northrop as well as his alternative to Northrop's comparative framework. It should be noted that, while Needham's is clearly the most prominent of such critiques, his position on the role of scientific thought in China was at least shared, if not anticipated, by scholars at the second conference. See, e.g., Hughes' argument in Moore (1951, 49–72), which is effectively a simplified version of Needham's argument.

57. Needham conceded that China ultimately failed to adequately develop its scientific thought but ascribed this failure not to a dearth of concepts by postulation but rather to a variety of other predominantly social causes. He wrote: "What went wrong with Chinese science was its ultimate failure to develop out of these theories forms more adequate to the growth of practical knowledge, and in particular its failure to apply mathematics to the formulation of regularities in natural phenomena. This is equivalent to saying that no Renaissance awoke it from its 'empirical slumbers'" (1954–2004, 2: 579). Compare this to Hughes' essay (Moore 1951, 70), which gives a very different account in largely the same terms.

58. For Northrop's responses to his critics, the reader is referred to Moore (1951, 153–54; also 379–80) and especially Moore (1962, 521–32).

59. Northrop might have been intrigued by the recent discovery of what appear to be Caucasoid mummies in China at Xiaohe, Xinjiang province (Mallory and Mair 2000).

60. It is important not to attribute this tendency in Northrop to his idealist influences. The reader will recall that Hocking, Northrop's teacher, was much more influenced by idealism and yet held such distinctions only provisionally.

61. It is worth noting, however, that the *Meeting* continues to serve as a text for many introductory courses with a comparative cultural emphasis, suggesting that Northrop's framework remains helpful at least as a starting point.

62. Indeed, it would not be until Hall and Ames developed their own alternative to Northrop's framework that a comparable framework would be made available.

63. The Comparative Religious Ideas Project is arguably the best example of such a method and will be discussed in further detail in chapter 4.

64. Actually, the move in the first conference was toward a quadripartite division between the West, India, China, and Japan, although the distinction between the last two appeared to exist for a primarily political reason; this reason, as well as the distinction, disappeared for the most part after the first conference (and the war that accompanied it), and a tripartite division became the norm thereafter. This tripartite division is the root of the current division among Western, South Asian, and East Asian traditions. See Masuzawa (2005) for a more recent study tracing the change from a two-civilization model of comparison to a three-civilization model.

CHAPTER 3

1. Although Hall and Ames do not appear to be aware of this, W. E. Hocking placed the same emphasis on the "interest" associated with ideas, over fifteen years before Whitehead penned this phrase. Hocking wrote that "a theory is false if it is not interesting: a proposition that falls on the mind so dully as to excite no enthusiasm has not attained the level of truth; though the words be accurate, the import has leaked away from them, and the meaning is not conveyed. Any such criterion of truth is based on a conviction or thesis otherwise founded, that the real world is infinitely charged with interest and value, whereby any commonplaceness on our part is evidence of a lack of grasp" (1912, xiii–xiv). In the spirit of highlighting connections among these comparativists, it is also notable that Neville used Whitehead's quote to open his *Recovery of the Measure* (1989), the preface of which acknowledges his indebtedness to his conversations with Hall.

2. *Ontologia generalis* and *scientia universalis* are formative terms for Hall and Ames' understanding of the Western philosophical tradition (1982b, 102; 1982a, 192–93; 1987, 199–200, 248, 291–93), and will be used to contrast their own distinctive approach to philosophy: *ars contextualis* (1987, 246–49; 1995, 273–75; 1998, 39–43, 111–12).

3. Early in his career, Hall's interest centered primarily around Chinese Daoism, but this interest gradually came to include—and even focus on—Chinese Confucianism.

4. Hall read the latter three as protopragmatists, especially insofar as they inherited concerns hitherto addressed most substantively by earlier pragmatists such as John Dewey (see, e.g., 1982a, 148). By contrast, Rorty received a relatively unsympathetic reception (see esp. 1982a, 104–05, also 144–45).

5. However influential Rorty was for Hall, there remained significant differences between them even at the end of their lives. See essays by Rorty, Neville, and Crosby in Chinn and Rosemont (2005) for evidence of these differences.

6. The tentative title of this unfinished work was "America's Broken Promise" (Chinn and Rosemont 2005, vi).

7. Evidence for their growing influence on one another can be seen by their mutual acknowledgments in publications shortly after their encounter (Hall 1982a, ix; Ames 1983, ix). Hall and Ames would write their first collaborative piece soon thereafter (1984).

8. They note that "[t]hough we shall have occasion to differ in some crucial instances with Fingarette's interpretation of Confucius, our principal purpose is quite similar to his" (1987, 6). They also refer to this as a "culturalogical method" (331).

9. This is not, strictly speaking, what Hall and Ames mean by a "problematic" method; this is more accurately reflected in the second and third levels of their method. Yet a broader notion of "problematic" allows these three levels of their method to hang together in a way that is not inconsistent with their more specific interpretation of that term.

10. Lau and Ames have subsequently worked together to translate the *Sun Bin* (1996), the *Yuan Dao* (1998), and portions of the *Huai Nan Tzu* (Ames, Chan, and Mau-sang 1991, 287). As far as I know, the portions of the *Huai Nan Tzu* that he worked on with Lau were not published—at least not in conjunction with Lau; it inevitably informed Ames' own publications pertaining to that text (1980; 1981).

11. Hall and Ames point to use of terms such as "Heaven," "Truth," and "Self" (1995, xiv); following Robert Solomon (1993), they maintain that such terms introduce into Chinese philosophy a "transcendental pretense" that is otherwise foreign to it. More on this *anon*.

12. "Importance" will be a crucial term for Hall and Ames, so great care is used throughout this chapter to use it only to indicate the precise meaning that they intended.

13. According to Hall, "Whitehead did not believe that the purpose of the systematic philosopher was first and foremost to 'get it right' " (1982a, 104). Hall (and later Ames as well) remained similarly indifferent to questions of truth: "My arguments are, for the most part, to be construed as seeking neither to establish truths nor to claim that no such establishment is possible" (1982b, xv).

14. Anyone familiar with Whitehead's *Adventures of Ideas* (1933) will readily recognize the strong influence of his work on the development of Hall's project.

15. They note that, while there have been occasional attempts in the West to engage in first problematic thinking—they point to Montaigne, Cusanus, Lovejoy, and others—this attempt was typically weak and half-hearted at best (see, e.g., Hall 1982a, 119–22).

16. When Hall and Ames refer to the "philosophical viability" of first problematic thinking, they do not mean to refer to such philosophy as it appears in the early accounts of the *physiologoi*—they readily admit that those early accounts "evidence serious flaws" (1982a, 123); rather, they mean the philosophical excellence of the ideas themselves as developed in all of their potential.

17. A more subtle reading of Hall and Ames, reading between the lines, would suggest that first problematic thinking did not flourish in early Greek soci-

ety because its "importance" was not able to be made adequately manifest in that cultural context.

18. Hall and Ames have undoubtedly been pleased with the resurgence of something like first problematic thinking in Western philosophy, as evidenced in postmodern (e.g., Derrida, Foucault) and neopragmatist philosophies (e.g., Davidson, Rorty). Referencing these figures, they note that, "though our primary concern is to illumine the contrasting assumptions shaping classical Chinese and Western cultures, we shall not be disappointed if a side effect of our discussion is to add some plausibility to the various intellectual movements which are attempting to reformulate important aspects of our own cultural sensibility" (1995, xviii).

19. This paraphrase is adapted from John Dewey's comment in "From Absolutism to Experimentalism" (1930) that "a chief task of those who call themselves philosophers is to help get rid of the useless lumber that blocks our highways of thought, and strive to make straight and open the paths that lead to the future" (Dewey 1998, 1:21).

20. The resonances with Northrop's theory are especially strong here. As suggested in the previous chapter, Hall and Ames have significant intellectual debts to Northrop, most notably on the distinction between East and West along the lines of the aesthetic and the rational (see, e.g., 1982a, 194). More on this *anon.*

21. It should be noted that Hall's argument for philosophical anarchism is not an absolute argument for its superiority; such an argument would be inconsistent with the very idea of anarchism. Rather, it is for the appropriateness of such a perspective in this particular context. Hall is careful to reiterate this point repeatedly (see 1982a, passim), but it is unclear—or, at least, uncompelling—that he would ever see a period in which a nonanarchistic view of the world should predominate.

22. Their work, if read outside of the appropriate context, can be very misleading. Hall and Ames make a number of statements about the character of Chinese philosophy that, taken by themselves, would seem to be intended to be normative statements about philosophy per se; however, given that their entire comparative framework is built on the respect for each tradition's unique and irreducible validity, these statements should rather be understood as being normative only within the Chinese philosophical tradition. At the same time—their protests to the contrary notwithstanding—one is never entirely sure that they do not *also* mean to insinuate a broader normativity in their claims.

23. The interest here was admittedly more of Hall's than Ames', so it will be interesting to see whether this strand of their collaborative work will persist in Ames' subsequent work.

24. It is important to note that, at least to my knowledge, Hall and Ames have never maintained this strong position in print. It is, however, a direct inference from their work: while it is possible for philosophers and sinologists to make advances that Hall and Ames may not see (they provide numerous example of cases in which they have been corrected in both respects), at the end of the day—all other things being equal—the combined philosopher-sinologist simply has more data at his or her disposal and is thus most likely to be able to make the most informed comparative judgments.

25. This change seems to be occurring—however gradually—on its own. As careful philosophical studies of Chinese thought become increasingly available to linguists, one can expect an increased philosophical sophistication in the translations

that are made available. Likewise, as translations of Chinese texts become increasingly critical and philosophically informed, one can expect students of Chinese
philosophy to develop a more accurate understanding of the precise character of
Chinese thought. Moreover, as sinologists and philosophers increasingly interact in
conferences, peer-reviewed journals, and so on, the academy itself comes to represent Hall and Ames' project writ large. Projects like that undertaken by Hall and
Ames thus do not bring about something that otherwise would not occur but rather
hasten the development of something that reflects a demonstrable and pressing need
within the subfield.

26. This can be seen, for example, in Hegel's changing attitude toward Buddhism: in the 1824 version of his lectures on the philosophy of religion, he classified Buddhism as a "religion of magic"; however, upon further study of Buddhism,
he revised his interpretation for the 1827 version of those lectures and classified it
instead as the "second form of nature religion, the more determinate and intensive
being-within-self" (562, [458]). See Hegel 1984–98, vol. 2, 303–16 [207–19]; 562–79
[458–76] for more details. Peter Hodgson, who edited a complete edition of Hegel's
lectures, has commented, "On the whole, the 1827 treatment of Buddhism is more
fully developed and balanced than in 1824, evidencing a better mastery of the available sources" (562 n. 138). See Hegel 1984–88, vol. 2, 303–16 [207–19]; 562–79
[458–76] for more details.

27. Hegel was, admittedly, working with only a very limited subset of available data about non-Western traditions and was far ahead of his time in terms of
engaging that data. While few modern-day scholars would endorse his conclusions,
most would laud what Hegel was able to accomplish with the limited cross-cultural
resources at his disposal.

28. For example, both Nishida (1986a, 1987a, 1987b) and Nishitani (1982)
argued for an underlying similarity between the Buddhist notion of śūnyatā ("empti-
ness") and the Christian notion of kenōsis ("self-emptying"); while there are certainly
at least vague similarities between these concepts, it is unclear whether the extent
of these similarities is the result of anything more than an unduly Zen Buddhist
reading of Christianity (or, perhaps, an unduly Christian reading of Zen Buddhism).
A similar case could be made for Nishida's use of William James' theory of "pure
experience" for interpreting Zen Buddhism (Nishida 1990), where James' notion is
so altered—admittedly, both creatively and constructively—that it is unclear how
fully the connection really holds between the two. See Odin (1987; 1989) for a fine
summary of the arguments of the Kyoto School in these respects, as well as some
commentary on their place in comparative philosophy.

29. Perhaps the key difference in Cheng's work is that its primary purpose is
not so much descriptive as it is constructive. Some of the concern about his work
should be mitigated if this distinction is observed.

30. Support for this can be found in Hall's prior work on philosophical
anarchism (1982a): while it clearly bears some affinity with pre-Socratic Greek
philosophy, it also bears the clear marks of a twentieth-century postmodern philosophical program.

31. Interestingly, the process is much like the dialectical process that Plato—
who is proclaimed by Hall the "hero" and "villain" of his work (1982a, xv)—typically undertakes in his own work. This is surprising, given that Hall and Ames do
not mince words in their rejection of the priority of dialectical modes of reasoning.

They write, for example, that "we believe comparative discussion cannot usefully depend upon dialectical argumentation" (1995, xx). To my knowledge, this tension remains unresolved in their work.

32. I employ the word *opposition* in addition to *contrast* because, while opposition overstates the difference (suggesting even some antagonism among the alternatives), contrast does not entail the strong sense of difference that I argue is meant to be communicated by these distinctions in their work. In making these distinctions, Hall and Ames seem to intend something that lies between mere contrast and actual opposition.

33. Using their "field and focus" terminology, this is to say that each tradition constitutes a particular foci within a common field but that only one of the foci can be drawn into focus at any given time (1987, 237–38). Thus, a better example of the sort of opposition I am describing here would be not logical/illogical but rather logical/analogical: both sides address logic but in sufficiently different ways as to be opposable to one another.

34. Of course, Hall would go on to describe an alternative way of characterizing traditions that purportedly avoids these difficulties. The critical question is whether his endorsement of first problematic thinking avoids the arbitrariness described above, as well as the practical results that issue from it.

35. Hall and Ames are particularly critical of Dilworth in this respect (see, e.g., 1995, 160–64; 197–98). Dilworth has been far more ambitious than Watson in his application of his transcendental framework across cultural boundaries and thus has been much more susceptible to the types of critique leveled by Hall and Ames.

36. Watson and Dilworth would both allow that they have made errors in the application of their frameworks, but Hall and Ames are pointing not to errors in application but rather to a more fundamental, methodological error in the use of the structures themselves.

37. Hall and Ames vigorously defend the notion that McKeon did not assert the transcultural validity of his typology (see, e.g., 1995, 298–99).

38. Interestingly, in what is perhaps a softening of Hall's previous anarchistic stance, Hall and Ames do not reject out of hand the possibility that there could exist a taxonomy that would adequately account for all philosophic traditions; more pragmatically, they merely insist that it is evident that no such taxonomy exists at present and that it is therefore detrimental to our understanding of philosophic traditions to pretend that it does.

39. See note 11 in this chapter for the intended meaning of the term "transcendental pretense."

40. There are, of course, also important differences as well. For example, Hall focuses more on cosmology (one-world versus many-worlds hypotheses) and argues that, while both ways of thinking are relatively adequate, they do not appear capable of being synthesized. Such differences notwithstanding, the strong similarities in terminology and structure of comparative framework bring Hall and Northrop remarkably close to one another methodologically.

41. Whitehead is able engage such a wide breadth of traditions in large part because of his understanding of philosophy as the "critic of abstractions" (Whitehead 1925, 87). This forces him to take seriously the abstractions of the Western tradition (e.g., its substance cosmology), but also to call them into question to the extent that they run afoul of the available evidence (i.e., in favor a process cosmology). Northrop

himself seems aware of this connection, as it is precisely his critique of Whitehead's theory of abstraction that causes him to develop his own two-termed theory of relation (see chapter 2, note 22). In this connection, it is surprising that Hall would favor Whitehead over Northrop, given his own use of two-termed contrasts.

42. In contrast to Northrop's example of the color blue (perhaps in deference to Hume) to show how epistemic correlation works with respect to experience of the color blue (see chapter 2, note 23), Hall used the example of the color red (even in his examples, Hall was a nonconformist!) to distinguish between Northrop's and Whitehead's views on abstraction (1982b, 189–91). He argued that both philosophers would distinguish between the aesthetic and theoretic component in the experience of that color and that both would want to demonstrate how the two components are epistemically correlated. (I find this argument dubious at best.) Only Whitehead, however, would make the further claim that the two are also *ontically* correlated. Again, given Hall's embrace of two-termed distinctions like the ones Northrop developed, it is surprising that he would endorse Whitehead's theory of abstraction over Northrop's.

43. As noted throughout the previous chapter, Northrop never maintained that the two sides of his framework were to be associated exclusively with any particular traditions. To the contrary, he tried to highlight the cases where lesser developed tendencies nonetheless found expression in traditions that historically privileged the other side of the contrast. Yet Needham's strong response to Northrop's distinctions (i.e., misreading his argument as if to claim that there was nothing like science in the classical Chinese tradition) is the key to the oddity of Hall's drive to associate himself with Whitehead. I believe he sees Whitehead as more capable of providing the flexibility in the interpretation of traditions that Needham's critique seemed to demand. Furthermore, I would argue that, if Hall better understood Northrop's argument—or, perhaps, if the broader academy (including Needham) better understood that argument—this temptation would not have been as compelling, and Hall would have identified more closely with Northrop in this respect. In short, I see his unexpected and ultimately inconsistent choice of Whitehead over Northrop as the unfortunate fallout of Needham's highly influential and equally unfortunate misunderstanding of Northrop.

44. Hall and Ames' reading of Northrop often presses the point about his Kantianism too far, suggesting that Northrop intended his terms to be as rigidly distinguished as they are often made out to be. It is unclear whether this is due to a misreading of Northrop or—more likely—a point overemphasized for rhetorical effect (i.e., to give emphasis to a subtle point that might otherwise be overlooked).

45. As the reader will recall from the chapter on Northrop, this differs from the latter in that, while Northrop also began with an empirical review of each culture, he ultimately allowed the review to be shaped in accordance with a preexisting theoretic framework. I say that Hall and Ames *try* to avoid this, because while they *intend* to do so, it is unclear that they can *effectively* do so (although the effort is an important difference nonetheless).

46. I quote Hall's own answer to the question raised above, because it is the most direct response available in Hall and Ames' corpus. That both Hall *and* Ames would agree with this response, however, is evident from the many affirmations of an equivalent pragmatist sensibility in their collaborative works (1987, 131–38; 1995, 116–19).

47. Technically, it is possible to highlight both similarities and incongruities through the medium of contrasts. One could, for example, point out that "tradition X and Y both address issue Z this way, whereas other traditions do not," or "tradition X contrasts with tradition Y in that it addresses issues of Z whereas tradition Y does not." The point here, however, is that such contrasts are seldom if ever made. For Hall and Ames' part, at least, the contrasts are constructed for the sole purpose of differentiating two cultural traditions.

48. One cannot do away with similarity altogether in comparative studies, and Hall and Ames never attempt to do so. This is evidenced at the very least by their tireless commitment to actually translating the terms and concepts of one culture into those of another, something that would be entirely impossible if there were no basis of similarity. Indeed, the acceptance of at least some basis of commonality is a precondition for the possibility of comparative philosophy itself. The point here is simply that, in comparison to other approaches to comparison, Hall and Ames put a clear emphasis on the differences.

49. Hall and Ames would, I think, be content with this characterization of their project. Such, they would say, is all that can be expected of any philosophical formulation: any claim to do more than this can only, in the end, do less.

50. The difference here could be rephrased as the difference between exploiting a contrast for the purposes of elucidating a cultural tradition and exploiting a cultural tradition for the purposes of elucidating a contrast.

51. Neville developed this critique more explicitly and in more detail in his later work, *Boston Confucianism* (2000).

52. Hall and Ames do not indicate that they are responding to Neville's critique in their defense, but the similarity of their response to his critique—both in topic and in terminology—suggests that they had in mind the sort of critique that Neville raised when writing the introduction to their second collaborative work. Although Neville would not publish the aforementioned critique (see note 51 in this chapter) for another five years, Hall and Ames would have been aware of his position both from their ongoing personal interaction and from unpublished conference papers on similar themes. Recalling these developments, Neville has commented, "I think you can take it that they knew of the arguments in *Boston Confucianism* from the prepublication days of *Thinking through Confucius*, if not of the careful formulation of them" (Robert Neville, personal correspondence, October 17, 2005).

53. Hall and Ames are certainly not alone in this concern to preserve the integrity of traditions in comparison; for example, see Grappard (1992) for a more extreme version of this argument with respect to Japanese religion.

54. The use of the terms *important* and *significant* are not innocent in this context. As noted earlier, Hall and Ames mean something very specific by the word *important* (see note 12 in this chapter and surrounding text); I use 'significant' here as an alternative term to signify ideas that may not be considered "important" by the precise definition given by Hall and Ames, but which may be important (in a very general sense) nonetheless. It is worth noting, however, that this is an imperfect solution, as Hall and Ames have occasionally used 'significant' in their earlier texts to indicate what they would later mean by 'important,' as when they assert "the lack of any significant recourse to the notion of transcendence" in classical Chinese culture (1987, 254).

55. Again, this is not to say that Hall and Ames maintain that these exceptions actually do not exist; rather, it is to say that, by treating exceptions only as the things that prove the (more important) rule, they effectively read the exceptions out of the comparative narrative they construct.

56. According to Neville, most of these critiques apparently arose in unpublished conversations (interview by Robert Smid, November 1, 2005), although Tu did apparently address the issue in a conference at Brock University at some point in the 1980s.

57. Hall and Ames are also not alone in arguing this position on transcendence. Perhaps the most formative ally for them in this respect is A. C. Graham, who has made similar arguments in his published work (e.g., 1989; 1991).

58. They make the point of defining "strict transcendence" in order to differentiate their philosophical definition from more general and less precise understandings of the term. For the purposes of this study, all references to transcendence are to the precise, philosophical sense of the term, so it will not be necessary to observe that distinction here.

59. Hall and Ames seem to undertake this task with a certain rhetorical flair; that is, they arguably overstate the case concerning the lack of any notion of transcendence in classical Chinese philosophy in order to provide an effective counterweight to the mistaken assumptions of the broader population. Presumably, if that population were to become effectively dispossessed of its transcendental pretenses, Hall and Ames would afford greater consideration to possible exceptions on the question of transcendence.

60. The key term in this disagreement is *accuracy*. Is comparative understanding in general more accurate if more of the precise features of comparative relations among traditions are made available, or if the more definitive features of those relations are understood more clearly?

61. While most of the debate hitherto has pertained primarily to the interpretation of data, surprisingly little has pertained to the proper character and role of the philosophy of culture; that is, Hall and Ames have been for the most part free to define the philosophy of culture and to defend their position from the perspective of that definition. Neville has, in conversation, noted that if the debate is to move forward productively, it will probably have to proceed in terms of critical engagement concerning the philosophy of culture itself (Neville, personal conversation, October 25, 2005).

62. Again, I am using 'significant' as an alternative to Hall and Ames' 'important' (see note 54 in this chapter): the whole point in Neville's critique is that their definition of 'important' is too narrow to include all of the relevant data in comparison.

63. Compare this to Neville's broader criteria, namely, whether something "catch[es] the main drift of cultural differences" (1987, xiv).

64. As the reader will recall, Hall and Ames alternatively defined importance as anything that "*significantly qualifies, defines, or otherwise shapes the culture*" (1995, xv, italics original).

65. The most likely explanation for this apparent discrepancy is that the emphasis on first problematic thinking in the West was able to serve a very practical, heuristic purpose for their comparisons; it is unclear, however, that such an

explanation is sufficient to justify the methodological inconsistency that results. To the contrary, any clarity gained in heuristics is arguably lost in the defensibility of the method, unless the method is to be defined primarily on the basis of its heuristic effectiveness.

66. The clearest example, though much lesser known, is found in the work of Allan Menzies, who, in his *History of Religion: A Sketch of Primitive Religious Beliefs and Practices, and of the Origin and Character of the Great Systems* (1895), traced the development of world religions from tribal religion to national religion to individual religion to universal religion; it is clear from his work that Christianity is the closest exemplification of universal religion and has all of the features necessary to embody such religion. See also Frederick Denison Maurice (1852 [1847]) and J. A. MacCulloch (1902) for similar approaches; Masuzawa (2005) provides excellent treatment of these figures. Comparable arguments for the superiority of Christianity can also be found in the early-twentieth-century missiologists, including James Dennis (1906), James Barton (1912), John Farquhar (1913), and Hendrik Kraemer (1957; 1962). For the most part, such arguments became more difficult to make after World War I: that war was fought primarily among supposedly Christian nations, whose seemingly limitless capacity for bloodshed and destruction—acted out on battlefields throughout the world—flew in the face of any pretensions to being among the foremost civilizing forces in the modern world.

67. Jonathan Z. Smith embodies these developments perhaps better than anyone else. In his *Map Is Not Territory* (1978), he argued that the priority given to congruency and conformity in religious studies not only privileges more structured religions but also ignores important facets of what it is to be religious; in response, Smith opts to focus his work on the incongruities of religion, thus hoping to broaden the purview of the study of religion (comparative and otherwise). His challenge for the development of more self-critical comparative methods (1982) is often misinterpreted as a resolute rejection of comparative methods per se; the inaccuracy of this interpretation can be seen in his subsequent work (e.g., Smith 2000, 2001). In the end, Smith endorses the continuation of the comparative study of religion but only if and when the biases in such study are readily acknowledged and critically addressed.

68. Although this commitment is expressed in their more recent works with reference to Richard Rorty, it was originally found in Hall's interpretation of Whitehead. There are many commonalities between their reading of Whitehead and Rorty, however, and for the sake of brevity this influence will be explicated here primarily with respect to Rorty.

69. Something of this can be seen in the fact that, while they want to "get on with it," they want to do so "in the most responsible manner possible (1995, 119). While this allows for a rejection of the quest for objective truth, it nonetheless maintains strictures of the possibilities for interpretation that ultimately stem back to the truth of what it interpreted (what else is there to be responsible to? Surely not cultural importances, for those are effectively whatever one understands them to be). Their rhetoric against getting it right seems to be a rejection not of those who would seek to provide a reasonably accurate description of philosophical traditions but rather of those who claim to have gotten it right and against those who maintain that one cannot proceed unless one has a surefire means for getting it right.

70. The tension between Rorty's philosophical commitments and those of Hall and Ames was made most clear at the recent Ninth East-West Philosophers Conference in Honolulu, Hawaii (2005). In a joint address with Gianni Vattimo entitled "Modernity and Technology: The West and the Rest" (May 31, 2005) Rorty effectively argued that, if philosophy were properly understood, there would be no comparative philosophy. There are simply no "prevailing philosophic ideas" that could be taken to have relevance across cultures; there is only the edifying discourse of each philosopher. (To my knowledge, their joint presentation is not yet available in published form).

71. This is something that Rorty would seem likely to embrace, as when he tells his readers that "if we take care of freedom, truth can take care of itself" (1989a, 176).

72. "Narrative commitments" is left intentionally vague here, in order to include both those who disagree with their commitments to a narrative approach to philosophy and those who disagree with the particular commitments of the narrative they provide.

73. It is somewhat ironic that Hall and Ames feel that "Martin's approach and philosophic temperament leave little room for discussion or debate" (343) when it is Martin who opened the discussion by means of his review of their work. Hall and Ames may be correct that the assumptions he brings to his review prevent an accurate understanding of Chinese philosophy, but—if so—then it is precisely these assumptions that should be considered in greater detail in the ensuing conversation.

74. Perhaps this remarkable shift should not be so surprising. For example, Hall and Ames are quick to remind their readers of how easily the definition of words can morph into its opposite. Moreover, Hall even noted in an earlier work how easily pluralism can turn into intellectual fascism: "Modern philosophy, born of the heuristic employment of doubt as a means of obtaining certainty, has progressed to a point where philosophic doubt has become a consequence of the realization that certainty is unattainable, or the realization that too many mutually contradictory "certainties" are possible of attainment. The most significant consequence of this realization is that without the authority of truth undergirding a given theory, that theory can only lead to commitment through the use of rhetorical persuasion, intimidation, or coercion. Meta-mentality invites a kind of intellectual fascism which elicits commitment to values and ideals, not because they are true, but for the sake of law and order, the harmony of society, or 'the destiny of a people.' The extreme of intellectual subtlety that finally succeeds in suspending belief in favor of the exercise of reason ends by affirming the necessity of arbitrary commitment if there is to be any commitment at all!" (Hall 1982b, 18).

75. Their argument rests on a broadened notion of how the terms *logic* and *logical* apply cross-culturally, so Hall and Ames were keen to dissociate their use of the terms from that employed by the currently dominant Continental and analytic philosophical traditions. It is my understanding that Paul and Martin drew from each of these traditions (respectively), so it would have been of particular importance for Hall and Ames to respond decisively to these critiques in particular.

76. One might also look to their response to a number of critical responses to their work in an issue of the periodical *Dao* that was dedicated to an analysis and appreciation of their work. See *Dao* 3, no. 2 (June 2004).

77. It is important to note that, while I disagree with Møllegaard's broader critique and find Ames' response to that critique generally compelling, I find that his critique of Ames in this respect is particularly insightful. It is unfortunate that Ames focuses so little on this facet of the critique in his response.

78. The internal citations in this quote are taken from Hall and Ames (1995, 144–45).

79. This argument has already been laid out in detail in the previous section; because it is relevant to the current discussion, I have included a cursory review of it here.

80. Again, the obvious exception here is Neville's concept of transcendence, which—despite substantive and longstanding interactions between them—is never substantively addressed in Hall and Ames' main texts. Neville has explicitly challenged their exclusion in this respect (2000, 148–49), but to my knowledge Hall and Ames have not officially responded in print.

81. See Møllegaard (2005, 329) for a similar critique.

82. It should be noted that, while Rorty takes postmodern insights seriously, he is not rightly understood as a postmodernist. As Hall argues, "In spite of his some-time self-description as a 'postmodernist bourgeois liberal,' Rorty does not identify himself with the postmodern movement" (1994, 51).

83. Rorty himself speaks more in terms of "historicization" and the "temporalization of rationality" than he does about cultural contexts, but I have used the latter terminology (which Hall and Ames use) to make the connection between them more clear.

84. Rorty refers to this as "holding one's time in thought," by which he means more precisely "finding a description of all things characteristic of your time of which you most approve and with which you unflinchingly identify" (1989a, 55). This idea is taken from Hegel, whom he sees as an early model for properly historicized narrative philosophy.

85. This is similar to the case with Derrida: self-proclaimed postmodernists have made a veritable cottage industry out of deconstruction, thus making of it precisely the logocentric entity that it was designed to do away with. Derrida is one of the few who has maintained with any consistency the idea that deconstruction is not an idea whose meaning can be fully present to consciousness.

86. Cf. Hall and Ames' "interesting and plausible" (1995, xx).

87. Something of this tension can be found when he acknowledges that "edifying philosophers have to decry the very notion of having a view, while avoiding having a view about having views." Rorty acknowledges that this is an "awkward" position to take but maintains that it is not an impossible one (1979, 371).

88. Hall's reading of Rorty is more balanced than this closing word would suggest. In his study of Rorty (1994), he follows this conclusion with the following caveat: "Why is this snide word not the last one? It cannot be since so many of us, often in spite of our own understanding of what we are really supposed to be up to, remain seated at Rorty's table, waiting for what comes next" (236). This caveat notwithstanding, however, there is a clear sense that, however much Hall appreciates Rorty's work, he wants something more from the practice of philosophy.

89. Rorty's own strong rejection of comparative philosophy suggests that the existence of such an approach is unlikely, but this is not sufficient reason to conclude that such an approach could not exist.

NOTES TO CHAPTER 4

1. In the epigraph, Neville is speaking on behalf of the Comparative Religious Ideas Project, which—as will be seen later—exemplifies his comparative method in its most developed form.

2. *Engagement* is a crucial term for Neville's comparative method (see esp. 2000; 2006). As with Hocking, the point is not simply to characterize other traditions but to take them in and learn from them as much as possible.

3. Neville acknowledges there that, due to limitations of his own experience (and, presumably, the space limitations of his first major book), it would not be possible to make this any more than just a suggestion. He does, however, leave open the suggestion that this may be followed up in subsequent work and follows up on it in extensive detail in many of his later works (see, e.g., 1982, 1991).

4. Neville did take a number of courses with Northrop, but this was during the later stages of Northrop's career when his philosophical interests in comparison were largely overshadowed by those in law and science. Neville recalls having been in Northrop's class when the latter was working on *Philosophical Anthropology and Practical Politics* (1960), as well as being in Northrop's last class at Yale (interview by Robert Smid, July 17, 2006).

5. Neville would later dedicate one of his most important comparative works, *Boston Confucianism* (2000), to his "mentor in world philosophy," noting that "Boston Confucianism is barely catching up with his long practice of world philosophy" (2000, xxxv).

6. As Neville notes, this increasing general interest in non-Western traditions had an influence on him as well, although his interest ultimately proved to be more than merely faddish. In his case, it provided him with the opportunity to study Taijiquan with Sophia Delza, who was offering classes at State University of New York Purchase; even after Neville moved to State University of New York Stony Brook, he continued to study weekly with Delza at her studio in Carnegie Hall in New York City over the next eleven years. Neville attributes much of his initial interest in Chinese philosophy to what he learned from Delza through Taijiquan and notes that his foreword to one of her books (1996) is his best essay on the metaphysical status of things as determinate yin-yang patterns (interview by Robert Smid, July 17, 2006).

7. "Opportunity" is a loaded word here: as Neville relates the story, a few students had expressed interest in learning Sanskrit, and—as head of the philosophy board at the college (State University of New York Purchase had "boards" rather than "departments")—he promised that if they could find twenty students willing to sign up for the course he would find them a teacher. The students found twenty-two who would sign up, Neville found that the board did not have money for a new Sanskrit teacher, so he taught the course (Neville committed to learning Sanskrit from Thomas Berry just far enough ahead of his students that he could teach them with integrity; in fact, he had one student ultimately go on to receive his Ph.D. in Sanskrit studies at Columbia).

8. This argument would be developed more completely in his later work (esp. 2000).

9. This essay was later revised and integrated into a larger collection of his essays, *The Tao and the Daimon* (1982), as "The Empirical Cases of World Religions"

(111–29). For the sake of clarity, all references will be to the revised version unless otherwise noted.

10. The scope of this essay pertains to comparative religions in particular; however, when one considers his earlier claim that abstract speculation "is the best interpretation of what is presupposed abstractly by [the historical particularities of religion]" (1992a[1968], 187; see also 186), it is fair to assume that the approach he develops in this essay has application to his philosophy work as well.

11. Some credit for this is also probably due to his interest in the work of A. N. Whitehead, who in like manner treated speculative claims as hypotheses (see, e.g., Whitehead 1929). Yet while Whitehead is one of the most prominent exponents of this approach to speculative philosophy, he can hardly be said to have initiated the approach in his own right and is arguably influenced by the pragmatists himself in this respect.

12. This is not to say that Peirce did not emphasize the role of experience in his own work or that that it was not made prominent in the work of pragmatists before Smith. Smith's significance in this respect is due to the fact that it is primarily through his interpretation and development of their work that Neville developed his own theory of experience. See (1992a [1968], xxv) and especially (1982, xiii; 257n. 1) for comments on the significance of Smith's influence on his work.

13. See note 9 in this chapter.

14. Neville is careful to note that determinacy need not indicate causal determinacy and that God need not represent an unchanging, personal being; both of these are specifications of Western traditions, which are no more necessary to the vague hypothesis of creation *ex nihilo* than they are to non-Western traditions.

15. It is worth noting that Islam is generally passed over in Neville's analyses. This lack of emphasis is understandable, however, given that Muslims specify the vague concept of God the creator in a manner very similar to that of most Jews and Christians. While there are differences here, it is understandable that Neville would focus his attention on traditions to which it is less obvious that his hypothesis has any significant application.

16. McKeon never published his architectonic, but its basic structure has been recreated from lecture notes and published in *Freedom and History and Other Essays* (1990).

17. Watson and Dilworth were not in complete agreement in their use of typologies, so Watson had his text revised in 1993 to include a response to Dilworth's text. Yet their positions are sufficiently similar that they can be considered in tandem here.

18. Neville acknowledges Hall's strong influence on his development in many of his works; the best such account is found in Chinn and Rosemont (2005, 21–34).

19. One could argue, for example, that Neville's choice of categories in this text is as reflective of a Platonist orientation as Watson and Dilworth's is of an Aristotelian one.

20. This selection of resources for moral reflection both reflects a broader ongoing interest in the relationship between American philosophy and Chinese philosophy and anticipates Neville's own subsequent work on this relationship.

21. The careful reader will note that Neville appears somewhat more apprehensive in associating all kinds of valuing with thinking than he is in associating the reverse. It is unclear whether this indicates an actual rift in the association of

the two, or whether he was simply unable to explicate all forms of the association in the text at hand.

22. "Unity" will later be replaced by "importance" as the guiding value for theory.

23. Neville's examination of theory constitutes the first half of *Normative Cultures*, which constitutes an effective blueprint for his comparative method.

24. This is the shift indicated earlier (see note 22 in this chapter). Neville acknowledges that the change "marks a major theoretical shift" in his account of theory (1995, 6), and it will have significant implications for his comparative method.

25. The influence of Scotistic realism is readily evident here, especially insofar as it differentiates Neville's understanding of importance from Hall's Whiteheadian understanding of that term (see previous chapter, esp. notes 12 and 64 and surrounding text).

26. See Neville (1995, 22–30, 38, 43–44) for a more detailed account of these critiques.

27. "Broad" here should be interpreted as "vague" rather than "general," in the sense described earlier.

28. Even with nonreductive theories, however, theorists will be faced with difficult choices, something that Neville readily acknowledges. In the infinite long run (to use Peirce's term), nonreductive theories are the ones fated to represent reality with the greatest accuracy and completeness; however, in the finite run—which is what each of us are faced with—even nonreductive theories will suffer from limited vision. In the meantime, then, theorists must seek to provide interpretations that recognize as much value as possible (i.e., values of the greatest importance), and it is nonreductive theories that are ultimately more conducive to the development of such an interpretation.

29. In drawing on Chinese traditions to improve Western traditions, Neville makes a move distinctly reminiscent of the work of Hocking (see note 2 in this chapter).

30. "Identification, vetting and improvement" are not stages identified in Neville's own work, but I have found them an instructive way to organize this part of his work.

31. As suggested by the close association of a theory of theories with a theory of cross-cultural comparison, theories and cultures are closely associated in this aspect of Neville's work. Of course, Neville is entirely aware that there is more to culture than the theories that might give them ordered self-expression, but the method by which they can be compared—indeed, by which anything can be compared—is nonetheless similar enough for the one to inform the other. Accordingly, this exposition will move rather lithely between the comparison of theories and cross-cultural comparison.

32. Interestingly, there appears to be room within Neville's method to assess the categories by which certain cultures can be compared (as opposed to simply developing and testing them). This can be seen, for example, in the move from considering what categories cultures *have* used to engage reality to arguing for what categories they *should have* used to do so. This move from passive description to normative theory construction may seem to slip the bounds of comparison proper, but it is not that far removed from what Hocking sought to accomplish in his essay

on Zhu Xi. It is arguably the fullest expression of Neville's comparative method, although it is seldom given expression.

33. There is strong precedent in *Normative Cultures* for understanding the comparative method as an ongoing process (see, e.g., 1995, 81–83), but this idea is developed more fully and explicitly in CRIP itself.

34. He notes that "there was a kind of suspicion [within CRIP] that the conception and method we employed had its status by my authority, genial as that might have seemed, rather than by actually exhibiting its worth" (2001c, 222). For Neville, however, the project was a *test* of the comparative method he laid out in *Normative Cultures* (1995), and while it constituted the starting point of the project, it should also have been considered—no less than the categories for comparison—subject to correction as necessary.

35. Neville admits being unable to bring as many disciplines to the project as he may have liked (2001a, xxiv), but this was an unavoidable, practical limitation of the project.

36. One of the notable characteristics of this group was that, with the exception of one scholar, each of the specialists represented traditions with which they did not themselves identify. Neville describes this as an intentional choice, made for the sake of allowing for the critical distance that was seen as necessary for comparison (2001a, xvi). Wildman, by contrast, notes that it was difficult to determine the value of that distinction, since there was no alternate rendering of CRIP to compare it to (Neville 2001a, 273).

37. CRIP modeled its method of inquiry in part on the natural sciences, which should not be surprising given the strength of this link in American philosophy (see Berthrong's note in Neville 2001b, 239).

38. See *The Human Condition* (2001a, xvi–xviii, 272–74, 309–10) for more details on each group and its constituent scholars.

39. Neville notes that many other categories could have been proposed and researched further but that the inquiry was limited to these for the sake of practicality (2001a, xviii).

40. Neville is particularly careful to point out that the identification of these subcategories is entirely the result of the comparative inquiry, rather than a prior set of subcategories for which each specialist was expected to find specification. This distinguishes his work from the typological approach advocated by McKeon, Watson, and Dilworth and bespeaks his pragmatist commitment to positions that are the result of investigation rather than their starting point (Neville 2001a, 5).

41. *Late modern* is Neville's term for the current period, suggesting that modernism and postmodernism share enough of the characteristics of modernity as to make it in no way clear that modernity is over. Better to let later historians of philosophy decide when modernity is over and—at least until it is clearer that the defining characteristics of modernity have been left behind—to merely call ourselves "late modern" (1992b, 5–6).

42. In this way, Neville exemplifies another characteristic of classical pragmatism: meliorism. This was a term used by James to express pragmatism's rejection of both optimism and pessimism on any issue, insofar as they short circuit the very process of inquiry that they should rely on. It is much better to do all that is possible to bring about what is in question and let the empirical data judge its possibility

(see, e.g., James 1975, 137–38). Later, in CRIP, he will again exemplify this commitment when he writes (with Wildman) that "the test of any comparative method
is whether that method helps to detect commonalities without bias for a legitimate
purpose. While some thinkers have philosophical commitments for or against the
possibilities of meeting these conditions, we do not" (Neville 2001a, 16).

43. For example, in consideration of the data from East Asian traditions, the
group decided to change the second categories investigated from "ultimate reality" to
"ultimate realities"; such a designation, they maintained, avoided the insinuation that
some single, divine figure was the ultimate reality for all traditions and furthermore
maintained the pluralism inherent among the traditions themselves (2001b, 1–2).

44. To be fair, his argument has changed slightly over his career. For example,
whereas Neville was initially much more inclined to use theistic language to refer
to the indeterminate ground, he now employs more neutral terminology in contexts
where theism cannot be taken for granted. Similarly, whereas he used to argue that,
if the vague hypothesis of creation *ex nihilo* was true, it should find exemplification in any comprehensive theory (even if not always in the same way), he now
seems more prepared to accept that there may be traditions with no clear corollary
(although if one reads between the lines, one can still see a normative suggestion
that such a consideration *should have* been part of that theory). Ultimately, however,
these remain mere amendments and elaborations of the theory and nothing like
fundamental reconsiderations.

45. Of course, Neville is not simply a Peircian and has built on this understanding
of truth in important ways (see esp. 1981, 1989, 1995, and 1996). In *Normative Cultures*,
for example, he defines it as "the carryover of value from the objects of interpretations
into the experience of the interpreters, as qualified by the interpreters' biology, cultures,
semiotic systems, and purposes" (1995, xi–xii). Even in this definition, however, the
focus is not on the individual inquirer but rather on the community of inquirers. The
difficulty of knowing when to reject a tentative hypothesis is echoed in the work of
CRIP, as Wildman comments with respect to the evaluation of comparative categories
(Neville 2001a, 279). Admittedly, he is not speaking about this with respect to the
broader community of inquirers in particular, but the difficulty is related. He notes that
this problem was not well developed in Neville's previous work, but he does maintain
that was it worked out to a greater degree over the subsequent development of CRIP
(280). To my knowledge, whatever was learned there has not yet been applied to the
more abstract ideas in Neville's thought (such as creation *ex nihilo*), and I am perhaps
less optimistic than Wildman that this problem can be adequately resolved with further
critical attention, at least with respect to these more abstract ideas.

46. As noted earlier, Neville's most substantive work on the construction and
defense of systematic speculative hypotheses is found in the Axiology series; however,
a clear and succinct account of the truth conditions for such hypotheses can also
be found in his *Highroad around Modernism* (1992, esp. 147–48).

47. This is the method Neville followed in his Axiology series, among other
works.

48. Actually, Neville gets his philosophical realism initially from Duns Scotus,
but Peirce has since become the primary conduit for Neville's interpretation of realism in the contemporary context.

49. The problem of the One and the Many can be described as the attempt
to account for the fact that reality is at once a diverse multiplicity of things that

cannot be reduced one to the other and yet is at the same time a single totality. In other words, how can something be both discretely individual and also parts of a broader whole?

50. The question of the presence of the problem of the One and the Many in non-Western traditions is still very much a matter of debate between Neville and his critics, but the possibility of arbitrariness renders the question of presences secondary to that of significance. It is a case that is by no means clear but that exemplifies the challenges of comparative philosophy itself.

51. As Wildman notes, however, many of the participants found it difficult to master Neville's comparative method, such that he and Neville were left—at least initially—to work out most of the comparative syntheses in accordance with the method (Neville 2001a, 274–75). This difficulty does seem to have been mitigated over the course of inquiry.

52. In this sense, Neville's admonitions to pursue a comparative method that is comprehensibly fallibilistic are little different than Rorty's admonitions to stop pursuing comparison altogether. There is a certain irony here, as comparative philosophy should be able to mediate precisely these sorts of disagreements.

53. Ask a classical pragmatist why he is a classical pragmatist, and he will likely give you classical pragmatist reasons. Ask a neopragmatist why she is a neopragmatist, and she will give you neopragmatist reasons. A neopragmatist could not have classical pragmatist reasons for being a neopragmatist, at least not positive and compelling ones, without thereby becoming a classical pragmatist of sorts. My own suspicion, following James, is that what makes people choose their respective philosophical commitments has ultimately to do with something as basic and less directly philosophical as temperament (1975, 9–26). While I agree with James—and Neville, for that matter—that (classical) pragmatism appeals to the best in every kind of temperament, I remain unconvinced that this is ultimately demonstrable outside of classical pragmatist commitments.

54. Of course, in reality the progression is not so simple; one also floats out ideas in discussions, presentations, and other means of scholarly interaction. Nonetheless, the progression described above arguably reflects a rift between individual scholar and broader community in the development of ideas that runs counter to the vision of communal inquiry advocated by the classical pragmatists.

55. It should be noted that "science" in this context should not be understood in terms of *Geisteswissenschaft*, a method of logical deduction based on demonstrably true premises; as far as the organizers of CRIP are concerned, this understanding of scientific method was aptly criticized by J. Z. Smith (1989). CRIP, by contrast, understands the importance of science for comparative religions as indicating that it is possible to develop a method for specifying comparative categories in a way that can be communicated beyond the traditions themselves compared. For a similar, though more pluralistic rendering of this commitment, see Tu Weiming's comments in Neville (2001b, xii).

56. This includes prefaces written by Peter Berger (Neville 2001a, xi–xiv), Tu Weiming (Neville 2001b, xi–xiv), and Jonathan Z. Smith (Neville 2001c, xi–xii), as well as excellent later chapters by Berthrong (Neville 2001b, 237–60) and Wildman and Neville (Neville 2001b, 187–210; 211–36; 2001c, 203–18).

57. This accomplishment is all the more remarkable given that, as Frank Clooney warned, "past projects of this sort have not succeeded when they have tried

to initiate readers into the process of the project" (Neville 2001a, 268). For his part, Wildman is uncertain that he has been successful in this respect (2001a, 268–69), but I believe that the appendices have proven surprisingly helpful nonetheless.

58. This tension is also mirrored in the difficulty associated with drawing on scholars from such a wide variety of areas of expertise (not only with respect to religious traditions, but also with respect to disciplines, familiarity with comparative religions, etc.) and trying to cull all of this diversity into broad representation within a single set of publications. Wildman also draws attention to the challenge of getting scholars with such different working styles to work together productively in a larger group setting (2001a, 272).

59. Tu Weiming picks up on this dual concern when he writes in the preface to the second volume, *Ultimate Realities* (Neville 2001b), "As students of religion, the reasons to participate in such a joint venture [as CRIP] are threefold. First, it is a pioneering attempt, guided by a *coherent vision*, to study a seminal religious idea cross-culturally. Second, it is meant to be an open inquiry, with a self-correcting methodological reflexivity. And, third, it addresses a core concern of human religiousness in a *pluralistic spirit*" (xii, emphasis mine). It is interesting to note that, while I have emphasized two poles in collaborative work, Tu has emphasized three; one might say that Tu's second point—that concerning the self-correcting methodology—is that which may allow CRIP to bring these otherwise competing commitments together.

60. Neville and Wildman describe the aforementioned tension between generalists and specialists as an intentional tension (2001a, xvi; 2001b, 261). They also describe the similar tension between the focus of specialists on ancient and medieval periods in their traditions and that of generalists on the contemporary application of comparisons about those traditions as a similarly "healthy tension" (xxii).

61. Of course, he follows this up with the consistent fallibilistic byline, "All of this is subject to further investigation" (2001a, 264), but the point is that the process was *in process* and that the competing goods of the generalists and specialists were in fact being brought to bear on the process of comparison (see also 279).

62. The tension examined here was more widespread than that simply between Neville and Fredriksen, (e.g., Frank Clooney, the expert in Hinduism and comparativist in his own right, expressed concerns similar to Fredriksen's, while Livia Kohn, the expert in Chinese religion, maintained commitments similar to Neville's), but it is their debate in particular that will be highlighted here. See Neville (2001b, 154) for more details.

63. Wildman notes that "the group found itself looking over its shoulder repeatedly at [a variety of] questions bearing on the advisability of spending time in comparing religious ideas across cultures," at least some of which "simply never dissolved in our group consciousness" (2001a, 277).

64. The task proved more than could be asked of individual scholars: Wildman admits his own inability to complete the task, as well as his amazement at Neville's ability to forge forward nonetheless (2001a, 283). Ultimately, it is an aspect of the tension that Neville and Wildman regard as "extraordinarily frustrating" (2001b, 3; see also 6).

65. Neville recognizes this problem from a different perspective when he notes that the second and third volumes lack the systematicity of the first volume. The systematic character of the first volume, he argues, enabled it to be subject to

critique in clearer, more precise ways, whereas the comparative conclusions of the next two volumes—dispersed as they were throughout the text—were thus more difficult to critique (2001c, 223).

66. Consistent with this nominalistic impulse, Eckel has also suggested that the project refer not to traditions generally (since traditions themselves do not "say" anything) but rather to individual authors or individual texts (2001b, 7; see also 155; see also 2001a, 274, for his similar suggestion to treat categories of comparison as constructions rather than something that is, at least potentially, true of reality itself).

67. See, e.g., Neville (2001b, 7, 155, 187–210).

68. As Eckel noted in the first year, "We begin the process of comparison of religious ideas in the middle, for we already possess comparative categories (by default, in translations and traditions of discussion). The aim must be to correct, sharpen, and enlarge the collection of categories rather than to start over" (2001a, 276, Wildman).

69. See Neville (2001b, 4–5) for a list of the many positive things learned from the "slow process" of having worked through the first year that were then applied to the second year's collaborative work.

70. Wildman hints at this when he suggests the "[p]eople with wicked imaginations, presumably mostly Bob Neville, designed the working group. Pandering to the aforementioned desire of the religious-studies gods for chaos and mutual incomprehension, perhaps, the project designers juxtaposed people with utterly different working styles" (2001a, 272), but he never develops this suggestion beyond this one tongue-in-cheek jab.

71. Peter Berger's earlier-cited comments about "natural reason" and "scientific methodology" are also instructive here insofar as they apply to both collaboration and comparison, although the collaborative dimension of the project was not Berger's primary concern in those comments (2001a, xiv). Tu Weiming also highlights this connection in his more pluralistic praise of the project: "I recommend the collaborative spirit embodied in this joint venture with a view toward 2001, the year the United Nations has designated to be the year of Dialogue among Civilizations" (2001b, xiii).

72. Neville recognizes this in *Normative Cultures* when he writes that "to get into my argument is like entering a strange country where people use familiar things in unfamiliar ways. Gaining access to a system requires a kind of suspension of judgment until the system is mastered and can be assessed; it is like learning a language in which much play and practice is required before sustained and nuanced speech is possible. Indeed, to be at ease thinking about and within a system requires inhabiting and taking on the system as one's orientation to be subjected to critical scrutiny" (1995, 113).

CHAPTER 5

1. Hall uses "methodology" in the epigraph to this chapter differently than I have been using it here, but that ambiguity plays into my own usage. Hall uses it to refer to what I have been calling a "method," and I think that he is right in his assessment of how such methods develop. I include his quote here, however, because it applies equally well to what I have been referring to as "methodology" (the study

of method itself). It always strikes me in reading this passage that Hall himself may also have intended both meanings.

2. Neville recalls taking multiple classes with Northrop, including the last class he taught at Yale (interview by Robert Smid, July 17, 2006). While I have no direct support for any such participation on Hall's part, it is inconceivable that he could have made his way through the Yale philosophy department without such exposure, especially in light of his budding interest in comparative philosophy. According to Neville, Northrop's influence on those interested in comparative philosophy at Yale was considerable even for those not directly involved in his courses (Kasulis and Neville 1997, 4).

3. The Korean War may also have had some effect. For example, Neville has acknowledged that it inspired him to learn more about Asian history and Asian forms of Marxism, although he notes that this took place too early in his life to influence the direction of his professional development (Neville, private correspondence, January 28, 2007). The fact that the two most significant American wars of the second half of the twentieth century took place on East and Southeast Asian soil cannot be divorced from the increasing interest in their traditions over that same time period, and the interest of Hall, Ames, and Neville in those traditions is arguably indicative of that shift.

4. Hall and Ames have made this more of a primary concern than Neville has, although the latter maintains that it is an important element of his work nonetheless. Along these lines, consider Hall's comment that he is "concerned to struggle against any sort of metaphysical colonization of China, which is no less suspect than are the commercial, political, or technological incursions that are its concrete correlates. . . . I will be urging Neville away from what I take to be his tendency to sympathize with that metaphysical takeover" (Chapman and Frankenberry 1999, 272).

5. Wing-tsit Chan recognized the significant advances in comparative philosophy in the fifty years since the first East-West Philosophers' Conference when he observed how the first conference "was a very small beginning. There were only five of us. . . . We dealt with generalities and superficialities and lumped Brahman, Tao, and Buddhist Thusness together. We hardly went beyond Spinoza in western philosophy and confined Chinese thought largely to the pre-Christian era. We saw the world as two halves, East and West [here he cites Northrop's work as the quintessential example]. . . . Contrast that conference in 1939 with the International Conference on Chu Hsi, held in Honolulu, two years ago [1982], and you will see the tremendous progress made in the past several decades. Eighty-six members participated instead of twenty or so. Almost all of the topnotch Neoconfucian scholars from China and Japan attended, along with authorities from other parts of the world. . . . Topics were discussed on a highly philosophical level, including some novel to the West" (Larson and Deutsch 1988, 230). Yet, as Larson and Deutsch note in their introduction, however questionable were the results of the first East-West Philosophers' Conference, "it was one of the formative events for the beginning of comparative philosophy as a field. *Indeed, we are the progeny of that conference*" (5, emphasis mine).

6. As noted in chapter 4, Hall and Ames acknowledge their similarity with Northrop in this respect (they call their shared approach an "intercultural approach") and express their appreciation for his recognition of the "irrevocable differences" among traditions (1987, 4–5). It is questionable whether Northrop felt these differences to be as irrevocable as Hall and Ames take them to be.

7. There are also differences here, as Hall and Ames focus on the distinction between immanence and transcendence, the causal and the correlative, etc., while Northrop focuses on the distinction between the concrete and the universal, but there is also a clear lineage between the two approaches.

8. Again, as noted in chapter 3, while Hall and Ames emphasize the presence of first problematic thinking in the West, they do not similarly emphasize the presence of second problematic thinking in the classical Chinese tradition. This is because they are interested both in countervailing the imposition of the dominant mode of Western philosophy on classical Chinese philosophy (and thus misunderstanding it) and in emphasizing the presence of the dominant mode of classical Chinese philosophy in Western philosophy (to thus promote it in the contemporary West). At first glance, this may seem contradictory, but it is reflective of a simultaneous commitment by Hall and Ames to maintaining the historical integrity of each tradition while also promoting the tradition deemed currently most suited to each culture.

9. Consistent with the standard set in chapter 3, I am using Northrop's terms for Eastern and Western traditions. His terms are often no longer politically correct, but using them allows my comments to remain consistent with direct citations from his work and can thus avoid confusion. The more politically correct correlates for these terms should be obvious.

10. One is reminded of Hegel's system, where after setting out his complex framework Hegel proceeds to designate himself as the autobiographer of *Geist*. It is perhaps unavoidable that the one who sets up a system receives a privileged place—if not the most privileged place—within it.

11. This is not an explicitly self-laudatory move for either Northrop or Hall and Ames. From everything that can be gathered from their written work, from personal interactions, and from accounts of personal interactions, all three scholars were nothing if not properly measured in their self-assessment and more than generous in their interactions with others. The point here is not how they carried themselves personally, but rather their assessment of the peculiar importance of their perspective given their ability to give voice to otherwise marginalized traditions.

12. It should be noted that Neville also lays out a philosophy of culture (see 2000, 25–40), but this is not as central a feature of his work as it is for Northrop and Hall/Ames. Moreover, it is of a very different character: for Neville, philosophy is in some sense prior to culture (philosophy that allows for the possibility of culture), whereas for Northrop and Hall/Ames it is posterior (culture as indicating what sort of insights will be developed in a culture).

13. Hall and Ames refer to this approach as a "transcultural approach," which they contrast with an "intercultural approach" they associate with Northrop (1987, 4). Although they do not name Neville explicitly in connection with the transcultural approach, it is clear that he is among their intended referents. Incidentally, Hall and Ames claim to share with the transcultural approach "the search for a single hermeneutical community serving as the context of viable philosophic dialogue" (5), but they have so emphasized the danger of that search as to make any lingering commonality superfluous.

14. It is important to disambiguate this from what Jonathan Z. Smith warns about when he refers to "the magic of comparison" (Smith 1982). Smith is concerned with the comparisons whose only defense is the insight of the comparativist itself,

to the exclusion of any underlying method; Wesley Wildman refers to something similar when he refers to "genius comparisons" (Neville 2001a, 278; 2001b, 231; 2001c, 222), which rely on the exceptional acumen of the comparativist rather than on the defensibility of the comparison itself. For their parts, both Hocking and Neville—and the latter in particular—have made concerted efforts to support their comparative insights with a clear method and adequate empirical evidence. What I am suggesting here is not that their comparative conclusions are merely asserted on the basis of rhetorical force, but rather that—whatever defense they provide for their conclusions—the initial insight informing those conclusions is either shared or not shared by one's peers (or "seen," to use Hocking's metaphor). I am thinking here of Hall and Ames' response to Neville's work in particular: how can Neville respond to characterizations that his comparative conclusions are "flat" and "uninteresting" except to insist—and to continue to argue, which is effectively the same thing—that they are not? In discussions among comparative philosophers, there is a real sense in which the conversation often fails to move beyond these initial, guiding insights.

15. Again, it should be reinforced, that this is not an observation on the personal character of either Hocking or Neville, both of whom give every indication of having been among the most humble and irenic scholars. Rather, the observation pertains to the perception of what constitutes comparative philosophy and why both Hocking and Neville feel particularly qualified to pursue it.

16. It is not without a sense of irony that I now try to navigate among these competing claims, perhaps setting myself up as the exemplar of the comparer of comparative philosophers. Heaven forbid that comparative philosophy achieve no further—and no better—self-reflective analysis than this inaugural study!

17. This is, of course, leaving open the possibility that there are cultures that have developed no capacity for philosophical thinking. However difficult it is to imagine, allowances for such a possibility must be made if one takes evolutionary biology seriously. For the purposes at hand, though, this is a merely formal allowance, as every known culture in existence has developed some capacity for critical thought that can be considered philosophical. The point at issue in the current consideration is not whether there are cultures that are not philosophical but rather whether the ways in which cultures are philosophical can be considered to be at all commensurate with one another.

18. While this is their intention, some of their work has been critiqued as being unduly Western—and Whiteheadian in particular, however unorthodox—in its orientation. For example, the Whiteheadian overtones of their *Zhongyong* (2001) have been well documented by their critics.

19. While both of these were listed as dimensions of the broader comparative project of Hall and Ames, it is clear by their latter works that the former (i.e., cultivating an understanding of classical Chinese philosophy) takes precedence over the others.

20. He wrote that "the Dutch Government, in order to preserve the artistic achievements of the natives of the East Indies, has prohibited in many instances the entrance of Christian missionaries. William Ernest Hocking reports a conversation with a Dutch Protestant missionary who persuaded the Dutch government to depart from its rule in his case because of his intense interest in encouraging the preservation of the remarkable artistic sense of the natives. He found to his dismay

that as his converts became more and more serious Christians, they proceeded to drop their traditional aesthetic interests and values. When he asked them why this was the case in spite of his admonitions to the contrary, they wondered why he had not realized that the acceptance of the Western Christian religious teachings, in destroying the native religious doctrine, thereby took from the native aesthetic and emotional cultural forms and practices the philosophical and Oriental religious basis which is their source and their inspiration" (1946, 430–31).

21. It is interesting to note the parallels of this project to CRIP: they consisted of roughly the same (large) number of regular participants, and experienced a similar split between generalists and specialists. In this sense, Hocking's experience in collaboration might be considered prophetic for Neville's later experience with CRIP.

22. Certainly, it is difficult to argue with attending a conference in Hawaii, but this conference spanned multiple weeks, which is a significant commitment for any academic. Suffice to say, Hocking would have shown up expecting to do some serious academic work with his fellow comparativists.

23. Given Northrop's training and background in the natural sciences, it is surprising that his work was not more thoroughly collaborative than it was; the American pragmatist emphasis on vulnerability to correction is itself taken from the natural sciences. The best explanation for this is that Northrop's work—both single-authored and collaborative—was oriented toward the step in inquiry where one develops the best possible defense of an idea, which is logically prior to subjecting it to critique from the broader community of scholars. From my limited exposure, this seems to be the primary *modus operendi* in the theoretical sciences in particular, although I do not know enough about those fields to comment in any more detail. In any event, later comparativists such as Hall/Ames and Neville will seek to develop much more thorough-going collaboration in their respective comparative works.

24. The more recent East-West Philosophers' Conferences have been less directly collaborative in nature, due in large measure to their much greater size. At this point, their collaborative dimensions can consist only of ideas shared and relationships formed among scholars; any direct connections with official collaborative ventures are thus almost impossible to track.

25. When I note that their collaboration has lacked breadth, this is not meant to indicate that their collaborative work has been pursued at the expense of working with other scholars. Ames, especially, has been active in collaborating on other projects with other scholars (e.g., Ames and Young, 1977; Ames and Lau 1996; 1998; Ames and Rosemont, 1998), and there is good reason to believe he will continue to do so with Hall's passing (although most of Ames' other collaborations have hitherto pertained to textual translations). It is meant to indicate that, while such collaborative efforts have been ongoing, they have typically been limited to two-person partnerships, rather than taking place within the context of a broader community of inquirers. Evidently—as will be discussed further later—this has its strengths, but it also has its weaknesses.

26. As noted in chapter 4, this divergence between generalists and specialists was most pronounced in the first volume (Neville 2001a), but it persisted through the subsequent volumes as well.

27. As Santayana noted, "[T]hose who cannot remember the past are doomed to repeat it" (1998 [1906], 82).

28. As noted earlier (see chapter 3, note 1), Hocking anticipated Whitehead's sentiment about the importance of "interest" to philosophical ideas (1929, 259) when he wrote that "a theory is false if it is not interesting: a proposition that falls on the mind so dully as to excite no enthusiasm has not attained the level of truth; though the words be accurate the import has leaked away from them, and the meaning is not conveyed" (1912, xiii–xiv). While neither Whitehead nor Hocking wants to discount truth entirely, the sentiments in both statements seems to be the same: make your contributions interesting, and further inquiry into the truth of the matter will certainly be worthwhile. This seems to have been Hocking's strategy in comparison: so long as the comparison is mostly true, as Hocking's arguably was, it should inspire further, more productive, and ultimately more true studies on the matter. Thus, although Hocking would probably not agree with most of Hall and Ames' method, he would likely have appreciated their desire to "present a narrative which is interesting enough and plausible enough to engage those inclined to join the conversation" (1995, xx).

29. I say "the areas of the tradition they have studied" because Hall and Ames' work has focused in particular on the classical Chinese tradition up to the Han. Unfortunately, Hall passed away before they could continue into studies of Song Neoconfucianism.

30. The reader will recall that the categories developed in CRIP were proposed simply as helpful categories for understanding religious ideas cross-culturally and that while an attempt was made to specify the categories with respect to each of the traditions, much less of an attempt was made to relate the categories to one another.

31. "Simply allowing traditions to speak for themselves" sounds innocent insofar as it seems to indicate giving voice to the otherwise voiceless, but the "simply" in that phrase indicates a much more restrictive program: specifically, it indicates only allowing traditions to speak for themselves and restricting attempts to engage in further comparative investigation (something suggested in the previous points on Northrop and Hall/Ames).

32. In this respect, assessing comparative methods is akin to comparing philosophical traditions. One tradition may be better than all of the others, but that status would be well neigh impossible to determine; in any event, no tradition is better than other traditions in every respect anyhow. Comparative philosophy has done well to the extent that it has not pretended to be able to answer that question. Realistically speaking, one does better to identify the respects in which each tradition seems to excel relative to other traditions, which is where comparative studies has rightly flourished.

33. Incidentally, another way to have undertaken this study would have been to trace the discussions running throughout the journal *Philosophy East and West*. This not only traces the work of many of the most influential figures from the East-West Philosophers' Conferences but also tracks the smaller discussions and debates that took place in between. Indeed, these intermediary conversations are often more interesting and insightful than the more polished essays submitted at the conferences themselves. A good sense of the development of comparative philosophy could be extracted from a careful study of the history of that journal (although, again, it would have a scope restricted in its own right).

34. This is arguably true not only for comparative philosophy but also for other fields as well. For example, the same historical influences that have contributed to the development of comparative philosophy have contributed to the development of cross-cultural interests in other disciplines as well. See, for example the work of J. J. Clarke (1994, 1997, and 2000) and Hajime Nakamura (1965, 1975, 1986a, and 1986b) in history; Wilfred Cantwell Smith (1973, 1981, 1989, and 1997), Huston Smith (1991 and 1992[1965]) and Ninian Smart (1983, 1987, 1996, and 1999) in religious studies; and Randall Collins (1998) in sociology.

35. See Corless (2002) for an excellent study of Legge in light of his background in missions and contributions to sinology. It would be interesting—and, I believe, revealing—to determine how many comparativists at the beginning of the twentieth century were missionaries, had parents as missionaries, or were trained for some period of time in missionary-founded schools.

36. Here I refer to the startling difference between *The Meeting of East and West* (1946) and *Philosophical Anthropology and Practical Politics* (1960), although the contrasts can be seen among his less prominent texts as well.

37. This is related to what Hegel meant when he suggested, "The owl of Minerva spreads its wings only with the dusk" (Hegel 1967, 13). It is only once history has been made history that the philosopher—like the historian—can reflect on it and seek to understand it.

38. The sentiment that the Allied powers could lose the war, and could have lost the war, was not limited to a fear of the Third Reich; likewise, the Japanese proved themselves their equals in many respects.

39. Contemporaries seem to have inherited Aquinas' intellectual boldness in his interactions with the Muslim world but to have forgotten that this boldness took place in the context of—and perhaps as a response to—his awareness of Muslim cultural superiority at that time.

40. The similarities between these challenges and those faced by Northrop are notable.

41. Taken from the SACP website, http://www.sacpweb.org/, accessed February 2, 2007.

42. *Narrative philosophy* is perhaps the best term for Rorty's philosophy, whereby one attempts not to give voice to some underlying truths but rather to provide an interesting enough story about the use of some ideas rather than others that it convinces others to take that story as normative. Understood in this way, narrative philosophy can be understood as the very worst form of comparative philosophy, where the intent is not to understand the other but rather to replace it; indeed, it skips the hard work of understanding the other altogether and thus represents the caricature of Christian missions so readily embraced by its critics.

43. It is interesting to think what Northrop would have made of this distinction. On the one hand, one would think that he would find them conducive to the sorts of distinctions he made himself, but the fact that they are not so easily brought together in a broader framework would probably make him search for a better way to describe the distinction.

WORKS CITED

Ames, Roger T. 2007. "From Variety to Diversity: Chinese Philosophy and a Revisionist Understanding of Religious Pluralism." The Leroy Rouner Memorial Lecture. Public lecture, Boston University Institute for Philosophy and Religion, March 7.

———. 2005. "Getting Past the Eclipse of Philosophy in World Sinology: A Response to Eske Møllegaard," Dao 4, no. 2 (June), 347–52.

———. 2002. "Preface," He er butong: bijiao zhexue yu xhongxihuitong [Harmony Not Sameness: Comparative Philosophy and East-West Understanding], ed. Wen Haiming. Peking: Peking University Press, 1–10. Originally written in English, trans. by Wen Haiming into Chinese for publication; all citations taken from the original English draft, available at http://newton.uor.edu/Departments&Programs/AsianStudies Dept/ames-preface.htm, ©2004 University of Redlands.

———, ed. 2000. The Aesthetic Turn: Reading Eliot Deutsch on Comparative Philosophy. Chicago: Open Court.

———. 1983. The Art of Rulership: A Study of Ancient Chinese Political Thought. Honolulu: University of Hawaii Press. Reprint edition with forward by Harold D. Roth: Albany: State University of New York Press, 1994.

———. 1981. " 'The Art of Rulership' Chapter of Huai Nan Tzu: A Practicable Taoism," Journal of Chinese Philosophy 8, no. 2 (June), 225–44.

———. 1980. "Huainanzi 'Zhushu' pian de 'fa' guannion" ("The Concept of Penal Law in the 'Zhushu' Chapter of Huainanzi"). Dalu zazhi (Continent) 61, no. 4 (October), 1–10.

Ames, Roger T., Chan Sin-wai, and Mau-sang Ng, eds. 1991. Interpreting Culture through Translation: A Festschrift for D.C. Lau. Hong Kong: Chinese University Press (printed by Nam Fung Printing).

Ames, Roger T., and D. C. Lau, trans. 1998. Yuan Dao: Tracing Dao to its Source, intro. Roger T. Ames. New York: Ballantine Books.

———. 1996. Sun Pin: The Art of Warfare. New York: Ballantine Books. Reprint edition: Sun Bin: The Art of Warfare. Albany: State University of New York Press, 2003.

Ames, Roger T., and Henry Rosemont, Jr. 1998. The Analects of Confucius: A Philosophical Translation. New York: Ballantine Books.

Ames, Roger T., and Rhett Young, trans. 1977. Lao Tzu: Text, Notes and Comments, adapted from a popular edition by Chen Guying. San Francisco: Chinese Materials Center.

Auxier, Randall E. 2005. "Hocking, William Ernest." Dictionary of Modern American Philosophers. Bristol: Thoemmes, 1129–35.

Barton, James L. 1912. *Human Progress through Missions*. New York: Revell.

Berthrong, John H. 1998. *Concerning Creativity: A Comparison of Chu Hsi, Whitehead, and Neville*. Albany: State University of New York Press.

Blackwood, R. T., and A. L. Herman. 1975. *Problems in Philosophy: West and East*. Englewood Cliffs, NJ: Prentice Hall.

Bloom, Harold. 1997. *The Anxiety of Influence: A Theory of Poetry*. 2nd ed. New York: Oxford University Press.

Burtt, E. A. 1948. "How Can the Philosophies of East and West Meet?" *The Philosophical Review* 57, no. 6 (November 1948), 590–604.

Carey, William. 1988 [1792]. *An Enquiry into the Obligations of Christians to Use Means for the Conversion of the Heathens*, ed. John L. Pretlove, intro. Keith E. Eitel. Dallas: Criswell.

Chapman, J. Harley, and Nancy Frankenberry, eds. 1999. *Interpreting Neville*. Albany: State University of New York Press.

Cheng, Chung-ying. 1991. *New Dimensions of Confucian and Neo-Confucian Philosophy*. Albany: State University of New York Press.

Chinn, Ewing, and Henry Rosemont, Jr. 2005. *Metaphilosophy and Chinese Thought: Interpreting David Hall*. New York: Global Scholarly Publications.

Clarke, J. J. 2000. *The Tao of the West: Western Transformations of Taoist Thought*. New York: Routledge.

———. 1997. *Oriental Enlightenment: The Encounter between Asian and Western Thought*. New York: Routledge.

———. 1994. *Jung and Eastern Thought: A Dialogue with the Orient*. New York: Routledge.

Clooney, Francis X. 2001. *Hindu God, Christian God: How Reason Helps Break Down the Boundaries between Religions*. New York: Oxford University Press.

Collins, Randall. 1998. *The Sociology of Philosophies: A Global Theory of Intellectual Change*. Cambridge, MA: Belknap Press of Harvard University Press.

Copleston, Frederick. 1982. *Religion and the One: Philosophies East and West*. Gifford Lectures, 1980. New York: Crossroad.

Corless, Roger. 2002. *The Victorian Translation of China: James Legge's Orientalal Pilgrimage*. Los Angeles: University of California Press.

de Bary, William Theodore, and Irene Bloom, eds. 1999. *Sources of Chinese Tradition*, 2nd edition, two volumes. New York: Columbia University Press.

Delza, Sophia. 1996. *The T'ai-Chi Ch'uan Experience: Reflections and Perceptions on Body-Mind Harmony*, ed. with fwd. by Robert C. Neville. Albany: State University of New York Press.

Dennis, James S. 1906. *Christian Missions and Social Progress: A Sociological Study of Foreign Missions*. New York: Revell.

Deutsch, Eliot. 1991. *Culture and Modernity: East-West Philosophic Perspectives*. Honolulu: University of Hawaii.

Dewey, John. 1998. *The Essential Dewey*, ed. Larry A. Hickman and Thomas M. Alexander. 2 vols. Bloomington: Indiana University Press.

———. 1951. "On Philosophical Synthesis." *Philosophy East and West* 1, no. 1 (April), 3–5.

Dilworth, David A. 1989. *Philosophy in World Perspective: A Comparative Hermeneutic of the Major Theories*. New Haven: Yale University Press.

Ehrlich, Eugene. 1936. *Fundamental Principles of the Sociology of Law*, trans. Walter L. Moll, intro. Roscoe Pound. Cambridge, MA: Harvard University Press.

Emerson, Ralph Waldo. 1940. *The Selected Writings of Ralph Waldo Emerson*, ed. Brooks Atkinson. New York: Modern Library.

Farquhar, John Nicol. 1913. *The Crown of Hinduism*. New York: Milford.

Fingarette, Herbert. 1972. *Confucius: The Secular as Sacred*. New York: Harper and Row.

Flew, Antony. 1971. *An Introduction to Western Philosophy: Ideas and Argument from Plato to Sartre*. Indianapolis: Bobbs-Merrill.

Graham, A. C. 1991. "Reflections and Replies." *Chinese Texts and Philosophical Contexts: Essays Dedicated to Angus C. Graham*, ed. Henry Rosemont Jr. Peru, IL: Open Court.

———. 1989. *Disputers of the Tao: Philosophic Argument in Ancient China*. La Salle, IL: Open Court.

Grappard, Allan. 1992. *The Protocol of the Gods: A Study of the Kasuga Cult in Japanese History*. Berkeley: University of California Press.

Gruber, Carol S. 1975. *Mars and Minerva: World War I and the Uses of the Higher Learning in America*. Baton Rouge: Louisiana State University Press.

Hall, David L. 1994. *Richard Rorty: Prophet and Poet of the New Pragmatism*. Albany: State University of New York Press.

———. 1992. *The Arimaspian Eye*. Albany: State University of New York Press.

———. 1982a. *Eros and Irony: A Prelude to Philosophical Anarchism*. Albany: State University Press.

———. 1982b. *The Uncertain Phoenix: Adventures toward a Post-Cultural Sensibility*. New York: Fordham University Press.

———. 1980. "Praxis, Karman and Creativity." *Philosophy East and West* 30, no. 1 (January), 57–64.

———. 1978. "Process and Anarchy: A Taoist Vision of Creativity." *Philosophy East and West* 28, no. 4 (October), 271–85.

———. 1973. *The Civilization of Experience: A Whiteheadian Theory of Culture*. New York: Fordham University Press.

Hall, David L., and Roger T. Ames. 2003. *Dao De Jing: "Making This Life Significant": A Philosophical Translation*. New York: Ballantine Books.

———. 2001. *Focusing the Familiar: A Translation and Philosophical Interpretation of the Zhongyong*. Honolulu: Hawaii Press.

———. 1999. *The Democracy of the Dead: Dewey, Confucius, and the Hope for Democracy in China*. Chicago: Open Court.

———. 1998. *Thinking from the Han: Self, Truth, and Transcendence in Chinese and Western Culture*. Albany: State University of New York Press.

———. 1995. *Anticipating China: Thinking through the Narratives of Chinese and Western Culture*. Albany: State University of New York Press.

———. 1991. "Against the Greying of Confucius: Responses to Gregor Paul and Michael Martin." *Journal of Chinese Philosophy* 18, no. 3 (October), 33–327.

———. 1987. *Thinking through Confucius*. Albany: State University of New York Press.

———. 1984. "Getting It Right: On Saving Confucius from the Confucians." *Philosophy East and West* 34, no. 1 (January), 3–23.

Hegel, G. W. F. 1984–88. *Lectures on the Philosophy of Religion*, 3 vols., ed. Peter C. Hodgson, trans. R. F. Brown, T. C. Hodgson, and J. M. Steward, with the assistance of H. S. Harris. Berkeley: University of California Press.

———. 1967. *Hegel's Philosophy of Right*, trans. T. M. Knox. London: Oxford University Press.

Hocking, William Ernest. 1959. *Strength of Men and Nations: A Message to the USA vis-a-vis the USSR.* New York: Harper and Brothers.

———. 1956. *The Coming World Civilization.* New York: Harper and Brothers.

———. 1952. "On Philosophical Synthesis," *Philosophy East and West* 2, no. 2 (July), 99–101.

———. 1944a. *Science and the Idea of God.* Chapel Hill: University of North Carolina Press.

———. 1944b. "Value of the Comparative Study of Philosophy." *Philosophy: East and West.* Princeton: Princeton University Press.

———. 1940. *Living Religions and a World Faith.* New York: Macmillan.

———. 1937. "Philosophy: The Business of Everyman." *Journal of the American Association of University Women* 30 (June), 212–17.

———. 1936. "Chu Hsi's Theory of Knowledge." *Harvard Journal of Asiatic Studies* 1, no. 1 (April), 109–27.

———. 1932. *Re-Thinking Missions: A Laymen's Inquiry after One Hundred Years.* Laymen's Foreign Missions Inquiry Commission of Appraisal, William Ernest Hocking, chairman. New York: Harper and Brothers.

———. 1918. *Morale and Its Enemies.* New Haven: Yale University Press.

———. 1912. *The Meaning of God in Human Experience: A Philosophic Study of Religion.* New Haven: Yale University Press. Reprint version, 1913.

Hogg, William Richey. 1980. "Edinburgh 1910-Perspective 1980." *Occasional Bulletin of Missionary Research* (now *International Bulletin of Missionary Research*) 4, no. 4 (October), 146–53.

———. 1952. *Ecumenical Foundations: A History of the International Missionary Council and Its Nineteenth Century Background.* New York: Harper.

Huntington, Samuel P. 1996. *The Clash of Civilizations and the Remaking of World Order.* New York: Simon and Schuster.

James, William. 2007 [1890]. *The Principles of Psychology,* 2 vols, New York: Cosimo.

———. 1985 [1902]. *The Varieties of Religious Experience.* New York: Penguin Books.

———. 1975 [1907, 1909]. *Pragmatism: A New Name for Some Old Ways of Thinking* and *The Meaning of Truth: A Sequel to Pragmatism,* intro. A. J. Ayer. Cambridge, MA: Harvard University Press.

Kasulis, Thomas P., and Robert Cummings Neville, eds. 1997. *The Recovery of Philosophy in America: Essays in Honor of John Edwin Smith.* Albany: State University of New York Press.

Kipling, Rudyard. 1994. "The Ballad of East and West" (1889). *The Collected Poems of Rudyard Kipling.* Hertfordshire, England: Wordsworth Editions, 245–48.

Kraemer, Hendrik. 1962. *Why Christianity of All Religions?* trans. Hubert Hoskins. Philadelphia: Westminster.

———. 1957. *Religion and the Christian Faith.* Philadephia: Westminster.

Kuehl, Warren, and Lynne K. Dunn. 1997. *Keeping the Covenant: American Internationalists and the League of Nations, 1920–1939*. Kent: Kent State University Press.

Kuklick, Bruce. 1977. *The Rise of American Philosophy: Cambridge, Massachusetts 1860–1930*. New Haven, CT: Yale University Press.

Lachs, John, and D. Micah Hester, eds. 2004. *A William Ernest Hocking Reader: With Commentary*. Nashville: Vanderbilt University Press.

Larson, Gerald James, and Eliot Deutsch, eds. 1988. *Interpreting across Boundaries: New Essays in Comparative Philosophy*. Princeton: Princeton University Press.

Leidecker, Kurt. 1951. "Emerson and East-West Synthesis." *Philosophy East and West* 1, no. 2 (July), 40–50.

Liu, Shu-hsien, and Robert E. Allinson, eds. 1988. *Harmony and Strife: Contemporary Perspectives, East & West*. Hong Kong: Chinese University Press.

MacCulloch, John A. 1902. *Comparative Theology*. London: Methuen.

MacIntyre, Alisdair. 1988. *Whose Justice? Which Rationality?* Notre Dame: University of Notre Dame Press.

Mallory, J. P., and Victor H. Mair. 2000. *The Tarim Mummies: Ancient China and the Mystery of the Earliest Peoples from the West*. New York: Thames and Hudson.

Martin, Michael R. 1991. "A Rejoinder to Hall and Ames." *Journal of Chinese Philosophy* 18, no. 4, 480–93.

———. 1990. Review of *Thinking through Confucius* by David Hall and Roger Ames, *Journal of Chinese Philosophy* 17, no. 4, 495–503.

Masuzawa, Tomoko. 2005. *The Invention of World Religions: Or, How European Universalism Was Preserved in the Language of Pluralism*. Chicago: University of Chicago Press.

Maurice, Frederick Denison. 1852 [1847]. *The Religions of the World and Their Relations to Christianity*. 3rd ed., rev. London: Parker and Son.

McCulloch, Warren S., and Walter Pitts. 1943. "A Logical Calculus of the Ideas Immanent in Nervous Activity." *Bulletin of Mathematical Biophysics* 5, 115–33.

McKeon, Richard. 1990. *Freedom and History and Other Essays: An Introduction to the Thought of Richard McKeon*, ed. Zahava K. McKeon, intro. Howard Ruttenberg. Chicago: University of Chicago Press.

Menzies, Allan. 1895. *History of Religion: A Sketch of Primitive Religious Beliefs and Practices, and of the Origin and Character of the Great Systems*. New York: Scribner's Sons.

Møllegaard, Eske. 2005. "Eclipse of Reading: O the 'Philosophical Turn' in American Sinology" *Dao* 4, no. 2 (June 2005), 321–40.

Moore, Charles A., ed. 1962. *Philosophy and Culture: East and West*. Honolulu: University of Hawaii Press.

———. 1951. *Essays in East-West Philosophy: An Attempt at World Philosophical Synthesis*. Honolulu: University of Hawaii Press.

———. 1944. *Philosophy: East and West*. Princeton: Princeton University Press.

Nakamura, Hajime. 1986a. *A Comparative History of Ideas*. New York: KPI.

———. 1986b. *Buddhism in Comparative Light*. Delhi: Banarsidass.

———. 1975. *Parallel Developments: A Comparative History of Ideas*. Tokyo: Kodansha.

————. 1965. *Ways of Thinking of Eastern Peoples: India, China, Tibet, and Japan.* Honolulu: East-West Center Press.

Needham, Joseph. 1954–2004. *Science and Civilization in China.* 7 vols. New York: Cambridge University Press.

Neville, Robert Cummings. 2006. *On the Scope and Truth of Theology: Theology as Symbolic Engagement.* New York: T&T Clark.

————, ed. 2001a. *The Human Condition: A Volume in the Comparative Religious Ideas Project,* fwd. Peter L. Berger. Albany: State University of New York Press.

————, ed. 2001b. *Ultimate Realities: A Volume in the Comparative Religious Ideas Project,* fwd. Tu Weiming. Albany: State University of New York Press.

————, ed. 2001c. *Religious Truth: A Volume in the Comparative Religious Ideas Project,* fwd. Jonathan Z. Smith. Albany: State University of New York Press.

————. 2000. *Boston Confucianism: Portable Tradition in the Late-Modern World.* Albany: State University of New York Press.

————. 1995. *Normative Cultures.* Volume 3 of *Axiology of Thinking.* Albany: State University of New York Press.

————. 1992a [1968]. *God the Creator: On the Transcendence and Presence of God.* Chicago: Chicago University Press. Reprint edition with corrections and a new preface: Albany: State University of New York Press.

————. 1992b. *The Highroad around Modernism.* Albany: State University of New York Press.

————. 1991. *Behind the Masks of God: An Essay toward Comparative Theology.* Albany: State University of New York Press.

————. 1989. *Recovery of the Measure.* Volume 2 of *Axiology of Thinking.* Albany: State University of New York Press.

————. 1987. *The Puritan Smile: A Look toward Moral Reflection.* Albany: State University of New York Press.

————. 1982. *The Tao and the Daimon: Segments of a Religious Inquiry.* Albany: State University of New York Press.

————. 1981. *Reconstruction of Thinking.* Volume 1 of *Axiology of Thinking.* Albany: State University of New York Press.

————. 1980. *Creativity and God.* New York: Seabury. Reprint edition; Albany: State University of New York Press, 1995.

————. 1978. *Soldier, Sage, Saint.* New York: Fordham University Press.

————. 1973. "A Metaphysical Argument for Wholly Empirical Theology." *God Knowable and Unknowable,* ed. Robert J. Roth. New York: Fordham University Press, 215–40.

Nishida Kitaro. 1990. *An Inquiry into the Good,* trans. Masao Abe and Christopher Ives. New Haven: Yale University Press.

————. 1987a. *Last Writings: Nothingness and the Religious World-View,* trans. and intro. David A. Dilworth. Honolulu: University of Hawaii Press.

————. 1987b [1945]. "The Logic of *Topos* and the Religious Worldview [Basho-teki ronri to shūkyō-teki sekaikan]," trans. Yusa Michiko, pt. 2 of 2. *Eastern Buddhist* 20, no. 1 (Spring, 1987), 81–119.

————. 1986 [1945]. "The Logic of *Topos* and the Religious Worldview [Basho-teki ronri to shūkyō-teki sekaikan]," trans. Yusa Michiko, pt. 1 of 2. *Eastern Buddhist* 19, no. 2 (Autumn, 1986), 1–29.

Nishitani Keiji. 1990. *The Self-Overcoming of Nihilism,* trans. Graham Parkes and Setsuko Aihara. Alban`y: State University of New York Press.

———. 1982. *Religion and Nothingness [Shūkyō towa nanika (What Is Religion?)],* trans. and intro. Jan Van Bragt, fwd. Winston L. King. Berkeley: University of California Press.

Northrop, F. C. S. 1985. *The Prolegomena to a 1985 Philosophiae Naturalis Principia Mathematica.* Woodbridge, CT: Oxbow.

———. 1962. *Man, Nature and God: A Quest for Life's Meaning.* Credo Series, planned and edited by Ruth Nanda Anshen. New York: Simon and Schuster.

———. 1960. *Philosophical Anthropology and Practical Politics.* New York: Macmillan.

———. 1959. *The Complexity of Legal and Ethical Experience: Studies in the Method of Normative Subjects.* Boston: Little, Brown. Reprint Westport, CT: Greenwood, 1959.

———. 1954. *European Union and United States Foreign Policy: A Study in Sociological Jurisprudence.* New York: Macmillan.

———. 1952. *The Taming of Nations: A Study in the Cultural Bases of International Policy.* New York: Macmillan. Reprint edition: Woodbridge, CT: Oxbow, 1987.

———, ed. 1949. *Ideological Differences and World Order: Studies in the Philosophy and Science of the World's Cultures.* New Haven: Yale University Press.

———. 1947. *The Logic of the Sciences and the Humanities.* New York: Macmillan. Reprint edition: Woodbridge, CT: Oxbow, 1983.

———. 1946. *The Meeting of East and West: An Inquiry Concerning World Understanding.* New York: Macmillan. Reprint edition: Woodbridge, CT: Oxbow, 1979.

———. 1931. *Science and First Principles.* New York: Macmillan. Reprint edition with new preface: Woodbridge, CT: Oxbow, 1979.

Northrop, F. S. C., and Helen Livingston, eds. 1964. *Cross-cultural Understanding: Epistemology in Anthropology.* New York: Harper and Row.

Northrop, F. S. C., and Mason W. Gross. 1953. *Alfred North Whitehead: An Anthology.* New York: Macmillan.

Odin, Steve. 1989. "A Critique of the Kenōsis/Śūnyatā motif in Nishida and the Kyoto School." *Buddhist-Christian Studies* 9, 71–86.

———. 1987. "Kenōsis as Foundation for Buddhist-Christian Dialogue." *Eastern Buddhist* 20, no. 1 (Spring), 34–61.

Organ, Troy Wilson. 1988. *The Self in Its Worlds: East and West.* Toronto: Associated University Presses.

Paul, Gregor. 1992. "Against Wanton Distortion: A Rejoinder to David Hall and Roger Ames by Gregor Paul." *Journal of Chinese Philosophy* 19, no. 1, 119–22.

———. 1991. "Reflections on the Usage of the Terms 'Logic' and 'Logical.' " *Journal of Chinese Philosophy* 18, no. 1, 73–87.

Peirce, Charles Sanders. 1998. *The Essential Peirce: Selected Philosophical Writings,* 2 vols, ed. Peirce Edition Project. Indianapolis: Indiana University Press.

Pirsig, Robert M. 1999. "Subjects, Objects, Data and Values." *Einstein Meets Magritte.* Brussels: Kluwer. 79–98.

———. 1974. *Zen and the Art of Motorcycle Maintenance: An Inquiry into Values.* New York: Morrow.

Reck, Andrew J. 1968. *The New American Philosophers: An Exploration of Thought since World War II.* Baton Rouge: University of Louisiana Press.

————. 1964. *Recent American Philosophy: Studies of Ten Representative Thinkers.* New York: Pantheon Books.

Riepe, Dale. 1970. *Philosophy of India and Its Impact on American Thought.* Springfield, IL: Thomas.

————. 1967. "The Indian Influence in American Philosophy: Emerson to Moore." *Philosophy East and West* 17, no. 1/4, 125–37.

Robert, Dana. 2005. "The Great Commission in an Age of Globalization." *Considering the Great Commission: Evangelism and Mission in the Wesleyan Spirit,* eds. W. Stephen Gunter and Elaine A. Robinson. Nashville: Abingdon.

————. 2002. "The First Globalization: The Internationalization of the Protestant Missionary Movement between the World Wars," *International Bulletin of Missionary Research* 26, no. 2 (April 2002), 50–67.

Rorty, Richard. 2006. *Take Care of Freedom and Truth Will Take Care of Itself: Interviews with Richard Rorty,* ed. with intro. Eduardo Mendieta. Stanford: Stanford University Press.

————. 1999. *Philosophy and Social Hope.* New York: Penguin Books.

————. 1998. *Truth and Progress.* New York: Cambridge University Press.

————. 1989a. *Contingency, Irony, and Solidarity.* New York: Cambridge University Press.

————. 1989b. Review of *Interpreting across Boundaries: New Essays in Comparative Philosophy,* ed. Gerald James Larson and Eliot Deutsch. *Philosophy East and West* 39, no. 3 (July), 332–37.

————. 1979. *Philosophy and the Mirror of Nature.* Princeton: Princeton University Press.

Rosenblueth, Arturo, Norbert Wiener, and Julian Bigelow. 1943. "Behavior, Purpose, and Teleology." *Philosophy of Science* 10, no. 1 (January 1943), 18–24.

Rouner, Leroy S., ed. 1969. *Within Human Experience: The Philosophy of William Ernest Hocking.* Cambridge, MA: Harvard University Press.

————. 1966. *Philosophy, Religion, and the Coming World Civilization: Essays in Honor of William Ernest Hocking.* The Hague: Nijhoff.

Royce, Josiah. 1977 [1912]. *Sources of Religious Insight.* New York: Octagon Books.

Saher, P. J. 1970. *Eastern Wisdom and Western Thought: A Comparative Study in the Modern Philosophy of Religion.* New York: Barnes and Noble.

Santayana, George. 1998 [1905]. *The Life of Reason, or the Phases of Human Progress.* Amherst, NY: Prometheus Books.

Scharfstein, Ben-Ami, Ilai Alon, Shlomo Biderman, Dan Daor, Yoel Hoffman. 1978. *Philosophy East/Philosophy West: A Critical Comparison of Indian, Chinese, Islamic, and European Philosophy.* New York: Oxford University Press.

Seddon, Fred. 1995. *An Introduction to the Philosophical Works of F. S. C. Northrop.* Problems in Contemporary Philosophy 27. Lewiston, NY: Mellon.

Shryock, J. K. 1936. Review of *Harvard Journal of Asiatic Studies* 1, no. 1 (1936). *Journal of the American Oriental Society* 56, no. 3 (September, 1936), 381–82.

Sinclair, Gregg. 1936. Letter to Sarvepalli Radhakrishnan, November 20, 1936. Archived at the Philosophy Department of the University of Hawaii.

Smart, Ninian. 1999. *World Philosophies.* New York: Routledge.

————. 1996. *Dimensions of the Sacred: An Anatomy of the World's Beliefs.* Berkeley: University of California Press.

————. 1987. "Comparative-Historical Method." *Encyclopedia of Religion*, ed. Mircea Eliade. New York: Macmillan.

————. 1983. *Worldviews: Crosscultural Explorations of Human Beliefs*. New York: Scribner's Books.

Smith, Huston. 1992 [1965]. *Forgotten Truth: The Common Vision of the World's Religions*, 2nd ed. San Francisco: HarperSanFrancisco.

————. 1991. *The World's Religions: Our Great Wisdom Traditions*. HarperSanFrancisco.

Smith, John E. 1992. *American's Philosophical Vision*. Chicago: University of Chicago Press.

————. 1983. *The Spirit of American Philosophy*. Revised edition: Albany: State University of New York Press, 1983.

————. 1978. *Purpose and Thought: The Meaning of Pragmatism*. Chicago: University of Chicago Press.

————. 1973. *The Analogy of Experience*. Annie Kinkead Warfield Lectures. New York: Harper and Row.

————. 1970. *Themes in American Philosophy: Purpose, Experience, and Community*. New York: Harper and Row.

————. 1968. *Experience and God*. New York: Oxford University Press. Reprint edition w/ new preface: New York: Fordham University Press, 1995.

————. 1961. *Reason and God: Encounters of Philosophy with Religion*. New Haven: Yale University Press.

Smith, Jonathan Z. 2001. "Foreward." *Religious Truth: A Volume in the Comparative Religious Ideas Project*, ed. Robert Cummings Neville. Albany: State University of New York Press.

————. 2000. "The 'End' of Comparison: Redescription and Rectification." *A Magic Still Dwells: Comparative Religion in the Postmodern Age*, eds. Kimberly C. Patton and Benjamin C. Ray. Berkley: University of California Pres.

————. 1982. *Imagining Religion: From Babylon to Jonestown*. Chicago: University of Chicago Press.

————. 1978. *Map Is Not Territory*. Chicago: University of Chicago Press.

Smith, Wilfred Cantwell. 1997. *Modern Culture from a Comparative Perspective*, ed. John W. Burbidge. Albany: State University of New York Press.

————. 1989. *Towards a World Theology: Faith and the Comparative History of Religion*. Philadelphia: Westminster, 1981. New edition: Maryknoll, NY: Orbis, 1989.

————. 1981. *Towards a World Theology: Faith and History of Religion*. Philadelphia: Westminster.

————. 1973. "Comparative Religion: Whither—and Why?" *The History of Religions: Essays in Methodology*, ed. Mircea Eliade. Chicago: University of Chicago Press. 31–58.

Solomon, Robert C. 1993. *The Bully Culture: Enlightenment, Romanticism, and the Transcendental Pretense 1750–1850*. Lanham, MD: Rowman and Littlefield.

Sorokin, Pitirim A. 1947. *Society, Culture, and Personality*. New York: Harper and Brothers.

————. 1937. *Social and Cultural Dynamics*. New York: American Book Co.

Squarcini, Federico. 2005. "*Tradens, Traditum, Recipiens*: Introductory Remarks on the Semiotics, Pragmatics, and Politics of Tradition." *Boundaries, Dynamics,* and *Construction of Traditions in South Asia*, ed. Squarcini Federico. Firenze: Firenze University Press.

Van Norden, Bryan W. 1996. "Letter to the Editor." *Proceedings and Addresses of the American Philosophical Association* 70:2 (November), 161–63.

Watson, Walter. 1985. *The Architectonics of Meaning: Foundations of the New Pluralism*. Reprint edition, with a new preface: Chicago: University of Chicago Press, 1993.

Whitehead, Alfred North. 1933. *Adventures of Ideas*. New York: Simon and Schuster. Reprint edition, New York: Free Press, 1967.

———. 1929. *Process and Reality: An Essay in Cosmology*. New York: Macmillan. Corrected edition, ed. David Ray Griffin and Donald W. Sherburne, New York: Free Press, 1978.

———. 1925. *Science and the Modern World*. New York: Macmillan.

———. 1922. *The Principle of Relativity with Applications to Physical Science*. Cambridge: University Press.

Yates, Timothy. 1994. *Christian Mission in the Twentieth Century*. New York: Cambridge University Press.

Yearley, Lee H. 1990. *Mencius and Aquinas: Theories of Virtue and Conceptions of Courage*. Toward a Comparative Philosophy of Religions Series. Albany: State University of New York Press.

Yong, Amos, and Peter G. Heltzel. 2004. *Theology in Global Context: Essays in Honor of Robert Cummings Neville*. New York: Clark.

INDEX

abstraction, 11, 88, 97, 112, 127, 143, 150–51, 164–71, 172, 220, 238n22, 247nn41–42, 255n10, 258n45
aesthetic(s), 265; in Hall and Ames' work, 90, 95–98, 107, 111, 112, 127, 128, 200, 245n20; in Hocking's work, 28, 201; in Northrop's work, 49–53, 64, 66, 67, 200–201, 206, 207, 227, 239nn22–23, 240n37, 241n45, 241n49, 248n42; in Whitehead, 248n42. *See also* concepts by intuition; first problematic thinking
Althizer, Thomas J. J., 145
American Academy of Religion (AAR), 226
American naturalism, 77, 222, 231n4
American Philosophical Association (APA), 38, 226
American philosophy, 6–9, 14, 15, 17, 23, 32, 35, 38–39, 57, 80–81, 132, 134, 193–4, 196, 220, 222, 223, 255n20, 257n37; controlling the scope of this study, 6; decline of, 7, 77, 223; definition of, 231n4; reemergence of, 8. *See also* American naturalism; American pragmatism; process philosophy
American pragmatism: 6–8, 49, 77, 80, 92, 95, 97, 132, 134, 136, 143, 160, 176, 182–85, 193, 197, 209, 210, 211, 214, 217, 221–22, 236n43, 243n4, 255nn11–12, 257n42, 259nn53–54, 265n23; comparative philosophy in, 132; influence on this study, 9, 12–14, 217–18; and Hall and Ames, 8, 80, 85–86, 91–92, 102, 106, 110–11, 114, 122,

126, 131, 133, 247n38, 248n46; and Hocking, 6, 32–33, 236n43; "negative pragmatism," 33, 236n43; neopragmatism, 81, 160, 172, 175, 201, 245n18, 259n53; and Neville, 8, 141, 143, 159–66, 171–76, 257n40, 257n42; and Northrop, 7; "paleopragmatism," 160, 165, 174, 175, 259n53; protopragmatism, 243n4. *See also individual representatives*
Ames, Roger T., 7–8, 9, 79–139, 146, 167, 176, 194–229 *passim*, 231nn6–7, 231n9, 236n46, 238n13, 242n51, 243n62; 263n11, significance of, for comparative philosophy, 7, 8
analytic philosophy, 7, 81, 129, 132, 221, 223–24; comparative philosophy in, 10, 224; rise of, 7, 65, 77, 225, 252n75
anarchism, philosophical 96–97, 112, 146, 245n21, 247n38
Anaximander, 89
Anaximenes, 89
Aquinas, Thomas, 2, 267n39
area studies, 38, 50, 59, 89, 90, 198, 201, 214, 221, 226
Aristotle, 23, 89, 90, 108, 109, 110, 146, 201, 239n28, 255n19
Association for Asian Studies (AAS), 226
Atman, 69
Auxier, Randall, 233n9
axiology. *See* value

Barton, James, 251n66
Berger, Peter, 176, 259n56, 261n71
Bergson, Henri, 25, 27

33286592R00169

Made in the USA
Lexington, KY
22 June 2014